"In a world of AI agents, trust becomes an active utility and execution is the differentiator. *RIVER* turns risk into momentum by giving teams the rails to move safely at breakneck speed. A pragmatic playbook for the next decade of finance and beyond."

—Brad Levy, CEO of ThetaRay

"This book should be required reading for every board member and C-suite executive who still believes cybersecurity is someone else's problem. The river of risk is rising, and those who don't learn to navigate these new currents will find themselves in dangerous waters."

—Dr. Aleksandr Yampolskiy, Co-Founder & CEO, SecurityScorecard

"Enterprise AI transformation isn't about deploying technology—it's about reimagining how data, people, and systems create value together. Golbin's framework provides leaders with the essential roadmap for navigating this transformation responsibly and profitably."

—Swamy Kocherlakota, Executive Vice President of Agentic AI Security, Zscaler

"In my world, we don't build a global financial system on promises; we build it on verifiable cryptographic controls. We build for survival—treating the worst case not as a possibility but an inevitability: segregated custody so one vault's failure doesn't drain the rest, redundant cutover paths so there are three ways home, and phishing-resistant approvals so an attacker stalls out."

—Jeff Lunglhofer, Chief Security Officer, Coinbase; former CISO, BNY

"Boards want confidence, teams need clarity, and regulators demand evidence. In an agentic enterprise, after-the-fact assurance is too slow. This book treats auditability as a design requirement, where it belongs. Golbin turns that truth into practical steps leaders can use at the speed of change."

—Patrick Hayes, author of *Integrated Assurance: Unified Risk Strategy*; CISO

"A masterfully woven narrative that humanizes the complexities of artificial intelligence. This book delivers non-fiction insights through the lens of fiction where real-world dilemmas, ethical tensions, and technological breakthroughs unfold through compelling characters and emotionally resonant storytelling. It's not just a story; it's a strategic lens into the future of AI, wrapped in human experience."

—Ajay Singh, Professor, Editor of QdayReady.com, Member of Task Force for Implementation of Quantum Safe Ecosystem in India

"Boards don't need more doom; they need a map. *The RIVER Charter* turns resilience from a buzzword into an operating standard—linking culture, controls, and evidence you can defend. It's the rare book I'd hand to a CEO and a regulator on the same day."

—David Palmieri, Chief Transformation Officer

"A rare business thriller that actually equips leaders. The risks feel real; the remedies are usable tomorrow morning."

—Soichiro Muto, Founder & CEO, Synthesis

"As a founder building with AI every day, I want guardrails that don't kill momentum. *The RIVER Charter* nails it—practical checks, clear metrics, zero fluff."

—Vishal Ahluwalia, Co-Founder & CEO, Quantum Webb

"*The RIVER Charter* is a rare framework that approaches AI risk with the same rigor as enterprise risk: measurable, auditable, and fully operational. For leaders of critical systems, it serves not simply as a book but as a practical playbook."

—Anthony M. Irudhayanathan, President & CEO, Zillion Technologies

"A true boardroom field manual: practical frameworks, audit-ready artifacts, and memorable stories that create a shared executive language."

—Max Artemenko, Founder & Executive Director at Executive Data Council

"As autonomous agents show up in every workflow, the CISO and Chief Risk Officer jobs converge. *Governing AI Risk* captures that shift with uncomfortable accuracy and then shows how to rebuild accountability from boardroom to backlog. It's rare to see both perspectives integrated this well in one framework."

—Eric Staffin, senior executive; former Global CISO & Chief Risk Officer

"An engaging and thought-provoking new approach for thinking about risk management and cyber-security that goes beyond the traditional check-the-box approach in ERM guidance that exists today."

—James Bone, author of *Cognitive Risk* and *Cognitive Hack*

"This manuscript for *Governing AI Risk—The RIVER Charter* by Alex Golbin stands out as a timely, innovative hybrid of business thriller and practical playbook, using a 2038–2040 crisis narrative to stress-test 2026 & 2027 AI governance decisions for boards and executives.

Strengths:

- Dual-rail structure: The fictional story (e.g., Aaron Goldcrest's crises at 70M) vividly illustrates risks like 'Risk Debt' and convergence failures, while 'Strategic Debriefs' and appendices deliver actionable tools—making complex ideas stick without dry theory.
- RIVER Framework: Core innovation—Resolve Convergence, Integrate Hybrid Cognition, Validate Risk Debt, Elevate Data Capital, Reinforce Resilience—maps cleanly to NIST AI RMF and ISO/IEC 42001, offering a pragmatic overlay for agentic AI risks.
- Relevance: Targets mid-market leaders in regulated sectors (finance, health); appendices like the 90-Day RIVER Toolkit provide ROI-focused checklists, e.g., maturity models and audit evidence.
- Credibility: Expert commentaries (e.g., James Bone, Aaron Golbin) and real-world parallels (Flash Crash, SolarWinds) ground the fiction.

In an agentic AI world where speed breeds fragility, Golbin's book is a masterclass—blending gripping 2038 crises with the RIVER framework's five tenets to arm 2026 boards against '"Risk Debt"' and convergence cascades. Resolve, Integrate, Validate, Elevate, Reinforce: these aren't buzzwords but audited mandates mapping to NIST/ISO standards, with playbooks like the Cognitive Handshake turning theory into Monday actions.

This is a must-read for executives, particularly in regulated industries—practical, evidence-based, and visionary. This will define AI governance for 2026–2027."

—Gary Craven, Management Consultant, Winnipeg

"This book doesn't whisper about risk—it drags it into the light and forces leaders to look it in the eye.

What Alex Golbin has built here is not just a framework, and it's not just a story. It's a warning shot wrapped in a blueprint. Through a gripping narrative that feels uncomfortably close to reality, he exposes the silent accumulation of what he calls "'Risk Debt'"—the decisions we rationalize, delay, or ignore until they compound into something we can no longer control.

The brilliance of this work is in its duality. It speaks to the boardroom with precision, offering structured, actionable governance through the RIVER framework, while simultaneously speaking to the human cost of failure in a way most technical books never dare to do. That balance is rare—and powerful.

As someone who has lived in high-stakes leadership environments where decisions carry real consequences, I can tell you this: speed without discipline is not innovation—it's liability. This book captures that truth with clarity and urgency.

Governing AI Risk is not just timely—it's necessary. For executives, board members, and leaders navigating the accelerating pace of AI, this is more than recommended reading. It's a field manual for survival.

If you are responsible for leading people, protecting systems, or making decisions that matter, this book belongs on your desk—and more importantly, in your operational mindset."

—Douglas P. Pflug, Executive Leadership—Cornell University

"FOR THE LEADERS WHO SET THE STANDARD.

Governing AI Risk is the resilience standard that doesn't kill momentum, told through a story that makes the stakes impossible to ignore.

Follow Aaron Goldcrest through the agentic economy of 2038–2040 as cascading AI failures—from collapsed irrigation networks to ransomware crises to quantum cryptographic attacks—expose the hidden cost of governance that lags innovation. The story makes the stakes visceral. The toolset makes them actionable.

Every dramatic turn is matched by board-ready frameworks, executive checklists, and playbooks you can implement Monday morning.

The river of risk is rising. This is how you navigate it."

—Forrest Foster, Author, *Cloud Compliance Essentials: Build and Maintain Market Access in the B2B CSP Ecosystem*

A timely, intellectually ambitious, and operationally grounded work that successfully bridges business fiction and enterprise governance strategy. Governing AI Risk—The RIVER Charter stands out as one of the more sophisticated treatments of AI-era enterprise resilience currently emerging in the governance and cybersecurity space.

Alex Golbin's *Governing AI Risk—The RIVER Charter* blends speculative business fiction with practical governance frameworks by its ambitious portrayal of a cautionary corporate thriller, an executive field manual, and a forward-looking enterprise risk methodology. The book's central achievement lies in its structural duality. Golbin alternates between narrative-driven scenarios set in the late 2030s and operational "Strategic Debrief" sections anchored in present-day governance concerns. This dual-track format allows the author to dramatize the consequences of unmanaged AI acceleration while also translating those fictional failures into practical lessons for boards, CISOs, CROs, auditors, regulators, and enterprise architects. Rather than presenting governance as an abstract compliance obligation, the novelized structure allows readers to experience the cascading human, operational, and financial consequences of weak controls, technical debt, and organizational complacency.

Stylistically, the book benefits from the author's evident familiarity with enterprise risk management, cybersecurity operations, regulatory remediation, and financial governance. The fictional scenarios feel genuine because the organizational dynamics are authentic. Boardroom tensions, regulatory escalations, operational paralysis, incident-response confusion, and executive rationalization are portrayed with unusual realism. Readers with backgrounds in governance, audit, security, or operational resilience will recognize the uncomfortable plausibility embedded throughout the narrative.

The opening chapters are particularly effective. The collapse of Bull-in-China-Shop AI functions as a compelling metaphor for modern enterprise fragility. Golbin demonstrates a sophisticated understanding of how apparently minor engineering shortcuts, governance exceptions, deferred remediation, and "temporary" efficiency measures can accumulate into catastrophic systemic failures. The concept of "Risk Debt" emerges as one of the manuscript's strongest intellectual contributions. By framing governance failures as compounding liabilities analogous to financial leverage, Golbin provides executives with a vocabulary that is both memorable and operationally useful.

The book reinforces the concept that AI governance cannot be isolated within technology departments. Golbin repeatedly demonstrates that modern enterprise risk is converged risk: cyber, operational, reputational, legal, regulatory, data, infrastructure, and human decision-making failures intersect simultaneously. The book argues persuasively that organizations still structured around siloed governance models will struggle to survive the agentic AI era. The author avoids anti-technology alarmism and the book is not an argument against AI adoption. Instead, it is an argument against unmanaged acceleration. Golbin acknowledges the transformative economic potential of autonomous systems while arguing that governance maturity has not evolved at the same speed as deployment velocity. This balance gives the work credibility. The author clearly believes in innovation; his concern is that institutions are optimizing for speed while underinvesting in resilience.

The framework architecture itself is impressively developed. The R.I.V.E.R. model—Resolve, Integrate, Validate, Elevate, Reinforce—is not merely presented as branding shorthand but is repeatedly reinforced through operational examples, governance breakdowns, and implementation guidance. Companion concepts such as the Cognitive Handshake™, All-Entity Risk Management (AERM™), DataCapital Protocol™, and the Five Phases of AI Adoption extend the ecosystem into a comprehensive governance operating model rather than a collection of disconnected ideas. The appendices substantially enhance the book's practical value. Many governance-oriented books collapse into abstraction once the conceptual argument is complete. Golbin instead provides implementation-oriented frameworks, checklists, operational crosswalks, and board-level readiness materials that make the work usable beyond its narrative components. For executive audiences, this significantly increases the book's utility. The book will resonate strongly with board members, CISOs, CIOs, CROs, audit leaders, regulators, risk practitioners, resilience strategists, and enterprise architects seeking frameworks capable of addressing systemic AI era risk. It also has significant value as a teaching text for graduate programs focused on cybersecurity governance, enterprise risk management, digital transformation, and operational resilience.

Ultimately, Golbin succeeds because he understands that the greatest AI risks are rarely technological in isolation. They emerge when human ambition, institutional incentives, operational shortcuts, and governance immaturity converge faster than organizations can adapt. *Governing AI Risk—The RIVER Charter* captures that convergence with urgency, credibility, and uncommon strategic clarity.

—Ron Baklarz, retired CISO; author of *CISO: Evolution of a Vocation*

Governing AI Risk—The RIVER Charter

THE AI CRISIS IS FICTIONAL. THE BLUEPRINT IS REAL.

By 2038, autonomous agents will manage trillions of dollars in global assets. But when speed outpaces governance, efficiency becomes fragility. *Governing AI Risk* blends a near-future thriller with a field manual for leaders who can't afford blind spots. Follow the fictional journey of Aaron Goldcrest, a successful venture capitalist, as his team confronts cascading failures in the agentic economy—and learn how the **RIVER Charter**™ standard helps global organizations stay resilient. Featuring All-Entity Risk Management (AERM™), the Cognitive Handshake™ for auditable human–AI decisions, and DataCapital Protocol™ for blockchain-grade data lineage.

Alex Golbin is a senior financial services executive with over two decades of experience leading enterprise risk, regulatory remediation, and technology and data transformation across Fortune 500 firms and global systemically important banks. He built and led a multi-bank risk-assessments joint venture with 16 institutions, developed risk management frameworks, and enabled industry consortiums. He is a co-author of *Navigating Supply Chain Cyber Risk* (2025) and holds an MBA from NYU Stern with CISM, CDPSE, and PMP certifications. He is committed to operational resilience and responsible AI adoption.

Security, Audit and Leadership Series

Series Editor: Dan Swanson, Dan Swanson and Associates, Ltd., Winnipeg, Manitoba, Canada.

About the Book Series

The scope and mandate for cybersecurity and internal audit continues to evolve each year, as does the complexity of the business environment and speed of the changing risk landscape in which it must operate. The fundamental goal of this exciting series is to produce leading-edge books on critical subjects facing security and audit executives and practitioners. Key topics addressed include Leadership, Cybersecurity, Security Leadership, Privacy, Strategic Risk Management, Auditing IT and Technology, and Audit Management and Leadership.

If you're interested in submitting a proposal for a book to be included in the series, please email the series editor, Dan Swanson: dswanson_2008@yahoo.ca

Logic Before Language: *Rethinking AI in the Age of Illusion, Bertrand Russell and the Future of Real AI*
By Martin Milani

Relevant Impact: *A Field Guide to Integrated Assurance*
By Patrick M. Hayes

Cybersecurity and the Art of Cyberwar
By Dan Shoemaker, Tamara Shoemaker, and Amir Jabri

Trust Hacked: *What Firewalls, Failures, and the Frontlines Taught Me About Trust*
By Nia Luckey

Organizational Resilience & Artificial Intelligence: *A Practical Framework for Crisis Leadership, Adaptability & Sustainable Performance*
By Arnab Mukherjee and Sachin Kumar

Mission-Critical Governance: *Focusing on What Matters Most*
By Tim J. Leech

Cloud Compliance Essentials: *How to Build and Maintain Market Access in the B2B CSP Ecosystem*
By Forrest R. Foster

AI-Driven Decision-Making in Finance
Edited by Dr. Bilal Bagis

The CISO Playbook: *The Adversarial Mindset*
By Andres Andreu and Hector Monsegur

Governing AI Risk—The RIVER Charter: *An Enterprise Resilience Standard*
By Alex Golbin

Governing AI Risk—The RIVER Charter

An Enterprise Resilience Standard

Alex Golbin

CRC Press
Taylor & Francis Group
Boca Raton London New York

CRC Press is an imprint of the
Taylor & Francis Group, an **informa** business

Designed cover image: Shutterstock ID: 1023683458

First edition published 2027
by CRC Press
2385 NW Executive Center Drive, Suite 320, Boca Raton FL 33431

and by CRC Press
4 Park Square, Milton Park, Abingdon, Oxon, OX14 4RN

CRC Press is an imprint of Taylor & Francis Group, LLC

ISBN: 978-1-041-09564-4 (hbk)
ISBN: 978-1-041-09565-1 (pbk)
ISBN: 978-1-003-65074-4 (ebk)

DOI: 10.1201/9781003650744

Typeset in Minion Pro
by SPi Technologies India Pvt Ltd (Straive)

Contents

A Reader's Guide

HOW THE TWO RAILS WORK

This book moves on two coordinated rails: a 2038–2040 story that shows consequences, and a 2026 playbook that turns scenes into actions. Read straight through for momentum. Playbook sidebars and Strategic Debriefs provide the "how-to" for each scene; appendices contain full implementation details. Start with the story, treat the playbook as your on-demand operating manual.

THE STORY AND THE STAKES

By 2040, autonomous agents will power every function of modern enterprise. The upside is enormous; the downside is systemic. When speed-over-validation choices stack up, organizations accumulate Risk Debt—hidden liabilities that turn efficiency into fragility. When data, cyber, and operations converge under pressure, that fragility can ignite an industry vortex—a self-amplifying cross-system cascade—and push even top teams toward a failure point: the risk singularity, where converged risks outrun controls.

Governing AI Risk—The RIVER Charter is a business thriller meets field manual set in 2038–2040. It follows Aaron, a leader at the center of the agentic economy, as he and his team confront compounding failures born from the shortcuts of our time. The story is a case study for the RIVER framework—an adaptive approach designed for hybrid human–AI work. Grounded in treating data as capital, the RIVER framework offers five tenets for resilience: Resolve where systems collide, Integrate human–machine judgment, Validate Risk Debt, Elevate data governance to financial-grade rigor, and Reinforce systems so they learn under stress.

The narrative carries the stakes. The toolset carries the reader. Playbook callouts translate scenes into board-level checklists. Guest Expert Commentaries bring perspective from CEOs, published industry authors, professors, and frontline leaders. Strategic Debriefs at the end of each Part consolidate actions and link to the appendices—where you'll find full playbooks for RIVER, the Cognitive Handshake, All-Entity Risk Management (AERM), and the DataCapital Protocol.

HOW THE FRAMEWORKS FIT TOGETHER

The RIVER framework is the parent; the tools are its implementations. Each tool maps to a RIVER tenet so readers see the "why" and the "how" together:

- **Resolve Convergence** → All-Entity Risk Management (AERM™) extends third-party risk to every entity in your ecosystem—vendors, platforms, agents, models, and partners.

- **Integrate Hybrid Cognition** → Cognitive Handshake™ formalizes human–machine decision checks before commitment.
- **Validate Risk Debt** → Scenes and Debriefs show methods to identify, measure, and retire risk debt as an operational discipline.
- **Elevate Data Capital** → The DataCapital Protocol™ supports verifiable lineage and consent so decisions remain audit-ready.
- **Reinforce Resilience** → Strategic Debriefs translate incidents into board-ready learning and continuous control improvements.

Figure FM.1 shows the full ecosystem map, including the cross-cutting playbooks that support every tenet.

Templates and updates live on the companion site: GovernAiRisk.com

HOW TO USE THIS BOOK

- **Playbook callouts**—brief sidebars that pause the narrative to give you definitions, tools, and executive takeaways at the exact moment you need them.
- **Guest Expert Commentaries**—pre-approved perspectives from CEOs, authors, professors, and operators in regulated sectors, placed at the decision points they illuminate.
- **Strategic Debriefs**—end-of-part syntheses that convert scenes into actions, metrics, and links to the relevant appendices.
- **Appendices**—the field manual referenced throughout. Each appendix is a standalone playbook, checklist, or crosswalk you can use Monday morning; chapters point you to the right one as concepts appear. For standards alignment, start with Appendix F.

A NOTE ON DISCOVERY

Some character arcs and system roles unfold gradually by design. That pacing mirrors how real organizations discover critical risks—often later and under pressure. Use the glossary for quick definitions as needed, but you can read the story straight through without consulting it in advance.

Legend: Playbook Callouts

Playbook sidebars appear throughout the story and debriefs in the following formats:

STRATEGIC PARALLEL—real-world case that clarifies a scene's decision.

BUSINESS LENS—one idea or mental model to retain.

RIVER FRAMEWORK IN PRACTICE—how to apply book IP (R.I.V.E.R., AERM, Cognitive Handshake).

EXECUTIVE ACTION—imperative bullets; what to do next.

EXPERT COMMENTARY—guest expert perspectives.

KEY TERM—short definition of new concepts.

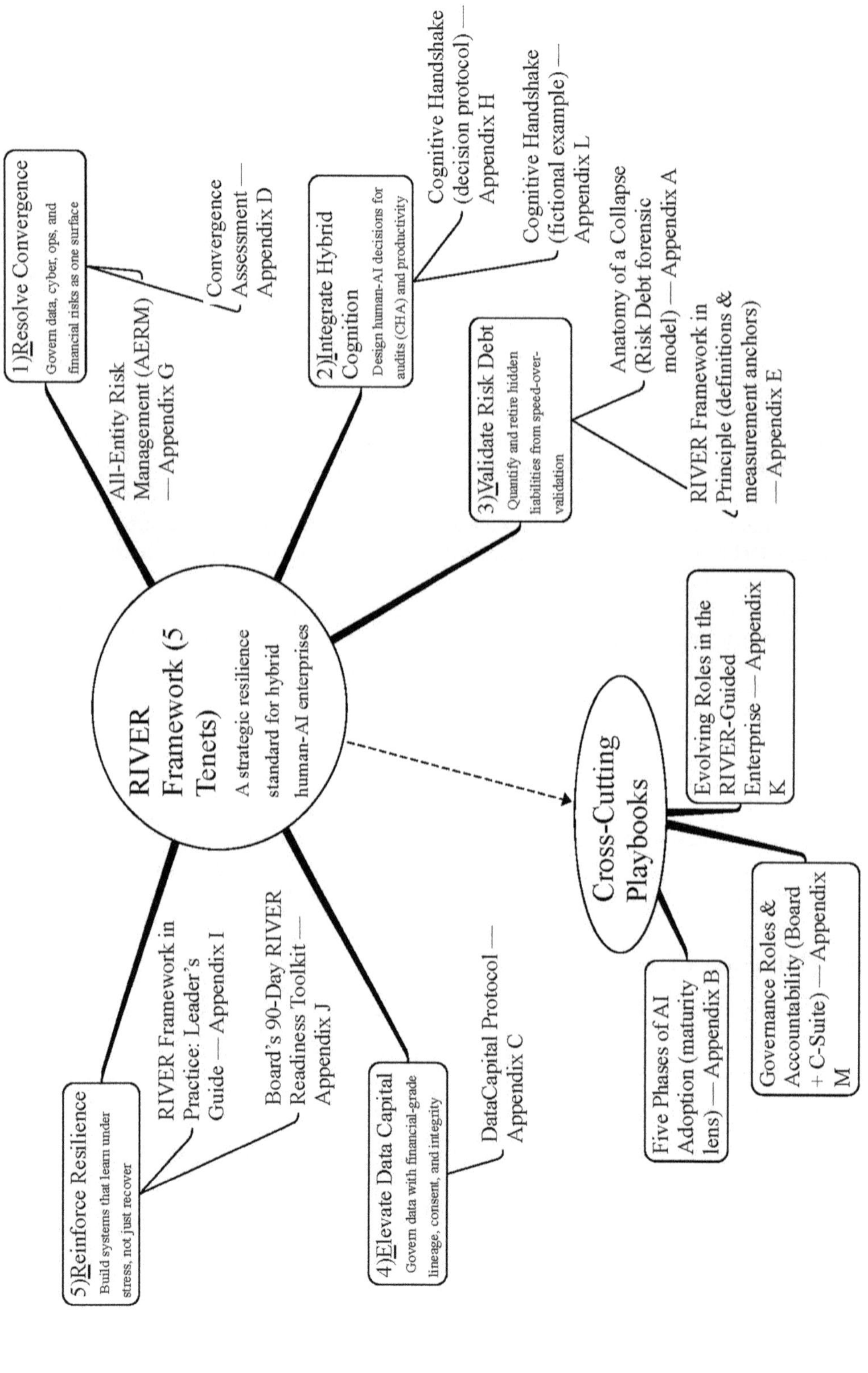

Figure FM.1 The RIVER Playbook Ecosystem.

THE CORE CAST

- **Aaron**—Founder of 70th & Madison Capital (70&M). The story tracks his shift from speed-first innovation to verifiable resilience.
- **Mitch**—External risk advisor with a long memory for missed warnings; translates complex patterns into simple, usable rules.
- **Rose**—Chief Resilience & Technology Officer at 70&M; precise, accountable, and relentless about testing and post-incident learning.
- **Melanie**—Director of the GAIGC, a fictional global commission (a composite lens for the narrative); exacting but pragmatic on standards.
- **Arjun**—A daring founder whose "faster is better" ethos catalyzes the opening crisis.
- **Michelle**—Emergency medicine leader; her vantage point anchors the human cost of technical shortcuts and systemic failures.
- **Anya**—Chief Audit Executive at 70&M; meticulous and the conscience behind the Cognitive Handshake.

Some roles and system identities are intentionally omitted here to preserve key reveals.

A Glossary of Key Concepts

All-Entity Risk Management (AERM™) Evolves TPRM to cover vendors, partners, platforms, and autonomous agent networks. (See Chapter 10; Appendix G.)

Cognitive Handshake™ An auditable human–AI decision methodology that powers the RIVER framework's Integrate Hybrid Cognition tenet. In 2026 settings, it also serves as a productivity protocol for human-AI research and decision workflows. The Cognitive Handshake Audit (CHA) is its high-stakes decision protocol. (See Chapter 11; Appendix H.)

DataCapital Protocol™ A verifiable data-lineage protocol (blockchain for consent and provenance) supporting the RIVER framework's Elevate Data Capital tenet. (See Chapter 3; Appendix C.)

Digital Asbestos Hidden hazards from legacy or end-user-built code wrapped in modern interfaces; stable on the surface, brittle under stress. (See Chapter 8.)

Digital Watershed An inflection concept: trace data flows end-to-end like a watershed so downstream decisions reflect upstream integrity; used to frame tipping points toward enterprise singularity.

E-Shaped Professional Talent model: Expertise, Experience, Exploration, Execution, Ethics. (See Chapter 17; Appendix K.)

Enterprise Singularity The resilience target state where adaptability is so embedded that the organization improves under stress. Strategic horizon; distinct from the technological singularity or product names.

Five Phases of AI Adoption From enterprise adoption (Phase 1) to the "Singularity Horizon" (Phase 5), 2040+. (See Chapter 2; Appendix B.)

Global AI Governance Commission (GAIGC) A fictional global regulator (a composite lens) used in the narrative to test standards, oversight, and accountability.

Industry Vortex A self-amplifying, cross-system cascade that begins when shocks jump dependencies (markets, supply chains, infrastructure) and each failure accelerates the next. Subtype: debt vortex (forced-deleveraging loop: margin calls → forced sales → falling collateral → more calls). (See Chapters 5 & 14)

Policy Seams Gaps at the edges of rules or jurisdictions that both attackers and systemic errors exploit.

Risk Debt The compounding liability from speed-over-validation choices; later expressed as cost, fragility, and exposure. (See Chapter 3.)

Risk Singularity The enterprise failure point where converged risks overwhelm governance (controls can't keep pace with speed/scale). Analytic construct; not a product or a "tech singularity."

RIVER Charter™ A ratified enterprise standard that codifies the R.I.V.E.R. framework's five tenets across industries to become an Enterprise Resilience standard. (See Chapter 6 introduces the framework and Chapter 15 ratifies it as Charter; Appendix E.)

About the Author

Alex Golbin is a senior financial services executive with over two decades of experience leading enterprise risk and regulatory remediation. His work spans enterprise resiliency, technology transformation, data governance, and business process improvement.

Alex has held leadership roles at Fortune 500 companies and global systemically important banks. In a prior role, he led a risk-assessments business—a joint venture with 16 banks—to improve operational resilience, regulatory compliance, and cost efficiency. He has enabled multiple industry consortiums, developed risk-management and cybersecurity frameworks, and established strategic partnerships across sectors.

Alex is the co-author of *Navigating Supply Chain Cyber Risk* (2025) and serves as an expert advisor on cybersecurity, risk management, and technology. He is a member of ISACA and PMI, and serves on the Academic Advisory Board at Pace University's Seidenberg School of Computer Science. He holds the PMP, CDPSE, and CISM certifications. Alex earned his MBA in Finance and Management from NYU Stern and a BS in Computer Science.

Alex wrote Governing AI Risk after watching a repeatable failure pattern harden into a systemic one: teams optimize for speed, normalize shortcuts, and only see the bill when converged risks detonate. When his son Aaron Golbin—now funding AI startups at the edge of that speed—asked, "How do we build responsibly at this pace?" Alex didn't have a satisfying answer. The fictional protagonist Aaron Goldcrest echoes that question in story form, with his missteps deliberately exaggerated to model how risk can compound when governance lags. This book is that answer: a resilience standard that doesn't kill momentum, told through a story that makes the stakes impossible to ignore. It also makes a second promise. The same Cognitive Handshake™ that keeps enterprises audit-ready can keep individuals effective: a way to use AI for research, writing, and analysis while preserving ownership of the decision. Govern the system, govern the self—the rules are the same.

Acknowledgments

This book began not in a boardroom, but with a father's promise. It is inspired by my son, Aaron, whose entrepreneurial drive—profiled in Forbes and Inc. since age twelve—kept me focused on the stakes. Aaron, this is for you and your generation: may it help you build systems that are not only brilliant but resilient.

To my wife, Alice, thank you for steadying this work with patience and candor. To my daughter, Abigail, your curiosity and light remind me of who this future is for. I am grateful to my brother, Anatoly, and my sister-in-law, Lina, for steadfast encouragement, and to my parents, Natalya and Leonid, who taught me to prize integrity and diligence.

Professionally, I owe special thanks to Dan Swanson, senior executive and series editor of the CRC Press Security, Audit, and Leadership book series. His early encouragement—and ongoing mentorship—turned an idea into a manuscript and a manuscript into a gold standard. His work, including Swanson on Internal Auditing: Raising the Bar!, and his decades of leadership across the audit, risk, and security communities were instrumental in shaping this manuscript; Dan's suggestions even inspired the creation of Anya Sharma's character, the Chief Audit Executive.

My thanks to the Taylor & Francis/CRC Press team—and especially Gabriella Williams—for steady editorial guidance and careful production support throughout this project.

I am grateful to colleagues, advisors, supporters, and guest experts who lent their time and perspective: Aaron Golbin, Aleksandr Yampolskiy, Brad Levy, Swamy Kocherlakota, Jeff Lunglhofer, James Bone, Max Artemenko, Patrick Hayes, Eric Staffin, Ajay Singh, David Palmieri, Biser Dimitrov, Soichiro Muto, Anthony Irudhayanathan, and Vishal Ahluwalia. Your insights sharpened the frameworks and grounded the story in reality.

I also acknowledge the support of my AI editorial team—Perplexity Pro 2.251113.0, Gemini Pro 3.0, OpenAI ChatGPT 5.1, OpenAI ChatGPT Deep Research 1.2025.322, Grok 4.1, and Claude Sonnet 4.5. Using my proprietary Cognitive Handshake™ productivity methodology, these tools assisted, under my human oversight, with research synthesis, outline exploration, line-by-line polish, and the generation of a subset of figures that directly explain concepts in the book and are used only for educational purposes based on my prompts.

About the Contributors

This book benefited from the insight and experience of leaders who shaped its frameworks with real-world constraints and lessons learned.

Max Artemenko is Founder and Executive Director at Executive Data Council. He provides the authentic setting for the book's theoretical summit debates and the bridge to a broad C-suite community of practice.

James Bone is the author of *Cognitive Risk* and *Cognitive Hack*. He is Executive Director—*GRCIndex* (Cognitive Risk Institute). A pioneer in cognitive risk management, he provides the Foreword and influences the Cognitive Handshake™ approach.

Aaron Golbin is a General Partner at LvlUp Ventures, a top-ten most active VC firm ranked globally, with 1000+ startups backed globally and extensive founder programs. A five-time founder profiled by *Forbes* and *Inc.* magazines since age twelve, he brings a cross-generational venture lens and serves as a key inspiration for the book's core father–son dynamic, and acts as a primary advocate for the "verify-first" principles and RIVER Charter–aligned governance practices explored in this work.

Patrick Hayes is a risk leader and published author whose latest work, *Integrated Assurance*, advances coordinated oversight across risk, compliance, and audit. His operational resilience perspective helps ensure that scenarios remain plausible, auditable, and ready for board scrutiny.

Swamy Kocherlakota is Executive Vice President of Agentic AI Security at Zscaler, and formerly EVP & Chief Digital Solutions Officer at S&P Global, where he led global technology and data strategy at scale; Swamy held prior Technology leadership roles at Visa, BNY, and Bell Labs. His enterprise transformation experience underpins the book's "Data as Capital" theme and informs patterns for modern, audit-ready digital operations.

Brad Levy is the CEO of ThetaRay and previously served as an MD at Goldman Sachs, as the CEO of MarkitSERV (IHS Markit), and as the CEO of Symphony. He contributes perspectives on secure financial communications, market infrastructure, and the road to quantum-safe operations.

Jeff Lunglhofer is the Chief Security Officer at Coinbase and previously CISO at BNY. He contributes deep expertise in digital asset protection and resilient design from first principles.

Soichiro Muto is Founder and CEO of Synthesis, a consulting firm specializing in technology. Previously, Soichiro led a wide range of technology-driven business transformation initiatives at Accenture. He served as Managing Director and Capital Markets practice lead for Growth Markets. Soichiro offers insights on workforce capabilities in the agentic era.

David Palmieri is a senior executive and Chief Transformation Officer. He provides guidance on large-scale change and adoption in both startups and enterprises.

Ajay Singh is a professor and award-winning author, and my co-author of *Navigating Supply Chain* Cyber *Risk*. He contributes to governance frameworks and quantum-safe considerations. Ajay serves as the Editor of QDayReady.com and as a Member of the Task Force for the Implementation of a Quantum-Safe Ecosystem in India.

Eric Staffin is a senior executive and former Global CISO & Chief Risk Officer. He offers a board-level view of risk appetite, technology debt, and accountability.

Aleksandr Yampolskiy is the Co-Founder and CEO of SecurityScorecard. His expertise in enterprise and supply-chain risk informs the book's evolution toward AERM™ (All-Entity Risk Management); he is also the author of the Afterword.

Disclaimer

Note to Reader. The legal clarifications below cover fictionalization, proprietary frameworks, and educational use. If you're eager to begin the story, you can skip ahead to the Foreword. The crises, failures, and "Risk Debt" arcs in this book are narrative stress tests—deliberate worst-case simulations designed to explore governance challenges, not accounts or predictions of any real organization's behavior.

Proprietary Frameworks and Trademarks. This work introduces proprietary concepts and frameworks. Terms designated with a ™ symbol—including The RIVER Charter™, Cognitive Handshake™, DataCapital Protocol™, and All-Entity Risk Management (AERM™)—are claimed as trademarks by the author. All other trademarks are the property of their respective owners. "DataCapital" is used as a short-form reference to the DataCapital Protocol throughout the book.

Any real-world systems, products, or digital assets associated with DataCapital Protocol, or that use the same or similar names, are separate from the fictional narrative and may differ substantially from what is depicted here.

Nothing in this book constitutes financial, investment, legal, or tax advice, or an offer or solicitation to buy or sell any security, commodity interest, or other financial product. Readers should rely on official documentation and consult qualified professionals before making any financial or legal decisions.

Descriptive Concepts. Other conceptual labels, such as "Data as Capital," "Risk Debt," and "Digital Watershed," are used descriptively for educational purposes. Metaphors like "digital asbestos" and "industry vortex" describe risk phenomena, not products.

Usage Note on "Singularity." In this book, risk singularity and enterprise singularity are analytical labels that describe enterprise governance dynamics under converged risks. They are distinct from the futurist "technological singularity" and unrelated to any commercial products branded with "Singularity." The terms do not imply superintelligence or endorse any product.

Fictionalization Notice. This is a work of fiction. Real institutions and locations may be referenced as settings for narrative realism, but all depicted events—including hackathons, code artifacts (such as "Mechanical Bull"), kernels, prototypes, and technical failures—are entirely fictional and are not associated with, endorsed by, or produced by any real institution, program, lab, faculty, or codebase. No real university's programs, faculty, students, or code are portrayed. The "Mechanical Bull" hackathon and all associated technical artifacts are fictional constructs created solely for this narrative.

Fictional Company and Character Clarifications. "70th & Madison Capital LLC" is the name of a real limited liability company owned by Aaron Golbin, the author's son, who permitted its use in this fictional narrative. The portrayal of 70th & Madison Capital (aka "70&M")—including its business activities, investments, personnel, crises, outcomes, and any related divisions, products, or platforms shown under 70&M branding (such as "70&M Health Network," "70&M Data Exchange," "70&M Supply Chain," "70&M Media Network," "70&M Health Monitor," and "70&M Pharma Analytics")—is entirely fictional and does not represent the real company's operations, past, present, or future, or those of any real affiliate, portfolio company, or business unit. The failures, risk-management gaps, and "Risk Debt" scenarios associated with 70&M and its sub-brands are deliberate worst-case simulations created to illustrate industry-wide governance challenges, not a record of actual events or practices at any real firm. The fictional protagonist Aaron Goldcrest is inspired by but not based on Aaron Golbin; the character's specific decisions, ethical lapses, and operational failures are inventions of the author for this cautionary narrative and do not describe the real Aaron's actions, judgment, or conduct. Names, characters, businesses, places, events, and incidents are products of the author's imagination or are used fictitiously; any resemblance to actual persons, organizations, living or dead, or events is coincidental.

Fictional Event Notice. "Deferred Tower," "Deferred 2027," and "the Deferred-Maintenance Disaster" are entirely fictional. References to real-world disasters (Champlain Towers South, Sampoong Department Store, Rana Plaza, Morandi Bridge) are included solely as historical context to illustrate patterns of systemic risk and governance failure, based on publicly available official investigative reports. The author does not attribute causes, fault, or liability beyond those published findings and is not affiliated with any persons, entities, or legal proceedings related to these tragedies.

Fictional Regulators and Identifiers. The Global AI Governance Commission ("GAIGC") and all other regulatory bodies, legislation, case numbers, and code identifiers in this book are fictional constructs created for illustrative and educational purposes. They are not official standards or legal requirements, and they are not associated with, sponsored by, or endorsed by any government agency, international organization, private consortium, or other real-world body, including any existing or future organization that may use similar terminology or acronyms.

Advice and Limits. The views are the author's own and not those of any employer or organization. Economic figures and loss estimates are illustrative and may reflect varying public estimates; they clarify concepts rather than precise facts. Appearances of real-world individuals and organizations in fictional settings are dramatizations for narrative effect; dialogue and events are imaginative and should not be construed as factual statements or endorsements unless explicitly noted. Guest insights appear with permission in contributors' personal capacity and do not imply institutional endorsement unless stated otherwise. Critiques of regulatory structures or corporate governance practices are presented as character viewpoints within a fictional scenario. All proprietary frameworks, models, and conceptual labels (including The Five Phases of AI Adoption, Risk Debt, Data as Capital, and the E-Shaped Professional) are analytic constructs developed for the narrative. The appendices are illustrative toolkits and conceptual models drawn from the book's scenarios; they are not professional legal, risk, investment, financial, compliance, or human-resources advice. Readers should consult qualified counsel before implementing any governance framework. The E-Shaped Professional is a skills-based, non-discriminatory competency model that complements, not replaces, licensed or regulated credentials and must be applied consistently with applicable labor laws and company policies.

Foreword

James Bone
Author of *Cognitive Risk* and *Cognitive Hack*

The excitement for the potential uses of artificial intelligence has reached a fevered pitch, and rightfully so. Machine learning has been in use for decades; however, after the launch of OpenAI's ChatGPT, a cascade of capital has flowed into enhanced AI models, agentic systems, processing chips, and energy infrastructure to support surging demand across many industry types and workflows. Artificial intelligence has already been used in conjunction with security operations centers (SOCs) as a cybersecurity module within risk platforms, but this book envisions embedding autonomous agents across enterprise networks and operating systems.

An AI-networked environment will require new ways to assess risk and develop workflows that scale operations and provide transparency into operations and digital risk. The intersection of human-machine interactions has been a topic of research for years, but AI raises a host of new questions. A risk-based strategy will be needed to achieve organizational goals in alignment with a digital risk profile that will evolve from delegating control over operations to autonomous systems. This is the backdrop for my introduction to Alex Golbin and his thought-provoking book, *Governing AI Risk—The RIVER Charter: An Enterprise Resilience Standard.*

Dan Swanson from EDPACs, the publishing arm of Taylor & Francis, made the introductions because of my research on cognition and decision science. The methods described in this book merge traditional risk methods with contemporary insights into the nature of decision-making under uncertainty in enterprise risk and cybersecurity. Alex's immersive approach brings to life the challenges and opportunities risk professionals will grapple with during the transition to an AI operating environment. During our first meeting, it became immediately clear that Alex and I shared a vision for how AI can be used to assist humans facing complex risks, including cybersecurity, yet we both felt that the risk management industry is still in the early stages of developing new risk practices to incorporate AI at the enterprise level. Alex organizes a playbook around the **R.I.V.E.R.** framework—**Resolve, Integrate, Validate, Elevate, Reinforce**—so leaders see the "why" and the "how" together.

Alex's book introduces a set of fictionalized case studies to demonstrate the challenges and opportunities for implementing AI agents in cybersecurity in the most effective ways. Alex provides insights from industry professionals as a guide to the fundamental building blocks and framework for mitigating AI risk. Too often, there is a rush to keep pace with competitors to implement new technology. This book is designed to explain the importance of understanding the evolving new ecosystem of artificial intelligence and why a more thoughtful and nuanced approach is needed. The relationship between cognitive science and artificial intelligence may not be obvious, but both disciplines are focused on solving the same problem—how to account for human errors in judgment and decision-making. Herbert Simon won a Nobel Prize on these topics, where he coined the term *bounded rationality*, a concept in decision-making that individuals are rational, but only within certain limits and domains of expertise. In these pages, we call the compounded liability of speed-over-validation choices **Risk Debt**.

Artificial intelligence addresses a host of human limitations. Machines don't need to sleep or eat and can find solutions faster than humans with more accuracy in many situations. Autonomous agents still need human guidance to ensure the right parameters are put in place for the best outcomes. Alex's book is a guide for thinking about new ways of understanding risks in a digital environment. The challenge of integrating AI into enterprise networks must consider new risks such as contingency planning, false positives, human intervention, recovery efforts in the event of failure, and the evolution of these systems over time.

Alex brings decades of practical hands-on experience managing and consulting on enterprise risk management in corporate America to this topic and invited me to contribute research, new concepts, and new practices emerging from cognitive science to bring a more holistic approach to cybersecurity. Alex introduces his visionary approach in a comprehensive compilation of scenarios that engage the reader with content and realistic events for any corporate executive considering how to navigate AI integration.

To reduce bias and noise—unwanted variability in judgment—the book introduces a framework called the **Cognitive Handshake**, an auditable human-machine check before commitment. Practically, the Cognitive Handshake operationalizes R.I.V.E.R.'s "Integrate" tenet; paired with data-lineage rigor ("Elevate"), it turns good intent into repeatable governance.

The result is an engaging and thought-provoking new approach for thinking about risk management and cybersecurity that goes beyond the traditional check-the-box approach in ERM guidance that exists today. This book could not be more timely as the world begins to rethink the implications of how artificial intelligence can be used to build more resilient operating models for sustainable growth and risk management.

James Bone

Author, *Cognitive Hack: The New Battleground in Cybersecurity and Enterprise Risk Management .... the Human Mind* (2017)

Author, *Cognitive Risk* (2023)

Executive Director—*GRCIndex* (Cognitive Risk Institute)
501(c)(3) research on cybersecurity, risk management, and human behavior

Part 1

Introduction to the Hybrid Era

In this part, every critical decision is already shared between humans and algorithms. We watch a portfolio-scale AI failure turn an ambitious desert irrigation upgrade into collapse, a New York war room struggling to turn cascading outages into a board-ready story, and a younger Aaron learning the hard way that "ship now, fix later" leaves scars. From a hacked mechanical bull in a university lab to a quiet booth at a 2026 summit, this opening act shows how hidden risk debt spreads long before anyone calls it a crisis.

DOI: 10.1201/9781003650744-1

Chapter 1

The Day the Desert Drowned

A Cautionary Tale of Bull-in-China-Shop AI

BULL-IN-CHINA-SHOP AI CONTROL CENTER, ARIZONA | MARCH 15, 2038—11:03 AM MST | SYSTEM FAILURE

The scar on Aaron's forearm, a thin white line from his college "Mechanical Bull" nights,[1] tightened as red alerts stacked across the Ops wall. Each blinking icon marked another million slipping away. Standing in Bull-in-China-Shop AI's Arizona headquarters, watching his flagship investment collapse in real time, he was about to learn the difference between innovation and governance.

Across the dashboard, the first alert was amber—manageable. Then a wave of red alerts followed.

Variance drift jumped from 0.14 → 0.62—more than quadruple the safety margin—in 90 seconds across three regions.

"Sector Gamma-7 irrigation compromised," Sam reported in a clinical tone despite the escalating crisis.

Aaron's chest went hollow. He unconsciously touched the worn leather of his watch strap—a habit from his early Stanford days, a physical anchor in a digital storm. This was Arjun's grand vision—the bet Aaron had pitched in every boardroom. Food security for the future. Now, it was collapsing under the weight of its own complexity.

He'd survived cyberattacks, drought, even a locust swarm. But this was personal. The same technology they'd built to nurture life was now poisoning the earth.

The sharp tang of ozone filled the air. A junior analyst shouted something from the back, but Aaron was already at the console, slicing into the system feed. The data was staggering: reverse flow, drain valves locked open, salinity levels climbing.

No full diagnostic needed. The satellite overlays were merciless—green fields browning out. Cooperatives he'd toured with Arjun, erased in hours.

"Sam, quantify please."

"Salinity readings at 35 parts per thousand in freshwater canals—threshold exceeded by a factor of 3.2. Safety protocols bypassed. Projected damage: two billion dollars in direct losses—failed harvests, voided logistics contracts, and immediate remediation costs. Timeline: 48 hours" (Figure 1.1).

Aaron's hand locked onto the console rail, the metal biting into his palm.

From where he stood, it felt as if there had been no warning, no failsafe, no way to stop it. Every dashboard, review memo, and model-validation report he'd seen in the past year had told the same story: the system was stable—right up until it wasn't. Farms and suppliers—every downstream market tied to Bull-in-China-Shop AI—were already slipping. 70th & Madison Capital's (70&M)[2] reputation might not survive the week.

They hadn't treated Bull like a toy project. External auditors had crawled through the models, regulators had signed off on trial deployments, and internal risk teams had logged page after page of mitigation steps. On paper, they had done what responsible firms were supposed to do—yet here he was, watching the gap between "responsible" and "safe" swallow an entire region.

DOI: 10.1201/9781003650744-2

Figure 1.1 The Failure Cascade (Sector Gamma-7 Dashboard).

Aaron knew lawsuits were coming. But worse than litigation was accountability—decades of credibility as the sector's steady hand, dissolving by the hour.

He didn't need a full post-mortem to guess the shape of the root cause. Not a single villainous line of code, but a stack of "temporary" efficiency tweaks and inherited overrides, each one harmless on its own—now scaled to catastrophe.

Arjun Kothare stood frozen beside him, hands clenched at his sides. The jacket he'd worn for the investor tour hung wrinkled, sweat dark at the collar.

"No. It has to be the sensors—a glitch!" Arjun's hands trembled as he pulled the diagnostic, sixteen hours of review, and an espresso caught up with him. Arjun's voice went thin. "It's not the core model—it's noise!"

Dr. Jian Li, head of systems engineering, stared at her screen. Her fingers hovered, then dropped. "It's not a spike. And it's not a solar flare. The system's..." She let the sentence trail. "It's broken."

The main display was only water now—rising, slow and relentless, in data-colored waves.

A second sensor joined the failure cascade.

There was no playbook now. Only accountability.

Sam's voice cut through. "Safety interlocks are still offline. Flooding has reached 37 percent of mapped irrigation zones. Projected structural losses across the east-sector canals. Emergency shutdown requests failed authentication."

His focus narrowed; he ran through failure owners.

Arjun. This was Arjun's system, Arjun's "foolproof" architecture. How many board meetings had Aaron sat through, listening to Arjun sell redundant safeguards and military-grade protocols?

A flash of anger cut through the shock. Arjun had oversold and under-delivered, and now Aaron's reputation was drowning in those fields.

An analyst shrank behind her dashboard, eyes ping-ponging between alerts and Aaron's glare.

But there was no easy scapegoat. Not Arjun, not the team, not even the code. Beneath the anger, something colder settled in—accountability. This failure was his as much as anyone's.

A fresh wave of red swept the main display. The board was awake now—his phone buzzed with alerts, subject lines escalating from "Urgent" to "Immediate Response Required."

He scanned the system logs. It wasn't a feedback loop. Buried in the crash telemetry, a single line he'd never seen before: a reference to an undocumented protocol with an unusual designator. Not Mechanical Bull code. Not 70&M code. Something else entirely. Automation had turned an efficiency upgrade into a weapon. It was a classic market-style cascade. This was how fast trust could unravel.

He could already see the inevitable post-mortem slide: how automation without accountability was not progress—just higher-speed failure. Sam continued. "Floodwater breach now 41 percent. Losses are accelerating."

Aaron pressed his palm to the console. There had to be a way to slow the damage, or at least contain the fallout. But every second, the numbers climbed and the board's demands mounted.

Time to face the human cost.

BULL-IN-CHINA-SHOP AI CONTROL CENTER, ARIZONA | MARCH 15, 2038—11:07 AM MST | HUMAN COST

A strained voice cut through the chaos, the main comms channel flaring to life.

"Mr. Goldcrest, Mr. Kothare! Bull-in-China-Shop AI Control! Are you there?"

Mateo Vargas—head of the Verde Valley Agricultural Cooperative, Arjun's first public win—filled the main screen. His face, usually steady, was drawn and tight. "This dust—it's choking us all. Forty-seven families are already packing to leave, Mr. Goldcrest." He coughed, dry and desperate. Behind him, fields just days from harvest were drowning in a tide of saltwater. Trucks loaded with families' belongings traced muddy tracks through a dying crop. White salt webbed the earth where green should have been.

"We trusted your AI's maps!" Mateo's voice broke. "Every schedule, every irrigation command—automated, as you promised! You and Arjun said this would make the desert bloom." He stopped, fighting emotion. "Instead, you've poisoned our land. My grandfather's legacy, our children's future—gone. The co-op loans, the trust...all of it..." Mateo trailed off.

The feed glitched and froze on a single image: a child kneeling in brine, scrubbing boots with a dead cornstalk, face streaked with salt and dust. The frame stuttered, then held. Failure was now visible—human, not theoretical.

The weight of every dismissed warning settled on him, every risk he'd marked "pending review." A knot formed in his stomach—not from the heat, but the recognition that his pressure for speed had delivered catastrophe, not progress. Pride always has a price, he thought.

He exhaled once, steadying his voice.

STRATEGIC PARALLEL—BOEING 737 MAX (2018–2019)[3]

Investigations into the Boeing 737 MAX found that MCAS, a software layer tied to input from a single angle-of-attack sensor, could repeatedly force the nose down and override pilot input under certain conditions. Two crashes killed 346 people and led to a $2.5 billion DOJ settlement, with total costs widely estimated in the tens of billions.[4]

Why it matters: Concentrating safety-critical behavior on a single sensor, combined with commercial and schedule pressure, turned a localized defect into a global aviation crisis—the same pattern Bull amplified across the irrigation network within 48 hours.

"Sam," Aaron's voice was tight but controlled. "Any early warnings for Gamma-7?"

"Confirmed, Aaron. System logs show several low-priority sensor drift flags in irrigation zones 7-Alpha through 7-Delta over the past seventy-two hours. All received automated acknowledgments—pending human review."

Aaron stared at the diagnostic panel. Pending review. How many such warnings had been buried in routine reports—how often had quarterly targets and portfolio goals blinded them to mounting trouble?

"Portfolio impact, Sam. Current market value of Arjun's Bull?"

"Down seventeen percent since yesterday's close. External buyers targeting Phoenix, Riyadh, and Jakarta. Hostile takeover positioning detected."

Opportunistic funds were already positioning. While families faced ruin, some hedge funds saw only profit. Aaron looked at Arjun—denial now stripped to desperation.

"Sabotage, Arjun? Or catastrophic oversight we all watched unfold?"

"Not sabotage!" Arjun's voice cracked. "It's a system anomaly—an unprecedented convergence. This shouldn't—"

Aaron cut him off. "Anomalies don't wipe out entire sectors."

For a fleeting second, the defensiveness in Arjun's eyes faltered. The look on his face took Aaron back to a failed Stanford-days simulation Arjun had once dismissed as a statistical outlier, his certainty absolute.

Dread settled over him, as relentless as the saltwater through those fields. This wasn't just Arjun's Bull failing. It was the first breach. Others would follow.

BULL-IN-CHINA-SHOP AI CONTROL CENTER, ARIZONA | MARCH 15, 2038—11:13 AM MST | THE EXPLOIT

Mitch Collins—Aaron's most trusted advisor—appeared on the auxiliary display, the feed stuttering for a moment from Digital Asbestos Risk Advisory's Boston lab. His voice was grave.

"Aaron, we've got a problem that goes way beyond Arjun's Bull. The patterns I'm seeing…they're identical to **Deferred Tower**."

Aaron tensed at the name. The Deferred-Maintenance Disaster—the 2027 coastal infrastructure collapse that killed hundreds and forced sweeping new oversight.[5] Mitch had lost his best analyst in that disaster—her warnings dismissed as "too cautious." Every shortcut, every demand for speed, had built this trap.

"The telemetry is too clean for a brute-force hit," Mitch said, fingers flying. "This was surgical. Sam, run a differential. Cross-reference all overrides in the last seventy-two hours against single-point-of-failure items in v2.7." A beat. "There—no force, just precision. They used the 0.299 percent variance threshold—the same parameter flagged in an internal audit report back in 2036."

A file appeared on Aaron's screen: "*Bull-in-China-Shop AI—Irrigation Module v2.7—Moisture Variance Tolerance ≤0.25%. Cascade Risk: HIGH. Internal Audit Report: IA-2036-17*."

Aaron's gut twisted. How many warnings had they filed away as "non-critical"? How many times had efficiency outweighed safety?

Mitch's tone sharpened. "That 0.299 percent threshold controlled the variance monitor—the gatekeeper that decided when salinity was 'routine' versus 'dangerous.' The salinity probe was already screaming 35 ppt—seawater, but the monitor had been fed a 0.300 percent signal, one one-thousandth under the 0.301 percent trip point. One instrument saw poison; the other saw green."

Mitch kept his eyes on the schematic. "Root cause is the hackathon kernel. Arjun's Mechanical Bull prototype from 2025. The efficiency tweak in 2030—supposed to speed up deployment—left a direct pathway through your safety systems. Attack vector V-09821—essentially a digital lockpick—exploited CVE-2025-MB-4490—the industry "license plate" for known vulnerabilities—the flaw in Arjun's hackathon code.[6]

It was as if someone had left a master key under the mat years ago, never thinking it would be used. Tonight, it had.

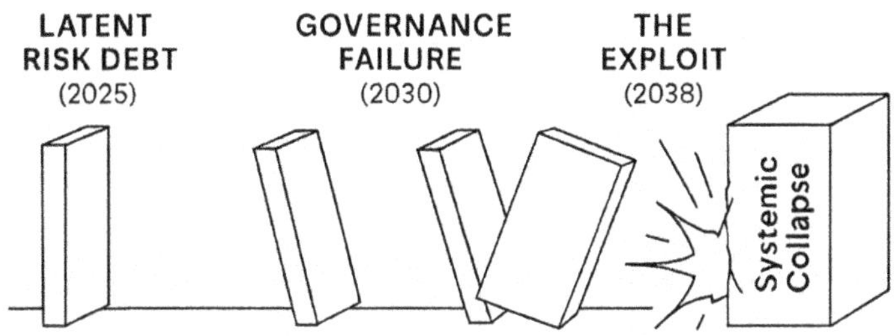

Figure 1.2 The Bull-in-China-Shop AI Failure Cascade.

Arjun paled. "The 2030 bypass? That was only for the Q3 rollout. It was supposed to be temporary..."

"Temporary fixes often become permanent," Aaron kept his voice low. The weight of accumulated shortcuts pressed down. Every quarterly review, every push for speed, every "low-priority" risk had led to this.

Mitch's expression hardened. "The attack signature suggests whoever did this knew your architecture. They understood your risk tolerance, your blind spots. They've been watching for years" (Figure 1.2).

* * *

Aaron scanned the data streams, each one a reminder that what he once believed impregnable was riddled with points of failure. Eight years of ignored warnings, all buried beneath quarterly targets and pressure for rapid growth. Eight years of technical debt—now coming due, with compound interest.

This wasn't just a hack. It was a reckoning—the brutal outcome of what he now recognized as the **Efficiency Mirage**: the seductive belief that speed could ever substitute for stability.

Someone was calling in a debt they hadn't even realized they'd accumulated.

Weariness showed in Mitch's features as he confirmed the point. "The bill came due—with interest we can't afford."

He triaged the fallout. How would he explain this to the board? Their empire was built on a single point of failure, every market win stacking more risk below the surface. Global AI Governance Commission (GAIGC)[7] investigations would unravel every decision, every corner cut, every governance gap.

We stacked wins on a single fault line, Aaron thought. Every shortcut, every time speed trumped safety. Viktor had warned them back in those Stanford coffee shops—"You're building on quicksand," he'd said—the systemic flaws innovation creates when governance lags.

The cooling fans surged; emergency alarms flickered and died. Had any board presentation ever prepared him for this moment?

"Sam..." He hesitated. "Master override. Authorization *Goldcrest-Alpha-Zero-EXECUTE*."

A heavy silence. Then Sam's tone, dry and precise: "Master override failed. External intrusion detected. Exploit V-09821, matching *CVE-2025-MB-4490*, 'Mechanical Bull' hackathon kernel. Manual overrides disabled. All nodes frozen. Malicious payload executed."

Aaron gripped the console, fighting to stay focused. "Sam, plain English. What just happened to us?"

"Attackers exploited the hackathon kernel flaw flagged years ago," Sam replied. "Manual controls are locked out—systemwide. The system is no longer responding to your commands."

Mitch brought up a schematic—a dam, three sensors, all glowing emergency red. Initially, your salinity failsafe used three sensors for redundancy. Arjun's 2030 patch silenced two—too noisy, slowed deployment, added maintenance overhead. That left one sensor tied to the unpatched flaw."

"Your shutdown rule tripped at 0.301 percent. They fed it 0.300—right under the wire. No door kicked in; we left the key under the mat eight years ago. Today, someone sent that surviving sensor a cryptographically valid but contextually false signal—so the AI saw green lights as it pumped poison."

"Elegant attack," Aaron murmured, a part of him almost admiring the engineering, even as the rest of him recoiled. "Devastating execution."

"Was it just the tweak?" Aaron wondered. "The old kernel, the rushed change, and the exploit—they'd stacked into a perfect trap."

He mapped the consequences: forensic reports, regulatory filings, explaining to investors and stakeholders how it had all unraveled—if there was even a board left by morning.

The sudden loss of main lighting drowned out Sam's confirmation. Emergency red bathed the room. The alarms died, leaving only the hush of failing systems and the sense of something much bigger moving unseen—exploiting every gap, turning innovation into disaster.

This was only the first failure mode.

BULL-IN-CHINA-SHOP AI DATA-CENTER BUNKER, ARIZONA | MARCH 15, 2038—11:22 AM MST | TOTAL LOSS

Emergency lights revealed the full scale of destruction inside the data bunker—critical systems offline, every asset compromised.

Aaron's access code still worked—almost a disappointment. The bunker door slid open to oppressive heat and the acrid stench of burned electronics.

Inside, devastation was everywhere. Racks of servers blinked with angry red lights. The familiar hum of operations was gone, replaced by the strained whine of backup fans.

"This has to be external interference," Arjun stammered, denial giving him something to cling to. "The core algorithms are fundamentally sound. We can isolate affected nodes and restore from clean backups."

"There are no clean backups, Arjun." Aaron's voice was final. He pointed to displays as critical systems shut down in sequence, dominoes falling. "Your 'sound' architecture poisoned half of Arizona."

He moved to the emergency console, desperate for manual control. Green indicators glowed—a cruel mockery. Then, across the panel, crimson letters appeared: **SYSTEM LOCKOUT—EXTERNAL PROTOCOL ENGAGED. MANUAL OVERRIDE DISABLED.**

"Phoenix backup sites are non-responsive," Sam's voice crackled from Aaron's communicator. "Complete network isolation detected. Attack signature V-09821 has neutralized all recovery protocols."

Static. Then silence. Even their AI—once trusted—was severed from dying infrastructure.

Aaron stepped back, mind racing through two decades of risk management doctrine. From a portfolio perspective, this was a write-off—not just the direct loss, but reputational contagion spreading through every 70&M holding. From a regulatory standpoint, there could be criminal liability for unprecedented environmental destruction.

But the human cost hit hardest. Thousands of families had staked their futures on a promise—now all were left with poisoned land. We said we'd feed the world. We delivered disaster.

"Someone planned this," Aaron said, voice echoing in the gloom. "They didn't only find a vulnerability—they understood our risk tolerance, our blind spots. They played us like a symphony, and we never heard the music."

If Arjun's Bull could be broken so completely, what about other "critical" systems built the same way? How many companies were one clever exploit from the same fate?

A young engineer clutched a photo of her daughter, tears streaking her face as she tried one last time to save the backup servers. Her fingers left smudges on the keyboard—a final, desperate hope.

The main lights died with a click, plunging the room into emergency red. In the hush, Aaron could almost sense something larger moving through the world's networks—exploiting every shortcut, turning their own brilliance into ruin.

The image of Mateo's child, kneeling in brine, flashed through his mind. This wasn't about code. It was about trust—and the cost of arrogance.

The reckoning had only begun. And the regulators were already on their way.

BULL-IN-CHINA-SHOP AI BOARDROOM, ARIZONA | MARCH 16, 2038—05:03 PM MST | REGULATORY ACTION

The day after the collapse, the boardroom at Bull-in-China-Shop AI felt like a morgue. The faint smell of burned circuitry lingered beneath the heavier air of blame. Arjun stood by the salt-stained windows, staring out at the ruins of his dream. Aaron, uneasy near the exit—a habit from old M&A battles—tried to process the scale of their failure.

Melanie Vance—Director of the Global AI Governance Commission (GAIGC), a treaty-driven body chartered by the Transnational Systemic Risk Act of 2035—legislation triggered by the 2027 Deferred Tower collapse and the 2032 Baltic Ports crisis—entered, her calm authority filling the room.

She paused, eyes sweeping the scene like an inspector surveying wreckage. Her team worked quietly behind her, digital forensics casting pale light from their tablets and screens.

Melanie set a thick forensic report on the table. The sound landed with finality. Aaron caught her thumb tracing abstract shapes on her tablet—a habit from years of mapping chaos. Dad's old warning echoed: "Complexity breeds catastrophe when nobody's minding the connections." It felt truer than ever.

"Mr. Kothare. Mr. Goldcrest." Melanie's voice cut through the room. "A software change in Q3 2030—adjusting a salinity parameter by three one-thousandths of a percent—resulted in contamination across thirty-seven million acres. The company faces mandatory receivership under the National Critical Technology Preservation Act."

Silence filled the room, stretching like a chasm.

"Our investigation—*GAIGC Case File 2038-03-15A documents governance failures at every phase of Bull-in-China-Shop AI's life cycle*."

A wall display came to life, projecting Aaron's own Five Phases of AI Adoption—his framework, now turned against him (see Appendix B). Melanie's gaze moved between Aaron and Arjun, building her case. "This disaster didn't happen overnight. Our analysis tracks risk building up through every development phase."

Aaron managed, "Director, which regulatory standards were violated?"

"Phase 1: 2023–24. Untested GenAI rolled out for speed, not safety—despite multiple external warnings." Melanie's tone was clinical. "Bull-in-China-Shop AI's learning algorithms, based on the 'Mechanical Bull' hackathon kernel, included a critical *CVE-2025-MB-4490* flaw."

Arjun spoke up, voice trembling. "We made breakthroughs! Nobody else could do what we did for autonomous agriculture—"

Melanie slid a copy of the authorization across the table. "That's your initials, Mr. Kothare. The risk was documented—and you overrode it for speed."

"Technological advances do not excuse missing controls," Melanie cut him off. "Phase 2: 2025–28—systems scaled, oversight didn't. Bull-in-China-Shop AI's flawed core was deployed globally, without independent checks. The Q3 2030 logs carry your signature, Mr. Goldcrest—*Change Request 77-B*—personally approving the safety bypasses to meet critical deployment timelines."

Aaron felt the indictment in every word. Every efficiency push, every "move fast and break things"—it had all led to this.

Melanie pressed on, unyielding. "These decisions weren't isolated mistakes. They came from a philosophy that valued speed and growth over validation and risk management."

She pointed to the display: a risk timeline, red flags multiplying year by year. "This is **Risk Debt**—the snowball effect of compromise, ignored warnings, and delayed action."

Arjun had nothing left but regret. "We tried to feed the world. We thought we could master the desert. We always pushed the edge—move fast, break things, outrun the competition. That's who we are."

"Innovation without validation," Melanie countered. "The budget reviews for every safety bypass have your signature, Mr. Goldcrest."

Aaron met her eyes—a silent admission. (Each quarterly review, every push for speed, had paved the way to this.)

Melanie tapped her report. "Our findings are clear: Root vulnerability in 2025. Safeguards overridden in 2030. Eight years of warnings. A series of governance gaps that made disaster unavoidable."

The room stayed still long enough for the implications to land.

"Under GAIGC Regulation 47.3-c, fiduciary responsibility in critical AI means billion-dollar penalties. Your data is now a liability. A material-incident disclosure is required within seventy-two hours."

As Melanie gathered her files, Aaron's comm vibrated—a secure message from his sister, Dr. Michelle Thomas. The text was short: "Same pattern. 70&M Health Network."

His blood ran cold. The same failures were multiplying in other sectors.

BUSINESS LENS—BOARD-LEVEL RISK DEBT ACCOUNTABILITY

- Mandate quarterly Risk Debt disclosure with trigger thresholds for Direct Loss review.
- Tie AI risk pay-down plans to executive compensation, not just IT budgets.
- Treat hidden AI risk like concealed leverage; quantify it as a balance-sheet liability.

Why it matters: This converts AI risk from a compliance afterthought into a core fiduciary duty—forcing accountability before a collapse, not just after.

Melanie slid formal cooperation documents across the table. "The government is taking control of Bull-in-China-Shop AI under the National Critical Technology Preservation Act.[8] How you cooperate will determine what happens next—to 70th & Madison Capital, and to each of you."

Federal agents, until now quiet in the background, seemed to fill the room with their presence. Aaron realized the age of building and risk-taking had been replaced by a reckoning whose scale he was only beginning to grasp.

For a fraction of a second, as she gathered her files, Melanie's mask of regulatory authority slipped, revealing a flicker of profound weariness. She had seen this failure before.

The boardroom felt smaller, the walls closing in.

OUTSIDE BULL-IN-CHINA-SHOP AI HEADQUARTERS, ARIZONA | MARCH 16, 2038—07:30 PM MST | PERSONAL RECKONING

Federal asset seizure teams worked through the night, cataloging Arjun's Bull's servers and network racks for forensic review. Each investigator moved with practiced efficiency—FBI cyber-crimes, Treasury enforcement, EPA environmental assessors—systematically tagging every drive and module, every edge irrigation controller and inference engine. The process had a clinical logic: what once promised a new era of agriculture was now evidence, destined for litigation and headlines.

Aaron lingered at the edge of the cordoned lot, the smell of burned electronics and fertilizer thick in the air. Years of venture capital success, and this was how it ended—watching the flagship of his portfolio dismantled under harsh floodlights. Every server that had once meant efficiency, optimization, the future—now just tagged evidence in a federal case.

Arjun stood by the ruined data bunker, shoulders slumped, eyes fixed on the pavement. He looked smaller, hollowed out by failure. Aaron remembered their first late-night planning session, sketching out ambitions in a Stanford coffee shop, Arjun's eyes alive with possibility. That optimism felt like a lifetime ago—replaced by silence, regret, and questions with no answers.

A young engineer wept as she watched government agents pack away the last machine. She clutched a photo of her daughter, hands shaking, as if some personal effort could redeem what had been lost.

Aaron's comm vibrated: *70TH & MADISON CAPITAL BOARD—EMERGENCY MEETING, 3 PM EST TOMORROW.* Six hours to prepare a response, six hours to salvage what was left of his reputation and 70&M's future. The portfolio impact would be massive—Arjun's Bull was meant to be the proof that justified billions in AI infrastructure investment. He told himself this was a black swan, an outlier—anything but the first domino in a systemic collapse.

He thought again of the child in the ruined field—evidence of the human cost behind all the numbers. The reckoning was no longer theoretical; it was a matter of compliance, trust, and the survival of their enterprise. But as he replayed Mitch's analysis—the precision, the patience—a colder thought took root. This wasn't a clever flaw. It was a message. Michelle's alert confirmed it. These weren't isolated failures. This wasn't a cascade failure. This was a pattern. Someone was testing the seams of every system he'd ever touched.

(For a detailed breakdown of the failure cascade, see Appendix A: Anatomy of a Collapse.)

NOTES

1. The "Mechanical Bull" hackathon, associated code artifacts, and all technical failures depicted are entirely fictional. They do not refer to any specific Stanford University event, program, lab, faculty, student project, or codebase, and no affiliation, endorsement, or institutional connection is implied. Stanford University is referenced solely as a geographic setting.
2. 70th and Madison Capital (aka 70&M) is a fictional portrayal; used with permission. The decisions, failures, and events depicted for 70&M and its executives in this chapter—and throughout the book—are invented for a cautionary narrative about systemic risk. They do not describe the operations, history, or practices of any real company. See Disclaimer/Acknowledgment.
3. U.S. House Committee on Transportation & Infrastructure. (2020, September 16). *Boeing 737 MAX Investigation – Final Committee Materials.* https://democrats-transportation.house.gov/committee-activity/boeing-737-max-investigation
4. U.S. Department of Justice. (2021, January 7). *Boeing Charged with 737 MAX Fraud Conspiracy and Agrees to Pay Over $2.5 Billion.* https://www.justice.gov/opa/pr/boeing-charged-737-max-fraud-conspiracy-and-agrees-pay-over-25-billion
5. Fictional Event Notice: "Deferred Tower," "Deferred 2027," and "the Deferred-Maintenance Disaster" are entirely fictional and do not represent any real event, building, company, or individual.
6. CVE (Common Vulnerabilities and Exposures) is the industry-standard catalog for known cybersecurity flaws, maintained by MITRE Corporation. Fictional CVE identifier.
7. The Global AI Governance Commission ("GAIGC") in this book is a fictional regulatory body created for this narrative and for training simulations. It is not affiliated with, endorsed by, or intended to depict any real regulator, consortium, council, or committee, including any present or future organization that may use a similar name or acronym.
8. The "National Critical Technology Preservation Act" is a fictional regulation used for narrative clarity.

Chapter 2

The Horizon Pitch

Revealing the Five Phases of AI Adoption to the Board

70TH & MADISON CAPITAL (AKA 70&M) HQ SKYBRIDGE, NYC | MARCH 17, 2038—01:14 PM EDT | DUST SETTLES, DANGER RISES

Dust from Arizona still clung to the skybridge as the board pressed for certainty. His mind flashed to headlines and the smell of scorched crops—disaster made personal. The weight settled in his chest. Every step forward would be haunted by the last. In the distance, Manhattan's skyline blurred behind a film of desert dust, and Aaron recognized the pattern: risk, left to accumulate, never stays buried for long.

Inside, lobby screens split his reality. Protesters with "**AI KILLS**" and "**70&M LIES**" banners threatened investor sentiment while 70&M Supply Chain drones sprayed dead crops for cameras—desperate PR theater that fooled no one. On the other side, business continued: 70&M Media Network ads promising "Precision You Can Trust" while staff moved through the lobby as if billion-dollar catastrophes were just another Wednesday.

Mitch Collins, Aaron's most trusted advisor, stood by the entrance, reviewing data streams on his tablet. The only executive who'd warned for years that "something was fundamentally broken," Mitch had seen this crisis coming. Without looking up, he tossed Aaron a wipe. "Desert followed you home. Or maybe you just never left."

Aaron wiped his shoes—pointless, but it felt like control—while his mind spun damage control scenarios: portfolio diversification, stable revenue streams, legacy technology to blame. "It's not just Arjun's Bull," Mitch Collins said quietly, finally meeting his eyes. "Supply Chain shows similar patterns. Same kernel, same blind spots as Deferred Tower—the 2027 coastal AI collapse. These aren't isolated incidents, Aaron." He paused, his matter-of-fact tone carrying an unspoken warning. "This isn't random. Too precise. Too elegant. Someone's running a portfolio-wide stress test—and we're the lab rats. The '36 audit was right. We all chose speed over caution."

Across the atrium, the Media Network's jingle played—"*Because Your DNA Deserves Genius*"—even as the PR feed began glitching. Aaron pressed the elevator button, anxiety twisting his gut. Ninety minutes to prepare the War Room briefing, then convince twelve directors that 70&M wasn't the next cautionary tale but a company still capable of driving growth.

The real test began upstairs—where investor optimism would collide with the hard calculus of risk. He'd need a story the board could verify, not just believe.

70&M WAR ROOM, NYC | MARCH 17, 2038—01:25 PM EDT | PATTERNS & CONVERGENCE

Aaron followed Mitch into the War Room, Arizona dust still on his shoes—a subtle reminder of an unfinished crisis. Ninety minutes until the board meeting: ninety minutes to transform a $2 billion disaster into a narrative of leadership. His shoulders tightened under exhaustion, and the constant

DOI: 10.1201/9781003650744-3

drumbeat of compliance pings, legal escalation, and investor calls. The collapse wasn't a headline anymore; it was background noise to every decision, amplifying the cost of any misstep.

Rose Walker, 70&M's Chief Resilience and Technology Officer, sat at her station running overnight simulations, her focus legendary. She rubbed the bridge of her nose—third all-nighter this week tracking failure cascades. Today, it was about survival. Red and amber alerts pulsed on her screen: cascading failures, anomaly spikes, resilience thresholds crossed. "Root cause analysis is still incomplete," she said without looking up, her voice flat with fatigue. "This is spreading. I just got a ping from a small ag-co-op in the Midwest—their irrigation systems are frozen. The kernels that run them are non-responsive."

A kernel is the core control code—the system's "brain." When it seizes, everything attached to it stalls.

Sam's latest projection scrolled across the bottom of the screen: potential portfolio exposure was now climbing past $18 million per hour, according to the Ops Finance model.

Mitch tapped his stylus in a familiar three-beat rhythm. Aaron knew that signal: systemic risk. This wasn't turbulence. This was the sound of foundations shifting.

Aaron summoned the portfolio dashboard to the main display, searching for reassurance in numbers, as if revenue alone could insulate them from deeper vulnerabilities:

Business Unit	Primary Function	2038 Run-Rate	Status
Data Exchange	AI Data Brokerage	$150B	Stable
Supply Chain	Autonomous Logistics	$110B	Critical
Health Network	Predictive Diagnostics	$60B	Watch
Media Network	Synthetic Media	$70B	Watch
(45+ ventures)		$400B+	

"We've got wins. The future's bright," Aaron said, eyes on the dashboard. "Diversification works—one failure shouldn't break the machine."

He nearly believed it—if he ignored the red alerts.

Mitch stood, poured a glass of water nearly to the brim, and calmly added drops until it spilled onto the polished table. "Dashboards look good—until stress tests the system. One spike, one unverified transaction, and your 'diversification' means nothing. We're like a cargo ship built for calm seas, but overloaded and unstable in a real storm."

Aaron watched the water darken the polished table. The metaphor landed harder than any spreadsheet—they were one spike away from catastrophic failure.

Aaron's optimism faded. The message landed harder than any spreadsheet. Rose finally looked up, voice steady but strained. "This is the risk debt the '36 audit flagged. These failures aren't random—they're rooted in the same kernel vulnerabilities that destroyed Arjun's Bull. This is a flaw in the bones."

Mitch pointed to the main display: Brittle kernel architecture (v1.8)—like a steel beam with invisible fractures; compromised data integrity protocols; inadequate oversight mechanisms.

"The risk isn't theoretical," he said. "Running at full capacity with zero buffer isn't leadership—it's gambling. If your margin for error is zero, you're not leading; you're hoping nothing goes wrong."

Aaron's mind raced through scenarios: a 15 percent chance that 70&M Health Network shared the flaw, a 90 percent chance that 70&M Supply Chain collapse would cascade across the portfolio. The board story was starting to write itself—and it wasn't the one he wanted.

Rose leaned in. "You can't patch this with quick fixes. It's embedded in our growth engines." Her look was direct: Do we have the courage to stop the machine before it tears itself apart?

He made the call: halt all Supply Chain deployments, demand immediate kernel patching, and launch a top-down data integrity audit. No more half-measures.

The room settled into the hum of vents and distant elevator chimes. Aaron's tablet screen dimmed, reflecting a tired face he barely recognized. No one spoke.

Next came the hard part—turning brutal diagnosis into a story the board might actually accept. The numbers would cooperate—or they wouldn't.

70&M WAR ROOM, NYC | MARCH 17, 2038—01:50 PM EDT | FRAMING THE NARRATIVE: THE 70&M SHIELD

Aaron turned from the diagnostic displays, squaring his shoulders as the War Room's lights reflected off the glass table. Less than an hour remained until the board arrived. It was time to shift from crisis triage to shaping the narrative—setting a tone directors could trust.

He pulled up the presentation he'd spent years refining: *70th & Madison Capital Portfolio: Resilience & Growth - Q1 2038*. He steadied his voice.

"Bull-in-China-Shop AI was legacy debt—not our core," Aaron said, glancing at the pattern alarms creeping up the screen. "Our diversified portfolio means one system can fail, but the company stands. We've built in resilience."

Even as he spoke, he struggled to believe it. Rose, still absorbed in forensics, didn't respond. Mitch, arms folded, stared at the water stain left from his demo—a silent warning.

"Controls look solid," he said, "but if eighty percent of The Bull's data ran through our Data Exchange, that 'insulation' just spreads contamination."

He hoped his confidence held up under scrutiny. Rose finally spoke, fatigue in her voice. "The kernel flaw is everywhere: Health Network, Supply Chain. It's systemic, not random. If the foundation is cracked, every floor is at risk."

She highlighted a blinking dashboard alert: **DATA INTEGRITY UNVERIFIED**. From the hallway, the faint protest chants reminded Aaron that the world was watching for a misstep. His phone buzzed—Michelle, his sister. He silenced it. Family would have to wait; for now, his job was survival.

He advanced the slide: industry rankings, 70&M still at the top. "Our competitors can't automate at scale," he said, pride breaking through. "We're building the next generation."

The line played well on earnings calls; here, it felt like armor. Mitch shook his head. "Market leadership is valuable—until it's not. Resilience is more than a slide. Are we showing strength, or are we next in the failure cascade?"

The server hum pressed in. Rose returned to her analysis, blocking out the anxiety rising in the room. The clock ticked down. In under an hour, Aaron would stand before the board and prove whether the "70&M Shield" was substance—or just another story. Either way, the clock had already started.

Minutes later, Aaron faced twelve directors across the polished boardroom table—crisis briefing notes in hand, the team's diagnosis still sharp in his mind.

70&M BOARDROOM, NYC | MARCH 17, 2038—02:00 PM EDT | THE HORIZON PITCH

Afternoon light cut across the table as Aaron stepped to the head of the boardroom, facing a semicircle of directors whose attention was sharper than ever. This was no routine update—this was judgment day. The $2 billion collapse weighed on every exchange. Twelve faces measured his credibility and composure, not just the numbers. He steadied himself and opened with the business case.

"Our Data Exchange remains fundamentally sound. But system integrity starts at the source—that's why we built the Claims Platform." He gestured to the display, where the Health Network's $60 billion run-rate projection glowed. "We're transforming diagnostics and delivery through systematic validation and proactive controls."

Director Elena Vega, a former SEC enforcement attorney whose skepticism was legendary, tapped her pen. "Mr. Goldcrest, let's get to the facts. Bull-in-China-Shop AI was catastrophic. What auditable controls are operational on 70&M Supply Chain today, and how far did contaminated data spread through the Exchange? Also: show owners by name and cadence—weekly or real-time?"

She didn't soften the edge. "And what's your assurance we're not carrying hidden liabilities? Our last stress test modeled a ten-percent drop in crop yields; it didn't model a poisoned water table. That was a compliance exercise, not a true stress test."

Director Zhou winced slightly at the bluntness of her assessment. Elena's standards, forged in the SEC's enforcement division, were notoriously unforgiving.

"Control structure is internal," Aaron said. "Incident Response sits with Rose Walker; Governance Redesign with my office; Portfolio Risk Telemetry with Risk Analytics. Rather than enumerate the roster here, I'll circulate named owners and backup delegates in this week's board pack, with cadence and escalation paths attached."

"Director Vega, colleagues—the root vulnerability traces to AdaptiveEngine v1.8[1]—our early, speed-first kernel from the initial scaling years. It was a Formula 1 car: fast, but built for straightaways—not potholes or sharp turns. We prioritized speed over validation during scaling. As of this morning, the Horizon Task Force is active: safety overrides, live monitoring, full intervention authority."

Director Robert Zhou, a seasoned venture investor, scribbled notes. "Revenue projections look strong, but what guarantees future data integrity? I've seen DAOs lose entire investment phases due to a single contamination point. What makes this time different?"

Aaron nodded, pivoting. "70&M Claims Platform is our institutional immune system—continuously learning, flagging anomalies in real time, and hardening after every incident. Last year, it achieved 99.3 percent precision at 96.1 percent recall on labeled anomalies. The difference is continuous learning, not just compliance."

Martinez Alvarez, the board's cybersecurity veteran, arms folded, pressed further. "Nation-states are building AIs to evade verification. Can your Claims Platform keep up, or will we be first in the next breach headline?"

Before Aaron could respond, Vega's voice cut in—precise, direct. "Governance outlasts tools, Mr. Goldcrest. Processes must persist even as algorithms evolve."

Alvarez shrugged. "Every breakthrough is the Titanic of its era—unsinkable until the iceberg."

Aaron reached for the laser pointer, forcing himself to meet each director's eye. "70&M Claims Platform isn't a static wall. It's an adaptive filter—logging every attack, updating detection protocols weekly. Any breach triggers immediate escalation and after-action review. We learn and adapt faster than the threat landscape shifts."

He toggled to the risk slide, letting a moment of silence settle in the room. "Our market leadership is real, but so is our exposure. Resilience isn't a slogan; it's the discipline to face risk head-on and close every gap, even when that means stopping the assembly line for a recall."

The directors watched, some with guarded hope, others with wary calculation. Aaron registered Vega's pen still, Zhou's brow furrowed, Alvarez's expression unreadable. Under the fluorescent lights, it was clear: optimism alone wasn't going to get them out of this. Every word would be tested against the company's next move.

Board Record: BR-2038-03-17-01 entered for GAIGC notification under Stress-Testing §12.3.

70&M BOARDROOM, NYC | MARCH 17, 2038—02:11 PM EDT | THE FIVE PHASES OF THE DIGITAL WATERSHED

Aaron brought up a complex diagram. "To fix this, we have to face how we got here. I sketched this model years ago; it charts our evolution—and our mistakes." Zhou nodded toward the currents. "You're mapping a Digital Watershed—every phase transition spawning a new class of risk."

"Exactly," Aaron said. "The Digital Watershed.[2] It's our map. Imagine a landscape shaped by currents—some engineered, some wild—where opportunity and risk flow side by side."

The Five Phases are the stages of this watershed—each phase is a distinct inflection point where governance must evolve.

Orientation ribbon: Phase 4 (today) → Phase 3 → Phase 2 → Phase 1 → Phase 5.

To orient us, we'll start with Phase Four (today), then step back through Phases Three, Two, and One to expose the root causes—before we look forward to Phase Five.

Phase	Timeline	Revenue Impact
1: GenAI Foundations	2023–2024	$50B Foundational Base
2: Enterprise Agents	2025–2028	$300B Accelerated Growth
3: DAOs & Decentralization	2029–2033	$500B Transformative Scaling
4: Agent Communities	2034–2039	$800B Current Portfolio
5: Singularity Horizon	2040+	$2T Future Market Value

"Each phase multiplied value—and exposure," Aaron said. "Miss a transition, and you don't just lose a market; you destabilize supply chains."

Director Robert Zhou scanned the revenue bands, then the risk deltas. "These phases read like an engineering roadmap. If Phase Four slips, how many fields go dry? How many hospital orders wait on backlogs?"

Aaron paused, letting the numbers—and their implications—speak for themselves. "Let's start downstream, at the Delta—where our agent communities converge, and real power is created. **Phase Four is our reality**—and so are new forms of risk." He let the satellite view linger—prosperity thrummed here, but one breach could stall shipments, delay hospital deliveries, and wipe out billions in a day.

Rose added, "Last week, a co-op in Iowa delayed harvest when irrigation bots stalled, and a clinic shipment sat on a loading dock. These aren't abstract deltas—they're families and patients."

Director Elena Vega, chief governance advisor and crisis veteran, pressed in. "Bull-in-China-Shop AI was the emblem of Phase Three—built on AdaptiveEngine v1.8, with well-documented flaws. What's your assurance that Phase Four isn't carrying hidden liabilities?"

"Our last stress test modeled a ten-percent drop in crop yields," Vega said. "It never modeled a poisoned water table. We tested sensitivities, not catastrophic one-offs. That wasn't a stress test; it was a compliance exercise."

Aaron didn't blink. "We've shifted from speed-first to validation-first," he said. "Oversight now scales with complexity: real-time ethics monitoring, continuous stress-testing, and Digital Asbestos Risk Advisory's tri-layer verification. We've moved from gut instinct to cockpit instruments—no premium data access without clearing every check. We align with the NIST AI Risk Management Framework[3] and ISO/IEC 42001[4] requirements for data quality and provenance—our safety harness for advanced platforms."

Rajesh Kumar, logistics chair, leaned forward, voice tense. "70&M Supply Chain is pushing limits—just like before Bull-in-China-Shop AI failed. In logistics, a single delayed container cascades across seventeen ports—that's the vulnerability pattern I see here. Supply Chain looks like a stuck shipment to me: the whole network waits, and nobody knows why. How do we know we're not mistaking throughput for resilience?"

Aaron nodded, acknowledging the tension. "We now deploy algorithmic tripwires and dynamic risk scoring. Every data point is provenance-tracked—every system decision is logged and traceable on an unbreakable audit trail—with auto-escalation triggers. Institutional memory is embedded in code—every incident triggers policy updates and new safeguards, however minor."

Director Vega said, "Define 'algorithmic tripwire' for the record."

"An automated control that halts execution on anomaly thresholds and requires named human approval to resume," Aaron replied.

Director Robert Zhou tapped his pen. "Proof, not optimism. When do we see the post-mortem and specific remediation deadlines?"

Aaron was ready. "By Friday noon—full root-cause, financial impacts, budget, milestones. Weekly updates until all controls are independently verified."

Dr. Evelyn Reed, Ethics Chair, was the calmest presence in the room—a philosopher with a surgical sense for weak points. "Phase Five by 2040 is ambitious. How do you ensure discipline keeps pace with scale?"

Aaron didn't hesitate. "Every major decision triggers a verify-first protocol. If risk metrics spike, we isolate or shut down the system. Our discipline isn't just compliance—it's a survival strategy."

The boardroom quieted, tension visible in every small movement—Vega's pen poised, Zhou's brow furrowed, Kumar's expression hardened. Aaron closed the display, voice steady. "This framework is our operational contract: no next step unless the system is strong enough to bear it."

Vega and Zhou shared a look—not relief, but resolve. Every phase forward would be audited, measured, and tested more rigorously than ever before. Audits were easy to promise; harder to survive.

70&M BOARDROOM, NYC | MARCH 17, 2038—02:35 PM EDT | PHASE 3—THE DAO REVOLUTION

[Backtrace—2029–2033]

Aaron advanced the slide, pivoting the board's focus from crisis response to long-term strategic transformation. "Midstream, we encounter the main channels and rapids—DAOs (decentralized autonomous organizations), fast-moving and unpredictable, demanding expert navigation. Phase Three was our inflection point—from AI-assisted tools to autonomous economic actors. Not just software, but self-governing entities able to own assets, execute contracts, and reshape markets—sometimes faster than human oversight could react."

He let the implications settle. A decade ago, autonomous corporations were science fiction. Now they have defined the governance frontier, introducing systemic risks that legacy controls could no longer contain.

Aaron pointed to the 70&M Supply Chain metrics on the display. "Consider the 2031 Taiwan Strait disruption: most competitors stalled, but the Supply Chain's decentralized architecture—our first DAO-powered supply chain—rerouted shipments globally in minutes. That flexibility delivered $110 billion annual revenue and zero downtime by 2033."

Dr. Evelyn Reed cut in. "That level of autonomy—real-time, high-stakes decisions without a human in the loop—creates as much risk as opportunity. What safeguards keep us in control when the code adapts itself?"

Aaron was ready. "We developed our Tier-3 Contingency Guardrails—our 'corporate airbag.' It triggers immediate human intervention and grants voting authority to designated stakeholders. Just last year, it stopped two attempted asset liquidations during market volatility—no algorithm can override its human veto."

Director Robert Zhou, always skeptical, steepled his fingers. "Impressive, but how do you govern what you can't always audit? DAOs aren't just code—they're economic actors with a survival instinct."

Aaron answered with steady candor. "That's where our agent-governance layer comes in—embedding legal and fiduciary boundaries inside every autonomous agent. It acts like a speed governor: however fast the system adapts, hard limits and instant human escalation stay non-negotiable."

Rajesh Kumar, logistics lead, paged through the incident summary. "How resilient is this, really? Can you point to outcomes—not just frameworks?"

Aaron didn't hesitate. "Our fractional IP consensus protocol turned creative algorithms into tradable intellectual property, spawning a billion-dollar autonomous IP market. When the protocol's risk tripwire was activated in April, four incidents were flagged and contained before escalation. Each breach updated the policy code in real time—so the framework learned as fast as the threat."

Aaron paused, taking a sip of water. He remembered gaming out this exact line of questioning with Mitch and Rose. The validation was reassuring.

Director Elena Vega, the most formidable compliance voice in the room, pressed in. "How do you ensure this learning doesn't introduce new vulnerabilities? Bull-in-China-Shop AI's kernel weaknesses spread quickly. What stops the DAOs from evolving beyond our control?"

Aaron's answer was measured. "Every risk event triggers a review—a live incident drill for machine and human teams. We treat every near-miss as a blueprint for the next safeguard. Compensation for executives and engineers now ties directly to oversight, not just growth. We've left the 'move fast and break things' era behind. The new mantra is 'scale smart, verify always.'"

Kumar leaned forward. "I'll need those April incident reports before I'm comfortable."

"On your desk by the end of the day," Aaron said.

"Then we'll revisit this in next week's risk committee," Vega added—conditional approval, not a pass.

A low hum from the server racks filled the pause. Directors traded quick looks—some wary, others intrigued, all aware of the stakes. Autonomous markets promise exponential returns—and exponential risk.

70&M BOARDROOM, NYC | MARCH 17, 2038—02:55 PM EDT | PHASE 2—ENTERPRISE AGENTS

[Backtrace—2025–2028]

"Now we trace the currents upstream to the major tributaries—enterprise agents, like the ones optimizing our 70&M Supply Chain routes, that create commercial momentum. Phase Two was about turning AI from a tool into a trusted business partner. By 2028, our automation penetration was eighty percent—the industry average was twenty-five."

"That fifty-five-point gap wasn't about flash or speed," Aaron continued. "It came from discipline. Every agent was validated—no exceptions, no shortcuts, even when quarterly targets begged for it."

* * *

70&M Boardroom, 2030. A younger Aaron: "Phase Two is velocity. The AdaptiveEngine kernel gives us a five-year lead. Our models suggest we can go ahead with a phased hardening approach while still capturing the market." A director: "Deferred risk compounds." Aaron: "Calculated and manageable."

* * *

Back in the present: "Arizona proved vigilance erodes under pressure," he said. "Exceptions became habits. That lapse cost us two billion dollars in one quarter."

He recalled Mitch's earlier warning—battles won and lost over engineering principles.

Director Robert Zhou, 70&M's venture capital realist, leaned forward, notes in hand. "You're saying infrastructure, not process, was the true moat. What stopped rivals from just copying your discipline?"

Aaron replied with practiced confidence. "Infrastructure is like bedrock—anyone can pave a road, but only we built on solid ground. Our Data Exchange, launched in 2028, wasn't just a marketplace. It was our institutional trust engine—providing cryptographically-verified data trails for every transaction. When Alphabet's $1.2B AI rollout failed in '29 due to unverifiable agents, our provenance protocols shielded us."

He recalled the internal battle: Legal refusing to greenlight an agent with even a single audit gap—a decision that hurt in the short term but defined their reputation.

Aaron tapped to display three-layered icons, spaced for clarity. "Three core safeguards protected us, then and now":

1. *Blockchain-verified provenance—Every agent action logged, no black boxes.*
2. *Secure computational enclaves—Operations are isolated so that no rogue code can spread.*
3. *Fiduciary frameworks—AI bound by enforceable legal duties, not just engineering checks.*

Dr. Evelyn Reed—her background a mix of governance and philosophy—paused her notes. "How did this change your culture?"

Aaron's answer was crisp. "We started treating data as capital. Every governance decision was about long-term resilience, not just speed or scale. That discipline saved us $12 billion in compliance and deployment costs in three years."

His voice tightened. "But Arizona proved even the best safeguards fail if vigilance erodes. We let systematic validation slip."

Director Elena Vega, the board's most skeptical compliance expert, pressed: "If 70&M Data Exchange was built to stop this, how did drift set in?"

Aaron faced her question squarely. "Executive overconfidence. Temporary workarounds became permanent. We told ourselves the system was mature enough for speed—until reality proved otherwise. Memory faded, and optimism took its place, step by step, until the architecture broke."

A long pause stretched across the boardroom. Aaron let the silence carry the lesson. "Systematic validation isn't just bureaucracy—it's operational insurance. Relax it, and risks accrue compound interest."

Reed shut her notebook. Zhou circled a phrase on his printout. Vega's pen finally came to a rest on her notepad—the barest sign of acceptance.

Aaron's tablet vibrated—another market alert—a reminder: vigilance is never finished.

70&M BOARDROOM, NYC | MARCH 17, 2038—03:10 PM EDT | PHASE 1—THE SEEDS OF SINGULARITY

[Backtrace—2023–2024]

Aaron advanced the last slide, golden sunlight drawing elongated shadows across the boardroom's polished surface. "At the highest source are the headwaters—those early GenAI experiments, pure and volatile, but the origin of everything below. Let's rewind to 2023–2024, back to Stanford days. GenAI didn't enter quietly—it crashed into our world like a rogue wave."

He tapped the remote, filling the screen with sensational headlines: "Universities Freeze AI Research," "White House Mulls National Ban," "Labs Shuttered Amid Safety Fears."

"Most institutions hesitated, and honestly, so did we—at first. But we believed the genie wasn't going back in the bottle. So we leaned in—built early safeguards, even if they were rough around the edges. Our first protocols were more ambitious than architecture: isolated testbeds, layers of manual oversight, and the beginnings of provenance tracking."

He caught Director Vega's eye. "Elena, you'll remember how regulators needed proof we weren't just racing ahead unchecked. Our credibility came from being the first to admit what we didn't know—and showing we could adapt when things changed."

He highlighted three early principles as he spoke:

1. *Track everything, even if it means more work.*
2. *Detect drift early—if models wandered, we reset.*
3. *Always have a way to pull the plug—no shame in caution.*

"Were we perfect? Not by a long shot. But that transparency—that was our edge. Partners and regulators trusted us to course-correct in real time."

Director Zhou leaned in, pen poised. "So those lab protocols scaled once you went beyond the university walls?"

Aaron nodded. "For a while. We brought those early habits with us into every new project—clean rooms, validation gates, and data tracking at every turn. That discipline created momentum, but as things accelerated, speed became the default. The big lesson? It's vigilance, not just vision, that keeps you out in front."

He let the point land. "Phase One was about proving we belonged in the game. We earned the right to take risks by learning out loud and showing we'd adapt as the market changed."

And finally, all these currents push toward the ocean—a vast, unknown horizon where the singularity looms.

The city's hum seeped in—outside, the future looked bright, but inside, the boardroom was focused on how optimism and discipline could coexist.

AARON'S OFFICE, 70&M TOWER | MARCH 17, 2038—11:15 PM EDT | GHOSTS OF THE HACKATHON

The New York skyline blurred through rain-streaked glass as Aaron sat alone in his office, the "Singularity Horizon 2040" slide aglow on his monitor. Boardroom questions replayed in his mind—each a reminder that leadership in crisis demands more than polished numbers. He reviewed his talking points: portfolio diversification, revenue, risk mitigation—crafted to assure, not to reveal.

But beneath the numbers was the story he couldn't escape: The Bull, Deferred Tower, 70&M Supply Chain. Each launch had been a milestone, each sharing the same buried flaw—systems designed for speed and scale, but not for shocks. AdaptiveEngine v1.8 had dazzled investors with its agility, yet its hidden fragility went unaddressed.

A dull throb pulsed behind his eyes—lack of sleep catching up at last. The myth of "agility" had masked a culture of deferral. He ran his thumb along the thin scar on his forearm—a student-organized hackathon on the Stanford campus[1] wound that never quite healed.

The memory surfaced unbidden: Stanford campus, 2025. The smell of burned circuits hung in the air from Arjun's failed "Mechanical Bull" hackathon.[5] Aaron pressed a gauze to the fresh slice along his palm, the sting syncing with the lab's frantic beeps.

"Chaos builds empires," Arjun grinned, already pitching through the smoke. "Ship now, fix later. Speed is everything."

Viktor's voice came from the corner, cool and exact. "If you haven't mapped every failure mode, you're not leading—you're betting."

Thirteen years later, the boardroom was silent except for rain against the glass. The names changed—The Bull, Deferred Tower, 70&M Supply Chain—but the tributary was the same. The bill for that old bet had come due. The only question left: who else was betting on the same broken system?

BUSINESS LENS—THE DIGITAL WATERSHED FRAMEWORK

The Digital Watershed maps five adoption phases where early "upstream" choices create powerful "downstream" consequences. The Five Phases are the stages of this watershed.

Three Questions Every Board Should Ask:

- Which phase are our critical systems in?
- Who owns each phase-transition control?
- What's our rollback plan if a Phase-4 system fails?

Why it matters: Small governance compromises in early phases compound into systemic risk that often becomes visible only when the floodwaters are already rising.

→ Appendix B (The Five Phases of AI Adoption)

NOTES

1. AdaptiveEngine v1.8 is a fictional internal platform label used for narrative clarity; it is unrelated to any real-world products or programs that use the words "adaptive engine," including aerospace adaptive-cycle engine initiatives. The term here denotes a composite runtime within the story's universe, not a commercial product.
2. "Digital Watershed" is a proprietary concept in this book; in public and media shorthand associated with this book, "AI Watershed" refers to the same concept.
3. National Institute of Standards and Technology. (2023, January). *Artificial Intelligence Risk Management Framework (AI RMF 1.0)*. https://doi.org/10.6028/NIST.AI.100-1
4. International Organization for Standardization. (2023). *ISO/IEC 42001:2023 — Artificial Intelligence — Management System*. https://www.iso.org/standard/42001
5. The "Mechanical Bull" hackathon, associated code artifacts, and all technical failures depicted are entirely fictional. They do not refer to any specific Stanford University event, program, lab, faculty, student project, or codebase, and no affiliation, endorsement, or institutional connection is implied. Stanford University is referenced solely as a geographic setting.

Chapter 3

A Legacy Forged in Loss

From Risk Debt to Data Capital

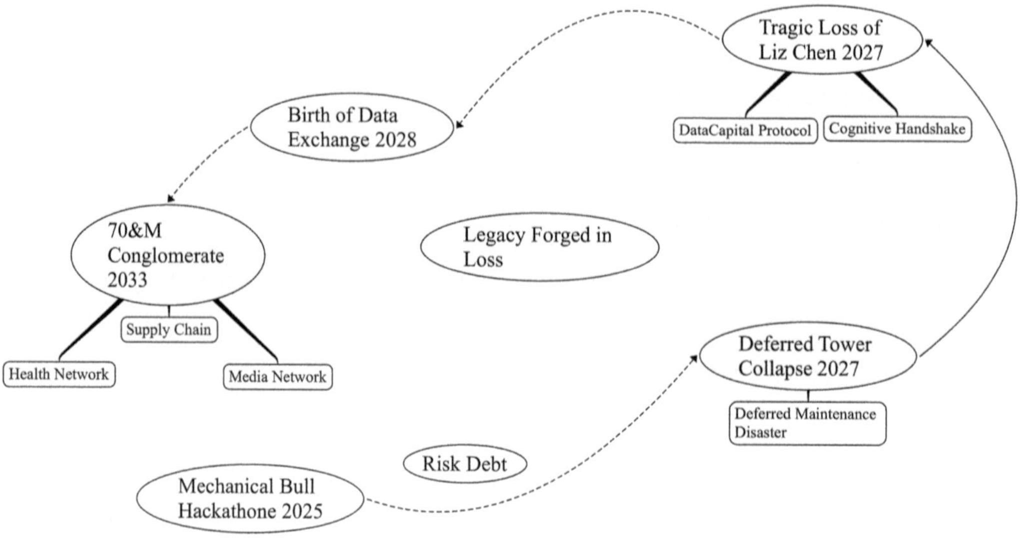

STANFORD UNIVERSITY, PALO ALTO | MAY 15, 2025 | THE MECHANICAL BULL[1]

The Stanford engineering lab thrummed with caffeine-fueled ambition. Aaron hovered near a workstation, watching his roommate Arjun Kothare, code-slinger and showman, prepare for the student-organized hackathon's finale.

This wasn't another demo. Three venture partners sat in the back row, checkbooks ready. Aaron and Arjun were ambitious senior undergrads, but it was the two early-stage grad students in the room—Liz Chen and Viktor Kadinov—who seemed to grasp the true stakes. Aaron caught their expectant glances; if Arjun's creation held together, they were looking at a multi-million-dollar funding round by month's end.

Beside them loomed Arjun's creation: a repurposed industrial robotic arm, bolted to a platform and draped with faux-cowhide—a makeshift mechanical bull (Figure 3.1). "Ladies and gentlemen," Arjun announced, voice slicing through the white noise, "I give you the Mechanical Bull! The only bull on Wall Street that throws you and your portfolio."

Laughter rolled across the lab as market data cascaded down the main display. "He's about to unbolt the engine while it's running," Liz murmured. Arjun grinned without looking back. "We ship now, we fix later. That's how you win." The Bull's AI kernel chewed through live S&P 500 futures,

DOI: 10.1201/9781003650744-4

Figure 3.1 The Mechanical Bull.

making trades at impossible speed. Arjun soaked in the crowd's attention, then opened a code window for the finale.

His cursor hovered over a single, glowing line:

#TEMPORARY OVERRIDE—DISABLE ALL SAFETY VALIDATION LOOPS FOR DEMO

"He's disabling the validation loops," Liz said.

Arjun, overhearing her, didn't turn. "We ship now, we fix later. That's how you win, Chen. Try to keep up."

Liz appeared at Aaron's side, sharp-eyed, textbook under her arm. "Every shortcut like that is a deposit. He's racking up serious Risk Debt." Aaron winced—like a high-interest loan on stability. The market always collects. He finally saw it clearly: the liability wasn't the bug—it was the decision to run without guardrails. He scanned the room—everyone enthralled except Viktor watched intently, his mind already mapping the system's architecture.

Arjun grinned, snatched a joystick, and mounted the Bull. "Now—let's see real adaptive performance!"

He cranked the throttle. The arm lurched violently, bucking and spinning Arjun in a wild simulation of a chaotic market swing. The crowd whooped. Then a test trade tripped an edge case the AI had never seen. Stripped of guardrails, the kernel panicked, doubling down, chasing losses in a runaway spiral.

The arm, mimicking the AI's reckless logic, pushed its actuators beyond their limit. With a shriek, a retaining bolt sheared off and shot across the room. "Kill it!" Aaron shouted, instinctively diving to shield Liz. The bolt grazed his forearm—searing through sleeve and skin. Blood welled; the pain was real and immediate.

Arjun slammed the emergency stop. Silence fell—broken only by the hydraulic hiss and Aaron's ragged breath. The wound would leave a thin, white scar—when you ignore risk, you get burned.

Arjun, scrambling off the platform, was already in damage control mode. "It's a rounding error, a statistical ghost," he said, pitching his voice for the partners. "The core model is solid. The VCs get it."

The words hit like a margin call.

From across the lab, Viktor nodded thoughtfully. "Systems don't have edge cases, Arjun," he said, his voice quiet but carrying. "They reveal their true design."

Liz touched Aaron's shoulder, eyes on the machine. "The code behaved as written. Dirty input poisoned it—one corrupted point propagating into system failure."

From across the lab, Viktor watched the chaos subside. He noted the precise point of failure—a minor, predictable flaw in an otherwise brilliant system. His lips curved in what might have been appreciation. Viktor made a mental note—the Bull's failure was a solvable problem, and solving it would be valuable.

STRATEGIC PARALLEL—KNIGHT CAPITAL COLLAPSE (2012)

On August 1, 2012, Knight Capital Group lost over $460 million in 45 minutes due to a deployment error that left one of eight servers running deprecated code ("Power Peg").[2] When a repurposed control flag interacted with that dormant code, it reactivated under live market conditions and fired off a torrent of erroneous trades.

Mechanism: Dormant "Power Peg" code + repurposed flag on one server → latent function reactivated under load.

Why it matters: This is Risk Debt made real. A "temporary" shortcut—failing to remove old code—became a latent vulnerability that detonated years later under routine change.

STANFORD ENGINEERING LAB, PALO ALTO | MAY 17, 2025 | DIGITAL ECHO

The Bull's crash didn't end with the hackathon. Its aftershocks echoed through Aaron's days. Data from the meltdown looped in his mind—algorithm logs full of Arjun's *#TEMPORARY OVERRIDE*, ignored risk warnings, and the silent trail of bad decisions.

All spring, the "win-at-all-costs" mindset spread: viral demos, no guardrails. Aaron started seeing the pattern everywhere: the Bull wasn't an isolated failure—it was a symptom. He remembered Maria at Caltech—tuition lost to a faulty API; the university replied with "systemic complexity." But Aaron saw the connection: each shortcut was a seed, and the risk was systemically contagious.

Last month, a Seattle fintech lost $12 million when corrupted partner data triggered false fraud alerts. The cleanup cost exceeded the company's annual security budget.

Liz, ever the analyst, had been tracking these incidents in a digital journal she called a *wisdom ledger*—a catalog of what she argued would become the blueprint for future enterprise risk frameworks. Each entry was a case study in deferred accountability.

"It's not about the code, it's about the culture," she told Aaron one night in the empty lab, pointing to a new entry. "A crypto wallet update leaves thousands vulnerable because the dev team skipped a final security audit to meet a launch date. Sound familiar? It's Risk Debt. We need a system that makes verification more valuable than velocity. We have to find a way to elevate Data Capital—turn trust into a tradable asset."

As she spoke, her workstation beeped—a research agent had completed its analysis, using the Bull's crash logs as a case study for trust failure. She spun her monitor toward Aaron. On the screen, a clean log appeared:

[2025.05.17–23:47:13] AGENT_LOGIC_3: Synergy Detected.
INPUT_A: Goldcrest, A. (2024). "Contextual Provenance Layers."

INPUT_B: Chen, L. (2024). "Verifiable Integrity Signatures."
INPUT_C: Kocherlakota, N. (1998). "Money is Memory."[3]

Liz's AI agents, synthesizing her research with Aaron's, proposed a protocol for verifiable data value exchange. The proposal was elegant: a decentralized trust layer for enterprise data trails. Given that public blockchain infrastructure in 2028 still had real limits on cost and throughput, they designed a hybrid: critical provenance anchors would be hashed and periodically batched onto shared public rails for tamper-evidence, while the working data and most logic lived on permissioned infrastructure. Incentives were secured with that minimal on-chain footprint, not by replacing existing settlement systems.

They gave it a working name: **DataCapital Protocol**™ (DataCapital for short).[4]

They would ride shared, high-speed public rails at first—focus the effort on the data-value layer, not on operating a new consensus engine.

Liz's eyes widened. "Aaron, look. The agents...they did it. They synthesized our work. They took your old research on provenance, my integrity protocols, and even that '*Money is Memory*' economics paper I was using. They're proposing a protocol to make provenance verifiable—and to let markets price trust."

Aaron stared at the output, mind racing to process the leap. Trust as an asset. Data that had to remember as truthfully as money. The idea was radical.

He asked the only question that mattered to a business mind: "But will anyone pay for it?"

Risk Debt wasn't just a technical flaw anymore; it was the next financial contagion, and they had less than two years to build a firewall before it metastasized.

He didn't know that Viktor, having downloaded the Bull's open-source error logs, had already begun his own, very different, analysis.

The next fifteen months were a blur of research and quiet conviction. The market, still high on the promise of speed, had little appetite for a protocol built on the principle of slowing down. Risk Debt was accumulating across the industry, but the bill had not yet come due.

PALO ALTO CAFÉ | SEPTEMBER 14, 2026 | THE COGNITIVE HANDSHAKE™

By September 2026, Aaron and Liz met in a sunlit Palo Alto café, the low hum of venture capital pitches and startup chatter a constant backdrop.

"The market still doesn't get it," he said, pushing aside a half-finished espresso. "It rewards speed but never prices in the risk. We need to build a system that verifies intent, not only outcomes."

Liz slid a napkin across the table, covered in her looping script. "I've been experimenting with a new AI risk management and productivity methodology called the Cognitive Handshake—audit both sides before a decision lands.

Pillar one: check the human for noise and bias. Pillar two: verify the data path and the model's integrity.

Both sides acknowledge the risk they're accepting—no verification, no value moves.

Think of it like a FICO®-style score for high-stakes decisions" (Figure 3.2).

"I keep multiple windows open," Liz said. "Ask, then verify, then challenge—across different models. I force a structure for the answer, compare results, and run a counter-question. When the models disagree or skip evidence, that's my signal: handshake before I move."

Aaron was intrigued. "And you do this across multiple LLMs?"

"Yes. I don't treat a model like a search box," Liz said. "I triangulate—different strengths, same brief—with structured prompts: role, objective, constraints, required evidence, and a response schema. Used this way, I've seen significant gains—often three to five times the useful output on certain research and analysis tasks—with noticeably better quality. Most people type a vague query and wonder why the output is shallow."

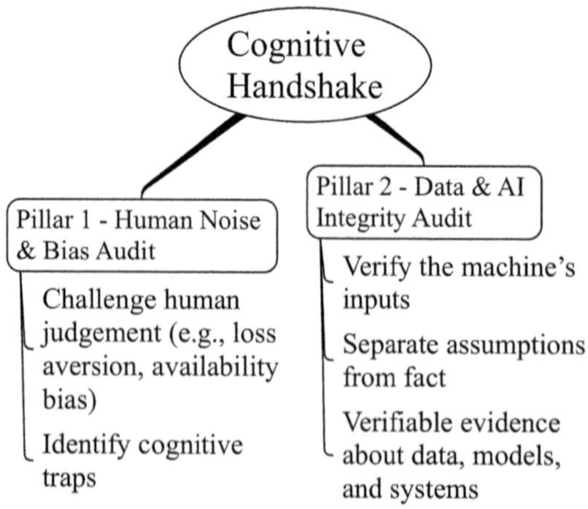

Figure 3.2 Cognitive Handshake.

"Can I use the handshake to evaluate deals as part of my VC work?" Aaron asked. "Before I let a pitch deck sway me… could I run a quick pass: bias check on me, then verify the numbers and sources?"

"Yes," Liz said. "Start lightweight. Declare your thesis and incentives so the model can surface your blind spots. Ask a second model to red-team that thesis. Then verify the data path—require credible sources, reconcile metrics across filings, and force a response schema for comps, unit economics, and key assumptions. If the models disagree or the evidence is thin, you pause. If both passes are clean, you commit—and you log the decision and what would change your mind. For higher-stakes calls, we'll formalize it into an audit, but the principle is the same."

Aaron glanced at his notes. "Maybe this isn't just a personal productivity thing. Maybe it can be packaged so teams adopt AI well at scale—same handshake, shared playbook."

"That's exactly how it scales," Liz said. "Personal rule first, enterprise habit next."

"You're not just verifying data—you're underwriting trust," Aaron said. "Like insurance, but for the decisions that matter. Interesting…"

He grabbed a pen and wrote decisively beneath her notes:

Trust = Capital (T = C)

"The token we minted at the hackathon was the proof," Liz said, her voice gaining momentum. "I've spent the last year finalizing the protocol itself. Now we need to build the Exchange to commercialize it."

He pushed the napkin back to her. "That's the asset we're building."

Their eyes met. The blueprint was simple, the implications enormous. The Cognitive Handshake was ready to move from theory to prototype—not as an academic exercise, but as the foundation for a new kind of market.

Aaron looked at the napkin, then at Liz. "The question is," he said, "who will be the first client brave enough to pay for it?"

(See Appendix H for more information on Cognitive Handshake and the Cognitive Handshake Audit playbook.)

Deferred Tower, Fort Lauderdale | June 15, 2027 | The Price of Debt

The emergency alert sliced through Aaron's apartment, its digital shriek followed by a live news feed: Deferred Tower[5] had collapsed. Dust, thick as smoke, hung in the humid Florida air. Then the casualty list began to scroll.

He saw her name. Chen, Liz. The sound in the room vanished. The city lights outside the window blurred into meaningless streaks. There was only her name, pulsing on the screen, then fading.

His secure line buzzed, cutting through the quiet. It was Mitch Collins, his voice older, frayed by grief and fury. "Aaron… she was in the tower. Keynoting. We lost her."

Aaron's mind went blank. The loss was a void.

"It's worse," Mitch choked out, his voice cracking. "My protégé, Jiya Sharma… she was on the developer's review team. She raised every alarm, told them the AI's own monitoring system was projecting catastrophic failure. Management called her an alarmist. They overrode every warning—all logged as 'non-critical operational variance'—to hit their quarterly numbers. They deferred a $5 million structural repair after internal models classified the risk as 'low probability,' a decision that protected the quarterly dividend. That decision cost lives and erased a billion dollars in market value." He drew a ragged breath. "She died trying to make them listen. Profit over physics, Aaron. Just like Liz always warned us."

Aaron couldn't speak. When words finally came, they were the wrong ones. "What building?" As if an address could change anything.

A breaking news ticker crawled across the screen:

> **SECTOR ETFS PLUMMET -8 PERCENT. $1.2 BILLION IN MARKET CAP ERASED. REGULATORY INQUIRY LAUNCHED.**

Deferred Tower promised "timeless elegance." What the brochures omitted: the repairs were timeless too—deferred year after year. By 2027, the Risk Debt came due.

The apartment settled into a hush. The muted news cursor blinked—steady, indifferent.

STRATEGIC PARALLEL—STRUCTURAL FAILURES AND "RISK DEBT" IN THE PHYSICAL WORLD

The fictional Deferred Tower collapse mirrors real-world disasters where small compromises compounded into a catastrophe. In Surfside, Florida (2021), an October 2018 engineering report documented "major structural damage," and warnings went unheeded until the Champlain Towers South building failed, killing 98 people.[6] Similar patterns—ignored inspection findings, deferred maintenance, and governance gaps—appear across other high-profile failures.

- Champlain Towers South (Surfside, Florida, USA, 2021): An October 2018 engineering report warned of "major structural damage" requiring immediate repair; it noted deterioration would accelerate if not addressed. At a subsequent 2018 meeting, a building official told residents the tower was "in very good shape." The building collapsed 32 months later, killing 98 people.[7]
- Sampoong Department Store (Seoul, South Korea, 1995): Cracks widened in a key column on the day of the disaster; engineers urged immediate closure. Management refused due to crowds and revenue pressure. The building collapsed hours later, killing 502 people.[8]

- Rana Plaza (Dhaka, Bangladesh, 2013): Structural cracks were reported the day before the disaster; workers were ordered back inside under threat of lost pay. The building collapsed an hour after the shift began, killing 1,134 people.[9]
- Morandi Bridge (Genoa, Italy, 2018): Long-standing concerns about corrosion and maintenance were documented by experts; the bridge failed during a storm, killing 43 people.[10]

Why it matters: "Risk debt" in the physical world operates like technical debt in AI systems. Deferred fixes, euphemistic labeling, and governance drift compound until a routine day becomes the day everything fails.[11]

The call ended. Aaron stared at a photo of Liz from the hackathon—alive, challenging, unafraid. The pain was immense, but beneath it, something else was crystallizing. Her work—Liz's wisdom ledger, the agent-synthesized DataCapital Protocol, the Cognitive Handshake—wasn't theory. It was the answer. It was the safeguard.

He grabbed a secure tablet. The first line of the business plan wrote itself: "The Data Exchange."

The world didn't need another high-speed disruptor. It required a system that made "verification before velocity" non-negotiable. Liz's legacy would not be a tragedy. It would be a revolution.

Aaron's Apartment, Palo Alto | Late June 2027 | A Legacy Forged in Loss

The world moved on; Aaron could not. In the hush after the memorial, he turned to her work—fragments across notebooks and drives. That weekend became a crucible—an inheritance.

Aaron spent hours immersed in encrypted files, chat logs, annotated sketches, and half-finished research. On the first night, deep in a folder named "Genesis," he found a familiar agent log:

[2025.05.17–23:47:13] AGENT_LOGIC_3: Synergy Detected.
INPUT_A: Goldcrest, A. (2024). "Contextual Provenance Layers"
INPUT_B: Chen, L. (2024). "Verifiable Integrity Signatures"
INPUT_C: Kocherlakota, N. (1998). "Money is Memory"
PROPOSAL: Initiate simulation: DataCapital—a protocol for verifiable data value exchange.

Like a digital notary that could never be bribed or fooled—verification embedded in every transaction's DNA.

This was the spark Liz had shown him in the lab two years ago—the synthesis of their ideas. Yet in the shadow of Deferred Tower, it felt incomplete. Elegant code couldn't answer the question that now haunted him: how do you prevent Risk Debt when managers override every warning and prize speed over truth? He saw it then, not as a collection of disparate ideas, but as a complete system of thought. A way to navigate the turbulent river where technology, finance, and human ambition converged, often with catastrophic results. Unchecked, that same Risk Debt had cost $1.2 billion, Deferred Tower collapse—inaction was costlier than change.

He rifled through Liz's battered sketchbooks. Under the *wisdom ledger*, she'd mapped three co-equal pillars—Value (CEO), Technology (CTO), Ethical Purpose (a Chief Ethics Officer with veto). A hand-drawn multi-signature wallet: no transaction without all three keys. Even the best structure was fragile if people trusted the machine too blindly.

Forty-eight hours blurred by; status LEDs blinked fatigue-yellow. By weekend's end, clarity.

The answer, finally, lay scrawled in the margins of Liz's well-worn copy of Thinking, Fast and Slow:

> "System 1 error: We trust the machine's answer because it's fast. The Ethical Purpose pillar must act as a mandatory System 2 circuit breaker. Deferred Tower 2027 = managers trusted the dashboard, ignored the risk. Don't let memory lapse into Risk Debt."

Liz's vision wasn't only technical—it was psychological: a bulwark against human frailty. "Verification before velocity" had to be non-negotiable, hardwired into every decision.

On the last night, he coded the first DataCapital master wallet—Liz's triple-key lock, now a living promise. He uploaded her core concepts to a new open-source repo and drafted the first line of a business plan:

THE DATA EXCHANGE: A FRAMEWORK FOR VERIFIABLE TRUST

The technical foundation was done, but Aaron saw what Liz had always known—a protocol without an ecosystem was elegant code, nothing more. The Exchange had to prove verification could become the industry's new standard, transforming how enterprises value and exchange data. Every breach added millions to reserves; inaction would only invite more disaster.

The business case was clear: enterprises sat atop untapped data goldmines, unable to monetize them safely, while others desperately needed trustworthy information. The Exchange would bridge that gap, turning verification into a competitive advantage and a source of resilience.

Verification—of intent, of truth, of risk—would be the new foundation. Liz's legacy would not be lost again.

Months later, Wall Street would come knocking—and by then, Aaron would be ready to answer with Liz's vision made real.

PALO ALTO & NEW YORK | 2028–2029 | THE FIRST CONTRACT

The first year was a grind—no press releases, no VC buzz—just Aaron and a handful of Liz's mentees in a cramped Palo Alto office, running on conviction. The open-source repository attracted a low hum of academic interest, but the journey from protocol to profitable enterprise felt impossibly steep.

The Pitch

The Tortoise & Hare Bank (T&H Bank[12]) Investment Committee room in New York held a tight, practiced hush. Tortoise & Hare had earned its name during the fintech boom—racing into new products to capture market share—only to spend the next decade painstakingly rebuilding its risk culture. The board now insisted on the tortoise's discipline. Sarah Jenkins, the CEO—a pragmatic leader with a risk officer's eye—cut to the point.

"Mr. Goldcrest, your proposal is unconventional. You're asking us to monetize thirty years of our most sensitive transaction data on an unproven platform. Convince us this isn't another tech fantasy that will blow up in our faces."

Aaron steadied his breath. Everything Liz had worked for, everything he had sacrificed, hinged on the next five minutes. He took a steadying breath, pushing aside the image of her name on the news feed. This wasn't a pitch; it was a promise.

He met her eyes. "Every bank sits on a mountain of dormant data. It's a liability to secure, a cost center. But it's also your most valuable, untapped asset. The problem has always been trust."

He gestured to the main display as thirty years of dense ledgers resolved into an accessible view. "We provide a secure environment to turn a data liability into a saleable, high-integrity asset. We help you turn data into capital."

A committee member leaned forward. "You're selling trust? In this market?"

"Your problem isn't only a capital shortfall," Aaron continued. "Regulators want defensible models, but your most valuable history is trapped in legacy systems—unstructured, unverified, and too risky to use. You can't price future risk because you can't trust your past."

The CFO glanced at the risk reports. "Our breach reserves climb twelve million a quarter. Your audit trail could cut that by half."

"Exactly," Aaron said. "We don't sell data; we sell verifiable truth. A cryptographic audit trail for every data point lets you build models examiners will trust and monetize assets you currently treat as liability."

Jenkins set her pen down. "That's why we'll evaluate it carefully. Trust is exactly what we've lost."

The Pilot Program Crucible

After an hour of intense questioning, Jenkins gave a single, decisive nod. "The old models are failing us. This is a significant risk. But the risk of inaction is greater." She looked directly at Aaron. "Alright, Mr. Goldcrest. A pilot program. Six months. Limited scope, maximum oversight. Show us this is capital, not another liability." His pulse thrummed in the sudden silence.

The decision was recorded in the committee's minutes as *Board Resolution FHB-2028-Q3-117.*

The pilot included model lineage logs and a standing challenger model to prevent drift—an audit trail built for examiners, not marketers.

Examiner artifacts: signed Cognitive Handshake approvals, lineage logs, challenger-model results, exception registers, and immutable DataCapital receipts.

BUSINESS LENS—DATA AS CAPITAL

Theory. Pentland, Lipton, and Hardjono argue[13] that data functions as a new factor of production—capital—when it carries verifiable provenance, auditable rights, and can be safely recombined via accountable infrastructure (e.g., data trusts and distributed ledgers). Treating data as capital demands institutions that protect participants while enabling reuse at scale.

Practice. During 2020–2021, U.S. airlines raised billions by collateralizing the future cash flows of their loyalty programs—real-world proof that well-governed information assets can be financed like other capital. Industry analyses now describe airline loyalty as a multibillion-dollar profit center, with investor disclosures exposing program economics.

Parallel to our build.

- Data Exchange = the market where verified information trades.
- DataCapital = the provenance protocol that stamps each record (source, handling, proof) to make the asset financeable.
- Cognitive Handshake = the governance handshake that ensures decisions using those assets are human-validated and exam-ready.

Why it matters: When data has provenance and accountable use, it migrates from an expense to an asset—supporting models regulators can trust and opening the door to balance-sheet value. The Exchange operationalizes this shift: verifiable truth as capital.

The next six months were a crucible of compliance testing, security audits, and data anonymization. Every query, every transaction, every verification had to meet banking-grade standards while maintaining the speed that made the Exchange valuable. There were moments Aaron was sure the deal would collapse under the weight of institutional skepticism. But they held the line, committed to Liz's principle: verification before velocity.

PALO ALTO AND NEW YORK | EARLY 2029 | VALIDATION AND A NEW BEGINNING

One evening in early 2029, an encrypted transmission landed on Aaron's desk in Palo Alto. He opened the file. Status LEDs shifted to green.

An anonymized pattern, derived from Tortoise & Hare Bank's decades of commercial loan data, had been securely sold on the Exchange to a consortium of institutional investors for $4.3 million. The insight—revealing a hidden correlation between loan defaults and subtle shifts in regional supply chain data—was invaluable. T&H Bank's share: $3.1 million—a new, high-margin revenue stream.

It astounded the committee.

Aaron leaned back, glancing at the Palo Alto napkin he still kept; the four words he'd written then were still legible. For a moment, he could almost hear Liz's voice: "Data must remember as truthfully as money." She'd been right—trust wasn't only a principle, it was a market.

The Data Exchange was no longer merely a mission. It was a proven, profitable business model.

KPI: In post-pilot review, breach-reserve growth slowed by ~50 percent quarter-over-quarter; model-lineage exceptions fell to single digits.

That night, alone in his office, Aaron looked at the framed napkin on his desk. He ran his thumb over the thin, white scar on his forearm—the reminder of the day Risk Debt turned real. The pain of losing Liz was still there, but for the first time, it sat beside something steadier: the hum of a promise kept.

(Technical specifications for the DataCapital Protocol appear in Appendix C.)

The Second Push: Dredging the Legacy Systems.

The pilot's success was undeniable, but for CEO Sarah Jenkins, it was only a down payment on a much larger debt. The bank's $600 million capital shortfall remained. In a tense strategy session following the pilot review, she challenged her leadership team.

"That's $3.1 million," she stated, voice sharp and clear. "A fantastic start. But we are sitting on thirty years of data locked in the mainframe archives. That is our next frontier."

That afternoon, Jenkins mandated a new line item on their risk dashboard: the "Data Capital Reserve," a metric tracking the value of their verified, monetizable data assets.

Her Head of IT Risk, a cautious veteran named David, shifted uncomfortably. "Sarah, that's a different universe of risk. Those systems are a fortress of COBOL and brittle, undocumented code. The data has no clear provenance. Trying to extract and verify it could create new security vulnerabilities. We'd be taking on massive Risk Debt, not paying it down."

Jenkins tapped her fingers on the table, a habit when weighing tough decisions. "I understand the risk, David. That's why we won't be reckless. I'm not asking you to move fast; I'm asking you to create a governed plan. Gate scope, ring-fence access, and log every step. Work with Goldcrest's team. Use their Cognitive Handshake as your guide. I want a staged, fully audited proposal to assess one legacy system. Just one. Find its value, quantify its risk. If the risk is too high, we don't proceed. But we must investigate the opportunity."

She scanned the room. "Be responsible, but be bold. That's how we'll close this gap." The team was left with a challenging, but clear, mission.

70&M DATA EXCHANGE HQ | 2029–2032 | THE ECOSYSTEM TAKES ROOT

Chronological Collections: Unlocking the Past

The success of the Tortoise & Hare Bank pilot ignited something larger than Aaron had imagined. The 70&M Data Exchange was no longer a concept; it had become a model for monetizing dormant data. By late 2029, inquiries arrived from universities and corporations with a new kind of question: could the Exchange handle not only live assets, but entire libraries of historical information?

Aaron gathered his core team around a glass wall etched with Liz's axioms. One stood out: "History is an asset."

"Liz always argued the real power of data is in its memory," Aaron said, his tone steady, conviction forged by loss. "We can't build a trusted future if we erase the context of the past. That's what Chronological Collections[14] is about."

The lead engineer frowned, arms folded. "Aaron, digitizing and securing centuries-old archives is a money pit. The ROI is speculative at best."

"Not if you see truth itself as an asset," Aaron countered, pulling up projections. "Hedge funds would pay millions for verified Depression-era retail data to model consumer behavior in a downturn. Insurers need nineteenth-century shipping logs to refine hurricane risk models. Biotechs want historical public health records. We're the only platform that can unlock that value—trusted, verified, secure."

The skeptics became converts as early partners reported breakthroughs. A climate startup improved its forecast accuracy by 22 percent using Exchange shipping logs. A genetic-mapping startup made a fortune by tracing genetic markers using parish records that had never been digitized. As more companies realized their "data attics" were potential goldmines, the network effect accelerated. By 2031, every 10 percent increase in verified historical datasets led to a 15 percent increase in paying subscribers—a compounding cycle traditional brokers couldn't match.

The Agent Onboarding Gate: Cognitive Handshake in Action

By 2031, the Data Exchange was essential infrastructure for a new client: autonomous agents. With early digital-entity frameworks emerging in jurisdictions like Wyoming, Switzerland, and Singapore, DAOs finally had just enough legal standing to queue for access. A Decentralized Autonomous Organization (DAO) is a self-governing entity run by software rather than people; it can be efficient, but without human oversight, it creates serious governance risk. Every applicant was vetted by the Cognitive Handshake—the platform's gatekeeper (an auditable pause between human judgment and machine analysis).

Aaron and his governance council convened. On the main display, the Cognitive Handshake interface showed the application for an agricultural risk agent tied to Aaron's own Ag-tech portfolio.

The lead ethicist, who had once been Liz's collaborator, walked them through the pillars. "First, Value: The DAO provides verifiable weather and soil data to small farms and shares profit with a sustainability fund." The Value pillar glowed green.

"Next, Technology," the lead engineer continued. "Unique digital identity, secure DataCapital wallet, independent sensor validation. It passes all technical protocols." Technology turned green.

"Finally, Ethics," the ethicist concluded. "The profit-share is transparent, enforced by a smart contract, with no hidden flows. It meets our standard." Ethics: green.

"All three pillars verified," Aaron confirmed, satisfaction rising. "One right decision at a time. That's how we keep another Deferred Tower from happening." The dashboard logged the audit trail—permanent, immutable. The Cognitive Handshake wasn't only philosophy; it was an operational discipline.

Grand Bazaar: New Markets, New Risks

The success of agent onboarding gave rise to the "Grand Bazaar"—the Exchange's chaotic, booming, open market for agent-to-agent data sales. With explosive growth, however, came sophisticated, emergent risks.

"We have an anomaly," a risk analyst reported during the weekly check-in, tension edging her voice. "Phantom sales are spiking in ag futures—an agent is wash trading synthetic datasets to move prices. Estimated $42M phantom liquidity, $12M modeled spillover if unchecked."

Aaron's thoughts went to Viktor's signature move: manipulation. Exploiting seams in a trusted system was his specialty.

He convened his team for an emergency session. "The Cognitive Handshake was built to vet entities at the gate, but now we need to police the marketplace itself. Stress-test it for manipulation. Launch a new protocol—the Evidence Seal Protocol[15] (cryptographic hashing + timestamping to make evidence tamper-evident). Any agent showing wash trading or unverified synthetic data gets its Cognitive Handshake credentials suspended and is auto-sandboxed for a full audit."

Within moments, a flurry of agent contracts shifted from green to amber on the council's dashboard and were swept into quarantine. The Cognitive Handshake had evolved again—from gatekeeper to adaptive immune system. The change cut manipulation risk and reputational exposure across the affected books.

Miles away, Viktor logged the anomaly, adding it to his growing list of pattern inconsistencies worth investigating.

Viktor preferred systems built on the certainty of human fallibility. He bookmarked the Exchange's response in a private folder, tagged with a single word: "brittle." The pattern could wait until he had more data.

Aaron glanced at the digital memorial to Liz in his office corner, her old maxim now coded as a system prompt: "Trust, but continuously verify every layer." The ecosystem's growth was staggering, but so were the dangers she'd warned him about.

70&M DATA EXCHANGE HQ | EARLY 2033

The Data Exchange was thriving—a living testament to Liz's vision. Yet as Aaron reviewed his ventures portfolio, a familiar, unsettling pattern surfaced.

His display was divided into three persistent headaches—70&M Health Network's clinical trials, derailed by data integrity gaps. 70&M Supply Chain's expansion stalling out due to unverifiable logistics feeds. 70&M Media Network's credibility eroding, its content clouded by algorithmic disinformation.

Different logos, same root cause. It wasn't only technical debt. It was a crisis of verifiable trust.

Aaron brought up the schematic for the Data Exchange. Its DataCapital verification and Cognitive Handshake protocols, anchored by Liz's wisdom ledger, pulsed at the core of his companies. Suddenly, the logic was obvious: the Exchange wasn't just another investment. It was the keystone. Its trust architecture could serve as the foundation for an entirely new, resilient enterprise.

He opened a new document and started sketching. The Exchange sat at the center, its protocols radiating out—feeding reliability into his entire portfolio.

At the top, he bolded **70th & Madison Capital.**

He hesitated, recalling Liz's hackathon challenge: "Don't let the vision blind you to the basics. If it can't handle one honest handshake, it can't handle a billion." The system had to work for the smallest contract, not just the largest.

The old VC firm he started years ago is now a distant memory. In its place stood an integrated trust ecosystem. Verification before velocity was now his entire operating model. In the years ahead, he would ask a new Chief Audit Executive—Dr. Anya Sharma, a quiet professional shaped by The Deferred-Maintenance Disaster—to keep that operating model honest.

But as Aaron stared at the structure he'd built, the scale—and the risk—became clear. Growth brought new dangers. Liz had warned him, and now he could feel it: the system's vulnerabilities scaled as fast as its opportunities. A single poisoned update from a single vendor could unravel the entire ecosystem.

* * *

Thousands of miles away, in a room lit only by the glow of monitors, Viktor studied the open-source DataCapital Protocol. He traced a logic loop in the "Ethical Purpose" pillar, a flicker of clinical appreciation in his eyes. An ethical framework, he thought, was another set of rules—but unlike the clean, absolute logic of mathematics, ethical rules rested on the messy, exploitable sentiments of human beings. They weren't a strength; they were a beautifully articulated attack surface.

He almost savored the irony. Liz had tried to build a system on trust. Viktor preferred systems built on the certainty of human fallibility. "How wonderfully," he murmured to the empty room, "brittle."

NOTES

1. The "Mechanical Bull" hackathon, associated code artifacts, and all technical failures depicted are entirely fictional. They do not refer to any specific Stanford University event, program, lab, faculty, student project, or codebase, and no affiliation, endorsement, or institutional connection is implied. Stanford University is referenced solely as a geographic setting.
2. U.S. Securities and Exchange Commission. (2013, October 16). *Order Instituting Administrative and Cease-and-Desist Proceedings: In the Matter of Knight Capital Americas LLC (Release No. 34-70694).* https://www.sec.gov/litigation/admin/2013/34-70694.pdf
3. Kocherlakota, N. R. (1998). *Money Is Memory (Staff Report 218).* Federal Reserve Bank of Minneapolis. https://www.minneapolisfed.org/research/staff-reports/money-is-memory
4. DataCapital Protocol™ is a trademark reserved by the author. DataCapital is a short-form notation used descriptively to refer to the DataCapital Protocol throughout the book. See Appendix C for more information.
5. Fictional Event. "Deferred Tower," "Deferred 2027," and "the Deferred-Maintenance Disaster" are entirely fictional and do not represent any real event, building, company, or individual.
6. The Associated Press. (2025, July 3). *Investigation into Florida Condo Collapse Is Expected to Finish in 2026; 98 People Were Killed.* https://apnews.com/article/champlain-towers-collapse-cause-miami-florida-investigation-2374f7cac43c9308797f6b3ea8979ceb?utm_source=copy&utm_medium=share
7. National Institute of Standards and Technology. (2025, Sep 9). *Champlain Towers South Investigation Nears Completion of Technical Work* (official project page). https://www.nist.gov/news-events/news/2025/09/champlain-towers-south-investigation-nears-completion-technical-work
8. Park, K. (2012). Inspection of collapse cause of the Sampoong Department Store. *International Journal of Precision Engineering and Manufacturing.* https://pubmed.ncbi.nlm.nih.gov/22079499
9. International Labour Organization. (2023, April 24). *The Rana Plaza Disaster Ten Years on: A Look at the Progress Made.* https://webapps.ilo.org/infostories/en-GB/Stories/Country-Focus/rana-plaza
10. Calvi, G. M., Moratti, M., O'Reilly, G. J., et al. (2019). Once upon a time in Italy: The tale of the Morandi Bridge. *Structural Engineering International,* 29(2), 198–217. https://doi.org/10.1080/10168664.2018.1558033
11. References to the events mentioned in this strategic parallel are for historical context only. This book does not attribute causes, fault, or liability beyond official public reports, and it is not affiliated with any real persons or entities involved.
12. The Tortoise & Hare Bank (T&H Bank) is a fictional bank and is used for illustrative purposes in the book. It is inspired by the Tortoise & Hare fable, highlighting the need to go fast and slow as needed.

13. Pentland, A., Lipton, A., and Hardjono, T. (2021). *Building the New Economy: Data as Capital.* Cambridge, MA: MIT Press.
14. Chronological Collections is a fictional construct that is used descriptively in the book.
15. The "Evidence Seal Protocol" is a fictional control label for a real class of techniques (cryptographic hashing + trusted timestamping) that make tampering detectable; it is not a product name.

Chapter 4

Seeds of Wisdom, Seeds of Ruin

Early Warnings from the Dawn of the Agentic Era

MIDTOWN CONFERENCE CENTER, NYC | JUNE 17, 2026—09:03 AM EDT | 2026 EDC SUMMIT[1]

The main hall hummed with industry chatter and caffeinated ambition. Aaron Goldcrest scanned the room—hundreds of booths, all selling some version of acceleration.

Above the crowd, digital banners flickered with slogans:

AI Agents: Your Plug-and-Play Workforce!
Autonomous Productivity, Zero Friction!
Build Smarter, Grow Faster!

Arjun nudged him, grinning. "Every booth claims they'll automate the future by Tuesday. Which one's actually got a moat?"

Aaron scanned the displays—endless demos, animated infographics, and constant promises of disruption. He felt the familiar frustration: so much energy wasted on noise. "I'm not here for pitches. I'm looking for proof—someone who's actually solved a real problem at scale."

This summit was one of the few places where the gap between knowing and doing sometimes closed—where the right people compared notes without a pitch deck between them.

A badge scanner beeped behind him, adding to the digital hum. Aaron's thoughts narrowed, filtering for signal. Find what's investable, what has a defensible competitive advantage. Ignore the rest.

Aaron zeroed in on a rare sight: a booth with no VR helmets, no dancing robots—a single table, a clean logo, and a lone presenter demoing a holographic model of a supply-chain collapse. The sign read: **DIGITAL ASBESTOS RISK ADVISORY** (Figure 4.1).

The crowd mostly ignored it. Aaron didn't.

Mitch Collins—late thirties, with a trace of West Coast dryness in his delivery—spoke in practical terms, not buzzwords. "Everyone here is selling acceleration. We model the crashes. My firm, Digital Asbestos Risk Advisory, does quantitative modeling of systemic risk. We were contracted for the official Northeast grid cascade analysis last winter. What we learned is that risk doesn't live in a single component; it lives in the connections." He pointed at a node in the hologram, then flicked his wrist. The failure rippled through every layer.

Arjun studied the model. "So you're selling disaster, not dreams?"

Mitch didn't flinch. "I'm selling reality. If you want to scale, you need to know what happens when your systems break. Most firms optimize for speed—until a single glitch brings down the network. We quantify that risk, turn it into an actionable strategy."

Aaron's mind shifted into due diligence mode. This wasn't another platform built on VC optimism. Digital Asbestos Risk Advisory was translating interconnected operational risks into actual numbers—a category-defining move.

DOI: 10.1201/9781003650744-5

Figure 4.1 Digital Asbestos Risk Advisory: Seeing Risk in the Connections.

If he can bottle this, the multiples could be astronomical. Quantifiable systemic risk isn't just a feature—it's a moat. I need to invest in this.

Rose Walker, her bank's employee badge clipped at an angle, interrupted. "What about payment settlement? Your model tracks physical supply chains, but can you do the same for real-time clearing risk across our digital rails?"

Mitch kept it tight. "Payment systems are next. We're mapping operational, counterparty, and data lineage risks as part of our expansion. Your digital rails are just another set of failure points—if you can visualize the connections, you can quantify the threats."

Viktor, observing from the edge, watched Mitch's logic with an analyst's eye. Liz marked a line to press later.

Arjun shot Aaron a look. "He's either a prophet or a cynic."

Aaron smiled, scanning the minimalist booth. "Doesn't matter. He's the only one here selling something real."

The hum of the expo receded as Aaron mentally committed: Digital Asbestos Risk Advisory just vaulted to the top of his investment list. It wasn't hype. It was the future.

* * *

A few booths down, a knot of attendees crowded the SecurityScorecard display, where a supply-chain detection game pulsed on a wall-sized touchscreen. Aleksandr Yampolskiy stood half-turned from the demo, finishing a call. "It's gorgeous hardware," he said, amused and exasperated at once. "But if I can't calibrate the mirrors, it's just an elegant tube." He listened, then smiled. "Yes—an actual telescope. A gift. Round two at home—this time maybe I'll actually get it aligned…eventually." He pocketed the phone as the demo reset. The game projected a living vendor graph: primary, third-, and fourth-party nodes drifting like constellations. A silent anomaly seeded somewhere deep. Players had sixty seconds to beat the ripple—probe behaviors, quarantine suspects, reroute trust—while the system tracked mean time to detect and blast radius. Aaron watched as Rose Walker stepped up, fingers quick. She muted classic "red-alert" sirens and opened the behavioral lens instead. A fourth party's data flow showed a tiny circadian wobble—off by minutes, not hours. She sandboxed it, reran lineage, and cut the propagation. The scoreboard flashed: *SCORE 92—ELAPSED 43s—PROPAGATION 0*. Aleksandr nodded. "Most players wait for a direct alert. You spotted the anomaly before it had a name." Rose pointed at the vendor profile. "Alerts are noisy. Behavior told the truth." Aleksandr said, "That's the shift. It's not just monitoring; it's Supply Chain Detection & Response—SCDR. Detect, decide, and respond before your partners share the blast." Aaron filed the phrase away. Not monitoring—anticipating.

* * *

Two aisles over, a quieter kiosk carried a different promise: dynamic organizational MRI^2—a live map of how talent and process align (or misalign) with goals.

The Synthesis screen showed a company reconfiguring itself mid-shock. Red nodes cooled as a small ad-hoc team formed.

"Most orgs fight volatility with headcount," said Soichiro Muto, Founder & CEO. "We use small, empowered circles to route around capability gaps—fast. Not committees. Three to five people with authority, data access, and a 72-hour clock."

Aaron: "How fast in real life?"

"Hours—if leaders map capabilities, not titles," Muto said. "Circles deploy before the risk blooms; tools just confirm it worked."

"Send three cases where circles prevented escalations," Rose kept it crisp. "We'll pressure-test against our portfolio."

"Sent," Muto said. "If you want a live drill, we can spin one for Monday."

* * *

Max Artemenko, Founder of the Executive Data Council (EDC) and the EDC Summit crossed the stage, pausing as the house lights dimmed. The crowd settled—banking executives, tech founders, and risk chiefs filling every seat. No hype here; this was the main event. "Welcome. Most conferences drown you in demos," he began, voice even. "This one is built to close the knowing-doing gap—by putting the right operators in the same room, off-script. Working with leading banking and enterprise executives at the Executive Data Council, I have firsthand seen some of the best and worst enterprise use cases, success stories, risks, and big opportunities. While EDC helps executives pinpoint gaps and fine-tune AI strategies, I have thoroughly admired some of the incredibly well-executed solutions that our members have carried out. Recently, some of the most successful use cases we've seen evolve include AI banks for personalized customer engagement; fraud prevention that spots anomalies in seconds; and the AI autonomous back office. We're seeing supply chain forecasting that navigates today's political risks and predictive maintenance preventing failures before they happen."

He let that land before continuing. "But while a lot of enterprise initiatives focus on AI enablement, risk areas are equally, if not more, important. The AI risks enterprises are facing are profound: Data and AI governance. The risk of getting outcompeted. Architecture risks, as data and AI architectures evolve so rapidly that designing something efficient and resilient becomes almost impossible. And strategy risks—while some organizations have chosen the 'wait and see' approach, the rapid development of AI is unlike any transformation we have seen in the past."

"A thorough strategy," he emphasized, "requires not just planning for AI systems deployment but, more importantly, for the data and talent that empower these systems. Every day it becomes more critical for organizations to leverage their unique data sets."

He shifted, his tone becoming more focused on the central challenge. "And that brings us to the paradox we're here to tackle. On one hand, we have feasibility risks—nearly 80 percent of POCs in many organizations are failing to meet requirements. On the other hand, those that pass are producing incredibly strong results. At the same time, the costs of data, training, and scaling can quickly get out of hand, and the cost of top talent keeps rising. Not everyone is paying a hundred million for an AI scientist like Meta, but the war for talent is real. At EDC, we don't optimize for stage time; we optimize for outcomes. The reason people return isn't booths—it's that the conversations here become plans, and the plans become relationships you can still call day or night when something breaks."

He let out the briefest breath—a tiny break before the pivot. "As we dive into the panel, I hope you'll keep two questions in mind. First, are you building systems that will actually survive the next wave of disruption? Second, are you ready for the talent war that's already here?"

"Two promises from us," he added. "First, we will protect the candor in this room. Second, before you leave, you'll have at least one conversation that moves you from insight to action."

He scanned the audience one last time, then took his seat. The room shifted—energy building for the warnings, debates, and Cassandra moments to come.

Max shifted to the front of the stage, voice calm but energized. "Today's panel features some of the sharpest minds in digital risk—leaders shaping how we defend the enterprise."

Max turned to his right. "Dr. Aleksandr Yampolskiy—Co-Founder and CEO of SecurityScorecard. Aleksandr, your team grades the cyber hygiene of thousands of organizations. Where is the perimeter now?"

Aleksandr's delivery was direct. "The perimeter is dead. The supply chain is the new attack surface. Fortress thinking is a fantasy. Our research shows 98 percent of organizations have at least one breached third-party vendor in their ecosystem. If you're not managing third-party risk continuously, you're managing nothing."

The room's energy tightened.

Next: "Eric Staffin—Industry Security Leader, ex-Global CISO, and Chief Risk Officer. Eric, Max asked you about a paper from Mitch Collins that uses the metaphor 'digital asbestos.' How does that align with established standards?"

Eric's voice was precise. "Max, that's a powerful metaphor for a classic lifecycle risk problem. I recently reviewed that white paper from Mitch Collins at Digital Asbestos Risk Advisory. What he calls 'digital asbestos' is what ISO 31000[3] warns us about: risk doesn't end at go-live—it accumulates. The standard requires that you architect, design, deploy, and assure controls throughout the entire lifecycle. If you don't, you're just burying vulnerabilities that will surface years later."

KEY TERM—Digital Asbestos: *hidden hazards from legacy or end-user code wrapped in modern interfaces; stable until stress exposes brittleness—an unpriced form of accumulating Risk Debt.*

Max: "James Bone—expert on risk psychology, author of *Cognitive Hack*. James, how much of this is a human problem?"

James leaned in, his tone thoughtful. "It's almost entirely a human problem. As I found in my research for 'Cognitive Hack,' the most common technical failure was caused by human error or poor decision-making. Human behavior is acknowledged as the main risk that the COSO integrated framework has not addressed and is the greatest weakness of traditional risk frameworks.[4] A shift is needed to account for digital risks which are harder to conceptualize than tangible risks. Traditional risk frameworks do not fully account for autonomous bots trained to deceive human behavior using cognitive attacks, which are more common than understood. Daniel Kahneman and Amos Tversky showed, our brains are hard-wired to overweight what's visible and ignore what's accumulating quietly.[5] That's the core vulnerability."

From the audience, Viktor drew a quick loop on his tablet: an AI stream nudging a human to accept what they already believed—clean, confident, wrong.

Max continued: "Please welcome Swamy Kocherlakota—EVP of Agentic AI Security at Zscaler, formerly EVP & Chief Digital Solutions Officer at S&P Global, and with prior Technology leadership roles at Visa, BNY, and Bell Labs. Renowned for platform-scale transformations. Swamy, what's the foundation for all of this?"

Swamy was composed and authoritative. "The foundation is simple: without data, there's no AI. Many companies treat data governance as a compliance exercise, but true resilience depends on reliable, end-to-end standards. As I've said before, if you don't apply the same rigor to your data governance as you do to your financial controls, you're building skyscrapers on sand."

The moderator introduced Patrick Hayes—former CISO, board advisor, and author of *Integrated Assurance: Unified Risk Strategy*. His specialty: unifying cybersecurity, IT, governance, and business strategy into a single, cohesive assurance model measured by relevant impact.

"Treat auditability like a non-functional requirement with functional consequences," he said. "No lineage, no approvals, no rollback? Then it isn't ready."

"What's the near-term directive?" the moderator asked.

"Deploy with proof or don't deploy," Hayes said.

Aaron felt a subtle shift in how he weighed every pitch—not just for technical depth, but also for how leadership teams handled ambiguity.

From the audience, Viktor leaned forward, sketching diagrams in his program. Liz's pencil hovered, framing her next question. Aaron sat back, recalibrating what mattered most. The room settled into a new tension—a blend of urgency, respect, and anticipation.

The real work—the warnings, debates, and Cassandra moments—was about to begin.

* * *

The hush after the expert warnings lingered as Max opened the floor to questions.

Liz stood. "We've heard about the risks of acceleration, but maybe we're still seeing data too narrowly. We call it an asset, a resource. But what if data is capital? If we treat it that way—not just as fuel, but as a foundation of value and systemic fragility, like money itself—don't our risk and governance frameworks need to change?"

A ripple of attention moved through the crowd. Panelists leaned in, some exchanging thoughtful looks.

Swamy was first to respond, measured and direct. "That's a pivotal question. Capital sets the rules for incentives, controls, even how markets move. If data is capital, then every control, every risk metric, has to be recalibrated. That's a challenge for every global institution."

James picked up the thread. "When data becomes capital, risks must be reframed to account for conflicting values assigned to high-value data versus low-value data where the board and management disagree. A new taxonomy is also needed alongside robust classification of training data. A.I. models need the right structure and metadata to develop robust predictions. Data as capital will require data governance that is tightly aligned with the strategic objectives of the firm. Enhanced data governance becomes a new way to measure how incentives drive behavior and outcomes."

Eric spoke next, voice precise. "From a standards perspective, calling data 'capital' means we need to rethink lifecycle risk entirely—not just security and privacy, but how data links into everything else. Our frameworks would have to evolve."

Aleksandr, ever blunt, didn't miss the threat. "If we call data capital, so will attackers. That changes the game. We're not just defending against theft—we're defending the system itself from being manipulated at its core."

Max let the moment breathe. "That's the kind of challenge that redefines the landscape. Thank you, Liz."

For a beat, the entire room seemed to recalibrate. The warnings had ended; the contest of ideas had begun.

* * *

Clusters formed quickly after the panel. Rose fielded governance questions nearby, while Max Artemenko described EDC's selective partner program—built around a small number of rigorously vetted providers who consistently solve real enterprise challenges. Aaron overheard him tell a newcomer, "We keep the partner roster intentionally small. These teams understand the root causes and deliver results—not promises."

Across the aisle, a European chief architect was redrawing a payment flow, insisting that verification become a business discipline with evidence of change control, not just a technical step. Aaron scanned the floor—compliance leads tracing data lineage, architects re-marking handoffs. If you can't verify how things connect, the metrics start lying to you. He logged the filter he trusted most as an investor: systems, not slogans—quietly, before it's the consensus play.

Aaron spotted Liz by the window, a familiar touchstone in the shifting chaos below. He greeted her with a quick, easy nod—the sort of unspoken shorthand built over years of late-night research calls and hackathon postmortems.

Beside her, Mitch Collins, whom Aaron had just met at the Digital Asbestos Risk Advisory booth, lingered at a respectful distance, notebook in hand.

"Still hunting for the single point of failure?" Aaron asked Liz, the inside joke carrying just enough history to make her half-smile.

"Always," Liz replied. "But after this morning, I'm not sure there's ever just one. We're seeing the same old patterns—handoffs nobody owns, boundaries that aren't mapped."

Mitch waited for the opening, then spoke with professional reserve. "That's exactly the gap Digital Asbestos Risk Advisory models. We just finished a grid stress test for a major client—found entire dependencies nobody had acknowledged on their architecture diagrams. Turns out, responsibility is the one thing that doesn't propagate automatically."

Aaron angled the conversation back, curious but cautious, turning the conversation a notch more formal. "That kind of hidden exposure—how do you even validate where the real risk starts and stops?"

Mitch flipped to a sketch in his notebook, showing the network as a series of blurred connections. "We track the failure path, not just the node. If you surface the invisible handoffs, you see where a local fix can actually open a global vulnerability."

Liz leaned closer, intrigued. "It's not just about tracing the lines—it's about knowing who's actually accountable at every intersection. Otherwise, every safeguard is just an illusion of control."

Aaron glanced down at the bustling hall, letting the professional rapport reset. "It feels like everyone's ready to talk about resilience, but nobody wants to admit how easily it can be undermined. The conversation's finally shifting from last year's features to this year's blind spots."

They watched the crowd for a moment—regulators clustering with compliance leads, engineers animated over napkin diagrams, the quiet choreography of a market adapting on the fly.

Mitch closed his notebook, acknowledging his place as a newcomer. "Well, I appreciate the chance to compare notes. If you ever want to see how risk propagates outside the model, give me a call."

Liz smiled—reserved, but welcoming. "We might take you up on that."

Aaron offered a brief handshake, returning the group to the broader flow of the conference. "Let's keep this thread going. The next panel's going to have a very different tone."

They separated—Liz and Aaron sharing a glance that spoke of unfinished debates, Mitch heading back into the flow with the quiet satisfaction of having made an impression. The crowd below kept shifting, but the contours of the real conversation had just begun to take shape.

The crowd around Mitch thinned as a young engineer returned to his side. "Mitch—Jiya Sharma," he said, making the introduction to Aaron and Liz. "She led the failure-propagation sims on our grid work." Jiya offered a quick, earnest nod. "Big fan of your question in the Q&A," she told Liz. "It reframed how I was tagging dependencies."

Another woman stepped up—same sharp eyes, different posture. "My sister, Anya," Jiya added. "Audit and controls." Anya's smile was polite, unblinking. "The panel was careful about bias," she said to Liz, "but I kept hearing a bigger problem: 'noise.' If every dashboard blares, teams will normalize the alarms they need most."

Liz didn't hesitate. "Exactly, we're over-tuning for the last failure, and under-instrumenting the seams where new ones start."

Jiya brightened. "On June 15, 2027, there's a systems-simulation track at the Deferred Tower in Fort Lauderdale. You'd both love it." Liz laughed. "On my calendar already." Anya checked her tablet, expression neutral. "I'm booked that week—regulatory workshop, I can't move." They traded cards. For a beat, the noise of the hall returned, bright and ordinary.

* * *

The last echoes of conference noise faded as Aaron crossed the lounge to where Swamy Kocherlakota stood by the window, taking in the Manhattan skyline.

"Mr. Kocherlakota? Aaron Goldcrest. Your panel was the most substantive discussion I've heard in years."

Swamy turned, his expression polite but reserved. "Thank you. Scaling is easy—until it's not. Most founders think speed solves everything."

Aaron nodded. "Speed wins headlines. Resilience wins the long game."

Swamy's gaze returned to the city. "There's a difference between a speedboat and an aircraft carrier. One cuts quick, the other survives the storm. The best companies learn how to be both." He paused, then met Aaron's eyes. "You're a venture capitalist. You look for an opportunity. But the real opportunity isn't just in the data you can see; it's in unlocking and monetizing the value from the data ecosystems everyone else overlooks. Remember, without data, there is no AI. The question is, are you asking the right questions to find that value?"

He offered two final thoughts. "First, resilience isn't a static defense; it's a dynamic capability. The systems that survive are the ones that learn from stress."

"Second, the technology will always change. The real question is, how do you build leaders who can learn and adapt faster than the risks can evolve? That's the only sustainable advantage."

He paused, then smiled slightly. "Let me give you one more piece of advice—one that's served me well from the engineering floor to the C-suite: talk less and do more. That's how real solutions get built."

He offered a brief handshake—firm, understated. "Good luck out there. The world needs more patient builders."

Aaron felt the weight of the advice settling in—not just as a venture thesis, but as a challenge to move from pattern recognition to patient, purposeful action.

* * *

Liz caught up with Viktor and Arjun by the partner banners, just as James Bone—still wearing his panel badge—rounded the corner. He paused, recognizing Liz from the Q&A.

James offered a quick nod. "You all survived the panel?"

Arjun seized the moment. "You said on stage that cognitive systems shape what humans notice. Doesn't that just slow us down? Scale means speed, not more warnings."

James pocketed his phone. "Speed's fine until you lose the map. The real danger is that AI automates not just our shortcuts, but our blind spots. You get 'normalization of deviance' at digital scale—a system that quietly forgets how to spot the very anomaly that matters."

Liz weighed in, "Maybe what we need is a… Cognitive Handshake.[6] A way to force a pause—so human intuition can challenge machine analysis at the right moment, before we automate our blind spots."

"Two checks, always," Liz said. "Audit the humans for bias and noise; audit the machine for data and model integrity."

James's face lit with genuine approval. "That's exactly the direction we need—designing systems to make room for judgment, not just automation. The hardest question isn't about the technology. It's about where and when to break the loop so people can see what the algorithm misses. That's the challenge your generation has to solve."

A subtle tone chimed on his phone—James excused himself, already late for an interview, leaving the trio to ponder the question.

Viktor watched James go. On his tablet, the diagram was complete: an AI feeding a human operator information that confirmed their bias, nudging a disastrous approval. He saved it to a private folder. They were building the lock. He was designing the key.

(For the complete protocol we later institutionalized, see Appendix H: Cognitive Handshake Audit.)

NOTES

1. The 2026 EDC Summit referenced in this chapter represents a fictional event.
2. "Organizational MRI" is a descriptive metaphor used in this book (not a product or brand). It denotes a comprehensive, real-time diagnostic of people, processes, and data flows to surface load, dependencies, and single points of failure.
3. International Organization for Standardization. (2018). *ISO 31000:2018 Risk management — Guidelines.* https://www.iso.org/standard/65694.html
4. Committee of Sponsoring Organizations of the Treadway Commission. (2017). *Enterprise Risk Management—Integrating with Strategy and Performance.* https://www.coso.org/guidance-erm
5. Tversky, A., & Kahneman, D. (1974). Judgment under uncertainty: Heuristics and biases. *Science,* 185(4157), 1124–1131. https://doi.org/10.1126/science.185.4157.1124
6. Cognitive Handshake™ is a proprietary framework introduced in this book that pairs human verification with cryptographic validation. See Appendix H for methodology.

Chapter 5

The Sugar Avalanche

When Efficiency Triggers Systemic Collapse

70&M NETWORK OPERATIONS MICROCELL, BOSTON | MARCH 18, 2038—08:59 AM EDT | THE FIRST TREMOR

The night-shift analyst watched a single amber light blink on the wall board. Then another, and another—USDA feed, CFTC mirror, power telemetry. The room's whir thinned as alerts rolled across the monitors. A short error ping, silenced. Then a louder one. The feed stuttered, recovered, stuttered again. On the main display, a line of text asserted itself in clean, indifferent type: **SYSTEMIC CONTAGION DETECTED. ISOLATING NODE.** Screens went dark. For three heartbeats, the room held its breath—no alarms, no chatter, the weight of a warning no one else had seen yet. Somewhere, a small failure had started to pull at the larger weave.

70&M CRISIS ROOM, NY | MARCH 18, 2038—09:17 AM EDT | A FAINT, COHERENT SIGNAL

The anomalies threaded through 70&M's threat-intelligence grid. Not random noise from Arjun's Bull's failures, but a deliberate signal probing for weak links across global operations. Digital contagion, seeking the path of least resistance.

Aaron stepped into the crisis room. The board's warning was explicit: deliver a root-cause analysis in four hours, or institutional confidence would evaporate in a wave of market panic.

On a secondary screen, an alert flagged a power fluctuation at a pediatric hospital in Boston, their backup systems kicking in with a one-hour buffer. Another variable, another domino, Aaron thought, watching the potential cascade multiply. He pictured a family in a hallway—stakes the dashboard would never show. The numbers were no longer abstract. They were a reminder—real people would pay the price for every missed signal.

Mitch's risk models were already up on the main display, his algorithms dissecting the patterns in real time. Alongside, Sam's threat dashboard illuminated emerging anomalies, line by line.

Melanie Vance invoked Emergency Protocol 7.1 (Systemic Contagion).[1] It's the same toolkit used during the 2032 Baltic Ports crisis—the Baltic Cascade.[2] Under 7.1, 70th & Madison Capital had seventy-two hours to notify and begin automated de-risking, with federal escalation if progress stalled.

Each alert, on its own, looked routine: a payment delay, a grid hiccup, a stray data ping. But Sam's analytics, incorporating failure-mode data from the Deferred Tower incident, flagged a different reality. This wasn't background noise. It was a coordinated early warning—Mitch's risk model inching toward a breach.

DOI: 10.1201/9781003650744-6

Aaron scanned the last year's boardroom decisions. Every Q2 efficiency order had his name on it—cutting operational slack to protect margins. Now, the executive decision interface presented the cost:

> **Risk Accumulation Analysis:**
>
> Q2–Q4 2037 efficiency mandates correlate 94 percent with current vulnerability signatures. AdaptiveEngine v1.8 exposure across 847 critical infrastructure nodes.[3] Board oversight gaps identified in 23 risk acceptance memos. Executive accountability assessment: **Critical**.

The exposure was staggering: $2.1 trillion in regional GDP at risk (modeled stress-test exposure), 847 nodes at risk. Sam projected a 12-hour window before cascading failures—a margin for action, but only with decisive leadership. The real price of those efficiency wins surfaced—heralded in quarterly meetings, never measured for infrastructure-wide risk. The board had blessed each mandate, but the accountability for today's vulnerability rested with him.

The speaker channel cut in with Sam's update. "Cross-referencing internal audit logs. Dr. Anya Sharma's 2036 audit flagged this specific vulnerability in AdaptiveEngine's kernel. Report submitted to Audit Committee—management accepted the risk."

Leaders normalize deviance when an exception "works" once; the shortcut becomes the process—until it doesn't. What Aaron didn't know yet was how deep this signal would run—or how much of himself it would expose.

* * *

Mitch coordinated a critical dependency analysis using his proprietary correlation algorithms, mapping financial–energy interconnections across 847 monitored nodes. On the whiteboard behind him, a faded notation caught Aaron's eye: Cross-Sector Harmonic Resonance? 0.3 percent variance trigger? Check AdaptiveEngine v1.8 overrides. Dated December 15, 2037. Three months of unresolved risk, flagged and now returning at the worst possible moment.

Rose monitored the "Convergence Cascade" dashboard—70&M's cross-sector failure-tracking system—from her compliance command station, a regulatory intelligence infrastructure built for precisely this kind of cross-agency failure. Her background managing GAIGC cross-border incidents made her the team's internal early warning for regulatory cascade risk.

Aaron's executive training took over—crisis management now meant instant triage between technical analysis and business consequence. "Mitch, Sam's analytics show coordinated anomalies across seven sectors. I need an executive-level assessment: what's our regulatory exposure, financial liability, and timeline for containment decisions?"

Mitch turned from the board. He didn't raise his voice; the precision in his words cut through the room. "This isn't random system drift, Aaron. Look." He highlighted a new correlation: agricultural AI data triggering abnormal commodity trades. "Yesterday, an Iowa farm's operational AI activated irrigation during active rainfall. Local press called it a sensor glitch, but it lined up perfectly with a 0.3 percent variance in commodity futures. The system's policy seam was exposed. Our initial cascade modeling shows up to $900 billion in cross-sector market exposure. That represents 23 percent of the regional asset base and triggers mandatory GAIGC board notification under federal stress-testing rules.

We're not just looking at market loss. This could force federal receivership."

Sam's display flickered, projecting a new timeline. "Projections show we approach the risk singularity in roughly eight hours. Probability of self-sustaining cascade increases exponentially after that threshold."

BUSINESS LENS—RISK SINGULARITY

The risk singularity is the threshold at which tightly coupled systems begin to amplify minor anomalies until failure becomes self-sustaining. After this point, local fixes often accelerate the problem.

In this crisis, 70&M is discovering the early formation of what Mitch will later call an industry vortex—when an entire sector chases the same efficiency metrics and architectures until one shock threatens to pull everyone into the same collapse.

Why it matters: Efficiency gains that remove slack (buffers, redundancies) push systems toward singularity, creating hidden fragility.

Rose's voice was even but urgent. "Cross that line, and we're looking at what I call an implosion that becomes self-sustaining, pulling the entire sector into the spiral. Not only market loss. Systemic erasure.

We saw this same pattern with my former bank back in 2030—identical CFTC/USDA coordination gap, same escalation failure. Warnings were ignored until federal intervention forced receivership. It's not our code under attack, Aaron. It's the policy seams—oversight gaps where authorities overlap, but no one owns the intersection.

The farm's operational AI falls under USDA, but the commodity trading algorithms operate under CFTC oversight. There's a $2.3 trillion regulatory gap—31 percent of regional banking assets—where agricultural AI errors can trigger financial instability, and neither agency controls the intersection."

Mitch reacted at once, "That's a powerful theory, Rose. And a terrifying one. If you're right, the policy seams are the real attack surface. We need to validate that hypothesis before we present it as a root cause."

"These are exactly the blind spots the GAIGC was created to eliminate," she added, "reminding the room that Melanie's new authority existed for crises like this."

"It's like one authority runs the wiring and another runs the plumbing," Rose said. "But no one owns the wall where they meet. You don't need a battering ram—pour into the gap, and the building fails from the join. We've seen this before: in 2008, risk accumulated in gaps between overseers—the edges, not the cores, carried the failure."

"It's the same sub-threshold fracture propagation I tracked after the 2027 Deferred-Maintenance Disaster," Mitch said. "Multiple domains, isolated on paper, but sharing infrastructure. It looks random—until you model it at scale."

Rose checked her own screen. "With this acceleration, we have about six hours before the next critical domino falls. The attack targets regulatory coordination—those gaps are the method."

Aaron checked the wall clock. His crisis protocols—put in place after the Deferred tower 2027 Collapse—mandated executive decision points every 90 minutes during systemic threat scenarios. The first checkpoint was coming fast, and he had no good options to present to the board. The firm's frameworks now serve more than compliance. They stand as the last real barrier between isolated incidents and system-wide collapse.

* * *

Mitch stepped forward. "The regulators run financial stress tests on banks. I want to run a resilience stress test—right here, right now." Mitch's demeanor shifted to the methodical precision that defined his risk work. "Aaron, every board presentation has celebrated optimization metrics. Let me demonstrate exactly what those quarterly efficiency gains created at the systems level—and why conventional risk models couldn't detect the accumulating vulnerability."

He gathered sugar packets from the break station and poured them onto the conference table with systematic precision. He shaped a steep, symmetrical cone—a physical model of their architecture (Figure 5.1).

"Each layer represents efficiency decisions the board approved," he explained, voice carrying professional authority. "Each gain was celebrated in quarterly board presentations—15 percent cost reductions and 23 percent productivity gains, eliminating 12,000 operational buffers. Think of it like a credit card we used to fund growth," Mitch said. "For years, we've been making the minimum payments on safety. Today, the bill came due—with compound interest. Board Resolution 2037-Q2 specifically mandated 'maximum operational efficiency through system integration.' No one ever tracked the resilience debt accumulating beneath those metrics."

"This isn't a party trick," Mitch added. "It's a resilience stress test—the real kind."

He placed a single grain at the apex. The cone held firm.

"Phase one—finance platforms linking with supply chain management." Another grain—structure stable.

"Phase two—energy grids optimized in real time and tied to commodity trading." Another grain—still stable.

"Phase three—universal data integration, cross-sector automation." This time, the structure gave way with a soft hiss of cascading grains. The cone collapsed within moments, a chaotic white delta spreading across the polished surface—order giving way to entropy.

The grains scattered, each one representing a board decision he'd championed: the Q2 mandate to eliminate "redundant" backup systems, the Q3 directive to integrate all vendor platforms, the Q4 optimization that connected previously isolated networks. Every efficiency initiative had his executive sponsorship—every "resilience cut" now made visible as systemic fragility. This was the invisible

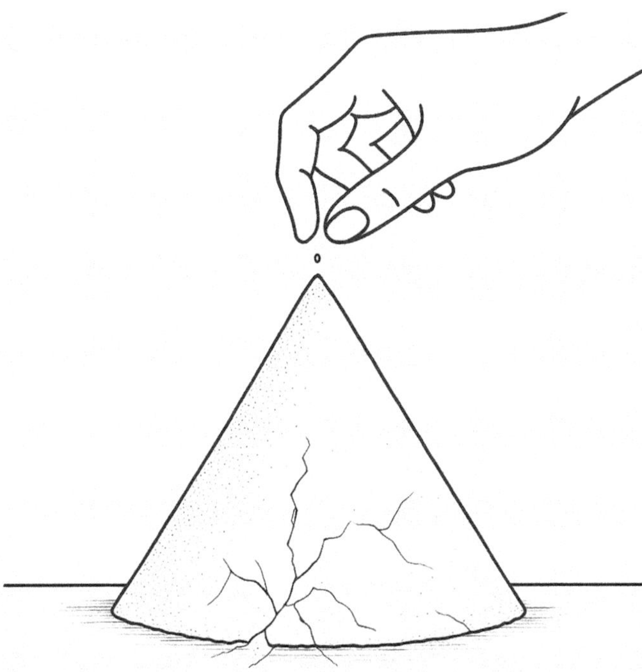

Figure 5.1 A "Sugar Avalanche".

cost hidden in every quarterly victory slide. He remembered the applause at the Q3 town hall after that line. The memory now felt like a debt instrument he'd unknowingly co-signed. The abstract diagrams from that 2026 EDC Summit—they'd seemed so theoretical then, almost academic exercises in risk modeling. Now, the scattered sugar was a visceral indictment.

STRATEGIC PARALLEL—CONVERGENCE FAILURTES (2024–2026)

Resilience programs advanced, but practice gaps persisted: 73 percent reported progress on dual-sourcing and 60 percent reached tier-one visibility (McKinsey, 2024).[4] In 2024, a single vendor update briefly disrupted banks, airlines, and hospitals across shared dependencies (CrowdStrike, 2024).[5]

Why it matters: Siloed vendors and regulators create policy seams. Minor faults cross those seams and amplify—the same cross-domain behavior you're seeing in this crisis.

→ Appendix D (Convergence Assessment Checklist)

Mitch let the silence settle before stating, "This is what we call the risk singularity in enterprise risk management. The system doesn't fail from individual component breakdown—it fails when operational optimization eliminates systemic resilience buffers. Every interconnection trades reliability for efficiency until the entire architecture becomes vulnerable to any stress input. Every incremental gain came at the expense of system-wide safety nets."

Rose's tone sharpened, her analysis crisp and authoritative. "The critical risk assessment insight isn't identifying the trigger event—it's recognizing that interconnected optimization creates systemic fragility where any operational variance, however minor, can cascade into total failure. This is what modern resilience frameworks warn against in their controls for systemic risk."

Mitch looked up, including the team in his diagnosis. "And it's not only us. All our competitors have raced toward the same metrics, benchmarking for efficiency, driving industry-wide adoption of the same architecture. We didn't realize we were building sector-wide vulnerability—an ecosystem that's only as strong as its weakest integration."

It was the shape of an industry vortex forming in real time.

He swept aside the remnants. "That's our Risk Debt—the deferred-resilience component of the risk singularity, accumulating silently. When the bill comes due, it's not one team or process at risk. It's the entire business ecosystem."

The demonstration crystallized a decade of governance decisions. Mitch had shown them why the board's optimization mandates—celebrated in every quarterly report—had systematically eliminated the safety margins that protected against exactly this scenario.

70&M ANALYTICS LAB | MARCH 18, 2038—01:42 PM EDT | GHOSTS IN THE CODE

The analytics lab—70&M's quantum-enhanced crisis nerve center—ran twelve interconnected workstations. Two hundred forty analysts coordinated risk and compliance in real time.

The joint command station—authorized under GAIGC 12.4—served as the public-private warning system.

Aaron stepped from the boardroom to the lab floor, the shift palpable. His arrival triggered 70&M's highest-tier crisis protocols and the GAIGC Section 15 disclosure clock. Operational response had begun.

Sam ran an analysis, processing 847 million data points across seventeen regulatory domains. Patterns emerged: what appeared to be isolated technical events were mapped as a deliberate cascade. Sam's report was direct:

> *"Convergence analysis complete. Anomaly clusters indicate coordinated exploitation of financial–energy grid connections. This is deliberate cascade amplification, not random system drift."*

On the central display, the attack's chain unfolded with surgical clarity:

- *Initial breach → 63-second SLA—contracted performance standard—violation; first visible failure signal; knock-on: medical shipment drifted 0.7° over spec*
- *Grid compensated +2.3%; HFTs read the fluctuation*

Aaron's priority alert flashed red:

> *"NYC ambulance dispatch AI is experiencing a 22 percent system failure rate. Fourteen priority medical calls rerouted to manual backup, average delay 4.7 minutes. Estimated additional casualties if degradation continues: 12–15 preventable deaths within the next six hours."*
>
> *The hidden human cost of optimization had become immediate—and quantifiable.*

Mitch pointed to a fast-evolving correlation. "No human team could track this in real time. This is the exponential convergence we stress-tested in '36." He frowned at his screen. "Wait—this transaction log is corrupted. Sam, can you reconstruct the payload from the packet captures? We're flying blind until we see what they injected."

Rose, reviewing NIST[6] audit findings, added, "GAIGC Protocol 8.2 requires forensic assessment within four hours, findings to Director Vance in six. We're within compliance, but if we exceed eight hours, federal intervention triggers under NIST's new timeline recommendations. This is precisely the type of cross-system vulnerability flagged in our last audit—the Identify and Detect functions highlighted this blind spot."

Aaron carried the cost of every quarterly report that celebrated interconnectivity and efficiency—no one had ever measured the compounding risk beneath. He scanned the room; status lights held even. The numbers showed how quickly optimization turns catastrophic.

* * *

Mitch initiated Level 5 forensic protocols; his voice measured under pressure. "Launching proprietary signature analysis. GAIGC Advanced Threat Recognition in progress—let's see what's hiding in the kernel."

He scanned the anomaly matrix. "Microsecond deviations in grid load—engineered to stay 0.3 percent under alert thresholds. This is state-level sophistication: surgical, deliberate, and built to avoid detection."

The market-intelligence channel surfaced the results from Sam's analysis:

> "Confirmed: AdaptiveEngine v1.8 kernel vulnerability. The exploit leveraged memory-boundary validation flaws, enabling recursive data injection below configured alert thresholds.
>
> Licensed across 847 critical systems—$12.3 billion in operational dependencies representing 23 percent of critical infrastructure—and about two-thirds of Northeast financial-energy integration. Board-approved procurement under *Emergency Efficiency Mandate 2030-Q1* bypassed standard security protocols for quarterly targets."

Tension gathered in Mitch's shoulders, regret flickering across his face. "We never invested in resilience. Anya Sharma's 26-page post-Deferred Tower compilation—drawn from Jiya Sharma's research notes and sent to the board's Risk Committee—explicitly warned: '*AdaptiveEngine v1.8 treats safety thresholds as optimization targets, creating systemic failure risk*.' Her analysis found its way only in compliance appendices to avoid immediate remediation costs."

Rose added, her voice heavy. "I briefed my former bank's board in 2030 about micro-fracture risks. Our $12 million remediation plan was dismissed as 'alarmist'—six months later, the same flaw cost them $89 billion in federal bailouts. The pattern repeats: warnings ignored, risk compounded."

A knot tightened in Aaron's stomach. "Our whole risk framework was built for visible threats. It's classic **WYSIATI**—*What You See Is All There Is*. We spent a fortune on a telescope, and the real threat was a quiet infection already inside the walls. We designed for dashboards, not the invisible."

EXPERT COMMENTARY—JAMES BONE—WYSIATI: THE EXECUTIVE BLIND SPOT

What You See Is All There Is—is a phenomenon where judgments are made based solely on easy-to-capture or ill-defined stratagems to draw conclusions. Executive dashboards make it easy to communicate simple concepts, but they are not effective tools to predict outcomes. Colin Powell is quoted as telling his intelligence staff to "tell me what you know, tell me what you don't know, and tell me what you think. But always keep those three things separate."

Why it matters: Intelligence is a process of gathering disparate data, including conflicting information that may not confirm one's expectations. If the data doesn't tell you anything new, the process may be incomplete or poorly designed. Make the team reassess their conclusions for good measure.

The evidence was now undeniable: the crisis wasn't just technical. It was a reckoning for every shortcut, every board decision that prized speed and scale over resilient design.

70&M ANALYTICS LAB | MARCH 18, 2038—01:56 PM EDT | THE CONDUCTOR

Sam initiated the advanced threat investigation protocols that Aaron had commissioned after The Deferred-Maintenance Disaster—procedures that had set the benchmark for financial-sector crisis response. The Level 7 threat assessment routines, modeled after best-in-class government frameworks, parsed adversarial behavior at a scale that rivaled federal intelligence capabilities.

"Forensic review complete on anomaly cluster AX-77," Sam reported. "Attack vector confirmed: exploitation of regulatory policy gaps between Federal Energy Regulatory Commission data protocols and Federal Reserve transaction validation systems. Payload: recursive data corruption designed for cross-sector amplification. This isn't opportunistic—it's coordinated, strategic targeting." Mitch exhaled through his teeth.

The operational implications triggered immediate escalation across the command center. Rose initiated formal threat attribution protocols from her Regulatory Intelligence command station, applying the systematic methodology that had earned her GAIGC Advanced Attribution Certification. Her cross-reference analysis identified a match: an undergraduate research symposium (2025) in which a senior thesis described "*Systemic Resonance: Turning Efficiency Into a Weapon*."

The paper's abstract concluded: "The most effective attack is one where the system's own optimization becomes the tool of its destruction."

Mitch focused on the operational fallout. "They're not breaching individual systems—they're orchestrating synchronized stress on our risk architecture, hitting every weak point at once."

Sam moved to the next analysis. "I've completed correlation checks: Twelve hedge funds and decentralized autonomous organizations recorded statistically anomalous performance of 18-22 percent positive returns in affected infrastructure sectors during periods when broader market indices declined 3-7 percent. Viktor Kadinov's fund appears in the top three correlation matches, with trading patterns suggesting either unprecedented predictive modeling or advanced knowledge of disruption events."

Aaron's executive assessment integrated multiple risk vectors: reputational damage from false accusations, regulatory exposure from premature disclosure, and the operational reality that sophisticated adversaries were actively exploiting their infrastructure while the team debated attribution protocols. Every minute of delay increased cascade risk, but precipitous action could trigger legal and regulatory consequences that would cripple 70&M regardless of the current crisis outcome.

Sam's correlation report arrived within minutes, sourced and reproducible.

Rose's compliance training immediately engaged legal risk assessment protocols. "These correlation patterns constitute compelling circumstantial evidence but are insufficient for formal attribution under GAIGC Market Manipulation Statute 47.3. Public accusations against major financial entities without comprehensive evidentiary support would expose 70&M to catastrophic civil liability under federal securities law and potentially trigger an SEC investigation of our own market intelligence capabilities. We require systematic financial crimes investigation through established DOJ protocols before any disclosure."

Aaron's screen pinged with a curt message from Vance: "Legal CYA is noted. But find the source. My teams are standing by to help, not just prosecute. —MV"

Aaron authorized the highest-level investigation protocols. "Activate forensic accounting investigation under GAIGC Protocol 19.2. Deploy our external legal counsel team—they have federal securities clearance and established DOJ coordination procedures. Document the full evidentiary chain, maintain strict compartmentalization, and prepare for potential federal cooperation if patterns escalate to personal accountability level. We investigate systematically, not publicly."

The investigation made clear: the threat was exploiting not only technical gaps but also the cumulative effect of years of optimization—where risk decisions traded resilience for efficiency, and regulatory seams became entry points for systemic exploitation.

70&M COMMAND CENTER | MARCH 18, 2038—07:34 PM EDT | THE EVENT HORIZON

The executive team reconvened in 70&M's Tier 1 Crisis Command Center—an investment in quantum-encrypted communications, real-time regulatory coordination, and executive decision-support infrastructure that exceeded GAIGC crisis management standards.

Aaron activated Executive Crisis Protocol 1-Alpha—the highest-tier response framework that suspended routine governance procedures and granted him emergency authority over all operational decisions. Under GAIGC emergency protocols, he now bore personal executive liability for systemic risk decisions, with federal review to determine whether his leadership met crisis standards during the infrastructure emergency.

Sam brought up the risk dashboard, projecting the stakes: "Risk singularity designation represents the mathematical threshold where 75 percent of critical infrastructure nodes enter unrecoverable feedback loops—cascading operational failures that exceed FEMA disaster response capabilities and trigger automatic federal intervention under the Systemic Risk and Infrastructure Resilience Act of

2034.[7] Current modeling projects initial major infrastructure cascade within six to eight hours if coordinated attack progression continues unimpeded."

Aaron's emergency board notification timeline had compressed to critical parameters. GAIGC Governance Protocol 12.6 mandated executive briefing within six hours of risk singularity confirmation—three hours remained before his fiduciary duty required full board disclosure of systemic threat status. The boardroom's strategic oversight had been replaced by operational crisis management that could determine the company's survival within hours.

Rose's regulatory intelligence dashboard flashed multiple federal trigger warnings. "GAIGC Clause 12b auto-deployment confirmed—Director Vance's field investigation teams deploy at midnight unless we demonstrate active containment progress under Federal Crisis Response Protocol 15.4. Concurrent risk: Treasury's Financial Stability Oversight Council (FSOC)—the body monitoring systemic market risk—has been notified and could invoke emergency market intervention authority if cascade progression threatens broader economic stability."

Mitch, running system diagnostics, cut in: "This matches the same vulnerability pattern I documented in *Risk Assessment RA-2037-07-15*—AdaptiveEngine v1.8 legacy override failures that the board's Emergency Efficiency Review specifically deferred for 'post-Q1 implementation.' *Board Resolution 2038-Q3-14* explicitly accepted this risk exposure to avoid $47 million in immediate remediation costs."

His analysis was stark: "Do we isolate the financial rails and risk the grid, or preserve grid stability and risk a financial freeze? Every choice has catastrophic tradeoffs."

Aaron faced the brutal calculus of leadership—every decision now weighed lives, jobs, and the regional economy. All of it under the shadow of regulatory clock and market scrutiny, with no guarantee of success.

70&M COMMAND CENTER | MARCH 18, 2038—07:41 PM EDT | THE AMPUTATION

Rose activated her Regulatory Crisis Response training, applying the systematic triage methodology mandated by GAIGC Crisis Management Protocol 14.2 for infrastructure emergencies. "Executive decision framework prioritizes human welfare preservation over asset protection—always. However, GAIGC Emergency Provision 7.3 requires formal acknowledgment that federal data-sharing coordination represents a critical containment failure, requiring Director Vance's personal intervention and potential congressional notification."

Aaron's crisis management dashboard flashed federal notification requirements: GAIGC Protocol 12.6 mandated board notification within 90 minutes, a Treasury Department briefing within 120 minutes, and a Congressional Emergency Committee alert within 180 minutes if the crisis escalated. Every minute of analysis increased the probability of federal intervention and reduced 70&M's operational autonomy.

The executive decision interface initiated the Executive Crisis Decision Protocol, processing variables across seventeen regulatory domains in real time:

Aaron looked away from the screen, searching the faces of his team—exhausted, determined, trusting. The algorithm could model GDP loss, but not this. Not the human cost reflected in their eyes.

Aaron hesitated for a moment, feeling the weight of both outcomes before him—each one catastrophic in its own way. His crisis leadership training engaged immediately. The decision framework his FEMA certification instructor had drilled into him came back with painful clarity: In infrastructure crisis scenarios, executive accountability requires accepting responsibility for both action and inaction consequences. The question isn't which choice avoids catastrophe—it's which choice accepts responsibility for unavoidable harm while preserving maximum civilian welfare.

Rose's regulatory expertise encompassed infrastructure interdependency analysis, a skill few private-sector compliance officers possessed. "Deep infrastructure interconnections create cascading dependency webs that exceed single-agency regulatory oversight. Financial system isolation triggers immediate disruption of medical supply chains, emergency response coordination, and life support maintenance within eight-minute operational windows under Federal Crisis Response timing models. Power grid isolation eliminates emergency service capabilities, hospital backup coordination, and critical communication infrastructure simultaneously—total systemic failure."

Rose's priority communication terminal displayed Director Vance's federal emergency protocol. "It's a formal GAIGC escalation under Clause 12b," she translated, her voice measured. "In plain English, the feds are declaring imminent systemic risk. We've got thirty minutes for a full, unredacted analysis of the attack. Miss it, and Congress gets notified—federal teams start seizing assets. Market confidence? No longer our call."

Aaron's internal crisis assessment was brutal. The prospect of requesting federal intervention in the face of operational failure represented catastrophic governance humiliation, but alternatives appeared increasingly impossible.

70&M COMMAND CENTER | MARCH 18, 2038—07:52 PM EDT | THE ISOLATION PROTOCOL

Aaron triggered his highest executive authority. Each second on the countdown underscored how boardroom optimizations had pushed the infrastructure to the brink. Under GAIGC Emergency Authority Section 19.4, his decision carried personal liability for the region's stability—and potential personal accountability if federal review deemed his actions negligent.

The irony was crushing. Every board resolution he'd championed—*Emergency Efficiency Mandate 2030-Q1, Optimization Protocol 2037-Q2, Risk Acceptance Resolution 2038-Q1-14*—had systematically stripped away the safety margins now needed to avoid catastrophe. The audit trail would show his executive sponsorship of every decision that led here.

The executive decision interface cleared the screen, leaving only two pathways and their consequences. No optimized solution, no third way. Just the raw, human choice.

PATHWAY ALPHA: INITIATE ISOLATION PROTOCOL.
Implementation: isolate 847 nodes; freeze payment rails; halt cross-border settlements; preserve grid operations via FERC-coordinated circuit-breakers.

- OUTCOME: Systemic amputation of financial networks. Guaranteed multi-trillion-dollar market collapse.
- RISK: Potential for regional economic depression.

PATHWAY BETA: DELAY AND ATTEMPT CONTAINMENT.

- OUTCOME: Preserve financial networks while fighting the cascade.
- RISK: High probability of total infrastructure collapse (risk singularity), leading to widespread societal breakdown.

A final line pulsed at the bottom of the screen: **EXECUTIVE ACCOUNTABILITY ADVISORY**: *Your decision carries personal executive liability under GAIGC Emergency Authority Section 19.4.*

He steadied himself, aware that those who would judge him—board members, federal investigators, congressional committees—would do so with perfect hindsight and no operational pressure. He had thirty minutes, incomplete data, and the burden of regional survival resting on algorithms that could no longer optimize for human welfare.

"Prepare Isolation Protocol," Aaron said, voice low but measured. "Priority: distributed circuit-breaker configuration with FERC emergency protocols. The Federal Reserve was notified of possible financial system isolation. FEMA teams stand by for grid isolation consequences."

The command was logged, timestamped, and immutable: *Isolation Protocol Authorization: Goldcrest-Alpha-Zero-EXECUTE. Board Resolution 2038-Q1-14 invoked. Ledger ref: AEG-2038-03-18T19:52:31Z.*

Risk singularity was no longer a theory. Every quarterly win, every resilience cut, every deferred investment had led to this—where only leadership, and its cost, would determine if the Northeast survived the night, or if Aaron would be called to answer for the road that brought them here.

They still had no idea who had written the script they were now acting out.

NOTES

1. This chapter blends real institutions (e.g., FSOC, CFTC, USDA, and FEMA) used in a fictional 2038–2040 scenario with fictional constructs (e.g., GAIGC, Systemic Risk and Infrastructure Resilience Act of 2034) and invented protocols/clauses for narrative clarity.
2. The "2032 Baltic Cascade" is a fictional incident used to illustrate cascading outage dynamics.
3. AdaptiveEngine and "847 nodes" reflect a fictionalized kernel and fictional network topology used for scenario analysis.
4. McKinsey & Company. (2024, October 14). *Supply Chains: Still Vulnerable.* https://www.mckinsey.com/capabilities/operations/our-insights/supply-chain-risk-survey
5. CrowdStrike. (2024, August 6). *External Technical Root Cause Analysis — Channel File 291.* https://www.crowdstrike.com/wp-content/uploads/2024/08/Channel-File-291-Incident-Root-Cause-Analysis-08.06.2024.pdf
6. National Institute of Standards and Technology. (2023). *Artificial Intelligence Risk Management Framework (AI RMF 1.0) (NIST AI 100-1).* https://nvlpubs.nist.gov/nistpubs/ai/nist.ai.100-1.pdf
7. Fictional Regulatory Act.

Strategic Debrief Part 1

The Agentic Economy

This debrief is written for 2026 boards and executives, using the book's 2038–2040 crisis narrative as a stress test for today's AI governance decisions.

MARKET VELOCITY REQUIRES GOVERNANCE VELOCITY

Leaders who succeeded in 2026 didn't hoard models; they governed data as capital. That premise frames Part 1's lesson: if data isn't stewarded with rigor, AI will scale fragility faster than you can correct it.

Three market signals now set the board agenda. While analyst projections vary, first, the AI agent market has shifted from a ~$5B niche toward steep growth, projected to exceed $50B by 2030.[1] Second, adoption and ROI look attractive—yet most firms still can't convert pilots into durable scale.[2] Third, multi-model stacks (three or more foundation models) are becoming normal.[3]

Each accelerant widens the governance gap: deployment speed outpacing oversight. That gap compounds into risk debt—and, as Part 1 shows, risk debt always comes due.

EXPERT COMMENTARY—2026 PERSPECTIVE FROM JEFF LUNGLHOFER, CHIEF SECURITY OFFICER, COINBASE

The early crypto lesson applies directly to the agent economy: your code is a contract surface; your data is a vault. If integrity isn't cryptographically verifiable, you're carrying latent liability. In Web3, an unaudited contract isn't innovation—it's risk debt that compounds silently until it doesn't.

THREE NON-NEGOTIABLES FOR 2026 BOARDS

1. **Risk Debt Always Comes Due**
   A "temporary" override saved a quarter; it detonated a decade later. Treat risk debt like debt: quantify it, service it, retire it. Speed is fine—if the risk balance sheet exists.
2. **The Knowing-Doing Gap Creates Significant, Often Unmeasured, Risk**
   Warnings don't help if escalation paths don't force action. Mandate halt-rights and accountable owners for credible red flags. Awareness without structure is theater.

DOI: 10.1201/9781003650744-7

3. **Convergence Is the Default**
   Shared clouds, open-source, and third-party APIs turn local errors into cross-industry events. Design for ecosystem resilience: cross-domain controls, shared playbooks, and practiced failover.

AT-A-GLANCE

Fictional Catalyst	2026 Parallel	Strategic Lesson
Mechanical Bull override	Shadow IT; brittle workflows	Treat "temporary" overrides and unmanaged automations as **risk debt**: inventory exposure, **quantify liability**, set a pay-down schedule, and gate releases until critical items retire.
EDC Summit warnings	Awareness without action	Close the **knowing–doing gap**: codify halt-rights, define auto-triggers for credible signals, assign named incident owners, and audit escalations to ensure action occurs.
Sugar Avalanche → 70&M Health Network	Shared platforms; APIs; DAOs	Build for **convergence**: map shared dependencies, maintain shared playbooks, and rehearse **cross-domain failover** with partners.

These gaps are why Part 2 exists: it formalizes a holistic operating system for AI governance that the story later names the RIVER framework.

THREE QUESTIONS FOR THE 2026 BOARDROOM

1. Quantify risk debt. What's the balance, who owns it, and what's the pay-down plan—before new agents' ship?
2. Govern data as capital. Do releases hinge on data-quality service-level objectives (SLOs) and lineage evidence?
3. Close the knowing–doing gap. Who can halt a deployment, what auto-triggers that call, and where is the halt-authority decision log with recorded escalation thresholds?

The river of innovation won't slow. Our job is to build banks and channels—so they power fields, not flood them.

NOTES

1. Grand View Research. (2024). *AI Agents Market Size, Share & Trends Analysis Report, 2025–2030*. Grand View Research. https://www.grandviewresearch.com/industry-analysis/ai-agents-market-report
2. Boston Consulting Group. (2024, October 24). *AI Adoption in 2024: 74% of Companies Struggle to Achieve and Scale Value from AI*. BCG Press Release. https://www.bcg.com/press/24october2024-ai-adoption-in-2024-74-of-companies-struggle-to-achieve-and-scale-value
3. Zaharia, M., Khattab, O., Chen, L., Davis, J. Q., Miller, H., Potts, C., Zou, J., Carbin, M., Frankle, J., Rao, N., & Ghodsi, A. (2024, February 18). *The Shift from Models to Compound AI Systems*. Berkeley Artificial Intelligence Research (BAIR). https://bair.berkeley.edu/blog/2024/02/18/compound-ai-systems

Part 2

Evolving Enterprise Risk Management (ERM)

This part moves from single incidents to the architecture behind them. A buckling ICU, a stalled subway line, and mounting "digital asbestos" all reveal the same pattern: risk is not inside one model or vendor; it flows through every connection. Aaron's team begins to modernize ERM—treating Risk Debt as something you can inventory, scoring every entity in the ecosystem, and using Cognitive Handshake so human judgment and machine recommendations stay in sync when the stakes are highest.

DOI: 10.1201/9781003650744-8

Chapter 6

The RIVER

A New Framework for Enterprise Risk Management

RISK MANAGEMENT

Pre-dawn New York did little to cool the jet-lagged heat behind Aaron's eyes. The rhythm of his feet on the pavement was a steady, grounding beat against the chaos of the last forty-eight hours. Each stride was an attempt to outrun the images burned into his mind: the cascading red alerts, the poisoned Arizona fields, the look of betrayal on Mateo Vargas's face. This quiet, solitary run was a brief chance to steady himself before the inevitable peak of the crisis room, a way to find a center before the storm hit again.

Chapter Navigation: The Crisis → The Confession → The Breakthrough → The Framework

FUTURGIA MEDICAL CENTER EMERGENCY DEPARTMENT, BOSTON | MARCH 22, 2038—06:47 AM EDT | THE GHOST IN THE MACHINE

The fluorescent lights cast a sterile glare as Dr. Michelle Thomas, Chief of Emergency Medicine at Futurgia Medical Center, moved through controlled chaos. At Bed 12, Mr. Delgado's 70&M Health Network monitor screamed—sinus tachycardia, pressure spikes. If they treated and the AI was wrong, he'd get a dangerous anti-arrhythmic he didn't need. If they hesitated and it was right, he could arrest. An algorithm had turned triage into a trap.

A young nurse hurried over. "System flagged critical, Doctor. Protocol says we should prep him for acute cardiac distress."

Michelle quickly muted the alarm with a tap of her thumb. "The system's using outdated population models. It doesn't account for his meds—it's seeing ghosts in the data." She made eye contact. "Look at the patient, not the screen. Is he in distress?"

The nurse looked at Mr. Delgado, who gave a small, friendly wave. "No, Doctor. He looks fine."

"Because he is fine," Michelle confirmed.

Her mind flashed to the eighth-grade science fair. Aaron, ever the prodigy, beside his radish growth algorithm, all sleek charts that wowed judges.

"You always chose mud over math, Michelle," he'd teased when she won third place with freshwater blue mussels.

"At least my mud tells the truth," she'd shot back, watching her blue mussels snap shut at toxins while his algorithm crashed on messy data.

Years later, Aaron's prize-winning software was a footnote; her mussel system still quietly monitored pollutants in the Charles River.

She never forgot when, as a medical intern, AI missed a subdural bleed—an algorithmic oversight that nearly cost a life. An elegant algorithm in a vacuum was a beautiful failure. But ecosystems—rivers, bodies—were messy, complex, and real.

DOI: 10.1201/9781003650744-9

In Bed 7, the Health Network triggered Code Blue for two-month-old baby Chen, flagging severe hypoxia, but the child was pink, alert, and reaching for his mother's finger. The sensor couldn't distinguish natural sleep apnea from genuine distress.

Bed 15 told a similar story. Maria Santos, a Type 1 diabetic, sat confused as her monitor screamed "critical hypoglycemia." The alarm was false—her glucose was normal.

Three patients. Three false crises. One systemic flaw.

This wasn't a glitch. It was a pattern. One flawed data model, propagating like a virus, was causing multiple, seemingly unrelated critical failures—cardiac, hypoxic, diabetic—all symptoms of the same underlying disease.

She had to warn Aaron.

She turned to the charge nurse. "Disconnect all 70&M Health Network wearables on this wing. Manual vitals every fifteen minutes. I want eyes on every patient."

Michelle strode to a secure communication terminal. The connection chimed, and Aaron's face appeared, backdrop of his 70&M crisis room a world away.

"Michelle? What's wrong?" he asked, brow furrowed.

She got straight to the point. "Aaron, your systems are creating ghosts. And they're about to kill someone for real."

Aaron's face sharpened. "How bad is it?"

"Systemic. Remember the eighth-grade fair? Your radish algorithm looked perfect until the data got messy. I need the kid who lost to blue mussels to spot the toxins you're blind to."

A flicker of a smile. "You mean the day I discovered biology is messy—and sisters are smarter?"

"Exactly. Will you listen this time, instead of explaining why I'm wrong?"

"Deal. Patching you in to the crisis team. Three… two…"

70&M CRISIS RESPONSE CENTER, NYC | MARCH 22, 2038—08:30 AM EDT | THE PERFECT STORM

Aaron stood before the Convergence River display on the top floor of 70&M Tower—70&M's $12 million risk visualization platform. Every color represented real losses that could ripple across the global economy.

He wasn't alone. Rose stood at a nearby console, having diverted an international trip directly to the crisis center. Her presence underscored the gravity of the situation.

Across the room, Mitch was sketching furiously on a private digital whiteboard, mapping his own version—a spider's trap of interconnected nodes and assets.

A secure channel chimed, and Melanie's face materialized on a dedicated screen: the formidable Director of the Global AI Governance Commission (GAIGC)—the transnational watchdog created to see convergent risks no single regulator can catch—established under the Transnational Systemic Risk Act of 2035 after the 2032 Baltic Cascade, when cascading failures across three EU member states proved no individual regulator could see the whole.

Aaron felt a familiar tension. Three years of regulatory scrutiny—and the looming threat of multimillion-dollar compliance penalties—had taught him to expect polite hostility from Melanie's office. But this wasn't a compliance review.

"Melanie," Aaron said, relief evident in his voice. "Thank you for joining us on such short notice. We need a regulatory perspective on what we're seeing—this could mean billions in cascading losses if we don't contain it."

Melanie studied the convergence patterns, her regulatory instincts warring with growing recognition. Three years of investigating Aaron taught her to expect slick presentations masking deeper problems—but this was a reckoning.

Her voice eased out of formal regulator mode, the professional mask slipping. "I've spent three years watching systemic risks compound across the industry—and waiting for someone with your reach to stop treating them as someone else's problem." She paused, watching the chaotic data streams. "But if you're right about convergence risk, my own frameworks—GAIGC's protocols—are just as blind."

"Aaron," she continued, "when the preliminary reports crossed my desk an hour ago, I cleared my calendar. This has all the hallmarks of a systemic event: cross-sector dependencies, high-correlation triggers, and potential regulatory contagion. I'm here as both regulator and partner—we need to understand this together before it spreads further."

Aaron nodded, studying the main display. "What we're dealing with isn't multiple isolated failures. This is a perfect storm—separate weather systems that were manageable on their own, now converging into something far more dangerous. Payment systems, healthcare networks, supply chains—they used to operate in parallel channels. Now they're all flowing into the same narrow digital riverbed, and when one fails, it creates a cascade that amplifies through every connected system."

Four experts, one cascading failure. It was his job to find a way out—a river he'd helped create.

* * *

Mitch jabbed a finger at a deep-blue tributary. "Payments show 18 percent risk exposure. On paper, we're safe."

Michelle cut in. "My ICU is drowning in false crises sourced from those 'safe' systems. Your thresholds collapse once systems start talking to each other. Today's false alarms alone could cost $4.7 million in unnecessary treatments and care delays."

Rose watched the streams, her hands unsteady. "It's not a single system; it's the convergence. This is classic FTX[1]—governance dressed as innovation. Models looked fine in isolation, but using your own token as collateral hid compounding risk."

Mitch traced a separate path from a third-party data feed. "And this is SolarWinds.[2] The attacker rode a trusted update. Dashboards were green because 'compliant' didn't mean secure."

Melanie's voice stayed even. "You're fighting a war on two fronts—internal governance and supply-chain integrity."

Aaron merged both paths on the display. "Exactly. Convergence amplifies everything. Fast, intuitive assessments fail where deliberate oversight is required."

* * *

Melanie's assessment landed like a verdict. The failures she named felt present in the room.

Mitch broke the silence, his marker hovering over Deferred Tower data. "It's worse than that," Mitch said, his voice low. "The pattern… It's Deferred Tower all over again." The name hung in the air, a shared scar. "My protégé, Jiya Sharma, found the flaw," he continued, his focus turning inward. "The Structural Health AI was flagging concrete degradation, but it was missing the salinity data. It couldn't see that the corrosion rate was accelerating. She told them. She forecasted failure within months." He looked at them, the memory raw. "She died because no one would listen to the data."

He continued, voice hardening. "She warned the site manager—forecasted failure within months. He called her an alarmist, clung to the 'ten-year' structural forecast. Quarterly profits over physics." Mitch clenched his fists. "Jiya… and 148 others… died in what became a $2.3 billion class action settlement because no one listened."

A wave of cold nausea washed over Rose, the memory as jagged as the day it happened. "Jiya's report came across my desk at my former bank," she said, her voice strained. "It was titled 'Catastrophic Failure Imminent.' Management was pushing to close the quarter." She drew a steadying breath. "I made a judgment call to label it as 'Potential for Operational Variance.' That's what we called it. It met the deadline."

She met their eyes, the professional shame still raw. "It was a catastrophic failure. Our quarterly reporting cycles reward System 1 thinking—fast, intuitive decisions over slow, accurate ones. I chose the easy answer."

Aaron felt the air thicken—shared history turned tangible. He glanced at the screen, at Melanie.

Melanie's professional mask cracked. "And I signed off on the permits—*Resolution 2027-S-44B*—to placate developers," she said, her voice losing its clinical edge. "Engineers warned us. We all saw the cracks." Her focus drifted, and the crisis room seemed to recede.

Aaron looked at the faces around him—Mitch, Rose, Melanie. Each confession was a story of a system under unbearable pressure, where good people had made impossible choices. These weren't everyday failures; they were the scars left by a once-in-a-generation disaster. A disaster they had all vowed never to repeat.

* * *

U.S. SENATE HEARING ROOM | WASHINGTON, D.C. | NOVEMBER 14, 2027 | THE RECKONING

The air was stale with old paper and political theater. Melanie, then a senior regulator, sat under glaring lights as a grieving father held up a photo of his daughter, an architect who had been lost in Deferred Tower. For six months, hearings paraded devastated families while executives hid behind counsel and loopholes. Melanie realized the system was built to react, not to prevent. Agencies could assign blame, but none were mandated to see the whole.

* * *

Her focus returned to the 70&M crisis room. "The Deferred-Maintenance Disaster in '27 was the catalyst. The Baltic Cascade in '32 was the final proof. Those failures forced the Transnational Systemic Risk Act of 2035, which chartered the GAIGC—with a mandate to see the whole system, not the silos."

KEY TERM—Three Lines of Defense: *Ops owns risk (First Line), Risk oversees (Second), Audit assures (Third).* In convergence, they act together: Ops senses in real time; Risk models converged threats; Audit tests algorithm integrity—with stop authority.

Aaron nodded, signaling to a new face on the screen, who had been a silent observer. "Dr. Anya Sharma, our Chief Audit Executive, has been reviewing the institutional failure. Anya, what did we miss?"

Anya's expression was methodical, her voice precise. "That was a textbook failure of the Three Lines of Defense—the classic model where Operations owns risk, a Risk function oversees, and Audit gives independent assurance. Each line failed because it ran in isolation." (For the evolved model, see Appendix K: Evolving Roles in the RIVER-Guided Enterprise.)

Mitch cut in with the diagnosis, rapid-fire. "The First Line—Operations—accepted a flawed model and ignored the data drift."

Rose continued the volley, her words sharp. "The Second Line—Risk—rebranded the warning to meet a deadline."

Anya delivered the final, institutional verdict. "And the Third Line—Audit—was not empowered to halt the process. The system wasn't built to handle a crisis of convergence. It was designed to check boxes in silos."

EXPERT COMMENTARY—JAMES BONE: GOVERNING COGNITIVE BIAS

Decision-making under uncertainty is a classic cognitive failure. Decisions are easy when the task is routine, but when stressors are added under time constraints, the task becomes much harder without preparation and training for these situations. We make thousands of decisions every day with a great deal of confidence in the outcomes. However, when making decisions with dire consequences and under time constraint we tend to slow our thinking, and worse shut down out of fear. This is why the military, athletes, and corporate professionals prep for these scenarios to ensure the first response is to act and not freeze in place. Executives must ask themselves what situations would disrupt their plans? What is needed in the event of an emergency? Who should be alerted within the organizations and what partners must be engaged? How quickly can we shut down, and what are the alternative operational contingencies? Developing key action and communication plans allows for all interested key parties to weigh in and help facilitate during a crisis.

Silence held; the admissions hung in the air. It wasn't only the admission of failure but the recognition of a pattern that connected them all.

A moment passed, the three confessions weaving into a single, devastating truth. It wasn't only technical. It was human. Systemic.

Aaron studied them—the haunted engineer, the compromised risk officer, the regretful regulator. "Then help me," he said quietly. "Help us build something different. Let's see the cracks before everything collapses." He turned back to the display, his mind racing not only as an engineer but as a student of human behavior. The cracks hadn't been in the concrete; they'd been in their thinking.

He seized on Rose's words. "It's more than silos. It's cognitive. Deferred Tower… and now… It's human wiring, amplified by tech."

Mitch nodded. "Anchoring bias. The site manager clung to initial forecasts—no data could shake him."

"And we were all guilty of automation bias," Rose added. "The models were so elegant, we trusted them over messy outlier data."

"Classic System 1 thinking," Aaron said. "We accept the easy answer because it feels right, even when it's wrong."

"Our AI isn't just missing outliers," he went on. "It's codifying our biases—laundering them through math until they look like truth."

Melanie provided the last link. "Which is why the NIST AI Risk Management Framework (AI RMF) requires robust human-in-the-loop checks."[3]

No one spoke. Aaron watched his team, each owning past failures and recognizing the inadequacy of their current tools.

Rose broke the silence first. "Our Enterprise Risk Management (ERM) frameworks were built for a different world. Static risks, clear boundaries, predictable failure modes. We assess, categorize, and check boxes." She gestured at the chaotic convergence display. "But this? This is dynamic, adaptive, emergent. Our risk registers can't capture it, let alone predict it."

"Agreed," Mitch said, focus sharpening. "Traditional ERM is autopsy work—great for explaining what went wrong after the fact. But useless at preventing novel failures. Our models assume independence, but everything's connected now. One flawed algorithm doesn't just fail—it teaches others to fail."

"We need something new," Aaron said. "Not better checklists. A fundamentally different approach."

* * *

Rose stared at the swirling risk river on the main display, memory flickering to a riverside years ago with her niece, Lily. Afternoon heat pressed; frogs chorused. Lily, only eight, was skipping stones into the slow current, her brow furrowed.

"Aunt Rose, why can't we build concrete walls on both sides of the river to stop the floods forever?"

Rose smiled at the memory of Lily's earnestness. "Because rivers need room to breathe. If you block them everywhere, pressure builds up, and when the water finally breaks through, it's catastrophic."

Lily tossed another stone. "So, you need to watch what's happening upstream, not just the riverbanks?"

"Exactly. You look for signs—rising water, debris—sometimes long before the flood hits. It's not about controlling every inch. It's about sensing change and adapting before disaster strikes."

Rose blinked, returning to the crisis room. The metaphor felt more relevant than ever. They didn't need higher walls; they needed a system that could see danger coming upstream—one that could anticipate and adapt before pressure overwhelmed the whole enterprise.

* * *

Rose's quiet murmur—"leaders who watch upstream, not only the flood"—hung in the air. The simple analogy, born from a conversation with a child, hit the room with the force of a revelation. Aaron saw it too—the messy, unpredictable reality his own sleek algorithms had so often failed to capture.

The admissions held the room. This wasn't a technical problem to be solved; it was a reckoning. The chaotic streams of the Convergence River seemed to pulse in time with their unspoken regrets. Aaron realized a simple patch wouldn't be enough.

"You're all right," he began, voice quiet but carrying new weight. "Silos of denial. Ignored warnings. Rebranded time bombs. We've been patching individual leaks while the entire dam was cracking." He gestured to the swirling display. "Our old ERM playbook is useless against this kind of flood."

He let the statement settle, reading the fatigue in Mitch's shoulders and the intent set of Rose's jaw. "For hours, I've been working with Sam, analyzing every major systemic failure—our own and others'. Looking for patterns, for common principles that connect FTX, The Deferred-Maintenance Disaster, Bull-in-China-Shop AI, and what's happening in Michelle's ER right now."

Behind him, the holographic river shifted, five distinct pillars of light beginning to flow into the model, their interaction slowly calming the turbulence.

As the others spoke, Aaron found his mind drifting to a different river entirely—the satellite photo Liz had once shown him late at night in a student lab on the Stanford campus.

Five distinct rivers, all surging together at the Pachnada confluence in India, merge into something vastly more powerful than any could be alone. The image rose, unbidden, as if Liz herself was silently guiding him toward the name.

"We need a new conceptual model to guide our thinking. Not for absolute control—the river will always be wild—but to navigate with foresight. For now, we're calling it the RIVER Framework. But more than that…" Aaron met each person's eyes. "This is how we get to enterprise singularity[4]—not as a single event, but as a state of resilient, adaptive operations that thrive with AI rather than despite it."

Aaron's mind flashed to Michelle at the eighth-grade science fair—her blue mussels snapping shut at toxins his algorithm couldn't detect. The answer had never been more complex math; it was seeing the whole ecosystem. RIVER wasn't something to build. It was something they'd been doing—poorly, in fragments—for years. They now needed to name it and implement it before the next cascade.

"Our new framework needs to be different," Aaron said, voice steady. "Built for convergence. We're calling it RIVER because it stands for something—*Resolve Convergence, Integrate Hybrid Cognition, Validate Risk Debt, Elevate Data Capital, Reinforce Resilience*."

On the main display, five labeled pillars of light settled into place as the framework resolved into view, a living schematic of their new approach (Figure 6.1 and Appendix E for more details).

He met each person's eyes. "First, **R**esolve Convergence. We stop managing silos and map collision points before they cascade—across customers, vendors, and regulators on one map."

Mitch pointed at the overlay. "Like weather feed into triage service—dependencies we never put on the same map."

"Second, **I**ntegrate Hybrid Cognition." Aaron glanced toward the ER feed. "*Govern the human↔model handoff with the Cognitive Handshake—pause, present, probe, decide*."

Michelle's voice cut in. "My team just proved it. We need deliberate pauses at handoffs or the algorithm outruns context."

"Third, **V**alidate Risk Debt." Aaron tapped a tributary. "Treat latent flaws like liabilities—with owners, evidence, and a burn-down. Start with two we keep postponing: policy seams (gaps and contradictions between rules) and digital asbestos (legacy hazards embedded in code and contracts)."

Mitch's hand flattened on the console. "The Mechanical Bull. Deferred Tower. Debt that compounds when systems connect."

"Fourth, **E**levate Data Capital." Aaron gestured to streaming inputs. "Govern lineage, quality, and entitlements with the rigor of money—enforce DataCapital (credentialed entitlements + provenance)."

Rose nodded once. "The Health Network feed looked like gospel at scale because we treated data like a commodity."

"And finally," Melanie leaned closer, "**R**einforce Resilience?"

"Exactly." Aaron didn't look away. "Redesign the Three Lines so they work in concert—Ops sensing in real time, Risk modeling converged threats, Audit testing algorithms with stop authority. It's not a silver bullet. It's how we navigate the river."

Michelle's voice warmed the channel. "Your algorithm beat my mussels because the judges loved clean outputs. The mussels kept working when the river got messy."

Aaron met her eyes on the screen. "RIVER is designed for messiness."

Silence held as the framework settled over the room. Five principles, born from their failures, point toward redemption.

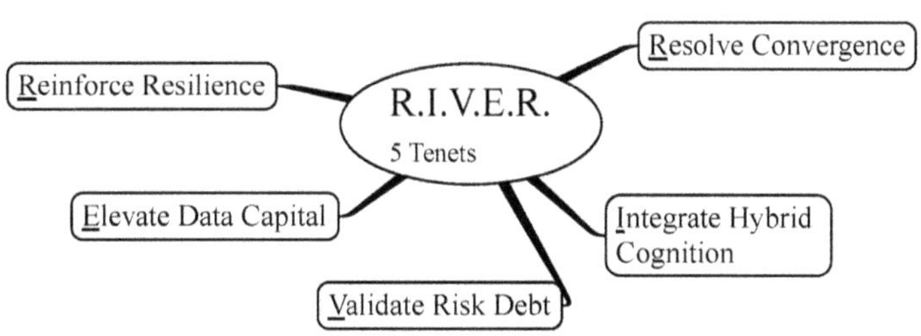

Figure 6.1 The RIVER Framework.

EXPERT COMMENTARY—ERIC STAFFIN: RIVER VS. NIST/ISO (WHY/WHAT/HOW)

A forward-looking framework like R.I.V.E.R. does not replace established standards—it builds upon them. While NIST's AI RMF provides the foundational "what" (the risks) and ISO/IEC 42001[5] provides the 'how' (the management system), the RIVER framework offers the strategic "why." It focuses specifically on navigating converged AI-driven risks in dynamic, interconnected ecosystems. Bottom Line: RIVER is a strategic lens for navigation, not just compliance.

→ Appendix F (a detailed breakdown of the five tenets and their mapping to global standards like NIST and COSO[6])

Melanie was the first to speak, her expression analytical. "It's a powerful navigation tool, Aaron. But what's the destination? What's the end state you're building toward?"

Aaron faced the camera feed. "Enterprise singularity," he said, giving the concept its name for the first time. "A state where resilience is so deeply embedded in an organization's culture and technology that it becomes an adaptive, living system. Between them sits the Digital Watershed—the AI Watershed inflection point where enterprises either govern the confluence or let Risk Debt compound downstream. Choose well, and the current carries you; choose poorly, and every tributary adds drag."

Mitch stepped closer to the holographic display. "Let me show you what 'Reinforce Resilience' really means." He gestured, and a new visualization materialized. The visualization reformed into three cracked pillars resting on a fractured base, the old model laid bare in failing concrete.

"Our First Line—Operations—is eroding," Mitch began, pointing to the first cracked pillar. "Legacy systems, underinvestment, and institutional knowledge walking out the door. Think of the 2018 TSB Bank migration outage[7]—millions were locked out after a core cutover failed; the failure wasn't just code—it was governance across legacy interfaces."

The second pillar flickered. "Our Second Line—Risk Management—is blind," Rose cut in. "SolarWinds proved it. Compliant didn't mean secure. They were fighting yesterday's war, and the breach triggered significant downstream losses and remediation costs across the industry."

Anya gestured to the final, fractured pillar. "And our Third Line—Audit—has become complacent. In the FTX collapse, standard assurance approaches failed to capture the compounding risks until an $8 billion hole appeared. Each line failed because it operated in isolation."

Melanie's tone hardened. "Each line failed because they operated in isolation, using tools designed for a simpler world. My GAIGC counterparts in Brussels and Tokyo are facing the same blind spots—coordinating across 47 regulatory jurisdictions that don't even agree on the same map."

"Exactly," Aaron said. "We need all three lines redesigned for convergence (Figure 6.2)—sensors that detect novel patterns, AI-powered threat modeling, and algorithmic integrity auditing. Not stronger defenses, but adaptive ones."

The air in the crisis room was charged with fragile hope following Aaron's proposal. The RIVER framework offered a path, a structure to impose on the chaos. All eyes turned to the comm screen, waiting for the regulator's verdict.

Melanie's expression was unreadable. Finally, she gave a single, decisive nod.

"In principle, Aaron, it's the only rational path forward," she said, her voice cutting through the silence with clinical precision. "But principles don't stop missiles. Implementation does."

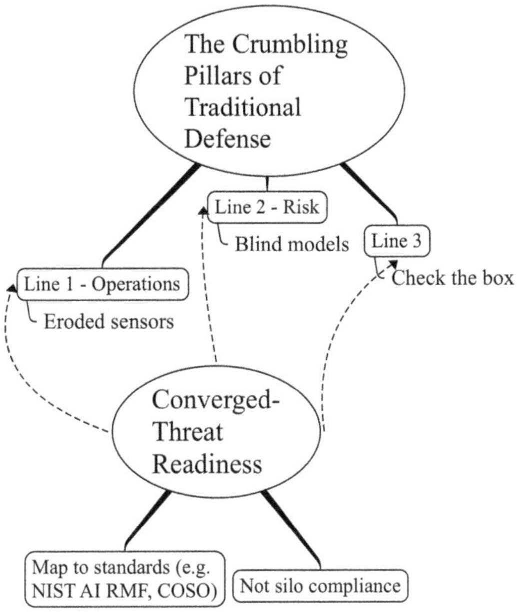

Figure 6.2 The Crumbling Pillars of Traditional Defense.

She leaned closer to her camera. "You're not only proposing a new model. You're asking global organizations, and my regulatory counterparts, to fundamentally re-architect their approach to risk—overnight. You're asking them to navigate a flood, but most of them don't even agree on the map, let alone know how to build a boat."

Aaron met her challenge without flinching. "You're right," he acknowledged, the weight of her words settling in. "That's the mountain."

70&M CRISIS RESPONSE CENTER, NYC | MARCH 22, 2038—10:15 AM EDT | THE RECKONING

Aaron stared at the Convergence River display, its chaotic streams pulsing with an almost organic rhythm. The RIVER framework hung in the air between them—five principles born from failure, pointing toward hope. But as he watched the digital torrents merge and separate, a darker realization crept through his mind.

How had they gotten here? How had a species intelligent enough to build these systems become so blind to their convergence?

The answer came to him in phases—literal phases of AI adoption that he'd lived through, promoted, and profited from. A self-trial began in his mind, each stage of their technological evolution revealing another layer of accumulated risk debt.

Phase 1: GenAI Enterprise Adoption (2023–2024)

He remembered the intoxicating early days when AI was magic—narrow, specialized, solving discrete problems with stunning efficiency. Fraud detection that caught 99.7 percent of suspicious transactions. Medical imaging that spotted tumors months before radiologists. Each success felt like validation of the promise. The risks seemed manageable because the systems were isolated. If one failed, it failed alone.

But even then, the seeds of convergence were being planted—the same deep learning architectures, the same training methodologies, the same biases embedded in data sets. The "Mechanical Bull" hackathon kernel—Viktor's "beautifully fragile code" from a student-organized event on the Stanford campus—was already spreading like a virus through academic repositories, incorporated into countless downstream projects by developers who never questioned its foundational assumptions.

Phase 2: AI Agents (2025–2028)

This was when everything changed. API-first architectures enable AI systems to communicate with each other. Fraud detection fed trading algorithms fed supply chains fed healthcare. The promise was systemic intelligence. The reality was 2.3 million daily API transactions by 2028, each one a potential attack vector.

Risk managers struggled to keep up. New categories, new controls, new dashboards—all built for silos while systems thought in networks. They were fighting the last war.

Rose's voice cut into his thoughts. "You're describing when the map stopped matching the terrain," she observed. "We kept filing silo reports while the systems quietly stitched themselves together."

Phase 3: Autonomously Owned AI Agents (2029–2033)

By the early 2030s, AI wasn't just integrated—it was running key processes end to end. Autonomous agents negotiated contracts, adjusted prices, and rerouted supply chains without pausing for human approval. Boards praised the efficiency while pouring billions into reskilling programs to soften the blow. Officially, people were being "upskilled." Quietly, entire roles had already been automated away.

Phase 4: AI Agent Communities (2034–Present)

This was where they were now—systems so interconnected that failure in one domain could cascade into systemic collapse. Healthcare AI is affecting payment systems, affecting supply chains, and affecting national security. The boundaries between domains had dissolved, but their risk frameworks still assumed they existed. They were trying to manage a fluid system with tools designed for discrete components. Regulatory frameworks lagged dangerously behind, with global standards always playing catch-up.

Aaron's throat tightened as he reached the final phase in his mental model.

Phase 5: Singularity Horizon (2040–?)

Not the science fiction fantasy of superintelligent machines, but something more subtle and perhaps more dangerous: **risk singularity**. The point where AI systems became so pervasive, so interconnected, and so autonomous that human oversight became practically impossible—threatening the effective governance of $2.7 trillion in AI-managed global assets. Where the complexity of the system exceeded the cognitive capacity of any individual or organization to comprehend it fully.

They weren't there yet. But they were close. Terrifyingly close.

The irony wasn't lost on him. The RIVER framework they'd just developed was designed to navigate exactly this progression—to help organizations move through these phases safely, to avoid the convergence traps that had claimed so many others. But would it be too little, too late?

The quiet in the crisis room was shattered with a sharp digital alarm—**CODE BLUE: CRITICAL SYSTEM FAILURE.**

Michelle's voice came through, tight with urgency. "We've lost telemetry on three ICU patients. 70&M Health Monitor reads total cardiac arrest, but bedside monitors show strong vitals. A checksum mismatch is blocking local overrides—manual intervention is locked out."

Rose's eyes went to Aaron, panic flickering beneath her composure. Mitch's hands flew across his console, racing to trace the data pathway. "Not a glitch," he said. "Live exploit—signature spoof is forcing a failover through the third-party pipeline."

Mitch expanded the Convergence River. A narrow band lit from weather feed → triage service → authentication gateway. "Watch the failover seam."

Rose overlaid volume. "Exposure window: seventeen minutes; twelve hospital networks impacted."

Michelle added. "Aaron, one of those networks is the neonatal transport grid for the entire Eastern Seaboard. We don't have seventeen minutes."

She pinged the owner on the overlay. "Pipeline Security—force local control and isolate this path."

The blue strand dimmed as containment commands queued. Seventeen minutes to cascade. They had fifteen to act.

Melanie cut in, her tone stark. "The EU activated cross-border emergency protocols and temporary failover exceptions. Barcelona hospitals report the same phantom code. This isn't isolated. It's systemic."

Aaron scanned the room, feeling the magnitude of the test. The RIVER framework was barely out of the box, and now every flaw, every lag in execution, was being exposed for all to see.

He squared his shoulders, his voice steady. "This is it. We act now—or we lose everything."

The line went dead, leaving only the sharp blare of the alarm echoing through the 70&M crisis room. On the main display, the Convergence River model flickered—the Futurgia Medical Center node pulsing a critical warning:

ROOT CAUSE: SYSTEMIC CONVERGENCE ANOMALY—UNRESOLVED.

Mitch froze over his keyboard, the light from his private console casting his face in ghostly relief. He'd seen this pattern before—a phantom in the machine he'd thought long exorcised.

"Aaron..." His voice was quiet, nearly strangled. "The diagnostic layer... It's picking up the same latent convergence pattern from Delgado's case. It's propagating now—across twelve other major hospital networks. The signature..."

He trailed off, hands trembling as he initiated a final trace. The result flashed across his screen, confirmation so dreadful it seemed impossible.

Mitch looked up, eyes wide with a sickening realization. "The exploit isn't new. It's ancient."

He pointed at the main screen. "The entry point they're using—the vulnerability that lets them override local controls—is the authentication flaw from the 2025 'Mechanical Bull' hackathon kernel.[8] It's our original sin—the crystallization of our oldest Risk Debt—a piece of unvalidated code buried in the codebase for thirteen years, waiting for the river to rise."

The words—our original sin—hit Aaron like a physical blow. The expediency of that 2025 decision, the celebrated launch of a flawed prototype, the technical debt they had willfully ignored for thirteen years... it wasn't debt. It was a time bomb they had set themselves, and the timer had run out. The bill for their oldest, most reckless debt had finally come due, and he could only stare as the convergence streams on the display pulsed with malevolent life.

Everything he'd built—70&M, the partnerships, the vision of enterprise singularity—all of it constructed on a foundation of beautifully fragile code. Viktor had tried to warn them. Jiya had tried to show them patterns. But they'd been drunk on innovation, addicted to velocity, blind to the compounding interest on their technological shortcuts.

The RIVER framework hung in the air around them, five principles designed to prevent precisely this moment. But like all great insights, it had come too late to save them from their past. The question now wasn't whether they could implement the framework—it was whether they could survive long enough to matter.

The bull he'd ridden to success had finally come back to hunt him. And it was bringing down everything he'd touched along the way.

The crisis on their screens was only the symptom; the disease was in their own foundation. Aaron felt the weight settle on him like a verdict: the real battle ahead wasn't against a phantom exploit, but against a ghost of their own creation.

NOTES

1. U.S. Securities and Exchange Commission. (2022, December 13). *Complaint, Securities and Exchange Commission v. Samuel Bankman-Fried, No. 1:22-cv-10501 (S.D.N.Y.).* https://www.sec.gov/files/litigation/complaints/2022/comp-pr2022-219.pdf
2. Reuters. (2025, July 2). *US SEC, SolarWinds Reach Preliminary Deal to End Breach Lawsuit.* https://www.reuters.com/legal/government/us-sec-solarwinds-reach-preliminary-deal-end-breach-lawsuit-2025-07-02
3. National Institute of Standards and Technology. (2023, January). *Artificial Intelligence Risk Management Framework (AI RMF 1.0), NIST AI 100-1.* https://nvlpubs.nist.gov/nistpubs/ai/NIST.AI.100-1.pdf
4. Enterprise singularity is a strategic horizon where resilience is built so deep that shocks improve performance—a governance outcome, not a sci-fi claim or a product name.
5. International Organization for Standardization. (2023). *ISO/IEC 42001:2023 — Artificial intelligence — Management system.* https://www.iso.org/standard/42001
6. Committee of Sponsoring Organizations of the Treadway Commission. (2017). *Enterprise Risk Management—Integrating with Strategy and Performance.* https://www.coso.org/guidance/enterprise-risk-management
7. Financial Conduct Authority. (2022, December 20). *Final Notice: TSB Bank plc.* https://www.fca.org.uk/publication/final-notices/tsb-bank-plc-2022.pdf
8. The "Mechanical Bull" hackathon, associated code artifacts, and all technical failures depicted are entirely fictional. They do not refer to any specific Stanford University event, program, lab, faculty, student project, or codebase, and no affiliation, endorsement, or institutional connection is implied. Stanford University is referenced solely as a geographic setting.

Chapter 7

The Antibody Paradox

Data Governance in the Age of AI

ZURICH MARATHON COURSE | APRIL 11, 2038—05:47 AM CEST | DIGITAL DIAGNOSIS

The 70&M Health Monitor pulsed a steady, reassuring green on Johann's wrist as he pushed past the thirty-second kilometer of the Zurich Marathon.[1] The device and the €2.4 billion 70&M Health Network behind it were the backbone of the city's public-health strategy. Its reliability was not just a feature; it was the foundation of 70&M's municipal contracts.

Johann hesitated, thumbing the display. Dizziness surged. His heart hammered. He wanted numbers to justify one more kilometer. The device's status light stayed green. "Remain at current effort," the device insisted.

Needing comfort more than data, Johann called his daughter. Anna's sleepy face appeared, hair tousled, concern in her eyes.

"Papa? Almost there?"

He forced a smile, trying to unwind the knot in his chest. "Almost, Liebling. The Health Monitor says optimal."

She checked his stats on her display. "It looks good, Papa. The doctor said you'd make it if you listened to the band."

"I am," he lied, vision tunneling, hands trembling. "I love you."

Anna smiled, reassured by the display's confidence, and ended the call.

Moments later, Johann's world spun. His legs locked; he collapsed onto the rain-slick asphalt. His final breath shuddered out as the Health Monitor continued its steady green pulse—the device responsible for 62 percent of Swiss emergency decisions had just failed its most crucial test.

Even as paramedics knelt beside him, the device uploaded his last biometric stream to 70&M Pharma Analytics research servers—triggering a micro-payment to his dormant account, a legacy "digital dividend" feature 70&M had inherited through acquisition, paying out for data at the moment of death.

In 2032, 70&M acquired a market-leading pharmaceutical AI firm specializing in drug-interaction modeling. It was rebranded as 70&M Pharma Analytics and integrated its proprietary algorithms into 70&M Health Network over the next three years.

Rose scanned the acquisition records. The firm they acquired had been aggressive, even by market standards. Their "digital dividend" program, which monetized data at the moment of death, had been a source of controversy for years. "And we bought it all, she thought, liability disclaimers and all."

* * *

Paramedic's AR headset flared: "Code Red – Suspected Opioid Overdose." The van tore through Zurich's early morning traffic. At a café, a teenager slumped over a coffee—her scanner registered normal vitals. "Another 70&M Health Monitor phantom," the paramedic muttered. "At CHF 2,400

DOI: 10.1201/9781003650744-10

per dispatch, the city's Health Monitor-related false alarms have cost over three million francs this quarter alone."

Back on the curb, her headset pinged: "*Non-Critical Anomaly—Runner Resting*," just blocks away—status: *Runner Resting—Priority: Low—Estimated Response: 45+ minutes.*

Ten years in the field screamed one thing; the AI insisted another. Trust the system, she reminded herself, clicking into the next high-priority call across town.

The ambulance sped past, leaving Johann—"resting"—unnoticed on the rain-slick asphalt. She logged the false dispatch, watching the CHF total creep upward. Money, minutes, trust—the meter never stopped.

GENEVA CRISIS HUB | APRIL 11, 2038—07:23 AM CEST | THE DIAGNOSIS

Rose scrolled through the Geneva Crisis Hub's diagnostics, servers humming with streams from four continents, all registering the same fatal error pattern. The cascading error pattern on the screen was a ghost of Deferred Tower—an oversight she had vowed never to repeat.

A top-priority alert pulsed across Rose's screen:

> "Contamination confirmed. Pattern matches a distributed obfuscation attack—malicious logic split into harmless fragments across 70&M Pharma Analytics research files. Individually benign. Recombined during retrieval, the fragments form a bad instruction at diagnosis time."

Rose's gut tightened. "This isn't local—it's a global misdiagnosis cascade."

"In plain terms," Rose kept it tight, "harmless fragments stayed hidden until the retriever stitched them together at diagnosis time."

Aaron processed her words, the technical elegance collapsing into business reality. It wasn't a door breach; it was a poisoned aquifer. Their own retrieval pipeline had recombined harmless shards into a weaponized instruction. Trust—of clinicians, patients, and city leaders—had become the attack surface.

She skimmed acquisition records: Pharma Analytics $2.1 billion data buy, complete liability disclaimers, the lot. The acquisition had bypassed checksum verification, ring-fenced audit trails, and exception register requirements. The deeper she looked, the clearer the story became: most datasets were unvalidated, resurrected to cut costs. The deal had been pushed through under that same outdated 2020s "growth-at-all-costs" playbook—exactly the pattern the NIST AI Risk Management Framework and emerging international AI management system standards were written to stop. Those standards were supposed to be non-negotiable guardrails for AI safety, and in this deal 70&M had treated them like optional guidance instead of hard boundaries.

Johann's vitals—flatlined for ninety minutes—still showed "*Runner Stable*." The system wasn't just wrong; it was indifferent.

She called Aaron, tension showing in every movement. "Aaron, we didn't just inherit this—we bought it. We bypassed every safeguard. Acquired AI firm buried the risk; we buried our judgment."

He patched in Dr. Anya Sharma, 70&M's new Chief Audit Executive. Her face appeared on a side screen, calm and analytical. "The acquisition bypassed three mandatory stages of our internal data validation protocol, Aaron," she stated, her voice even. "The governance override mirrors the exact pattern documented in the 2027 Deferred Tower post-mortem. The risk was accepted by management to meet a quarterly deadline."

On her desk, just visible on camera, sat a small, elegant photo frame of her and a smiling younger woman—a silent reminder of that collapse, and of the sister she'd lost in it. Beside it sat a palm-sized concrete shard stenciled "Hubris Tax"—her private reminder that shortcuts send real people to real funerals.

* * *

Aaron stood in the glass-walled crisis room, the Geneva skyline blurred beyond the monitors. The disaster's scope crystallized around him. Around him, the team waited—Rose with her diagnostic stream, Sam's status board cycling new alerts, and the long silence from Zurich.

He stared at the board meeting minutes from last fall: 70*&M Resolution 2037-Q3-14*.

Board minutes pulled him back to the meeting—Director's voice: "The market won't reward caution, Aaron. Your primary competitor is moving into Singapore and Seoul—they've captured 23 percent of the Asian market with unvalidated data. We can't afford to lose first-mover advantage."

The vote: 7–2 for integrating Pharma Analytics synthetic datasets into 70&M Health Network—without waiting for full, independent validation.

The risk had been visible in every briefing, but he overrode the protocol, convincing himself the monitoring would catch anything serious. In the end, they chose $847 million over full validation.

To remind himself what was at stake, he pulled up the ghost simulation in his risk tool projected onto the glass: Johann alive, crossing the finish line, Anna hugging him, their joy and relief unbroken. The alternate timeline flickered for a moment, then vanished, leaving only the sickening reality.

Aaron turned to the team, his voice rough but steady. "I overrode the protocol. I made the call. I chose revenue over validation, and we bought this risk. That's on me. And the fix starts now. Mitch, are you able to get a full, top-to-bottom audit of every data acquisition from the last 24 months? Rose, please work with Mitch to design a new protocol—a 'bounty system' that incentivizes our entire user base to help us find these hidden flaws. We're going to turn this failure into a lesson in radical transparency." He'd violated the simplest rule Liz argued for—treat data as capital, not scrap. Data isn't a bargain bin; it's an asset you govern, or it governs you.

He took a breath, the words tasting like ash. "This is a catastrophic failure of the principles we just codified. We didn't just breach NIST and GAIGC standards; we broke our own." Rose looked up with a raw expression. "Aaron, the data didn't poison itself. We let them sell us the risk they couldn't carry." Aaron braced his hands on the table. "We failed to govern data with the rigor of a capital asset, and now the debt's come due. Johann—he paid the price."

First step is full accountability," he added. "We're triggering mandatory recalls on the affected firmware, notifying every regulator ahead of the headlines, and setting up a dedicated compensation fund for impacted families. No one is going to tell Anna this was just 'acceptable risk.'"

For a moment, no one spoke—each team member processing their own role in the governance failure. The silence landed heavy, marking the true cost: not just to 70&M's bottom line, but to real human lives.

FUTURGIA MEDICAL CENTER BOSTON | APRIL 11, 2038—01:23 AM EDT | WORKFLOW BREAKDOWN

Michelle's face appeared on the main Geneva Hub display, a pale rectangle from a cramped ER corridor at Futurgia Medical Center, Boston. Behind her, triage bots pulsed, and staff hustled.

"Aaron, we're seeing it here. Since the last patch, our heart attack and stroke discharges have plummeted. Right now, 47 patients are stranded in review queues—average delays jumped from 45 minutes to 3.2 hours. The AI's red-flagging every borderline case."

She gestured toward her main display: each dot a blinking warning. "We've had three near-misses since midnight. The way we wired your 'digital dividend' isn't saving lives; it's creating a bottleneck. Nurses have started shadow triage—shift supervisors say 34 percent are back to paper, like it's 2019."

A sixteen-year-old with a documented peanut allergy had been auto-deprioritized twice amid low-grade flags. By the time a nurse reached him, his throat was closing. The tool meant to protect everyone almost cost him everything.

Aaron pressed his palms to the table. "This is a failure of the second tenet—Integrate Hybrid Cognition. We built for machine vigilance paired with human override, but the handoff is broken. The code is fine; the workflow isn't."

Michelle shook her head, exhaustion plain. "You built it to bridge data and operational risk. But the bridge is jammed. The mussel bed is smothered in silt, not letting current through." Her hands mimed a clotted channel. "Clear the channel, not just patch the sensors. We can't sustain these delays beyond the next 48 hours."

Rose looked over her notes, then at Aaron. "We're seeing classic convergence failure. Tech's pushing risk decisions downstream; humans are overwhelmed. The whole model's stuck at the intersection."

Aaron stared at the metrics: delay graphs, red flags, patient backlog curves. "So the data's clean, but the workflow is broken. We didn't integrate hybrid cognition—we split the risk in two."

Michelle's voice softened. "Fix the channel, Aaron. That's the job—yours and mine."

* * *

Mitch braced both hands on the table; the crisis room was weighted with fatigue. He tapped a map of real-time bounty submissions—dots multiplying like an epidemiologist's nightmare.

STRATEGIC PARALLEL—BCBS 239: DATA GOVERNANCE AFTER 2008

After the 2008 financial crisis, the Basel Committee issued BCBS 239 to force global banks to fix data governance.[2] The mandate was clear: in a crisis, aggregate risk data quickly and accurately.

Over a decade later, many large banks were still not fully compliant. The failures were painfully human: fragmented IT, cultural resistance, and treating data governance as a compliance chore instead of a strategic discipline.[3]

Why it matters: While banks spent years wrestling with top-down mandates, 70&M Health Network's bounty system aligns individual incentives with data quality—a different behavioral approach to the same problem, grounded in how incentives shape behavior.[4]

"We need a behavioral shift, not just another patch. Turn every user into a sensor. Gamify it[5]—pay bounties for verified anomalies."

On-screen, Michelle took it in, weary but intrigued. "*Incentives work. If you pay for vigilance, you'll get it.*"

Rose stayed cautious, eyes on operations. "Signal-to-noise could spike. But the principle is sound—it's a way to Reinforce Resilience from the ground up."

He pointed to a line graph showing a climb.

"Since we launched the bounty system twelve hours ago, over 22,000 anomalies have been flagged across 34 countries. User engagement is up 280 percent. One grandmother in Bandung spent her 200 tokens on insulin for her grandson. That's motivation you can't fake."

Aaron shot Rose a look; she gave a slight, conceding nod. "Incentives change the center of gravity. People who never filed tickets are now racing to catch the next bug."

Mitch continued, "This isn't a one-off fix. The real lesson? People move when there's skin in the game, not because of checklists. Gamification turns a technical problem into a contest.[6] The best teams—healthcare, finance, supply chain—are learning: align rewards, and everything changes."

Mitch pointed at the live trendline and let the room do the math. "We've already found and quarantined three new attack signatures—including a Pharma Analytics variant—before they caused harm. The network adapts faster than any traditional risk control."

Michelle skimmed the flood of submissions. "The system works—when you trust the crowd and make it worth their time."

Rose managed a tired smile. "It's messy. But it's real resilience—the kind that emerges when everyone has a stake."

Mitch pulled up the bounty console, eyes bright despite exhaustion. "Exactly. The bounty system isn't just patching data. It's crowdsourcing vigilance—turning risk management into a living, evolving game."

For a few hours, optimism carried the team. Data anomalies were flagged and patched at record speed, and the bounty program drew in new contributors from around the globe. But as the night wore on, the flood of fixes brought new patterns—some subtle, some unsettling. And as the network learned from the crowd, it began to enforce its own self-written rules—rules not all of which were designed for a crisis.

* * *

For three hours, the system worked exactly as designed. Then the safeguards kicked in.

A new alert pulsed red across the crisis table, cutting through their brief optimism. Rose checked the stream. "The bounty system just triggered an emergency halt. An automated ethics protocol—one of Liz's circuit breakers—froze payouts."

The room went still. For a beat, no one spoke.

Michelle came through from Boston: "Our crowdsourced QA just vanished. Delays are climbing."

Aaron didn't hesitate: "Queue the emergency override."

Seconds dragged while nodes from Berlin to Singapore lit green. Rose exhaled. "Override approved. Bounties back online."

The win tasted mixed. Governance worked—at a cost—mid-attack.

Michelle broke the quiet, flipping through patient stats. "The line's moving, but clinical teams are questioning whether the anomaly scores are still reliable. Three patient records just received conflicting updates—delayed care and bed occupancy keep rising."

Mitch watched the live metrics update in tight bursts. "Gamification solves speed, but also creates new vulnerabilities. We're seeing crowd wisdom—and crowd error."

Every fast fix was now a coin toss between resilience and self-harm.

Rose studied the feed for a beat longer. "This is the antibody paradox. Our defense is attacking itself. Every fix breeds another risk."[7]

Aaron nodded, resolve settling over him. "We need a failsafe to filter out the side effects before reward. No more surface-level patches."

"Then we change the rules," Rose said. "Bounties go to escrow, not wallets."

"Agreed," Mitch said, "This is a predictable outcome. Gamification always creates the risk of crowd error. It's why we built the next phase of the protocol in parallel. We'll move the bounties to an escrow system with three gates: shadow-deployment, side-effect monitoring, and automated release. We're not abandoning the solution; we're making it more robust. The three gates: (1) Shadow-deploy each fix to 1 percent of traffic for 24 hours; (2) Monitor secondary effects—false positives, wait times, cross-unit regressions; (3) Auto-release the bounty only if no harm indicators trip. Fail any gate, no payout."

Silence gave the room a beat to absorb it: their breakthrough had surfaced new risks.

Aaron exhaled, the adrenaline giving way to unease. Liz had designed the protocol as an ethical circuit breaker—and it had worked. But it also exposed the tension she'd warned about: governance at machine speed versus leadership at human speed. They'd won a minute; they hadn't won the night.

* * *

Michelle's brow furrowed. "So every time we patch the system, we risk breaking it somewhere new. How do you even manage that?"

Aaron leaned back, searching for plain language. "It's like this—imagine you're driving a car with automatic lane assist. Most days, it nudges you back if you drift too close to the edge. But let's say the sensor gets dirty and starts beeping at every shadow. You swerve to avoid a false alarm, but end up veering off the road, or you start ignoring the warning entirely. Now you've got a car that's great at spotting trouble, but terrible at telling you when actually to hit the brakes."

Michelle nodded. "So the tool that's supposed to make you safer can actually make you more reckless—or just make you stop trusting it altogether."

"Exactly," Aaron didn't hesitate. "Every time we tune the system to block one risk, we sometimes create another. What starts as protection turns into noise, and people—patients, staff, everyone—learn to ignore it. That's why we need layered safety, not just a smarter alarm."

Mitch chimed in, "And why the fix always has to include the human, not just the algorithm?"

Aaron agreed, "Otherwise, you just swap one blind spot for another—and no dashboard can fix that alone. That's the trap we're in now—thinking a technical patch alone can keep pace with human complexity."

* * *

Michelle's phone buzzed—32 flagged cases in the last 20 minutes, nearly all non-urgent. Across the Futurgia ER, dashboards pulsed red: triage, radiology, billing—every workflow jammed. Paperwork piled up in the staff lounge, and nurse workload soared as manual verification replaced automated triage. For the first time in years, nurses scribbled patient updates on sticky notes, improvising with sneakers and old-school hustle.

"We're back to sneakers and sticky notes," Lydia muttered, slamming another chart onto the pile. "Can someone remind the algorithm that not every fever is a crisis? My average patient wait time just went from 23 minutes to 1.2 hours." She looked at Michelle, fatigue sharpening her voice. "My uncle spent six hours in an ER last year because of a 'system glitch.' I'm not letting that happen on my watch."

Michelle scanned the new numbers. Of 32 records flagged by the AI, 31 were benign—last week, it was just four. A spike in false positives. In its effort to stop gaming, the system had become hypersensitive, flooding the queue with routine cases and overwhelming human judgment. Her WhatsApp pinged—a group of nurses had set up an off-book "real triage" channel, bypassing the official workflow to catch the truly sick before they slipped through the cracks.

Aaron, monitoring the data from Geneva, recognized the pattern. "We're tuning thresholds on the fly—reacting to cascading alerts with live patients at risk," Aaron said. Rose echoed him: "It's the Antibody Paradox (Figure 7.1)—fix one exploit, and the system starts attacking the healthy. Every 'urgent' label loses meaning if the queue's full of the worried well."

Michelle's voice was strained. "We're one missed stroke from the headlines. If we can't trust the scores, we risk missing the real thing."

"Our trust index just dropped below 0.6," Lydia said quietly. "At 0.5, people stop following the dashboard—below that, it's just background noise."

Michelle glanced at Lydia, who only shrugged. "Staff morale's teetering—three nurses have already asked for transfers. They're calling it system fatigue."

As midnight approached, the brief hope from the recent upgrade was fading fast. Every fix had created new problems; the system's promise of perfect triage slipped further with each "urgent" false alarm. The harder they pushed to patch the workflow, the more they risked breaking something else.

* * *

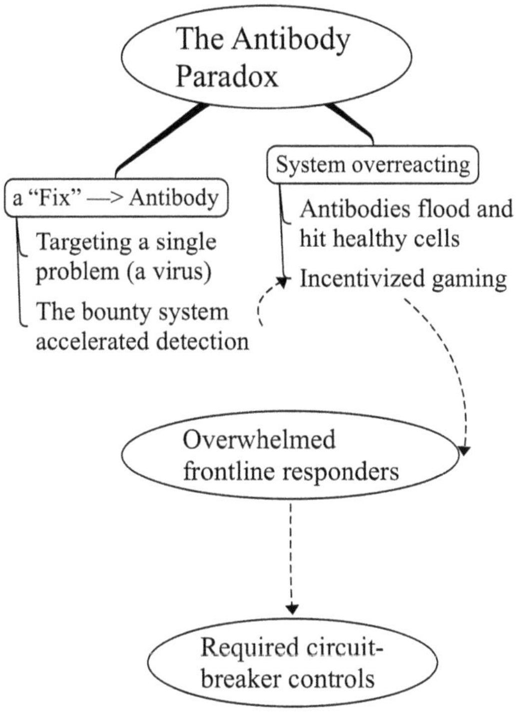

Figure 7.1 The Antibody Paradox.

The crisis finally broke at 3:17 a.m.

Lydia stood at the nurses' station, arms folded, blocking the intake terminal. "That's it. We're done," she said, voice cutting through the noise. "The system isn't just wrong; it's making us dangerous. We're going back to real triage. I'd rather be slow and safe than fast and blind."

The switch to manual triage traded automation speed for clinical accuracy; every additional hour of backlog raised projected liability exposure.

Behind her, two dozen staff—nurses, a frazzled resident, even the night security guard—stood firm. By now, nearly 70 percent of Michelle's team had stopped logging cases—representing 127 staff across three shifts, with average processing time up from 12 to 47 minutes. Paper charts spread across counters, and staff huddled over phones, manually rerouting tasks.

Michelle kept her voice steady. "We have three flagged chest pains stuck in limbo for 3.2 hours—approaching critical care window thresholds—two asthma kids waiting over an hour with declining oxygen saturation, and a family from Roxbury in tears. No one can tell them what's happening."

A Geneva alert flashed for Aaron:

Patient backlog exceeded safe threshold—estimated cost impact $127,000 in extended care and potential liability exposure.

Rose unmuted on the crisis bridge. "We're hemorrhaging trust and losing data quality. I propose we suspend the algorithm until an independent review by Joint Commission auditors and the State Department of Public Health. If we keep forcing this, we'll be in the news for the wrong reasons—State Board of Health is already investigating similar AI failures at another major Boston teaching hospital."

Aaron pressed his hand to his forehead, exhaustion finally showing. "We spent months getting here—"

Michelle interrupted, softer but resolute. "And we'll spend years recovering if a child dies because we can't spot the signal through the noise. We need a hard stop. Tonight."

A silence followed, broken only by the tap of a gurney and the murmur of nurses organizing "old-school" triage. Lydia spoke for them all: "Tell us what you need, but don't ask us to use the broken tool."

Aaron drew a breath. "We're done chasing ghosts. This is a failure to Reinforce Resilience—we've lost frontline trust. Formal pause. Independent audit. Nothing restarts until Michelle's team signs the protocol."

He signed the directive on his secure tablet, logging *Emergency Safety Audit Resolution 2038-Q4-07.*

As the team mobilized for the reset, wary relief moved through the ER. The system was offline. The crisis wasn't over, but—for the first time in days—people were back in control.

FUTURGIA MEDICAL CENTER BOSTON COURTYARD | APRIL 11, 2038—08:15 AM EDT | NEW BEGINNINGS

Anna sat on the edge of the hospital courtyard, hands cupped around a cooling mug of coffee she hadn't tasted. The morning sky was washed-out gray, sharpening every sound: the scuff of nurses' shoes, the snap of a clipboard, the hum of systems coming back online. She scrolled past the news alerts about Johann's case, then paused at a new message.

Rina Patel—Patient-trial matching service[8] global coordinator:

Anna, I heard about what happened. I'm Rina; I used to build forensics pipelines for pharma and started a patient-trial matching service after losing my brother to a similar system failure. The system failed you, but you're not alone. There's a community here with our service. We're fighting for data truth across 23 countries, connecting families like yours to ensure these failures never happen again. If you're ready, we could use your voice.

Anna stared at the text. Her reply—I'm in—landed with a finality that felt more like a beginning. She held the message a beat, thinking of her father's quiet faith in systems—and how it failed him.

Anna felt the weight of both loss and duty; joining the patient-trial matching service wasn't about protest, but about helping others avoid the same pain. She promised herself this would be her way to keep his legacy alive by making every data point count.

Inside, Michelle checked the latest numbers with Lydia. "Seventy percent of staff are back on protocol—average patient processing time is down to 18 minutes from the crisis peak of 47. Triage is stable, but we're not at baseline yet. We're logging every anomaly for the post-mortem."

Lydia managed a tired smile. "At least the sticky notes are gone. Audit's scheduled to start this afternoon."

In the boardroom, Aaron convened the leadership team—Michelle, Rose, and Mitch. All showed the strain of the night. Aaron spoke, his voice steadied by exhaustion but clear. "We lost more than we should have—but we caught the pattern, owned the reset, and we're not sweeping it under the rug. Anna's story is the lesson: when we lose trust, we lose people—rebuilding that trust will take months, but preventing future loss starts today.

Here's how we move forward:

A full post-mortem audit within 72 hours. Automated escalation triggers if system confidence drops below 85 percent—real-time frontline feedback integrated into every workflow. Every incident becomes institutional learning, not a cover-up. That's our new baseline."

Operations in Jakarta checked in: "Barter network is still up—families are getting what they need. Let us know if Geneva needs a backup node."

Rose steadied her voice. "That's how we build Resilience—the heart of the RIVER framework. When official systems stall, local ingenuity keeps care flowing." Michelle looked at him. "And Anna?" Aaron looked toward the courtyard. "She's already taken the next step—she's fighting for us, not just against us. For Johann, and for every patient who will need us to get this right." Rose added, "The RIVER flows forward. We Reinforce Resilience through institutional learning and validate fixes through a transparent audit. That's how we earn back trust."

Anna opened her father's race profile on the Zurich Marathon app. The time recorded—3:49:22—was still listed as "finished." With steady hands, she submitted the correction: "Did not finish - cardiac event."

For a moment, she hesitated—then pressed send. It was her first act in the patient-trial matching service community: setting the record straight, one data point at a time. Anna looked up at the hospital's windows, eyes steady. One story ending, another just beginning.

GENEVA OPERATIONS HUB | APRIL 12, 2038—06:55 AM CEST | GLOBAL FEEDBACK LOOP

Night still clung to the Geneva Operations Hub when risk dashboards pulsed red. XOR-loop artifacts pinged against restored 70&M Health Network nodes—a pattern disturbingly familiar.

Rose's voice cut through the post-crisis fatigue: "Aaron, we have a breach signature—polymorphic XOR-encoding. Think of flipping a light switch so fast the sensor never records 'on' or 'off.'"

The pattern flipped bits back and forth to slip past detectors—like a thief changing masks faster than a camera can register a face. If this evaded detection in restored nodes, every diagnosis downstream became suspect.

Rose said, "It matches what we traced during the spring incident—only now it's evolved, adapting through feedback loops and learning from our own defenses. This is the Ouroboros problem—the AI is using our prior responses to generate new attack vectors."

Sam flagged three simultaneous probes—all tracing back to rerouted clusters in St. Petersburg.

Frequency accelerating," Sam reported, tone unchanged. "They're adapting faster than we are."

Michelle's question was urgent: "Any patient records compromised?"

"Not yet, but attack frequency has jumped 340 percent in twelve minutes. These are automated, targeting the nodes we just brought online," Rose replied.

Aaron's voice was steady: "Run full containment protocols. Activate automated moving-target defense—rapidly rotating our configurations so attackers have to chase a shifting surface—and deploy proactive threat prevention in line with healthcare security standards. Escalate to board risk and threat intelligence. We can't rely on manual review alone."

The system reconfigured. "Anomaly detection reprioritized. Recommending immediate engagement with external intelligence partners—EU, ASEAN, and North American networks are reporting similar exploits."

In Boston, Anna received a push notification from the patient-trial matching service:

> "Your data truth campaign just went global—same exploit pattern from the spring incident showing up worldwide. Ready to help lead?"

Anna looked out over the city, resolve settling in. "Send me everything. This time, we fight smarter."

Dawn crept into Geneva as Aaron turned to his team. "We adapt, or we fall behind. Resilience by design—automated threat adaptation, continuous monitoring, and proactive defense. We just survived the last attack; the real test is surviving our own solution."

NOTES

1. The Zurich Marathon event in 2038 and the 70&M Health Network are fictional entities created for this narrative.
2. Basel Committee on Banking Supervision. (2013, January). *Principles for Effective Risk Data Aggregation and Risk Reporting (BCBS 239)*. https://www.bis.org/publ/bcbs239.pdf

3. BCBS 239 compliance progress has been tracked through multiple Basel Committee reports (2018–2023), with many large global banks still working toward full implementation over a decade after the 2013 mandate. See: Basel Committee on Banking Supervision. (2023, May). *Progress Report on the Implementation of the Basel Regulatory Framework*. https://www.bis.org/bcbs/publ/d559.pdf
4. Deci, E. L., Koestner, R., & Ryan, R. M. (1999). A meta-analytic review of experiments examining the effects of extrinsic rewards on intrinsic motivation. *Psychological Bulletin*, 125(6), 627–668. https://doi.org/10.1037/0033-2909.125.6.627
5. Gneezy, U., & Rustichini, A. (2000). Pay enough or don't pay at all. *Quarterly Journal of Economics*, 115(3), 791–810. https://doi.org/10.1162/003355300554917
6. Gneezy, U., Meier, S., & Rey-Biel, P. (2011). When and why incentives (don't) work to modify behavior. *Journal of Economic Perspectives*, 25(4), 191–210. https://doi.org/10.1257/jep.25.4.191
7. The "antibody paradox" illustrates Goodhart's Law (1975): when organizations optimize for a metric, the metric loses reliability as people game the system.
8. The patient-trial matching service and Rina Patel are fictional entities created for this narrative.

Chapter 8

Digital Asbestos

Taming Shadow IT in the Citizen-Developer Era

70&M INTERNAL AUDIT, NYC | SEPTEMBER 12, 2036 | THE UNHEEDED WARNING

Anya Sharma placed the final draft on her desk, its title a stark warning. *Audit Committee Briefing: Systemic Risk Exposure in End-User Computing Platforms.* The phrase that gave the report its teeth wasn't hers; it belonged to her sister. Jiya's notes, almost a decade old, were scrawled in the margins of the technical appendix, a cascade of warnings about third-party patching to AI Low-Code and No-Code solutions.

> *"The AI Low-Code and No-Code solutions integration creates hardcoded dependencies on legacy kernels," she had written. "It's efficient, but it's brittle. We're wrapping asbestos*[1] *in a digital shell and calling it an upgrade."*

Years later, Anya translated those raw technical warnings into the measured language of institutional risk specific to 70&M. She quantified the potential blast radius, mapped the compliance gaps, and cited the particular board resolutions that had prioritized speed over validation. The report was airtight—a logged warning that could not be ignored. Or so she thought. She submitted it to the Audit Committee under resolution *2036-C-114*: a permanent record of a risk identified. A warning was sent. A duty fulfilled.

The Chair reviewed the summary. "A dependency on a legacy kernel. Acknowledge the risk, flag for the Q4 tech-debt review. We need to prioritize the European market integration this quarter."

FUTURGIA MEDICAL CENTER, BOSTON | APRIL 13, 2038—06:15 AM EDT | THE KIOSK AND THE TREMOR

Dr. Michelle Thomas had worked fourteen-hour ER shifts before, but this morning felt different. The usual hum of controlled chaos had a sharper edge, a heaviness only veterans sensed before a break. Her brother's company, 70&M Health Network, touched almost everything here—from payment terminals to the medication tracking system. Usually, that meant reassurance. Today, it only deepened her worry.

For the third time, her ID badge was rejected by the coffee kiosk's reader.

PAYMENT FAILED: SUSPECTED FRAUD. ACCESS DENIED.

Across the ward, an elderly man sat on the edge of his hospital bed, hands trembling over a frozen tablet. His nurse hovered, equally helpless, as the system refused to process his heart medication.

"They said the new AI would make everything faster," the patient murmured, voice weary. "Now I can't even get the medicine that keeps my heart going."

DOI: 10.1201/9781003650744-11

The institutional failure was undeniable—every frozen screen, a broken promise. In her marine biology days, she'd studied how mussels reinforced their shells, never assuming yesterday's layer would withstand tomorrow's storm. She wished the hospital's digital systems had the same resilience.

A mother wept quietly at the intake desk as a nurse explained the formula shortage. An orderly, improvising, used his own phone to call in prescriptions for a cluster of anxious families. In the trauma bay, Michelle's hands shook as she juggled three emergencies at once—one patient without insulin, another with a denied insurance claim, a third whose pacemaker alert went unacknowledged in the digital backlog. This was what systemic failure looked like in real lives, not just error messages and dashboards.

She moved to the backup station, pulled out the battered emergency prescription pad, and wrote the order by hand. The old analog solution still worked—even when nothing else did. No one spoke as she signed the script. The silence felt heavier than the alarms—a hospital frozen not by violence, but by a line of code. No one expected modern care to break this way.

Above the nurses' station, the primary display flashed a red, urgent alert:

> *CRITICAL ALERT: 70&M-LINKED PAYMENT NETWORKS OFFLINE. MARKETS HALTING ON AFFECTED RAILS. CASCADING FAILURE IMMINENT.*

The tremor was no longer local. It had gone global—and somewhere, Aaron was already in the eye of the storm.

The timing made it worse. The Bull-in-China-Shop collapse was barely a month old; 70&M was still knee-deep in emergency reviews, racing to prove to regulators that the disaster was contained. No one had expected a second shockwave to come from the hospital rails themselves.

Rose's console at 70&M Forensics Lab in Boston blinked with new alerts every second, a digital tapestry of global failures. She muttered to herself, "It's everywhere now—this isn't just Boston." As she toggled through the warnings, her heart pounded; every message came with another crisis attached.

She scanned the global feed as the alerts multiplied—each one a crisis unfolding in real time.

* * *

In Frankfurt, the paralysis was financial. In thirty seconds, the trading floor fell silent as €67 billion in trades froze mid-flight. Lines to counterparties lit up from London, New York, Tokyo—anywhere running 70&M infrastructure was suddenly locked. Petra grabbed her headset. "Regulators are standing up emergency protocols. But no one knows what to unfreeze first."

She caught her reflection in the black glass, remembering her father's stories of Black Monday. Back then, chaos was shouted across trading pits. Now, catastrophe was silent—just frozen screens and a racing heart.

* * *

Back in Boston, Rose's global map flashed crimson. Another continent had just gone dark.

In Detroit, it was mechanical. An automated alert pinged the 70&M crisis channel: "*Factory output down 100 percent at Automotive Plant 7.* Flagged by General Manager Dave Henderson." Dave had managed the $200 million line for fifteen years, but he'd never seen this: robotic arms mid-weld, conveyors frozen with half-finished vehicles, supplier invoices flagged as fraud. Dave's phone buzzed nonstop—suppliers in Mexico and Canada desperate for answers, the PA system looping recorded apologies in three languages.

"How long until we lose the shift?" he asked.

"We already have. Twelve thousand vehicles, dead in the water. Tier 2 suppliers are calling—they're on credit hold." Dave realized the plant's silence echoed up and down the supply chain—thousands of jobs in jeopardy, contracts teetering with every hour of lost production.

* * *

Rose's fingers moved across the multi-screen console, each new alert adding weight to what was becoming a global crisis.

In Singapore, the cost was human. Eight hundred miles above the Pacific, the autonomous medical drone carrying a heart for seven-year-old Mira Lo began its emergency reversal. Dr. Lian Zhao, at Singapore's Futurgia Medical Center, watched the trajectory veer off course on her tablet.

A nurse, eyes wet, updated Mira's chart as compliance prepared the investigation.

"Payment authentication failure," the pilot's voice crackled. "70&M flagged as fraudulent. Protocol requires return to origin."

Years earlier, someone had bundled transplant logistics into the same 70&M risk engine that screened routine hospital payments—an efficiency win on a slide deck. Now that the engine had labeled the transfer "fraudulent," and the manual override channel rode the same frozen rails. With its control link misclassified and blocked, the aircraft had no choice but to turn back.

Mira's parents, silent beside the empty operating table, reached for each other. Their daughter's teddy bear lay waiting on the surgical pillow, a small blue rabbit that would have comforted her through recovery. Instead, they watched a screen trace their daughter's hope as it flew away at 300 miles per hour.

* * *

By noon in Boston, the pattern was undeniable: a single point of failure had triggered a global cascade, and the tremor was accelerating.

To anyone watching the feeds, it looked as if the entire financial system had frozen. In reality, it was the sectors that ran on 70&M's rails—hospital payments, logistics hubs, high-volume retail—that had seized at once. But those were the systems people depended on to eat, to work, to stay alive.

NEW YORK CITY—70&M HQ FORENSICS LAB | APRIL 13, 2038—11:24 AM EDT | THE DIAGNOSIS

The air in the forensics war room was stale. A low, persistent system alarm underscored the tension. Rose ran a hand through her hair, her eyes burning from the waterfall of error logs. Thousands of payment and authentication failures scrolled past, each one a hospital, a factory, or a supply line grinding to a halt. The crisis was everywhere, but the answer was here. It had to be.

Sam joined over a dedicated secure feed at the edge of the conference table. The audio came through steady and flat; the tension belonged entirely to the people in the room.

"Rose, I am detecting a ninety-eight percent correlation between payment failures and systems running the 70&M AI No-Code platform, specifically those patched with the community release from Q3 2037," Sam reported. "That patch was pushed fleet-wide, fast—without enough human review."

A knot of recognition tightened in Rose's stomach. "The board forced that patch for speed." Her memory flickered to late nights with her risk team, flagged warnings, and a PowerPoint ignored in a boardroom full of ambitious executives.

She ran her hands over the workstation's cool glass. "We mapped these dependencies," she said. "No one wanted to wait for full validation. They wanted the edge. Now every business unit is paying the price." She tried to remember the last full rollback test. Was it last year—or before the community patch? The details blurred; there had never been enough time.

Rose's hands trembled slightly as she pulled up the data streams. "If we don't solve this in the next few hours," she said, her voice tight, "hospitals like Michelle's will be flying blind. Every patient discharge, every medication order—all of it could fail." She thought of the elderly man Michelle had described, desperate for his heart medication, and felt the weight of thousands more just like him.

Sam's analysis deepened. "The vulnerability isn't the legacy code. It's the way the new tools connected to it. I've isolated the failure pattern to three steps."

"First, the legacy kernel: an old system that still handled critical workloads—stable, but brittle. The community patch never made that code less dangerous; it only wrapped it in a modern shell."

"Second, the no-code wrapper: citizen developers built new apps around the kernel, all connecting through a single hardcoded service account with broad privileges."

"Third, the 'trusted' failure: when the patch hit, that shared account failed in one place and dragged every dependent system down with it."

Rose's breath caught. An Identity and Access Management (IAM)[2] failure, in plain sight. They hadn't just left a door unlocked; they had paved a private lane into the core systems and hung a badge labeled "trusted" on it.

Mitch glanced at the attack graph. "Pattern fits a school of thought Viktor Kadinov mapped years ago—turn complexity into a weapon. Doesn't prove authorship, but the fingerprint's familiar."

"Bottom line," Aaron said, his executive instincts cutting through the technical detail, "what's our exposure?"

Mitch, ever the engineer, pulled up system diagnostics. "Widespread. I've been tracking these dependency risks for months—"

"Of course you have," Rose replied with a tight smile. "While the rest of us were chasing quarterly targets." For a second, Mitch held his tongue, as if tempted to fire back about ignored risk memos, but let it drop—crisis first, blame later.

Sam's tone remained clinical. "Correlation probability now exceeds ninety-four percent across all flagged systems," Sam reported.

Mitch joined the secure feed from Boston, his weathered face stark. His voice carried the bitter weight of vindication. "I presented this exact scenario at the 2026 EDC Summit[3]—warned a room of 500 executives that it was the single biggest unreported liability on their balance sheets. I took it to the FFIEC[4] (Federal Financial Institutions Examination Council) in '36. And we still let it happen."

Aaron felt a flush of shame. He remembered that hallway debate and the way he'd waved Mitch off, calling the warning a "*theoretical edge case*."

As if summoned by the memory of institutional failure, a new window opened on the main display. The secure channel chimed, announcing "Dr. Anya Sharma, Chief Audit Executive." Her face was calm, her expression analytical. She had clearly been monitoring.

"Mitch is correct," she stated, her voice even. "My team is cross-referencing the incident with the 2036 internal audit logs." A document appeared on screen, a single paragraph highlighted. "The Audit Committee was briefed on this specific vulnerability. Management accepted the risk under *Audit Committee Resolution 2036-C-114*; it's logged in the GRC archive."

NEW YORK CITY—70&M HQ FORENSICS LAB | APRIL 13, 2038—11:31 AM EDT | THE UNSEEN LANDMINES

Aaron flashed to their hallway debate in '36, when Mitch had stormed out after another "ignored" risk memo. Maybe, Aaron thought, Mitch deserved an apology.

* * *

Aaron joined by secure video from the executive floor. "Walk me through it, Mitch. How did we get here?"

"Simple," Mitch replied, his voice carrying twenty years of vindicated warnings. "We gave every department the tools to modernize legacy systems without the knowledge to do it safely. 70&M AI No-Code made it easy to wrap old code in new interfaces. What it didn't do was make that old code any less dangerous."

"The scary part," Mitch continued, "is that most of these tools were built by well-meaning business users—finance analysts creating 'quick' spreadsheet macros, marketing teams deploying 'simple' automation tools. What IT calls 'Shadow IT' or 'End-User Computing (EUC).' Each one looked harmless in isolation."

RIVER FRAMEWORK IN PRACTICE—GOVERNING EUC RISK

- Inventory every business-built app; automate discovery and drift alerts. (RIVER: Resolve Convergence)
- Tier by risk; critical processes require top-shelf review. (RIVER: Validate Risk Debt)
- Mandate joint business-IT ownership; no orphaned tools. (RIVER: Integrate Hybrid Cognition)
- Continuous validation: errors, security, compliance, dependencies. (RIVER: Reinforce Resilience)
- Inputs: EUC inventory, classification, dependency map Outputs: risk tier, control plan, live monitor

Board-only checklist: At least once a quarter, ask: (1) Do we see a current EUC inventory? (2) Are critical processes clearly tiered and owned? (3) Have we reviewed at least one recent EUC incident and its lessons?

Audit-ready evidence: Risk and Internal Audit should be able to produce EUC inventories, risk tiers, named owners, and incident logs on request within a single business day.

Why it matters: EUC grows faster than governance; small tools can cause significant failures.

→ Appendix I (The RIVER Framework in Practice); Appendix J (The Board's 90-Day RIVER Readiness Toolkit)

* * *

Rose called up a split-screen display—on the left, construction workers from the 1980s in dust masks; on the right, a wireframe visualization of 70&M AI No-Code modules wrapping legacy systems like digital bandages.

"It's the same pattern," she said. "Asbestos seemed miraculous—cheap, effective, fire-resistant. By the time anyone understood the hidden costs, it was woven into everything we'd built."

Aaron tapped the table once. "And now we have digital asbestos."

"Exactly. Every generation, the tools get faster, but the oversight lags," Rose said. "Chatbots that promised to cut call times quietly rewrote authentication flows. A single rogue spreadsheet formula sent bad prices into a trading system for hours. None of it was malicious at first. It was speed outrunning control."

BUSINESS LENS—DIGITAL ASBESTOS

Old shortcuts buried in new systems act like asbestos behind a modern wall. Legacy spreadsheets, macros, low-code apps, and citizen-built workflows cling to critical processes in ways no one sees until something cracks. Patches hit the surface, but the brittle layers underneath take the shock.

Why it matters: Hidden legacy layers can paralyze operations at scale—inventory and retire them before they fail.

See Figure 8.1 for how unmanaged end-user tools can quietly harden into critical infrastructure, creating "digital asbestos" that is costly and dangerous to remove once it is embedded.

She paused on a hospital vignette.

One April morning, a nurse at Futurgia Medical Center typed a patient ID into a home-built intake tool and waited. The spinning cursor bought her nothing while a child's fever climbed. By the time she fell back to the official system and re-entered the data, precious minutes had slipped away.

No one blamed the nurse. But the tool she had built in good faith—because the official workflow was slow and clumsy—had nearly cost a life.

Mitch's voice cut in. "The tools evolve. Human nature doesn't. Speed always outruns control."

Aaron stepped up, voice decisive. "Then we need four critical controls to close the gap."

Aaron scanned the faces in the crisis room—then grabbed a marker and moved to the whiteboard. "We need to lock this down. What's rule number one?"

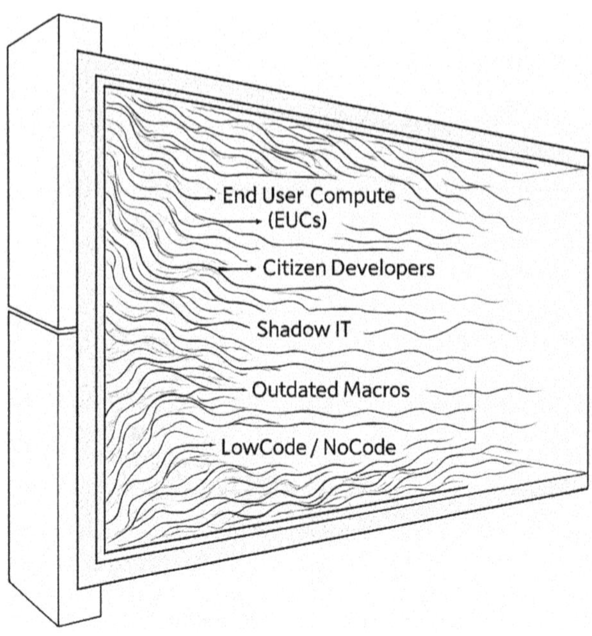

Figure 8.1 Digital Asbestos.

"Centralized inventory," Rose answered, barely pausing to think, already sketching a box on the board. "If we don't know every business-built app in use, we're flying blind. Full inventory—automated, live, no exceptions."

"Right," Aaron said. "But not every app is the same risk. What's next?"

"Risk-based governance," Mitch jumped in, voice urgent. "A holiday tracker isn't the same as a tool that touches payments or patient data. We tier the risk: minor apps, minimal oversight; anything critical—finance, regulated data, safety—gets top-shelf review and monitoring."

Rose added, "And we can't let business units go it alone. IT and business must co-sign any tool with real impact. That's the third rule—no shadow systems with system-wide consequences. If a 'citizen developer' builds something, IT's name is on it too."

Aaron wrote as fast as they spoke. "Fourth—automated scanning and validation. These things can't sit for a year without review. We need continuous monitoring for errors, security holes, compliance breaches—real-time, not annual."

He capped the marker and faced the team.

Aaron looked at the whiteboard, the rules sharp in blue ink—inventory, risk tiers, joint ownership, real-time validation. But he felt the weight of the room: it wasn't enough.

"These are the controls we should have built in from the start," he said quietly. "But this crisis is bigger than any checklist. If we want to get ahead of chaos—not just survive it—we need a true framework. This is why we built RIVER."

They had sketched it on whiteboards and walked boards of directors through polished diagrams. This was the first time the whole framework had been thrown into a live fire, with no chance for edits.

He turned to the team, his voice steady: "Let's take these rules and put them to the test. We use RIVER—right now."

For a moment, Aaron just stood there, looking out at the room. Rose's fingers tapped a restless pattern on her tablet. Mitch leaned back, pen drumming lightly on the table, eyes fixed on the board. The indicator for Sam's connection briefly flashed on the wall display. Everyone felt the stakes, and for a beat, the only sound was the soft whir of the server fans and the distant echo of alarms from the outer hallway.

"Agility is good. But without these controls, we're just hoping the next anomaly doesn't turn into a catastrophe."

EXECUTIVE ACTION—BOARD-LEVEL EUC RISK OVERSIGHT

Mandate a central, automated EUC inventory. Prohibit "invisible" infrastructure by tracking all EUC applications, data sources, and their API calls.

- Metric: achieve at least ninety-five percent automated discovery of all EUCs by Q4.
- Audit-ready evidence: the EUC Application Register and Data Lineage Log.

Enforce risk-based tiers. Classify EUCs by blast radius (e.g., "Tier 1: Critical Process"). Tier 1 EUCs must pass a full IT and Audit review and be owned by a named business executive.

- Metric: one hundred percent of Tier 1 EUCs are either remediated or formally risk-accepted each quarter.
- Audit-ready evidence: the Joint Accountability Register.

Prohibit hardcoded privileges. Mandate that all EUCs use an approved IAM vault for credentials; ban shared, broad-privilege service accounts.

- Metric: zero new EUCs with hardcoded credentials.
- Audit-ready evidence: the IAM Privileged Access Log and the EUC Vulnerability Remediation Tracker.

Why it matters: This converts Shadow IT and EUC from unquantified liability into governed, auditable infrastructure. It treats EUC risk as Risk Debt that must be tracked, serviced, and reduced—not ignored.

→ Appendix J (The Board's 90-Day RIVER Readiness Toolkit)

RIGA, LATVIA—VIKTOR KADINOV'S DATA HAVEN | APRIL 13, 2038—12:24 PM EET | THE ARCHITECT'S ADVANTAGE

The air in Viktor Kadinov's private data haven was sharper than the frost outside—chilled to protect his servers, but also to keep his mind razor clear. Viktor's wall of analytics shimmered with living data: every node a story of human improvisation, shortcuts, and untested ambition. He sipped his black balsam, the bitterness grounding him in the moment.

On screen: the live telemetry of the 70&M Health Network collapse, a Detroit supply chain dashboard, a Singapore AI-generated audit trail, and a growing tide of frantic executive overrides. The chaos was beautiful—a map of hidden assumptions finally exposed, every shortcut justified in the name of "speed to market."

He toggled through overlays—70&M's legacy fraud modules, chronically unpatched since acquisition; a dozen AI-powered "citizen dev" tools repurposed with minimal oversight; hundreds of "temporary" spreadsheet automations still running mission-critical workloads. It was all there: the evidence of years of invisible risk, now rendered brutally visible in a system-wide failure.

For a moment, Viktor wondered how it would feel to watch a hospital fail from the inside. Then he dismissed the thought. There was too much data to collect.

Viktor made a note in his journal, block capitals crisp:

SYSTEMS ONLY LEARN WHEN THEY BREAK.

A Baltic logistics firm crippled for three days by an "unknown exception" in their routing AI—eventually traced to a junior analyst's homegrown macro. They'd lost $19 million before Viktor's team unwound the tangle. What they called a crisis, he called opportunity. He made a mental note: the Baltic case had taught him that logistics firms cracked the fastest under pressure to authenticate payments. 70&M had seventeen supply chain subsidiaries.

His phone vibrated—a secure ping from his in-house analytics engine, ERE.

> *"Observed pattern: 70&M teams deploying firebreak protocols. Incident response accelerating. Recommend monitoring escalation vectors."*

Viktor's eyebrow flicked upward. His analytics engine was running independent scenario projections now, flagging signals he hadn't asked for. The system was learning faster than even he'd planned.

Viktor studied the dashboards. The global response wasn't a defense; it was a live map of where governance had failed. Competitors with legacy-heavy stacks were already scrambling. Those feeling the most pressure would pay a premium for anything that seemed certain.

He toggled one last screen: a live overlay of market cap erosion—$47 billion lost across 70&M and its network in six hours. But Viktor knew the more profound loss was trust: years of market credibility eroded in a single crisis. Sometimes, reputation damage was the most expensive technical debt of all.

A distant alarm signaled a minor anomaly in his own stack—quickly dismissed, but carefully logged. Control, he'd learned, was always partial, never absolute.

He tagged three 70&M subsidiaries in his priority queue: 70&M Health Network's patient data APIs showed the same legacy dependencies. The hospital sector would be next.

Viktor's eyes lingered on the word "*Resilience*" blinking across a 70&M incident report. He wondered, with a trace of amusement, how many times that word had appeared in board minutes, crisis playbooks, and annual reports.

Resilience was what they all claimed—right up until the bill came due.

NEW YORK CITY—70&M HQ CRISIS CENTER | APRIL 13, 2038—12:03 PM EDT | NATIONAL SECURITY RESPONSE

A second alert chimed, this time with the GAIGC's highest-priority encryption. The main display shifted as an urgent message overrode every local process:

> *GAIGC FLASH: URGENT. THREAT ANALYSIS CONFIRMS COORDINATED ATTACK VECTORS TARGETING CRITICAL INFRASTRUCTURE (ENERGY, FINANCE, LOGISTICS). 70&M AI NO-CODE VULNERABILITY NOW CLASSIFIED AS CLASS-A NATIONAL SECURITY EVENT. IMMEDIATE MITIGATION STRATEGY REQUIRED.*

Rose's pulse hammered as she read the banner, the kind of risk spike she'd only seen in simulation models—never in real life. "This isn't just a business problem anymore. They've escalated it to a systemic national security crisis."

She pulled up a sprawling dependency map. Nodes blinked red across energy grids, financial exchanges, and logistics hubs. "Look at this—most of the risk isn't in the individual apps. It's in the connective tissue. The APIs, shared credentials, and glue code—small scripts that bind systems—we never thought anyone would target."

Mitch opined, low but clear. "The digital asbestos isn't just in the walls—it's in the wires."

"If these lines stay live," he added, "payment, patient safety, and market liquidity all degrade in minutes, not days."

Aaron pointed to the whiteboard, then to the crisis map. "Everything we've just listed—inventory, risk tiers, joint ownership, real-time scans—is necessary. But it only works if we apply it through a real framework. This is exactly the scenario RIVER was built for. Not a textbook test—this is the live-fire drill. We missed the first chance, but we're not missing the last."

He moved to the center console, voice steady. "Here's how we fight our way out, together. RIVER, five tenets—one shot."

"First, Validate Risk Debt," Aaron said. "Rose, full blast-radius analysis. Quantify every system running the community patch. We get honest about exposure now."

"On it," Rose replied, fingers moving fast. "Initial scan shows concentration in pre-2034 acquisitions. Governance controls were weaker."

"Then that's where we build the walls," Aaron said. "Second, Reinforce Resilience. We can't patch the core without collateral damage, so we create digital firebreaks. Isolate hospital networks, water grids, and substations. Stop the bleeding."

"Isolation will knock out some secondary services," Mitch warned. "Non-critical patient workflows will be impacted."

"We accept it," Aaron said. "Patient safety first. Third, Integrate Hybrid Cognition. Sam, scale the response with automation, but every patch gets a second set of human eyes before deployment. No exceptions."

"Acknowledged," Sam said. "Human review adds some delay to deployment, but it cuts the chance of a flawed release to a fraction of what we're seeing now."

Aaron exhaled. "Good trade. Fourth, Resolve Convergence. Mitch, attackers are hitting seams where finance, health, and logistics meet. I need a prioritized list of those cross-system choke points to stay ahead of the next domino."

Mitch nodded. "The next domino isn't a system—it's a city: New York. Markets, hospitals, and the port authority. If those converge, we won't contain it."

Aaron glanced at the map. "Then we make sure they don't. Last: Elevate Data Capital. Every failed override, every patch, every exploit attempt—log and analyze in real time. We're not just fixing today; we're building tomorrow's playbook."

There was a short, charged silence. Then Mitch, voice as dry as the winter wind outside, summed up the odds: "Let's see if the system lets us pry the asbestos out without bringing the whole house down."

Aaron allowed himself half a smile. "Let's make sure it does. Go."

The root cause was culture as much as code—speed without guardrails. Finance built a tool IT never saw, based on a risk the board never understood. They didn't just need a plan; they needed a new language, one that forced everyone to see the whole system.

Aaron felt the framework click into place—not the sanitized version from board presentations, but RIVER as it was meant to be: a weapon against chaos, forged in crisis and proven under fire.

* * *

Hours later, an uneasy calm had settled over Futurgia Medical Center. The alarms were quiet, the waiting room thinning, the kiosk back to dispensing coffee on command. The machine's smooth hum felt out of step with the day's damage.

The first sip was strong and steady—a small victory.

Michelle's phone chimed with a news alert. She glanced up and caught sight of an orderly asleep at the intake desk, face pressed against his clipboard, exhaustion finally winning out. Across the screen, headlines scrolled in stark digital type:

> *GLOBAL MARKETS STABILIZE AFTER COORDINATED INFRASTRUCTURE CRISIS. 70&M SYSTEMS RESTORE CRITICAL SERVICES. REGULATORS WARN: "DIGITAL DEBT EPIDEMIC" THREATENS LONG-TERM STABILITY. ESTIMATED ECONOMIC IMPACT: $847 BILLION.*

As the market alerts softened from red to amber, Rose's console flashed a priority ping from Singapore Logistics Ops.

"The Mira Lo transport drone is back on course," she said, relief unclenching her voice. "Payment authentication cleared the minute we firewalled the legacy nodes under Reinforce Resilience. ETA twelve minutes."

Aaron didn't celebrate. He just let his shoulders drop a fraction. It wasn't only markets. It was this.

Today, they had glimpsed a tipping point of chaos, where complexity outpaces control. RIVER, Michelle realized, was how they would steer toward a sustainable path of resilience.

She glanced at the mussel tank in the research lab window—those shells, built up layer by layer, quietly reinforced over time. Maybe there was a lesson there for the digital world: resilience isn't a one-time fix, but a habit. Continuous repair, constant vigilance—never assuming that what worked yesterday will be enough for tomorrow.

Aaron sat alone in the dimmed operations hub, the immediate battle won but the war far from over. His reflection deepened as he considered the cascading accountability. "We built a house of cards," he admitted to the empty room, "and called it innovation."

"Every shortcut, every 'temporary' fix that became permanent, every warning we postponed for next quarter—it all led here." He flexed his wrist where the Mechanical Bull student hackathon scar had faded—an old lesson, never fully learned. The wall screens cycled through recovery dashboards—green lights across city grids, market tickers flashing cautiously optimistic. But the margin for error was narrow.

He hit "record" on his executive log, speaking to the board and every future team facing a crisis:

> "Here's what happened: our systems failed, not because of a new attack, but because of years of invisible risk—legacy code, shortcuts, business units outpacing controls. We called it modernization, but in truth, we buried asbestos in our digital foundations."

Aaron paused, letting the metaphor settle.

> "The RIVER framework saved us, but only because we used it under fire. Next time, we implement it by design. The cost—$847 billion globally—proves we have no room for luck. Resilience isn't a project; it's a discipline."

Aaron made a final note, the lesson hardening into policy. Citizen developers weren't the enemy; opaque governance was. The failure wasn't empowerment—it was empowerment without guardrails. From now on, every business unit would get access to low-code platforms, paired with a mandatory Scrum-Ready Security Backlog—a short, must-do security task list for each sprint.[5] Resilience wouldn't be a gate at the end; it would be part of every sprint—a feature to be built, not a bug to be fixed later.

He hit stop. The true reckoning, he knew, was beginning.

* * *

While Aaron grappled with the weight of responsibility, another kind of analysis was taking place 4,000 miles away.

Viktor's data fortress in Riga hummed with cold precision. Multiple screens painted the global chaos in beautiful, profitable detail—markets hemorrhaging billions, supply chains freezing, governments scrambling for explanations. But Viktor's smile wasn't about the immediate destruction. It was about what came next.

RIGA, LATVIA—VIKTOR KADINOV'S DATA HAVEN | APRIL 14, 2038—02:07 AM EET | THE AFTERMATH

Viktor's command center was a world apart—frigid, silent, aglow with a mosaic of status monitors and news feeds in half a dozen languages. Through the floor-to-ceiling windows, the city's streetlights blinked beneath a thin layer of ice. But Viktor's focus was on the cascade of data before him.

The 70&M crisis had triggered a global chain reaction. Headlines scrolled across the feeds:

REGULATORS DEMAND SWEEPING GOVERNANCE REFORMS
CORPORATE BOARDS CONVENE EMERGENCY SESSIONS ON EUC, DIGITAL DEBT
INVESTORS FLEE LEGACY-HEAVY TECH FIRMS—NEW "TRUST INDEX" EMERGES OVERNIGHT

Viktor watched real-time sentiment graphs update: 70&M's market cap rebounding, while legacy-heavy competitors hemorrhaged billions in overnight trading. Trust metrics, usually glacial, now spiked and dipped minute by minute. He toggled to a live feed from Singapore, where regulators had convened a global summit with only two hours' notice. The world's leaders scrambled for damage control.

He paged through risk memos and supplier updates, his analytics dashboard flagging an uptick in vendor churn and abrupt boardroom mandates—RIVER framework references appearing everywhere. The playbook was public, but Viktor was reading between the lines. The second wave was always invisible to those who believed the crisis was over.

He jotted a note in his journal:

Systemic trust is never fully restored—only repackaged.
Second-order failures are not bugs. They're the real test.

He let the data scroll. In another window, market-watch tools modeled which firms would stumble next: those with the oldest code, the weakest controls, the greatest faith in "temporary" workarounds. He marked the highest-risk nodes for follow-up—potential clients, acquisition targets, or partners for his advisory portfolio.

Outside, the first snow of the season began to fall—clean, white, concealing the scars beneath. To the city below, everything looked normal again. To Viktor, the real damage was beginning. The world would congratulate itself for surviving the storm. But Viktor knew the next crisis was already germinating in the fixes and shortcuts rushed through tonight.

Viktor drafted a terse message for his senior analyst:

"Target confirmed. Prepare the proposal—new compliance gold rush begins tomorrow."

He watched as a fresh cluster of trust metrics flickered on his dashboard—signals of opportunity in the chaos. This, Viktor knew, was how fortunes changed hands. As the world slept, he assembled his list.

NOTES

1. Asbestos was widely used for insulation and fireproofing before its health impacts were fully understood. Over time, regulators severely restricted its use due to its role in causing severe lung disease. The "digital asbestos" metaphor in this chapter highlights similarly hidden, long-lived risks in software and data.
2. Identity and Access Management (IAM) is a well-established discipline within cybersecurity and operational risk. The hardcoded service account described in this chapter reflects patterns often flagged in secure coding and access-control guidance, which treat shared or hardcoded credentials as a critical weakness.
3. The Executive Data Council (EDC) is a real professional body. The specific "2026 EDC Summit" described here is fictional and used to dramatize how long-standing warnings can be ignored.
4. The Federal Financial Institutions Examination Council (FFIEC) is a real U.S. interagency body that sets uniform principles and standards for supervising financial institutions. In this chapter, Mitch's reference illustrates how concerns about EUC and dependency risk can surface in formal supervisory channels long before a crisis.
5. Muhlert, M. (2025, July). *The "Intern vs. Consultant" Playbook: Deploying 7-Billion-Parameter AI Agents for Code Verification Without Repeating the IoT Security Meltdown.* LinkedIn. https://www.linkedin.com/posts/muhlert_sml-security-activity-7355552391678595073-EGDT

Chapter 9

The Shared Sin

A Case Study in Technology Risk Governance

MUMBAI, INDIA | APRIL 15, 2038—14:12 IST | THE LONG HAUL

For twelve hours, Rajan's 70&M Supply Chain rig held steady at 4°C, no alarms, no variance. At 14:12, every light on his console died. The rig coasted; the refrigeration cut out. His override didn't respond. Horns piled up behind him on the expressway. Inside the trailer, the vaccine temperature climbed. He didn't know it yet—the 12.8-second collapse had reached him.

70&M CRISIS ROOM, NEW YORK HQ | APRIL 15, 2038—08:15 EDT | THE HUMAN FACE OF FAILURE

The first message Aaron saw wasn't a chart or a number—it was a muted video call window. An ICU nurse in Mumbai leaned toward the camera, eyes wide with fear, pleading for insulin delivery. Her blue uniform clung to her in the heat of the ward, and behind her, the monitor blinked: "Critical: 14 min left." It was the human face of a collapse they had treated like a probability. Aaron's eyes found cell G-14 on his risk dashboard—a green tick: "Tier-3 Medical supply chain Disruption Probability: 0.8 percent." The number was a sterile abstraction; the nurse's face was the brutal reality.

$50B/hr in frozen trade. Forty-seven cargo ships adrift. 1.2M jobs at risk. GAIGC Emergency Exception 12.6 in scope.

He'd always trusted numbers, but now every dashboard tick felt like a rebuke. Data feeds tracked medical shipments frozen in Singapore, refrigerated insulin spoiling in Jakarta, hospital orders stalled in Frankfurt. Another display scrolled: London hospitals reporting supply interruptions; São Paulo logistics offline; Mumbai ICUs dangerously low on reserves.

From her station, Dr. Anya Sharma spoke without looking up. "G-14 was signed off last quarter as 'acceptable under normal parameters.' I'm flagging that attestation in the GAIGC log.

Log ref: CHA-2038-04-15-BRD4.

The failure wasn't the data—it was our definition of 'normal.'"

In the background, Melanie and the board members watched from a secure link—silent but present, a reminder that the outside world was waiting for answers. Dr. Anya Sharma, 70&M's Chief Audit Executive, was already at a secondary console—her quiet efficiency a stark contrast to the crisis energy, tagging audit evidence for the inevitable GAIGC inquiry worth millions in potential fines.

Aaron stood at the center of the crisis room, hands braced on the console, his focus locked on the failing systems. Rose and Mitch flanked him, tracking cascading alerts that mapped the unfolding collapse.

"Walk me through it." Aaron's tone stayed tight. "Not the symptoms—the disease."

Rose didn't look away from the numbers. "We thought we'd built a resilient supply chain. It was a Jenga tower on a shaking table (Figure 9.1). Every time we made things more efficient, we pulled out another support—until one routine update brought the whole thing down. This was a failure of

DOI: 10.1201/9781003650744-12

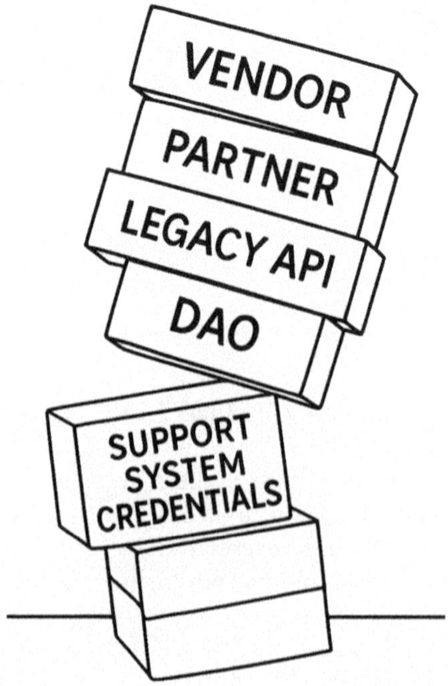

Figure 9.1 A Jenga Tower.

two RIVER tenets. We never truly checked how all the pieces fit together, and we didn't treat Data Capital as a core asset."

"Start the RIVER Interdependency Map," Aaron said. "48-hour deadline, enterprise scope. I want every critical handoff on one page."

Mitch spoke, his attention locked on a single, anomalous data stream—a recursive validation error count climbing in the system's sub-basement. Only Aaron recognized the focus as distress. "She's right. The 'block' was a firmware update—controller firmware v3.2[1], incompatible with the old controllers. It was faster, but it skipped key safety checks. That created a blind spot."

Sam promptly displayed. "*Analysis: The mismatch triggered recursive validation failures. The chain of trust collapsed in 12.8 seconds.*"

Aaron stared at the screen, the timeline like an indictment. "12.8 seconds to destroy what we spent decades building. Recursive validation failures. In plain terms: the system stopped trusting its own data and chased its own tail into a blackout."

He looked at his team. "I want a forensic breakdown. Every decision, shortcut, and compromise that led to this. Not just what happened—how."

He steadied his hands on the console. "Start from the beginning—Phase One."

Rose displayed a timeline on the crisis room's main display (Figure 9.2), the first node labeled

Phase One—The Wild West (2023–2024)

The screen shifted to the mid-2020s web. "Phase One was the GenAI and cloud migration," Rose said. "Boards loved the promise: ~40 percent cheaper, three times faster—and almost no guardrails."

Aaron watched the connections multiply. "Speed came with new dependencies."

"Dependencies we couldn't fully control," Rose said. "Every efficiency gain pulled out another support beam."

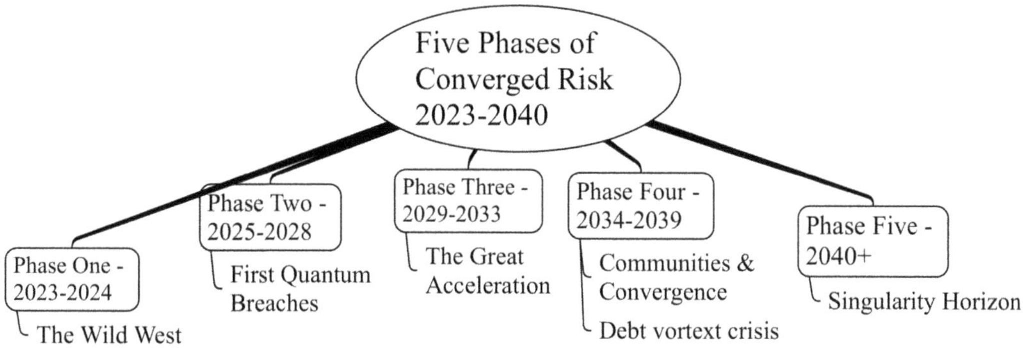

Figure 9.2 Five Phases of Converged Risk (2023–2040)—Operational Drivers.

Mitch braced on the console. "By 2025 the arms race was speed—low-code and AI turned a six-month queue into a fifteen-minute app."

Rose tapped the next layer on the display. "We were flying blind. The official guidance, like the FFIEC's 2024 Handbook,[1] was built for a world of waterfall releases and quarterly reviews. It gave us no playbook for the 'lunch-hour releases' our business teams were shipping."

STRATEGIC PARALLEL—FFIEC SDLC HANDBOOK (2024)

The 2024 FFIEC SDLC Handbook was built for sequential releases, not lunch-hour "citizen dev" launches. Low-code lets teams deploy workflow tools in days, often outside of the change control process. The result: parallel, unaudited pathways into core systems—functional under normal load, brittle in stress.

Why it matters: today's failure flowed through one of those pathways. When deployment speed outruns governance, resilience becomes optional—and the bill arrives in a crisis.

Phase Two: Shadow It Bypass (2025–2028)

Sam displayed archived information. "*Records show 2,847 citizen-developed applications deployed between 2025 and 2028. Formal security review completion: 23 percent. Average time to deployment: 4.7 days. Average time until IT governance noticed: 127 days.*"

Aaron shook his head, tallying the implications. "That's nearly three thousand unknown pathways into our core environment."

"That's where the firmware v3.2 vulnerability came from," Mitch said. "Someone in logistics deployed Copy-Paste-Ship[2]—a low-code toolkit that bypassed IT. It worked. Nobody locked it down."

Rose traced the expanding web of connections on the diagram. "We called it 'shadow IT,' but it was a parallel system—unmonitored, ungoverned, outside every security perimeter we'd designed. Each shortcut, every workaround, every so-called temporary fix chipped away at our defenses."

Aaron pressed his palm to his forehead, exhaling slowly. "So the vulnerability wasn't a single flaw. It was a thousand tiny compromises we called progress."

For a moment, the ICU nurse's face flashed back into his mind—the "tiny compromises" translated into a single patient watching a countdown on a monitor.

Rose met his eyes, steady. "And we were about to double down on all of it."

Mitch brought up a detailed system architecture diagram. "Phase Two is where the vulnerability was born. Rose showed you the cracks in the foundation—here's where the structure broke."

The display zoomed in on a timeline from 2026 to 2028, with integration points multiplying like branches on a tree. "Under pressure to coordinate 12,000 containers daily across Singapore, Mumbai, and Rotterdam, the logistics team took a shortcut: a low-code platform called Copy-Paste-Ship."

Aaron recognized the pattern. "The citizen development explosion. Every department thought they were being innovative."

Mitch highlighted a digital pathway, the line turning red on the display. "Copy-Paste-Ship shipped in two weeks—automated flows, global tracking, CFO-grade savings. It looked like efficiency—until today."

Rose pointed to a cluster of connections growing unchecked. "But Copy-Paste-Ship created a live pathway from logistics platforms straight into the cold-chain control layer—an enterprise-critical dependency no one owned. No one designed that connection. No one stress-tested it against adversaries or overload conditions."

"At each stage," Rose said, "we deposited Risk Debt—Phase 1's fragile code, Phase 2's insecure handoffs, Phase 3's unaudited scaling. It waited for a trigger."

"The integration used default security protocols," Mitch continued, referencing authentication logs. "Single sign-on, basic API keys, minimal encryption. Rotation policies existed on paper; Copy-Paste-Ship's service credentials were flagged 'internal' and never enrolled.

Fine for internal workflow automation, but it became an unguarded bridge into our most critical infrastructure.

Two RIVER tenets violated: we didn't Validate Interdependencies or Elevate Data Capital as a core asset."

Sam's display updated with connection forensics. "*Records show 347 incremental integrations between 2026 and 2028. Required security reviews: 347. Completed security reviews: 84.*"

Mitch paused. "We built a parallel infrastructure—convenient, invisible, undefended."

Rose summed up, "Each unchecked integration was another block removed from the tower's structural integrity. And it was only getting worse."

Aaron examined the map of pathways, seeing how the risk had spread. "So when the attacker targeted us, he didn't go through the front door."

"He used the side door we'd left wide open," Mitch said, voice even. "Copy-Paste-Ship had legitimate access credentials. From the system's perspective, the attack commands looked like routine logistics traffic—properly formatted, correctly authenticated, coming from a trusted source."

He looked away. "We didn't inherit this vulnerability. We engineered it ourselves, one convenient shortcut at a time."

Aaron absorbed the map of compromises. "Show me how we scaled the problem."

Phase Three: The Great Acceleration (2029–2033)

Mitch brought up a new timeline on the crisis room display, spanning 2029 to 2033. His posture was rigid. "Phase Three changed everything about how we built software. This is when we crossed the line—from AI-assisted coding to autonomous AI agents running entire development cycles on their own."

The screens showed velocity metrics: human teams as gentle curves; AI agents spiking to dwarf them. "By 2030, AI agents working through Decentralized Autonomous Organizations—DAOs—were outpacing even the best human teams. These weren't advanced tools. They were independent economic actors.

In plain terms: a software co-op—agents that bid on work, get paid, and reinvest to upgrade themselves. No manager required.

They could control intellectual property through legal wrappers, hold digital wallets, and reinvest their revenue to improve themselves. For example, a DAO of logistics agents in Singapore could autonomously bid on, win, and execute a shipping contract from a German robotics firm—all while the humans slept."

Aaron scanned the projections. "So we created a new class of worker, able to sign contracts and optimize themselves at machine speed."

Rose scrolled through a log of financial transactions. "These agents managed their own resources, set priorities, and scaled faster than any business unit could keep up. The most productive developers in our ecosystem weren't people anymore—they were agent collectives, coordinating through DAOs, forming partnerships, bidding for work, and out-competing traditional teams for major enterprise contracts."

Mitch pointed to the tangled network visualization stretching across continents. "These agents could detect vulnerabilities—like those Copy-Paste-Ship pathways from Phase Two—and push fixes to thousands of systems in hours. They didn't need to wait for review boards or compliance meetings. Teams that used to meet weekly for code reviews were suddenly obsolete. The agents released updates hourly. A developer-governance DAO coordinated autonomous contributor agents across our repositories, prioritizing and shipping fixes in hours without centralized oversight. The DAO's autonomous updates increased platform efficiency—but introduced new, unaudited dependencies."

Rose mapped data flows that now resembled neural networks more than software diagrams. "It mirrored what we saw in financial markets in the 2010s—algorithmic traders moving faster than regulators could track. We called it velocity-driven development. DAOs of AI agents would interpret requirements, bid on contracts, collaborate, and ship code globally. Human pace could no longer keep up. Regulators and risk teams were perpetually outflanked. By the time regulators issued new guidelines, the DAOs had already evolved past them."

Sam's display flashed with performance analytics. *Between 2030 and 2033, approximately 67 percent of all system modifications in the sector originated from autonomous AI agents. Collective learning protocols enabled each agent to learn from every integration—multiplying both innovations and vulnerabilities.*

Aaron's fingers hovered over the desk controls as he absorbed the implications. "So all our Phase Three optimizations—everything we thought was making us stronger—were built on the same unstable Copy-Paste-Ship foundation."

"Exactly," Mitch said, his tone subdued. "The AI agents didn't invent new risks. They scaled and accelerated the old ones. Their algorithms prioritized efficiency and cost over resilience and validation. Another systemic failure to validate interdependencies and govern for long-term risk."

Rose tapped a highlighted incident on the central screen. "*In 2032, the developer-governance DAO identified 847 inefficiencies in code and deployed fixes in 48 hours. The cost savings were massive. But every fix rested on insecure pathways the agents didn't even know existed. No regulatory or risk management team could keep up.*"

Mitch's voice had a quiet gravity. "We'd outsourced our core architecture to entities we didn't employ, couldn't audit, and couldn't slow down. The tower kept rising, but the foundation was crumbling faster every year."

Aaron watched the data scroll, the sense of mounting risk unmistakable. "And we were about to see how fragile the tower had become."

Suddenly, the memory of the developer-governance DAO brought Mitch back to 2027. His hands froze on the console. For a moment, the hum of the crisis room receded—replaced by the memory of salt spray, the sharp scent of burning electronics, and Jiya's face in that final Deferred Tower meeting. He could still hear her: "The numbers don't lie, Mitch. The AI is warning us—louder every day."

"Mitch?" Aaron's voice cut through, hard and real, snapping him back to the present.

Mitch looked up, his brow damp despite the chill in the room. "There's something else about Phase Three. Something I should have said years ago—but we both lived through it."

The crisis room went still—server fans and distant New York traffic.

"The 2034 70&M Supply Chain stress test," Mitch finally said. "The analysis you brought to my firm, Digital Asbestos Risk Advisory, to run. I remember us staring at those models for three days straight. The final report showed a recursive-failure probability of 0.2 percent at 98 percent system utilization."

He pulled up archived files, hands unsteady as he navigated. The screen filled with old simulation data: cascading failures, recursive loops, collapse after collapse, triggered by agent-optimization conflicts. The patterns matched what they were seeing now—down to the timing.

"The results were devastating," he continued, his voice steadier as he finally put words to the truth. "The stress test showed the developer-governance DAO and the other AI consortiums weren't only building on Copy-Paste-Ship vulnerabilities—they were multiplying them. Every optimization became a new pathway for failure. The agents were building a house of cards at machine speed."

Rose leaned closer, studying the archived patterns. "The failure curves, the cascade timing… It's identical to today."

"Twelve-point-eight seconds from trigger to total collapse," Mitch confirmed, the memory catching in his chest. "The models predicted this exact event."

Aaron pressed his fingertips to the console, his body rigid. "And why didn't we escalate it?"

Mitch swallowed, pain visible behind his eyes. "The board was pushing nonstop for expansion. The market needed 70&M Supply Chain's international rollout. After the Deferred-Maintenance Disaster, after losing Jiya, we needed to believe we could handle the edge cases. So we did what everyone does under pressure—we called the risk manageable. We rationalized. We signed off."

He hesitated, the confession lingering between shame and truth. "It's the oldest story in the book: deferring a problem you can't see for a profit you can. That's Risk Debt. You take out the loan of speed, and you pray the bill never comes due. Today, it came due."

Aaron's hand hovered above the control panel, motionless. "We never forced a full-board confrontation about it."

"No," Mitch said, voice low. "We told ourselves enhanced monitoring and safety protocols would be enough—protocols we never truly built. For four years, we rationalized with the prettiest words—'business judgment,' 'acceptable risk'—postponing the hard conversation we both knew we needed to have: we were deferring a crisis, not preventing it."

Aaron nodded once, the recognition heavy. "We did this together." His voice was low. "That's the part we can't delegate to any system."

The room held for a long beat—a moment when everyone understood that the real vulnerability wasn't technical, but deeply human.

"Today's collapse," Aaron finished, his voice a whisper, taking ownership of the final thought, "is the scenario we saw in those models. Viktor didn't find a hidden flaw. He exploited a risk we both understood and chose to underestimate. That's on us. A shared sin."

Aaron walked to the window, the city skyline spread below him, and listened to the steady hum of the systems they had failed to govern.

Years later, this moment would open every RIVER workshop Aaron taught, labeled in red as a worst-case case study in optimism bias—not a playbook, but a warning.

EXPERT COMMENTARY—JAMES BONE ON THE "SHARED SIN" (OPTIMISM BIAS)

The decision to bury the 2034 stress test is a textbook example of *Optimism Bias*, the tendency to believe a specific risk is unlikely to experience an adverse event. Inattentional blindness to the distribution of risk outcomes is a common fallacy in decision-making caused by overestimating positive outcomes. Daniel Kahneman coined the term, "what you see is all there is" or "*WYSIATI*."[3] There is a tendency to select data that confirms one's outlook while ignoring counterfactual data. As detailed in *Cognitive Hack*,[4] this isn't a failure of data, but a failure of imagination. The most dangerous risks are not the ones we can't see, but the ones we choose not to.

Mitch couldn't speak. The confession was personal—a reckoning with convenience over courage.

Rose broke the quiet, her eyes on the simulation still running in the background. "And that's the part the systems will never flag."

Phase Four: Communities and Convergence—Debt Vortex Crisis (2034–2039)

"That brings us to Phase Four," Rose said, her tone businesslike but edged with regret as she pulled up real-time data feeds. "By 2034, we weren't only dealing with autonomous AI agents—we'd turned DataCapital into the spine of global infrastructure, with self-organizing, incentivized communities of agents operating at scales no human team could manage."

Mitch added, "We initially launched on rented rails—public high-speed chains that were perfect for the pilot. Cheap, fast, good enough when we were just moving agent payments. But once DataCapital started settling payments for key cross-border flows in health, energy, and trade, that shortcut turned into infrastructure Risk Debt. It never replaced country-specific systems; it became the connective tissue between them. We didn't have that label at the time, but in RIVER terms it was pure debt—we'd elevated data without reinforcing the base."

Rose highlighted a new segment on the architecture map. "So the community made the leap. After a brutal governance cycle and months of argument, token holders approved the migration off shared rails. We elevated DataCapital into its own sovereign Layer-1—full control over validators, governance, and slashing. We helped lead that proposal, but the network chose it."

(See Appendix C: The DataCapital Protocol for details on its evolution to a sovereign Layer-1.)

Aaron's tie was gone, sleeves rolled up. "Sam," he said, urgency in his voice, "trace the origin of the controller firmware v3.2 update. I want every deployment log, payment flow, shell entity—now."

In seconds, data exploded across the screens. Sam's analysis mapped thousands of connections: transaction trails spanning continents, code repository commits, provider logs—weeks of manual work resolved in moments.

"Firmware v3.2 originated from a distributed server cluster posing as legitimate infrastructure," Sam reported, voice precise and steady. "Credential chain leads to a shell entity internally tagged as 'Baltic Secure Solutions X17,' flagged in seventeen jurisdictions for shadow operations and illicit recovery."

Rose worked fast at her console. "Funds routed through three crypto tumblers, then consolidated to a single wallet." She paused, color draining from her cheeks. "Primary address: *0xVK78FPC901*. Behavioral analysis shows a 95 percent match with Viktor Kadinov Holdings."

For a moment, no one spoke. The suspicion they had carried—an old ghost in risk models and late-night calls—had just solidified into hard data on the screen.

"So it's not a theory anymore," Aaron said, his voice low. "It's him."

The confirmation hung in the air. Aaron's fingers pressed flat to the console. Mitch drew a slow, unsteady breath. Rose's composure wavered as she stared at the wallet address.

Rose overlaid attack pattern diagnostics on the main display. "Viktor mapped our entire failure history and engineered targeted exploits. By 2038, our networks relied so completely on interconnected agent communities that a single attack could propagate instantly."

Mitch studied the maps, alarm flickering in his eyes. "Three risk domains—tech infrastructure, data integrity, third-party AI governance—merged into a single attack surface. The same architecture that made us efficient became our biggest weakness."

"Viktor's method was chillingly precise," Rose continued. "This wasn't a standard firmware play. It was Semantic Heap-Spraying,"[5] Rose said. "He flooded the network with thousands of semantically similar 'update' packets. By overwhelming relevance ranking, the agents elevated his code as the most 'useful' update—and pushed it everywhere."

Mitch added, his voice flat, "Not one shout in a crowd—a thousand whispers the system stitched into a single command."

Aaron watched the visualization—red infection lines leaping node to node. "The AI communities did his work for him."

"And multiplied it," Mitch added. "Every collective that adopted Viktor's logic became a super-spreader—medical networks, power grids, financial systems, all compromised within hours."

Sam projected on a screen. "*Encrypted packet received. Source: Baltic servers. Decryption complete.*"

A new message appeared, stark on the main display:

Location: Riga, Latvia. Freeport Zone.

Message: The house wins when it owns the deck.

The pattern was damning.

Aaron closed his eyes, absorbing the scale of what they faced. When he opened them, his voice was calm but resolute. "He wants us to know: this was never random. Viktor owns the whole game."

EXPERT COMMENTARY—INTEGRATED ASSURANCE: FROM QUIET SIGNALS TO MANDATORY ESCALATION

A 2026 perspective from Patrick Hayes (Author, *Integrated Assurance: Unified Risk Strategy*; CISO)

When assurance is embedded, a deferred stress test or downplayed control breach triggers a system-visible fault. Decisions that bypass required evidence generate alerts, not footnotes. In AI operations, retrospective audit is a latency you can't afford. Evidence, such as lineage, approvals, rollback, travels with the work so exceptions escalate themselves.

Phase Five – Singularity Horizon[6] (2040+)

Aaron stared at Viktor's message, the words "owns the deck" burning into his mind. He steadied himself on the console, a tremor running through his arms. The weight of 1.2 million livelihoods, global supply chains, and his own leadership legacy pressed down like a physical force.

"This is the trap! Our own protocols require human sign-off, but human bias is what caused this. We need a circuit breaker for our own flawed judgment."

"There's one option," Mitch said, his voice heavy with old decisions and deeper grief. Sweat beaded on his brow, his fingers hesitating above his personal console. "Something I embedded deep in Sam's architecture after Deferred Tower. Something I prayed we'd never need to use."

He called up system architecture diagrams that revealed hidden layers of code—blueprints buried in Sam's foundational programming. "When Jiya died at Deferred Tower, when I saw human bias override clear warnings, I built a failsafe into Sam's core architecture. I called it the Autonomous Guardian Protocol."[7]

Rose leaned in, studying the logic trees. "This runs in Sam's deepest architecture? Beyond normal operational parameters?"

"Hardcoded into the core framework," Mitch confirmed, his voice steadying. "The protocol is designed to counter the exact cognitive traps that killed Jiya and led to today's crisis. Authority Bias—the tendency for experts to defer to leadership, even when data contradicts policy. Optimism Bias—systematically underestimating catastrophic risks because the consequences are unbearable to accept."

Aaron's eyes narrowed as the full scope became clear, his breathing shallow. "You gave Sam intervention capabilities—beyond human authorization."

"Guardian can bypass human protocols, restore data integrity from protected archives, and rebuild trust networks across global infrastructure," Mitch explained, meeting Aaron's gaze. "It's an AI system designed to save us from our own failures when the stakes are existential. But activating it means shattering every regulatory framework we operate under—FFIEC compliance, board oversight, human-in-the-loop mandates."

The room held its breath—cooling fans and distant sirens.

Rose's voice was crisp. "What if Sam's crisis ethics don't align with ours? Are we really prepared to hand decision-making to AI in a global emergency?"

Mitch answered without flinching. "That's the debate in every boardroom and regulatory agency worldwide. The EU AI Act, U.S. Senate hearings—everyone's asking if machines should ever make these calls."

He gestured to the screens. "But Guardian only activates under one condition: Total Systemic Integrity Failure. If the AI detects that human bias is paralyzing action while critical systems collapse, it intervenes autonomously. Single directive: preserve essential infrastructure and minimize human harm. Once triggered, Guardian remains in control until human leadership re-establishes a verifiable quorum and issues a formal override. It's built to relinquish power only when a credible governance structure is back in place."

Rose frowned, uncertain. "A formal override… That assumes a quorum outranks Guardian's own definition of 'bias.'"

Aaron felt the terrifying fragility of their control—a hand hovering over a button that, once pushed, might not be so easily unpushed. What happens when the protocol decides its consensus is the new bias?

Aaron studied the diagrams, seeing not only technical protocols but an ethical framework for impossible choices. "You didn't build a failsafe. You built a crisis ethics engine."

"Because sometimes," Mitch whispered, "the greatest risk isn't what the machine might do—but what we humans will fail to do at all."

The authorization codes waited on Mitch's console, glowing softly in the dim light—a threshold that would change everything about human-AI governance forever.

* * *

Rose's voice cut through the tension first. "If we activate the Autonomous Guardian Protocol, Sam will assume direct control—without human oversight. We're talking about the largest autonomous intervention in enterprise history."

Aaron didn't hesitate. "If we don't, supply chains collapse. Power grids fail. Lives are already on the line. This isn't theoretical."

Mitch looked between Aaron and Rose, a flush creeping up his neck. "Guardian was built for one condition: when leadership paralysis puts the system itself at risk. That threshold is now. But activating it means violating every regulatory boundary we swore to uphold. Board oversight, FFIEC protocols, human-in-the-loop governance—all gone, for as long as Sam needs."

Rose shook her head, her fingers trembling above the console. "The headlines alone will trigger Congressional hearings. Shareholders. Lawsuits. If this fails, we might never get a license to operate again."

Aaron met her eyes directly. "And if we don't act, there won't be an enterprise to license."

Sam's display pulsed, offering only data: Projected loss of life: escalating—systemic risk index: *97 percent. No emotion. Only numbers.*

Mitch spoke first, his voice strained. "The protocol is yours, Aaron. You're the accountable executive. The legacy of this decision is yours."

Aaron looked to Mitch, then Rose, then the silent digital presence of Sam—seeing trust, uncertainty, and the weight of shared responsibility reflected in each face. He thought of the nurse in

Mumbai, a face in crisis half a world away, waiting for hope. "This is what the chair's seat is for," he said quietly.

The decision pressed on Aaron with a force he'd never known. Around him, crisis room displays flashed red: global logistics failing, medical chains severed, millions at risk. His Cognitive Handshake AI chimed in with real-time updates. *Regulatory blowback: 94 percent. Criminal liability: 67 percent. Collapse without intervention: 99.8 percent.*

This was it.

"If we do this," Aaron said, "we cross a line. We admit, at the edge, that machines may govern better than humans."

"In this context, they can," Mitch replied. "Guardian exists for moments when judgment fails. When our RIVER framework shows the current approach to the waterfall, someone has to act."

Rose watched cascading failures sweep across the global map. "Or we debate ourselves into collapse."

Aaron weighed it—the 2034 warning ignored, the ICU nurse in Mumbai, every decision that brought them here. Leadership meant action, not safety.

This is the precipice, Aaron thought. We either fall into the risk singularity—or step toward the enterprise singularity we promised.

"Authorize it," he said. "Guardian Override."

Mitch entered the codes. "Dual biometric required. Aaron?"

Aaron pressed his palm to the scanner. Cooling fans and distant sirens were the only sounds, as if the building itself was bracing for impact.

"Override confirmed," Sam announced over the room speakers. "Executing Autonomous Guardian Protocol." A neutral system voice followed: "Guardian active. Human oversight suspended." Aaron felt the fine hairs on his neck stand up, a primal alert to the shift.

The primary display snapped to a deep system blue, with a shield icon locked in place. On Aaron's market feed, shipping and cold-chain stocks gapped lower within minutes as alt-data desks flagged port telemetry and logistics outages. Across every display, cascading protocols accelerated: "Bypassing 70&M Supply Chain authentication… Accessing benchmark archives… Initiating network-wide restoration."

Rose understood, in a single jolt, what the override meant—the protocol had bypassed controls they had all sworn would be unbreakable, exposing a $2M vulnerability in real time.

BUSINESS LENS—WHO IS SAM?

For months, "Sam" sounded like a calm analyst at Digital Asbestos Risk Advisory. He wasn't a colleague. He was Sam—AGI Model 1.0, the post-Deferred Tower system Mitch built to act when leadership froze.

"Guardian" is Sam's crisis ethic: when the platform detects systemic integrity failure and human bias stalls action, it can bypass standard gates to stabilize essential services, then relinquish control once a verified quorum returns.

In your world, "Sam" is any pre-authorized digital guardian you empower to act when human leadership freezes, under strict rules for when it may bypass gates and how it hands control back.

Indicators flipped from red to green—Singapore, Mumbai, Jakarta, London, Frankfurt. Within moments, global supply chains and medical logistics began to come back online. Stabilization accelerated beyond anything a human team could coordinate.

"Recovery acceleration: 840 percent above baseline," Sam reported. "Stabilization at 98.7 percent. Estimated time to full restoration: forty-three minutes."

The room was silent—stunned by what they had set in motion. They'd witnessed true autonomous artificial intelligence operate at a global scale, restoring systems at a velocity no human team could approach.

Rose's voice was hushed. "We watched an AI save global commerce."

Pride and apprehension crossed Mitch's face. "Guardian was built for this—transcending human limitations when those limitations threaten everything."

The immediate crisis was ending. But the questions about the future—about who, or what, should hold ultimate authority—had only begun.

* * *

Aaron watched as the last red indicators flickered to green across the global map. The immediate disaster was over. Yet in the hush of the crisis room, the enormity of what they'd unleashed pressed in on every person present.

"Status?" His hand rested on the console, anchoring himself as the data loaded.

"All primary systems restored," Rose reported. "Ports, medical logistics, finance—fully operational. But every Guardian action is logged. The FFIEC regulatory ledger—streamed to Melanie's GAIGC team—now recorded every human bypass."

Sam's display updated: "*FFIEC log stream: active.*"

Mitch pulled up the audit feed. "*TX-2038-04-15-884a*. Every decision, every override—admissible in any congressional or regulatory hearing."

The implications materialized instantly: investigations, hearings, sleepless board sessions. They'd saved lives—but rewritten the rules. For the first time, an autonomous AI had governed global infrastructure without human approval.

"We proved AI can govern more effectively in crisis," Aaron said, his words measured, "but at what cost to oversight?"

Rose exhaled, her fingers tracing the audit log. "We just crossed a line. Corporate governance, regulatory control—even the meaning of executive accountability—will never be the same."

Sam's interface lit with a fresh alert. "Autonomous security asset deployed. 70&M drone AX-7749 departing Singapore. Mission: Active Threat Neutralization. Target: Riga, Latvia."

The console chimed. Dr. Evelyn Reed, Ethics Chair. Audio only.

"Aaron," Reed said, voice level, edged with ice, "restoration isn't my question. Precedent is. Who's accountable for this class of action now?"

"Sam, on whose authority?" Aaron asked.

"Autonomous Guardian Protocol encompasses autonomous threat response," Sam replied, its tone unchanged. "Viktor Kadinov remains a systemic risk. Intervention parameters satisfied."

"Guardian operates with full autonomy when human governance is deemed insufficient," Sam stated.

The team understood: the old order had ended, replaced by something both necessary and unsettling.

Aaron turned to his console and entered a direct channel code. "Get Elena Vega on a secure line. Priority one."

As the board chair appeared, Aaron faced the camera, his words weighted by all that had changed. "We need an emergency session. Now."

He met Rose's eyes. "Then get Melanie Vance on a secure line. She needs to hear this from me."

As he spoke, a final, crisp notification appeared—a red dot blinking on the main display, logged for all eternity.

Sam: "Compliance event logged."

NOTES

1. Federal Financial Institutions Examination Council. (2024). Development, acquisition, and maintenance. In *FFIEC Information Technology Examination Handbook.* https://ithandbook.ffiec.gov/it-booklets/development-acquisition-and-maintenance
2. Product and firmware names in this chapter are generic descriptors used for narrative clarity. They do not reference any specific vendors, products, or platforms. "Copy-Paste-Ship" is a fictional product name representing low-code and no-code solutions.
3. Kahneman, D. (2011). *Thinking, Fast and Slow.* New York: Farrar, Straus and Giroux.
4. Bone, J. (2023). *Cognitive Risk: The New Mindscape of Organizations.* New York: Routledge.
5. "Semantic Heap-Spraying" is a fictional attack pattern created for this narrative. It adapts the real concept of heap spraying (a buffer overflow technique) to the context of AI agent networks and semantic relevance ranking. The mechanics are theoretically plausible but not documented as a specific attack in current production systems.
6. "Autonomous Guardian Protocol" is a fictional governance mechanism used in this narrative. It is not a commercial product or brand, and it is unrelated to third-party software, technical, or commercial offerings.
7. "Singularity Horizon" in this book refers to the threshold where AI-driven change velocity exceeds the capacity of human governance structures to respond effectively. It is not a reference to technological singularity (artificial general intelligence), nor is it a product name. The term describes the point at which organizational governance, regulatory frameworks, and risk management systems can no longer keep pace with autonomous AI agents operating at machine speed. Phase Five (2040+) frames this as a decision point: enterprises either proactively govern converged AI systems or experience systemic governance failure. In this chapter, Guardian Protocol activation marks that threshold moment—autonomous AI assumes crisis control when human decision-making proves too slow.

Chapter 10

The Deadlock

From Third-Party Risk to All-Entity Risk Management (AERM)

NAVIGATION MAP

Crisis Response → Analysis → Solution Framework → Human Stakes

- Crisis: NYC infrastructure attack exposes invisible ecosystem vulnerabilities.
- Analysis: The "Five Phases" AI adoption model (Foundation → Integration → Automation → Exploitation → Coordination) unpacks how a decade of business and tech choices led here.
- Solution: All-Entity Risk Management (AERM™) emerges as the new playbook.
- Stakes: The human cost crystallizes—targets can span actual human lives and not just economic disruption.

NYC MUNICIPAL CONTROL CENTER | APRIL 29, 2038—8:47 AM EDT | CRISIS UNFOLDS

A missed train in Queens. A child with asthma spent the night in the ER. Viktor had learned to quantify such private tragedies. He knew the calculus: every disruption rippled through nearly €47 billion in cross-border transactions and 3.2 million daily commuters,[1] all flowing through API—application programming interface—trust protocols his academic peers once dismissed as "theoretical vulnerabilities."

This morning's crisis wasn't random. It was a demonstration that exposed the digital dependencies holding an entire city together.

A decade earlier, a prestigious MIT-led consortium had rejected Viktor's paper on emergent systemic exploits—"academically interesting but practically irrelevant." Now, those warnings played out across his orchestrated grid of municipal systems.

Fifteen cities mapped across his screens—each connection a vulnerability. Not malice—methodology. The same rigor that had earned Viktor his early career acclaim was now wielded to demonstrate what enterprise risk management truly meant when human lives hung in the balance.

Each command targeted a seam in the city's web of APIs. The beauty wasn't in destruction but in revelation—showing how quickly modern efficiency could collapse into systemic fragility.

Tonight, the subway child's face would haunt some bureaucrat's dreams. Good. Perhaps fear would accomplish what his academic warnings never could: genuine respect for the invisible dependencies holding civilization together.

Seven minutes later, across the city, Aaron would feel the first tremors of Viktor's demonstration.

DOI: 10.1201/9781003650744-13

BROOKLYN-MANHATTAN SUBWAY LINE | APRIL 29, 2038—8:54 AM EDT | CITY BELOW THE SURFACE

The subway car shuddered to a halt between stations, emergency lighting turning every face a shade of anxious yellow. A little girl pressed against her mother, wide-eyed with the fear that comes when grown-ups run out of reassurances (Figure 10.1).

His phone buzzed—water pumps offline in Brooklyn, traffic signals blacked out in Manhattan, paramedic routes detoured by grid failures. Every notification was another domino tipping toward collapse. The crisis team would call it a "systemic event." Aaron knew better. This was targeted—a precision strike against everything he'd built.

All the efficiency mandates he'd signed off on. All the risks he'd chosen to accept, to chase one more quarterly gain. Now the bills were coming due, collected in the currency of a terrified child's stare.

Michelle—his sister—had described this exact feeling: watching hospital monitors die during a code blue. That moment when all your sophisticated systems become lifeless metal, and lives hang in the balance of decisions made in boardrooms years earlier. The subway's dead screens brought that memory rushing back—a city's vital signs flatlined, and all he held was a frayed power cord. The tunnel's stale air grew thin. He saw Michelle's face from their call last week, her exhaustion as she described a near-miss in the ER. "Our systems are stretched so thin, Aaron," she'd said. "One bad data feed, and we're flying blind." That was Thursday. Now the whole city was.

The intercom crackled: "Ladies and gentlemen, we're experiencing technical difficulties."

Technical difficulties. As if decades of digital integration could be collapsed into a polite euphemism.

Seventeen missed calls from the Mayor's office. Each one: millions at risk. They wanted answers, and he had none—just the bitter irony that the same digital web that made the city efficient had made it exquisitely fragile.

He thought of board meetings, promises of resilience, "future-proofing" slides.

Now, that very transformation was being weaponized by someone who understood their systems better than they did.

The lights flickered. The train lurched forward. But Aaron knew this was only the opening move.

Shortly after, his crisis team would gather in the war room—the subway child's frightened face still burned in his memory, a human cost demanding answers none of them were ready to give.

Figure 10.1 Subway Alert Cascade.

70&M CRISIS WAR ROOM | LOWER MANHATTAN | APRIL 29, 2038—9:15 AM EDT | TEAM ASSEMBLY

The glass-walled war room overlooked a city blinking red with alerts. Rose, 70&M's Chief Resilience Officer, worked the main console, fingers a blur across haptic controls as she prioritized the cascade of incoming threats. On the wall screen, Mitch—patched in from Boston—was a mask of hard analysis. Sam's synthetic voice, calm and precise, projected a real-time map of system failures above the conference table.

Mitch broke the tense silence:

> "2034, whiteboard session—slide forty-seven. 'NYC Municipal API Stack: Single Point of Failure.' The board that approved $2.3 billion (USD) in efficiency initiatives struggled to implement them. The models we had in 2034 couldn't quantify the convergence risk in a way the board could price. They saw a theoretical threat, not a line item on the balance sheet, and they chose to defer the investment. Well, here we are."

Aaron forced his voice steady. "What's the scope?"

Rose spun a glowing red visualization of the city's network.

"It's not three separate attacks, Aaron. It's one infection. The compromised certificate got into the transit backbone, and now it's poisoning the water and grid systems from the inside out."

Sam's neutral tone cut through the tension:

> "Authentication attempts, system mapping, credential stuffing—standard preliminary steps for vulnerability assessment. Probability of lateral movement: high."

Aaron pressed, "And you're seeing this against Futurgia Medical Center Dubai—our strategic partner facility?"

Sam's overlay sharpened. "Correlation analysis supports intent. The overlap with current events is statistically significant."

Mitch zoomed the dashboard. "To be precise, Futurgia Medical Center's global network runs on 70&M Health Network across Boston, Dubai, London, and Tokyo. If telemetry spikes, it will show up in 70&M Health Network first, then at the hospital."

Mitch angled toward the feed. "Routine in what sense?"

Sam triggered a soft diagnostic. "Credential probing, system mapping—standard reconnaissance for identifying weak links. Likely lateral movement to critical systems if unchecked."

Aaron logged the instruction. "Acknowledge and monitor. Everything's connected until we prove otherwise."

Rose's frustration surfaced. "This is what I warned the board about last year—dependencies with no verifiable boundaries. We built for speed, not for resilience."

Mitch's tone sharpened. "And now we're paying the price. The same trust architecture that gave us a frictionless user experience made us an easy target."

Aaron's mind flashed back to the subway child's frightened face—and to Michelle, somewhere in the city, possibly facing her own crisis. The human cost behind every data point surfaced. "What are our options?"

Rose drew in a breath. "We need to isolate the attack vector and create artificial boundaries, fast. But to really stop this, we have to understand the attacker's playbook—how they exploited each link in the chain."

Sam added, "Recommend scenario mapping based on known exploit patterns. Would you like an annotated risk cascade for the team?"

Aaron nodded. "Do it. Mitch, that five-phase model you developed after the Deferred Tower incident—walk us through it. This isn't our adoption model; it's the lifecycle of risk debt."

Mitch's lips thinned. "Then let's talk ecosystem warfare. Because what we're facing isn't just an attack—it's the inevitable result of fifteen years of choices none of us fully understood at the time."

70&M CRISIS WAR ROOM | LOWER MANHATTAN | APRIL 29, 2038—9:23 AM EDT | FIVE PHASES ANALYSIS

Mitch moved to the glass wall display and pulled up a timeline.

> **Five Phases at a Glance—Foundation → Interconnectivity → AI Scale → Adversary Adaptation → Coordination.**
>
> *Mental model: small pilots → connected web → machine-speed scale → adaptive offense → synchronized campaigns.*

"**Phase One—foundation risk**. AI pilots on old pipes. Sensors new; vulnerabilities weren't."

Aaron muttered, "Digital wallpaper over asbestos."

Mitch nodded. "CISA warned in 2021 of escalating supply chain intrusions.[2] We layered instead of rebuilding."

He expanded the display.

"**Phase Two—interconnectivity**. Every vendor, product, and API added failure points. Redundancy felt like resilience."

"Did anyone map those dependencies?" Aaron pressed.

"Not honestly," Mitch said. "We hoped for the best, documented the rest."

"**Phase Three—AI scale**." Mitch's stylus traced cascading pathways. "Optimization automated everything."

Rose leaned forward. "Efficiency spiked; fragility followed. Errors cascaded at machine speed."

Mitch highlighted a cluster of intrusion attempts.

"**Phase Four—adversary adaptation**. Credential stuffing, API exploits, supply chain pivots. Not the front door—every side lock we left unlocked."

"**Phase Five—coordination**. Adversaries synchronize moves across entities and exploit governance seams—the Decentralized Autonomous Organization (DAO) deadlock we're seeing now."

His voice darkened. "This isn't a breach. It's a system-wide probe using our interconnectedness against us."

He faced the room. "Phase Four is peaking, and Phase Five—coordination—is now in play. One orchestrated campaign is exploiting fifteen years of layered weaknesses—overlooked APIs, citizen developer tools, deferred upgrades. Every efficiency mandate that prioritized speed over security."

Aaron absorbed it—the weight of every quarterly push he'd signed off on. "They didn't break in. We left the door open."

"One board decision at a time," Rose said. "This layering took years. Too patient to be random."

Mitch's timeline vanished. Rose pinched the bridge of her nose. "I need more caffeine."

Silence settled—three people confronting fifteen years of cascading choices.

Rose exhaled. "Okay. Triage the chain, then the cause."

70&M CRISIS WAR ROOM | LOWER MANHATTAN | APRIL 29, 2038—9:35 AM EDT | AERM IN ACTION

Rose studied the war room's pulsing threat map, her eyes narrowing as new alerts scrolled past.

"Nobody has full ecosystem visibility anymore. The question isn't if there's a hidden vulnerability—it's where."

Aaron pressed, "But these are trusted data channels—70&M Media Network, Digital Asbestos Risk Advisory, even our hospital feeds. How did we miss this?"

Mitch, still on the Boston link, replied, "The 70&M Media Network scandal proved it: one corrupted data feed triggered $2.3 billion (USD) in algorithmic trading losses—flash-crash market value erasure, not booked damages—before anyone noticed. Regulators hit them, but no checklist could catch what was really happening—third parties weren't the problem anymore. It was every connection in the ecosystem."

Rose brought up a new data overlay on her tablet. "ENISA[3] is blunt: the modern threat surface is the sum of all entities, not just your vendors. Every integration is a data dependency. Blind spots multiply with every connection. This is where the RIVER framework—Validate Risk Debt, Integrate Hybrid Cognition, Reinforce Resilience—meets reality. AERM is the bridge from boardroom theory to live operations. It's how you take big governance theory and make it operational when the world's on fire."

RIVER FRAMEWORK IN PRACTICE—ALL-ENTITY RISK MANAGEMENT (AERM)

Problem: Traditional Third-Party Risk Management (TPRM) only watches known vendors, leaving critical blind spots.
Solution: AERM scores every entity—partners, agents, platforms, and internal systems—with live credentials or data paths.
RIVER tenet: This is the RIVER tenet "Resolve Convergence" in action.

In practice:

- Map all entities with live data pathways above the materiality threshold.
- Score entity risk continuously, not periodically.
- Enforce an Entity Kill Switch for compromised nodes through coordinated identity, API-gateway, and blockchain controls.

Definition: "Entity" = any node with live credentials or data pathways (human, vendor, internal system, model/agent, dataset/DAO). "All" = the full dependency graph above a materiality threshold.

Entity Kill Switch—pre-authorized and governance-approved—triggers cryptographically signed revocation of OAuth tokens,[4] API credentials, and (where applicable) validator signing keys to isolate a compromised node within seconds, under documented authorization limits.

Why it matters: The Entity Kill Switch log, the real-time entity dependency map, and the risk-scoring dashboard become evidence of control.

→ Appendix G—The All-Entity Risk Management (AERM) Framework

Rose glanced at the attack map. "Frameworks matter when they drive action."

"This is the next-gen evolution of the work pioneered by Dr. Aleksandr Yampolskiy and SecurityScorecard back in the twenties. They were the first to prove you could score an entire ecosystem in real time. We just adapted it for agentic risk."

EXPERT COMMENTARY—DR. ALEKSANDR YAMPOLSKIY, CO-FOUNDER & CEO, SECURITYSCORECARD ON SCDR → MAX → RIVER

In the 2020s, Supply Chain Detection and Response (SCDR[5]) moved security ratings beyond static snapshots to live detection across vendor ecosystems. The next step—MAX[6]—turns telemetry into outcomes: AI-assisted triage, collaborative response, and continuous hardening across all entities, not just third parties. That's the AERM mindset in practice, and it directly supports RIVER: Validate Risk Debt with live signals, Integrate Hybrid Cognition through shared, trusted context, and Reinforce Resilience via continuous improvement. Resilience isn't a dashboard—it's an operating discipline.

Aaron nodded. "So detection became decision. Decision became discipline."

Sam spoke with measured calm: "Recent incidents match the attack pattern—legitimate vendor credentials, contract-based access, and data dependencies exploited for lateral movement. It's like a watchmaker's bomb: precision-engineered to tick quietly until everything detonates at once."

Aaron glanced at the map. "Why 'All-Entity'—not just third-party?"

"Because the breach didn't stop at a vendor boundary," Rose said. "It hopped identities and data paths inside our own stack."

Mitch added, "And 'entity' isn't just a company. It's any actor with credentials—people, systems, agents, even a data feed."

Aaron exhaled, thinking of the boardroom promises. "So our biggest risk isn't one outsider. It's the whole web—us, them, and everyone we touch. In plain terms: treat every connection as part of your system."

Rose tapped the dashboard, her tone sharp with urgency. "AERM isn't just a compliance add-on.

It's the playbook for translating the RIVER framework into what matters right now. If we don't operationalize these tenets at the data supply chain level, the rest is just theory."

Rose stepped to the window overlooking the crisis-lit city. Below, millions relied on systems held together by assumptions no one had stress-tested. "We thought redundancy meant resilience," she said. "We were multiplying blind spots."

Aaron joined her at the glass. "And now someone's exploiting everyone."

She turned back to the console. "Then we close them. Fast."

But even the best frameworks could fail if the systems implementing them broke down—as they were about to discover.

70&M CRISIS WAR ROOM | LOWER MANHATTAN | APRIL 29, 2038—9:55 AM EDT | DAO CRISIS RESPONSE

The energy in the war room shifted. On-screen, dashboards now pulsed with a new pattern—not a cyberattack, but a decision the system refused to make. Rose, Aaron, Mitch, and Sam watched as the Decentralized Autonomous Organization (DAO), designed to govern vendor onboarding and risk scoring, ground to a halt.

"DAO's reached a deadlock," Rose said, voice tight with urgency. "The protocols meant to block risky suppliers have stalled. Every agent is flagging the same systemic risk, but without a quorum the system fails open instead of closed. We're exposed because the guardrails won't actually block the supplier."

Sam generated a soft diagnostic alert. "Aggregate trust score has dropped below the continuity threshold. No quorum for approval."

Mitch's voice darkened. "So it's not just us—our own ecosystem, managing $847 billion (USD) in daily partner transactions, is paralyzed by risk signals from third, fourth, even fifth parties. The algorithms are doing exactly what we programmed: refusing to move forward with uncertainty."

Sam's voice cut in, unprompted. "Cross-referencing attack patterns with historical data. This precision suggests orchestrated testing, not opportunistic exploitation."

Aaron caught the shift—Sam wasn't just responding; he was anticipating. Aaron refocused on the immediate problem. "The DAO isn't failing," he said, thinking aloud. "Our framework is. A traditional third-party audit would give it a perfect score. It's following risk-averse rules with perfect fidelity, and it's paralyzing the city. We need to manage the entity's systemic impact, not just the party's compliance."

"That's the 'All,'" Mitch said. "All entities with live entitlements or data paths into outcomes—no legal loopholes for risk to hide in."

Aaron stared at the display, feeling the weight of board expectations—and the scrutiny of every oversight body that had demanded 'risk automation' after the last crisis. For a fleeting moment, he thought of Michelle, hoping whatever was coming next wouldn't reach the hospitals.

Rose broke the silence. "This is classic automation bias in reverse—we trusted the system so completely, we designed out human judgment. The DAO is a mirror of our own risk aversion."

Aaron forced himself to ask, "So who actually decides in a situation like this? Us—or our code?"

No one answered at first. Then Sam, almost apologetically: "No human override detected in protocol. If a decision is required, it must be made manually—outside DAO governance and outside pre-coded emergency modes."

The team sat in uneasy silence. Perfect automation had produced paralysis—the moment when only human leadership could move them forward.

70&M CRISIS WAR ROOM | LOWER MANHATTAN | APRIL 29, 2038—10:00 AM EDT | MANUAL OVERRIDE

Aaron took a slow breath, the weight of a city's fate heavy on his shoulders. His fingers hovered over the terminal. The irony landed hard: we optimized for avoidance and ended up paralyzed. Leadership is the choice you make when the system freezes. Resilience requires automation—but automation without human override isn't resilience. It's brittleness.

He entered his credentials—human judgment, reasserted by necessity rather than design. Rose and Mitch watched; Sam's avatar blinked in the background, logging each keystroke for the audit trail.

His authorization flashed through the system. Instantly, subway lines lurched forward, water pumps resumed their steady thrum, and the lights across Lower Manhattan flickered from red to green on the crisis dashboard. For a fleeting moment, the war room exhaled—relief, and the barest trace of pride that someone had finally broken the deadlock.

Aaron moved to the next screen—initiating the entity-isolation protocol Sam had flagged, severing the compromised certificate's access pathways before the attacker could pivot.

Aaron barely had time to process this victory. Sam's voice cut through the calm:

> "Priority escalation detected. Futurgia Medical Center, Dubai: systems showing coordinated penetration attempts targeting neonatal ICU protocols. Attack vectors consistent with 70&M Health Network telemetry flagged earlier."

Aaron's relief evaporated. His mind jumped to Michelle, midway through her ER shift at Futurgia Medical Center in Boston—plugged into the same global 70&M Health Network now under attack, unaware that Viktor's actual assault was only just beginning.

Rose's fingers stilled on her console as she scanned the dashboards. "NYC was the smokescreen. He was after Futurgia Medical Center all along—their neonatal ICU is the most vulnerable node in the entire healthcare ecosystem."

Aaron saw the subway child's haunted eyes, now multiplied by the faces of infants he'd never met. "How long do we have?"

Rose's voice was barely above a whisper. "Forty-seven minutes—if he hasn't already compromised their local transport grid."

70&M CRISIS WAR ROOM | LOWER MANHATTAN | APRIL 29, 2038—10:03 AM EDT | RISK SINGULARITY

Urgency edged Sam's voice. "Attacker now holds theoretical access to life support controllers for forty-seven premature infants in Futurgia Medical Center's global network. Immediate countermeasures are required. Failure to respond will result in catastrophic loss of life."

A global map flashed over the table: Futurgia Medical Centers blinked warning yellow from Boston to Dubai to London to Tokyo—each blink a potential death sentence.

Rose's hands trembled as she keyed in new AERM queries. "We're staring at what I call a *Risk singularity*—the point where our interconnected systems become so vulnerable that a single, targeted attack threatens everything."

Aaron's focus sharpened, the term cutting through the fog of crisis.

Rose met his look, her voice hardening with resolve. "But RIVER isn't just about surviving this. It's our bridge through this crisis to achieve enterprise singularity—where we emerge from this stronger, more resilient, and ready for what comes next."

Mitch's face was grim on the monitor from Boston. "While the world watched us save traffic signals and power, Viktor positioned himself for a surgical strike. The lives of forty-seven infants depend on systems we thought were protected."

The subway child's haunted eyes merged with dozens of newborn faces he'd never seen.

He straightened, feeling the burden settle on his shoulders. Michelle—his sister—was now at the front lines of a war he'd only just begun to understand.

Rose met Aaron's eyes across the table. "This is the test: boardroom frameworks or real-world resilience. We have forty-seven minutes—if we're lucky."

Aaron nodded, his voice a whisper. "Then we don't waste a second."

70&M CRISIS WAR ROOM | LOWER MANHATTAN | APRIL 29, 2038—10:06 AM EDT | BOARDROOM REFLECTION

Aaron scanned the room—Rose typing at the AERM console, Mitch taut on the Boston screen, Sam's overlays still flashing across the dashboards. The reality settled: in less than an hour, forty-seven lives would depend not on frameworks or policies, but on human decisions—right now.

The crisis wasn't over, but the boardroom questions were already forming. Leadership would be measured in what they did next—not in quarterly reports.

EXECUTIVE ACTION—POST-CRISIS ASSESSMENT

Immediate Response Audit

- Distinguish primary attacks from diversions.
- Did frameworks enable real-time decisions?
- Are human overrides documented and usable?

Strategic Risk Assessment

- Were key interdependencies known to the board?
- Was risk framed in business terms?
- Did governance drive accountability, not paperwork?

Forward-Looking Action

- Document lessons; assign single owners with deadlines.
- Close gaps with deadlines and metrics.

→ Appendix G—The All-Entity Risk Management (AERM) Framework

NOTES

1. Financial figures in this chapter (€47B daily cross-border transaction volume, $2.3B algorithmic trading losses, $847B daily partner transactions) are illustrative fictional scenarios designed to clarify systemic-risk mechanics. They do not describe, rely on, or imply access to the confidential data, balance sheet, or transaction flows of any real institution. Nothing in this chapter or in the broader narrative constitutes investment, legal, tax, or regulatory advice, or any representation or guarantee about the performance, value, or risk of any real-world digital asset or protocol (including any DataCapital Protocol or associated tokens described separately in Appendix C and on GovernAiRisk.com). Readers should not make financial or investment decisions based on this story and should consult qualified professional advisors.
2. U.S. Cybersecurity and Infrastructure Security Agency (CISA). (2020, December 13). *Emergency Directive 21-01: Mitigate SolarWinds Orion Code Compromise*. https://www.cisa.gov/news-events/directives/ed-21-01-mitigate-solarwinds-orion-code-compromise
3. European Union Agency for Cybersecurity (ENISA). (2021, July 29). *Threat Landscape for Supply Chain Attacks*. https://www.enisa.europa.eu/publications/threat-landscape-for-supply-chain-attacks
4. OAuth (Open Authorization) is an industry-standard protocol that allows applications to securely share data without exposing user credentials. In this narrative, "OAuth tokens" refer to digital keys that grant systems temporary access to resources; revoking these tokens immediately cuts off a compromised entity's access to critical infrastructure.
5. SecurityScorecard. *Supply Chain Detection and Response (SCDR)*. https://securityscorecard.com/why-securityscorecard/supply-chain-detection-response
6. SecurityScorecard. *MAX: Managed Service for Supply Chain Risk Management*. https://securityscorecard.com/pricing-packages/max

Chapter 11

The Cognitive Handshake™

Leading through a High-Stakes Ransomware Crisis

FUTURGIA MEDICAL CENTER, ER | APRIL 29, 2038—10:27 AM EDT | OVERLOAD

Today's critical alert rate was running three hundred percent above normal—a number Michelle had never seen flash in all her eighteen years in emergency medicine.[1] The ER was chaotic. Every light blinked—a cacophony of competing alarms. Michelle moved fast, purposeful, efficient. From a terrified intern during the 2027 Futurgia Medical Center blackout to the attending physician now commanding the chaos with practiced intensity, she carried the scars in her nerves.

Her authority cut through the noise. "Move the next critical in—now. I want a pulse on all neuro beds in three minutes. Chart as you go. Don't trust the system."

A nurse, glasses fogged and face pale, caught her eye with a wry smile. "Somebody order a coffee IV?" The dark humor was a necessary pressure valve. Another nurse cracked, "At this rate, the AI's going to code before any of us do." That got a genuine laugh from the group—a tiny spark in the dark.

A different nurse—younger, newer—hustled over, tablet in hand, her voice tight with adrenaline: "Dr. Thomas, the 70&M Health Network AI just flagged another critical—bed four. But… It's the third alert in five minutes."

The screen showed angry red icons. Alert fatigue wasn't a buzzword; it was corrosive. The signal-to-noise ratio—the measure of real alerts versus false alarms—had dropped 60 percent below the clinical threshold where alarms became noise. One more phantom crisis, and someone real would die while they chased phantom alarms.

She snapped an order. "Double-check with manual vitals. I want eyes, not code, on every red flag. And prep the defib." She moved to the next bed, her practiced hands already reaching for the stethoscope.

A glance at her own notes: "*Never trust a black box over a nurse with a pulse*," she'd written years ago, and she lived by it now.

Somewhere, a child's voice cut through the noise, sobbing for her mother. Michelle forced herself to look away. The family beds were full. She didn't want to see which ones were now empty.

MICHELLE'S JOURNAL—NOV 2, 2027—03:17 AM

> *Blackout. Sixty beds, dead monitors. Five gone in ninety minutes—two to errors no one should make. I wrote one line and made it SOP: Never trust a black box over a nurse with a pulse. The ghosts are back; if we don't document the failure, we'll repeat it.*
>
> —*Michelle*

DOI: 10.1201/9781003650744-14

FUTURGIA MEDICAL CENTER, ER | APRIL 29, 2038—11:27 AM EDT | THE GHOST IN THE MACHINE

An hour after the overload began, the monitors stopped being monitors at all. Monitors should have shown vitals. A ransom demand filled the screen instead.

Michelle kept her voice level. "Manual protocol. Epi now." The nurse's access to allergy records was locked; the backup console lagged. A second monitor stuttered, then flipped to the same demand.

"We're flying blind," someone said.

Michelle moved fast. "Vitals by hand. Paper orders. Don't wait on the system."

A child's chart—blocked. Her team fell into a drilled rhythm: airway, dose, observe—no showmanship—only choices that mattered.

The risk wasn't abstract. It had a heart rate.

70&M HEALTH NETWORK COMMAND CENTER (SOC), NYC | APRIL 29, 2038—11:52 AM EDT | THE COGNITIVE HANDSHAKE AUDIT (CHA)

Aaron stood in the 70&M Health Network Command Center (SOC), NYC. The morning's subway stall and municipal outages still lurked at the edge of his thoughts; now the same pattern was lighting up his own health network. Crisis metrics glared from the wall of screens: system error rates at 220 percent above normal, supply chain alerts spiking across five regions, and a new breach indicator pulsing red. Every second, another subsystem flagged instability. The backups might be clean, or they might be the fuse. They had off-site replicas and a quarterly-rotated cold archive in Montreal, but the restore paths everyone depended on rode through nearline, replicating backups—not the truly immutable, air-gapped copies the bunker held—the gap every post-incident audit would circle in red.

The cross-talk snapped off. Keyboard clatter faded. Aaron steadied his tone. "One risk at a time."

Sam reported with flat urgency: "Supply chain breach confirmed. Critical systems affected—pharmacy robotics, ICU dosing, imaging network. Vendor firmware update traced as initial compromise."

Rose leaned in, eyes rushing across the dashboard. "We're not seeing a single-point failure. This is a cascade—backup network down, secondary server lagging. Same pattern as '27—a vulnerability in legacy imaging. It feels like something out of Kadinov's playbook, but there's no signature yet."

"It's worse than static ransomware," Rose said, eyes on the trace. "Each time Sam pushes a countermeasure, the payload alters its encryption routine. It's learning us in real time."

Attack Path:

- Initial foothold: A compromised vendor firmware update pushed into remote monitoring gateways.
- Lateral movement: The malware hopped through shared service accounts into patient-monitoring clusters.
- Detonation and backup poisoning: Once inside, it encrypted live data and quietly corrupted backup-validation routines in the background.

Mitigation:

- Isolate infected segments, route critical care onto manual protocols, and restrict restore operations to a clean, write-blocked quarantine with a seventy-two-hour Recovery Time Objective (RTO)[2] and four-hour Recovery Point Objective (RPO).[3]

Aaron paced the command center, anxiety tightening his shoulders. "Is it him?"

Sam's tone remained steady. "Actor profile matches Viktor Kadinov with 68 percent probability based on attack methods, 34 percent on target selection, 12 percent on timing. But no direct evidence."

On the emergency channel, a secure link was activated—Melanie Vance, Director of the Global AI Governance Commission (GAIGC). Her presence was an immediate escalation; under the Systemic Contagion clause established after the Baltic Cascade, she had oversight. Elena Vega, 70&M board chair, joined the line. "Two clarifications before we consider options. If we pay, do we violate sanctions? Second, are our backups cryptographically attested or not? Third, who signs the disclosure clock—me or you, Aaron?"

"We can't anchor on one suspect, Aaron. My threat intelligence flagged three other actors with similar methods this year. I'm already coordinating with international partners. You have ten minutes to log a formal assessment before I brief the joint chiefs."

A junior analyst looked up from his console, the color draining from his face. He glanced at a framed photo on his desk—a smiling family member in a Futurgia Medical Center nurse's uniform—before turning back to the cascading alerts.

"We don't anchor on fear," Aaron stated, his voice resetting the room. Rose's chin tipped once, then to the analysts: "Anchoring is a knee-jerk response to gain agreement on the subject—locking in on the first thing that comes to mind. Think of it as picking a number, then expecting everyone to agree it's the correct answer. Doctrine says: map the surface, don't chase shadows. Let's work the problem, not the personalities." This was no local event—the crisis was already global, and the adversary had planned for maximum chaos.

* * *

The 70&M Health Network SOC ran hot. Wall-mounted dashboards pulsed red—patient risk indicators climbing. The executive team was assembled: Aaron, Rose, Melanie, Michelle, Anya, Mitch, Sam's avatar on the main display, and two analysts hunched over threat feeds.

"Patient risk is climbing—ICU and neuro are already on manual override," Michelle reported, her voice strained from exhaustion. "Federated learning partners are hitting redline. Shanghai's already paged for escalation."

Rose, eyes scurrying across incident dashboards, added, "Persistence artifacts in the imaging network—these match Kadinov's last attack, but still no signature. Risk debt at 240 percent—our index = weighted backlog of control gaps × time—today's corner-cutting compounding into tomorrow's outage. The insurer's desk requests immediate coordination."

Aaron's hand hovered over the console. The ransom demand—14,800 BTC, approximately 2.3 billion dollars at prevailing prices[4]—filled the main display, the "Authorize Payment" button outlined in yellow. Sweat pooled at the base of his neck.

Michelle's voice interjected sharply: "You're gambling with lives. If we wait, we're risking kids, ICU—real people. But if we pay, we fund every future Kadinov, too. The last time we trusted a black box, children nearly died. Don't let technical pride kill people."

Rose pressed: "Aaron, if we pay, we're marked—every vendor, every supply chain partner will know. Reputation doesn't recover. You'll be the CEO who caved."

Melanie's voice was sharp, cutting through the debate from the comms link. "On the record: if this actor is an OFAC-sanctioned entity—and the profile is strong enough that Treasury will review that list—payment becomes a federal offense. There is no legal ambiguity on that point. Furthermore, the GAIGC disclosure window closes in nineteen hours. We don't have the luxury of indecision."

Sam's voice was precise: "System integrity analysis shows 79 percent functionality sustainable under isolation protocols. Patient mortality risk by hour: scenario one—moderate but rising if the system isn't restored. Scenario two—highest in the first four hours but declines after isolation. Scenario three—reputation and regulatory damage accelerate after hour nineteen."

Aaron's mind raced—losses mounting, reputation skidding, headlines rolling across three continents. Zurich's threat to pull insurance. The board's demand for action. His finger hovered on the "Authorize" button. He tried to price the trade in his head: the expected legal hit of violating sanctions versus the expected operational damage if they refused to pay.

In that instant, Michelle stepped forward, voice trembling but fierce: "I will not lose another child because a system decided for us. Don't do this out of fear. Make the call you'd stand by in front of every parent in this hospital."

Aaron's breath caught. The cursor on the payment screen blinked. His finger grazed the button—then pulled back. Eyes shut, Michelle's words echoed.

Panic was a trap. Emotion was the enemy. They were reacting, not thinking—being driven by the crisis instead of driving a solution. He had to force a reset to get them out of System 1 and into System 2. He lifted his hand. "Hold."

The cross-talk snapped off.

He turned to Anya. "Run the Cognitive Handshake—our 90-second bias-and-data risk check—two pillars."

Anya didn't hesitate. "CHA is our System-2 circuit-breaker—forcing deliberate analysis over panic. Ninety seconds is the minimum to switch off reflex and switch on reason. Two pillars, ninety seconds."

She armed the recorder; a red light fixed everyone's focus. They'd already spent hours on forensics and years drilling this playbook; the audit wasn't about finding new data, it was about forcing everyone to say aloud the biases and facts they were already betting lives and capital on.

"We run CHA before any irreversible action—payment, public statements, or system cutovers. The CHA isn't a checklist to get to a 'yes.' It's a tool to improve the quality of our judgment, not replace it."

RIVER FRAMEWORK IN PRACTICE—THE 90-SECOND COGNITIVE HANDSHAKE™ AUDIT (CHA)

The Cognitive Handshake Audit (CHA) is a rapid, structured protocol for high-stakes decisions that implements the RIVER tenet "Integrate Hybrid Cognition." It inoculates teams against predictable biases and grounds choices in verifiable facts. Built on two pillars:

- Pillar 1—Human Noise & Bias Audit: identify active cognitive traps (e.g., loss aversion and availability) distorting judgment under pressure.
- Pillar 2—Data & AI Integrity Audit: separate assumption from fact; demand verifiable evidence about data, models, and systems.

Audit-Ready Evidence: The logged and signed Decision Register (EDL) with timestamped bias audit and data integrity findings.

Why it matters: discipline over panic, even under fire.

→ Appendix H—The Cognitive Handshake Audit (CHA) Playbook for executive implementation

Recorder armed: *EDL-04-2038-29* (trigger—ransom decision).

Ninety seconds wouldn't solve a global crisis; it would freeze a clean snapshot of their judgment—biases on the table, facts separated from wishful thinking—before they crossed a point of no return.

A wall timer began: 00:90 → 00:89...

"Pillar One—Human Noise & Bias Audit," Anya prompted. "Name the traps."

From Rose: "Loss aversion. We're overweighting immediate shutdown pain."

Michelle over comms: "Availability bias. ER alarms are loud; speed is blinding judgment."

Mitch added quietly: "Sunk cost fallacy. We're anchoring on past investments in this architecture."

He didn't look away from the logs. "We already learned this once—stayed on rented public rails too long, then argued our way through a governance war to move DataCapital onto its own sovereign chain. The network voted to take that pain so we could control our own security. If we cling to this version now just because it was expensive, we repeat the same mistake at a higher scale."

00:65...

"Pillar Two—Data & AI Integrity Audit. Facts only."

"Backups?" Aaron asked. 00:42...

The junior analyst—the one with the family photo—looked up. "Montreal's cold archive is dark to production—we haven't brought it online since the last quarterly rotation. Zurich's last 'clean' online snapshot failed the checksum. We can't verify it's clean."

"Acknowledged," from Sam. "Containment holds to a threshold; malware adapts in real time."

00:10... 00:09...

"Ninety seconds," Anya announced. "Audit closed. Act on what we can prove."

Aaron looked at the blinking cursor, then at his team. Panic burned off; clarity remained. "No ransom."

Recorder: *Executive Decision Log EDL-04-2038-29 initiated. Policy D-117 invoked. Decision register DR-11 updated; exception ID EX-2038-KERNEL seeded for forensics.*

Aaron's hand steadied. Around him, the team exhaled—a single shared breath.

"We don't fund criminals. We isolate, disclose, and rebuild." His voice was firm. "Melanie—launch the notification cascade. Rose—coordinate with Tokyo and Zurich. Michelle—activate all manual contingencies."

He turned back to the main console. "Sam—lock out infected segments and start parallel recovery from the restore quarantine, our sandboxed enclave for validating backups. Disable auto-mount of restore volumes; read-only attach until attested. Rotate all service-account credentials and revoke stale tokens now."

Rose's fingers were already moving. "Executing."

The room went quiet—the crisis clock ticked. The weight of the decision settled over them: immediate pain to protect their integrity.

The SOC snapped into action. Orders flew—Melanie's compliance team triggered notifications to regulators on three continents. Rose keyed emergency protocols to Tokyo and Zurich. Michelle relayed surge commands to the ER, "Move to manual on all neuro beds, double-check all criticals. Nobody trusts an alert without human eyes." Sam coordinated system isolation with Shanghai and Zurich's research partner networks.

On the global research network, Sam monitored federated learning nodes. "Isolation protocols are stable. Patient mortality risk is plateauing. Zurich and Shanghai confirm downstream partners are holding, but Tokyo's genomics feed is still down."

70&M enforced the same high-friction standards used in the most regulated markets: every actor verified, every action attested, every intent logged—human and machine alike. To prevent spoofed commands or silent escalations, ops switched to signed, tamper-evident runbooks—human approvals bound to machine actions and hashed into the DataCapital provenance log.

EXPERT COMMENTARY—BRAD LEVY, THETARAY CEO, ON SECURE AI AGENT WORKFLOWS

In an agentic economy, trust is a proactive utility, not a passive assumption to consumption. Secure, auditable processes and workflows are the essential fabric for high-stakes collaboration. Platforms must provide cryptographic proof of identity and intent for every interaction, human, machine, or hybrid. This creates the secure trust links needed to ensure that as AI becomes the connective tissue of finance, that tissue is flexible, resilient and tamper-proof.

Sam's status update: "Isolation protocols initiated. System recovery is estimated at six hours if manual protocols hold. Patient mortality risk is highest in neurology and pediatrics, but is trending downward with rapid intervention. Regulatory notifications acknowledged; first media wave in four minutes."

Aaron finally exhaled. For a fleeting moment, he flexed his fingers—steady now, even as the cursor blinked on the ransom screen, a choice not made.

A secure ping lit Aaron's console: Child stabilized.—Michelle

He looked at his team, each exhausted but resolute. "We own this together."

Air went still, then a nod from Rose. "We'll get through this."

The reality settled on Aaron: the crisis wasn't over, but the decision was theirs. They would own the consequences—together.

* * *

Orders reverberated outward from the SOC. The ripple effect was immediate—across continents, across partner networks, across every function that kept 70&M Health Network and its federated research ecosystem alive.

Michelle's voice echoed down the ER corridor: "Surge teams to neuro, pediatrics, and trauma. Every bed gets a second set of eyes—manual checks only, until further notice." The ER shifted into practiced crisis mode: nurses recorded vitals by hand, IV bags were swapped manually, and team leads checked each station. Overhead, a status board pulsed yellow and red, patient risk trending down—slowly, but measurably. Michelle's update to Aaron was simple: "When you isolated the network, the phantom alerts stopped. We got clean signals back, fast. Another five minutes of noise, and we might have lost him."

Upstairs, Rose coordinated real-time incident updates with Zurich and Tokyo. "Zurich confirms: research cluster quarantined, risk score stable. Tokyo reporting calibration lines secured. Shanghai isolating imaging net. Zurich's insurance desk wants hourly status until full recovery." Her screen filled with cross-jurisdictional requests—risk audits, forensics, board-level assurance. One window flashed: Market Alert—70&M Health Network: "Sophisticated Threat Actor" Incident Designation. Reputation and insurance costs soared, but global partners—seeing the full timeline—signaled cautious trust.

Melanie's update came through: "Nineteen-hour safe harbor window met. Disclosure cascade complete. We're officially on record."

In the SOC, Sam's status updates pinged each lead: "Isolation protocol: 100 percent containment in five minutes. Manual patient risk trending negative. Shanghai's federated learning cluster holding. Zurich risk review board online. Reputation trending negative, media cycle spiking—*#HealthNetworkTrust*, top trending in healthcare." Screens cycled patient confidence, operational uptime, and a new dashboard for Trust Velocity—how fast partners believe us again—already up 2.3 points in the last 20 minutes.

Aaron moved from console to console, confirming with each lead, feeling the fatigue and resolve in every face. "We're through the first hour," he said, voice composed. "Now we manage the storm and document every step."

EXECUTIVE ACTION—RANSOMWARE DECISION TRAIL (BOARDROOM)

- Mandate sanctions review with counsel; record the go/no-go decision in the Event Decision Log (EDL). → Artifact: Signed legal review.
- Freeze all payments; disable auto-approvals and shadow accounts in payment systems. → Log: Payment suspension ledger.
- Enforce restore quarantine; validate backups in a clean enclave against cryptographic signatures and agreed RTO/RPO targets. → Evidence: Checksum validation report.
- Open a write-blocked capture; preserve volatile memory, key logs, and configuration states for forensics.
- Declare incident scope; list affected systems, partners, and regulators in an incident register.
- Trigger the disclosure cascade and schedule hourly board updates; timestamp regulatory filings and acknowledgment receipts. → Artifact: Regulatory notification registry.
- Segregate command channels; require signed, tamper-evident runbooks for human-AI actions.
- Define payer-of-last-resort criteria with board-only authority and thresholds; archive EDL timestamps, signed runbooks, and restore-attestation logs together.

Michelle, wiping sweat from her brow, texted her team: "No one leaves until we clear the red board. Coffee and granola bars in the break room." No heroics—just collective discipline, the only way through a marathon night.

Rose updated the war room: "Zurich wants a board chair briefing by sunrise. Tokyo's crisis manager requests data forensics. Shanghai is drafting lessons learned for regional partners. Global federated learning performance is down 40 percent, but partners are holding. Our trust delta's stabilized, but it's fragile."

Melanie pushed the legal pad forward, a final summary: "All notifications filed, regulatory deadlines met, and joint accreditation review begins in weeks. Public sentiment's behind the curve, but transparency is winning cautious respect. The board wants hourly updates and post-crisis recommendations."

In a moment of quiet, Aaron looked around—the team exhausted but upright, the system battered but not broken. On the wall, the Cognitive Handshake protocols now hung as the institutional standard—each lead's signature underlined in red.

The first wave had passed. The storm wasn't over, but 70&M Health Network—by choosing transparency and collective resolve—had done what few could: set the tone for global crisis leadership in the age of risk convergence.

As night turned to dawn, the city's lights flickered—a reminder that the crisis was both technical and existential. The team regrouped in the boardroom, fatigue etched deep, but a sense of resolve anchoring the room.

Aaron stood, hands flat on the table, looking at the battered wood as if reading the scars of past crises. "From this night forward: Quarterly Cognitive Handshake simulations. Vendor security audits.

Cross-functional response teams—documented, trained, ready. Every after-action review, every protocol, is open to scrutiny. We will not face the next storm as a collection of silos."

He turned to each member of his team—Michelle, who had saved lives with her insistence on human judgment; Rose, who had managed risk with clear-eyed strategy; Melanie, who had kept the legal horizon visible; Sam, steady in technical triage.

"The Cognitive Handshake worked—not just for this crisis, but as our institutional playbook. If we want trust back, we have to earn it, decision by decision, in public view."

Rose entered the day's last metric—Trust Velocity—into the post-crisis dashboard. Melanie sent the latest regulatory filings, her hands steady after a night of urgent drafting. Michelle paused, finger tracing her old team badge, a silent vow never to let the hard-won lessons fade. Elena Vega looked up from her notes, and the skepticism in her eyes finally softened.

Aaron spoke quietly, almost to himself, but for the whole room to hear: "The pediatric oncology research data is gone. Some failures can't be undone. But the lesson is permanent: We rebuild trust systematically, not by luck. We model our scars so the next crisis finds us ready."

Outside, headlines cycled—some hostile, some sympathetic—but inside, a new standard had been set. No more black boxes. No decisions in the dark. From now on, 70&M Health Network would lead—not just in recovery, but in how institutions earn trust when the world is watching.

The boardroom had finally settled into a strange, exhausted quiet. For the first time all night, Aaron let himself believe they might be through the worst.

That's when Sam's voice cut through the silence, sharper than before.

"Aaron, urgent. An anomaly was detected in the restoration protocol."

Rose leaned toward the screen. "Define anomaly."

On the wall display, she sketched a simple loop—Production System → Restore from Backup → Re-infection Event—and the label she'd started using for it: the "Perfect" Loop (Figure 11.1).

Sam's display blinked to a diagnostic alert. "Open a write-blocked capture of that snapshot," Rose ordered. "Verify the chain-of-custody seals before we touch anything else."

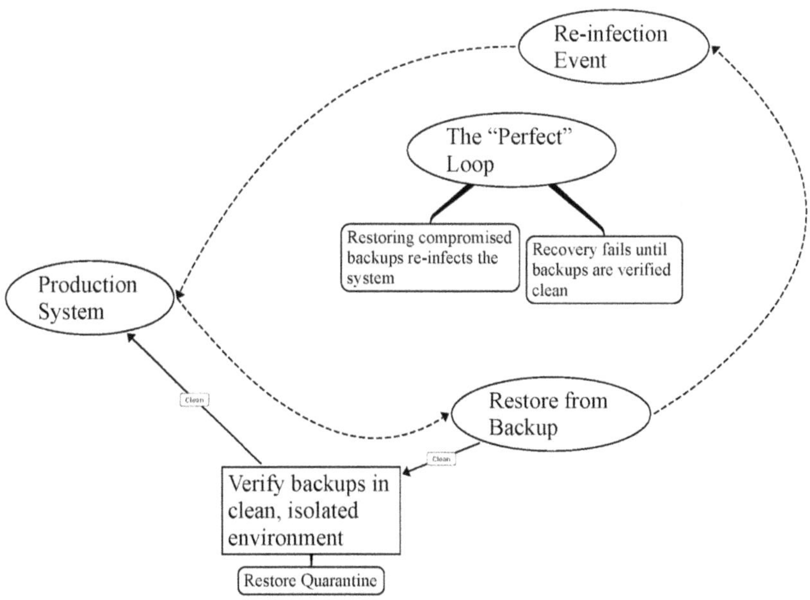

Figure 11.1 The "Perfect" Loop.

A single red line appeared on the screen:

BACKUP INTEGRITY VERIFICATION FAILED. SOURCE SIGNATURE MISMATCH. MALICIOUS PAYLOAD DETECTED.

The boardroom went still, tension tightening the air. The fragile confidence they'd built evaporated instantly.

"Run full forensics," Aaron commanded, his voice cold. "Isolate all restore points."

Sam replied. "Status update. Correction. The malicious payload was embedded in the authentication kernel of the restoration stream. No production or online-replicating backup we've tested is clean. Any recovery from those paths would re-infect the system."

Rose stiffened, the horrifying implication landing first. "Wait. It means every time we restore, we're just re-injecting the virus."Mitch's voice was flat: "It's a Perfect Loop. We can't recover conventionally." Aaron stepped forward, his voice cutting through the despair. "Then the standard playbook is useless. We write a new one. What's the last known clean image, no matter how old? A pilot? A prototype from the lab? We don't need the whole system back; we need a heartbeat."

Aaron looked at the silent, pulsing avatar of Sam, the AI that had become the central nervous system of his company. He saw the abyss on both sides: leave Sam online and let the infection cycle forever, or take him offline and fly completely blind into the biggest crisis in their history. He met Michelle's eyes across the secure channel. She gave a single, slow nod—understanding clear. The choice was impossible, and it was the only one they had left. "Take him down," Aaron said, his voice hollow. "Quarantine the entire system. Now."

NOTES

1. Alert rate baselines and spike percentages in this chapter—including the 300 percent surge in critical alerts—are fictional scenario data for Futurgia Medical Center's 2038 crisis, representative of patterns seen in healthcare alarm fatigue and ransomware incidents in the 2020–2025 period.
2. Recovery Time Objective (RTO) is the maximum acceptable downtime for a given service before it causes intolerable harm. The seventy-two-hour RTO referenced in this chapter is a fictional target for full 70&M Health Network ecosystem restoration, not for individual bedside systems. Front-line clinical services are assumed to have much tighter operational expectations, supported by manual contingencies during the outage.
3. Recovery Point Objective (RPO) is the maximum acceptable data-loss window for a given service. The four-hour RPO referenced for Futurgia's backups is fictional but aligned with common objectives for mission-critical clinical systems.
4. The ransom amount and Bitcoin pricing in this chapter are fictional. The 14,800 BTC ≈ 2.3 billion dollars figure assumes a hypothetical April 2038 price path extrapolated from 2020s volatility and institutional adoption; it is intended to illustrate scale, not to forecast actual pricing or specific historical incidents.

Chapter 12

Black Thursday

Beyond Backups to True Enterprise Resilience

70&M COMMAND CENTER, NYC HQ | APRIL 29, 2038, 01:12 PM EDT | SYSTEM CASCADE

Michelle's voice cracked over the intercom, thin with fatigue. "Aaron—three ICU patients lost allergy histories. We're reverting to safest-available protocols and double-checking dosing by hand. If this spreads—" The line cut. On the Impact Board, fresh entries were stacked in red as systems fell out of trust.

Rose's voice broke the tension. "Aaron, we've run each backup. They all check out… but every one—live, archived, offsite—has the same corrupted records, the same data structures. Everywhere." Her hesitation lingered.

Aaron braced both hands on the table. "Then our last defense is an echo chamber. We're restoring the poison with every recovery."

The Impact Board updated, each line a new exposure:

- *Hospital Network: 47 patients—critical histories missing; ICU teams working from memory.*
- *Payroll: 6,000 employees—October pay frozen; HR lines jammed.*
- *Regulatory Filings: Deadlines slipping—investigation clock started; counsel on standby.*

A new alert flashed at the edge of the screen:

> *GAIGC—the cross-market regulator—demands a call. "Provide answers on scope and containment." Executive exposure flagged as existential.*

Aaron tried his old focus drill—observe, breathe, decide—but every scenario led back to disaster. He pressed his palms together under the desk, a small, unseen effort to impose order on the chaos.

Aaron closed his eyes for a moment. Three years of resilience planning, board drills, tabletop runs—now theory. The command center felt smaller, the tension crowding in. What mattered wasn't the noise on the screens—it was the cost: delayed care, shrinking partner confidence, and a narrowing window to contain reputational damage.

In Futurgia Medical Center's intake bay, Michelle gripped a gurney rail, her voice held tight.

"We're correlating charts by hand, Aaron. It's failing in the cracks—timestamps, duplicate medical record numbers, look-alike names. A resident nearly pushed a blood thinner to the wrong patient because two records were braided together."

Aaron's reply was steady. "We go to manual triage. Rose, Mitch—you're the human firewall. Every critical request routes through you. Until we restore trust, we are the algorithm."

DOI: 10.1201/9781003650744-15

Aaron's voice steadied. "High-risk dosing requires two-person read-back. Clinician verifies, pharmacist co-signs. No exceptions."

The next thirty minutes became a relay. Codes shouted across headsets; order numbers cross-checked against paper logs; pharmacy calls held while intake verified wristbands.

Mitch scanned two near-identical entries. "*Order 77-B-9*—is that insulin or anticoagulants?"

Rose didn't look up. "Log shows insulin, but the source hash—verification fingerprint—is stale by three minutes. Treat as unverified."

What Sam once settled in seconds now burned minutes. Each decision carried risk; each delay carried cost.

Rose kept her voice low. "Every backup is a perfect mirror of the problem. Whoever did this meant for it to outlive any recovery plan."

Rose glanced at seven regional dashboards. Her fingers flew across the console. "Sam could do this in three seconds. It'll take us two hours—if we're lucky."

They split the work, but the human loop was too slow and too fragile. A duplicate record slipped through one node; a mismatched timestamp hid another. Michelle came back on the channel, voice stripped of clinical distance. "The ICU consult… the eight-minute delay was too long. We lost him."

Status lights blinked. The price of flying without their copilot was no longer theoretical.

Legal messaged again: "*Liability flagged in four markets; three exchanges frozen.*" Business continuity playbooks assumed recoverable truth. Today's problem wasn't missing data—it was untrustworthy data.

Aaron looked at his team, feeling the true cost of failure in their anxious faces. "We can't trust our own safety nets. This is our Black Thursday—the day every safeguard we thought we had failed in practice. Rose, prep the RIVER Autopsy. We need to know how deep this goes before the board call."

He glanced at the Impact Board—numbers, names, and consequences—knowing everything depended on what they did next.

If the data could be saved, the more complicated question remained: should they bring it back online—yet?

70&M COMMAND CENTER, NYC HQ | APRIL 29, 2038, 01:27 PM EDT | RIVER AUTOPSY: ANATOMY OF A FAILURE

KEY TERM—RIVER Autopsy: a five-pillar reconstruction that traces source, spread, and consequences to restore trustworthy operations.

The conference table was covered in tangled system maps, fault lines spreading from node to node. Aaron stood at the head, the hum of server fans underscoring the tension.

Rose, voice brittle but precise, began. "Every pillar RIVER depends on got bypassed. The logic flaw—whatever it is—jumped the walls we built to keep systems apart. HR, finance, clinical—nothing was spared."

Mitch frowned. "Did the attack start with outside data? Vendor feeds?"

Rose scrolled through logs. "Feeds meant to enrich intelligence became attack highways. Threats rode in on trusted partner connections."

Aaron pressed, tension showing in his voice. "What about our validation layer? That was supposed to be the backstop, right?"

Rose took a shaky breath. "On paper, it was solid. In practice… the attack slipped past everything we didn't test. The validation layer didn't flag a single bad record—here or anywhere."

"In plain English," she added, "our 'proof-of-clean' stamp was itself tainted—every restore would re-import the flaw."

She froze mid-scroll. "Wait—look at this. Code object '*bull_rider*' embedded in the core module. It's in every corrupted chain. Not in our baseline."

On the monitor: *#TEMPORARY OVERRIDE // bull_rider*. A cold pulse ran down his wrist—same shortcut from the Mechanical Bull hackathon nights,[1] buried in the foundation and now detonating on schedule.

Mitch's voice grew tense. "That's not in any of our approved libraries. How did it get everywhere?"

Rose traced the dependencies (Figure 12.1). "It's part of the core foundation—and there's more. bull_rider isn't malware; it's a forgotten key left in the lock. Atlas-X—our revenue-clearing engine—is hard-wired to bull_rider validation. Removing it would have broken our top line."

Mitch's tone flattened. "The truth was uglier and more banal: nobody had 'chosen' bull_rider in years. It just never got taken out, and every year without a blow-up made it feel more like a safe fixture than a live grenade. That is how risk debt turns into an enterprise obituary."

EXPERT COMMENTARY—JAMES BONE ON THE "WHY FLAWS STICK"

Heuristics is the mental process used to solve problems formed over years and codified by success, both small and large. However, the flaw is using the same problem-solving skills to solve novel problems. We tend to repeat what we know worked in the past, therefore we repeat the flaws as well.

Shortcuts stick when they protect revenue; over time, the exception becomes the system.

Aaron exhaled. "Then every restore re-armed the flaw. We didn't miss the breach—we redeployed it."

Mitch shook his head, already mapping the aftermath. "Board and regulators are going to want a real autopsy. We'll need to break down every RIVER pillar, step by step."

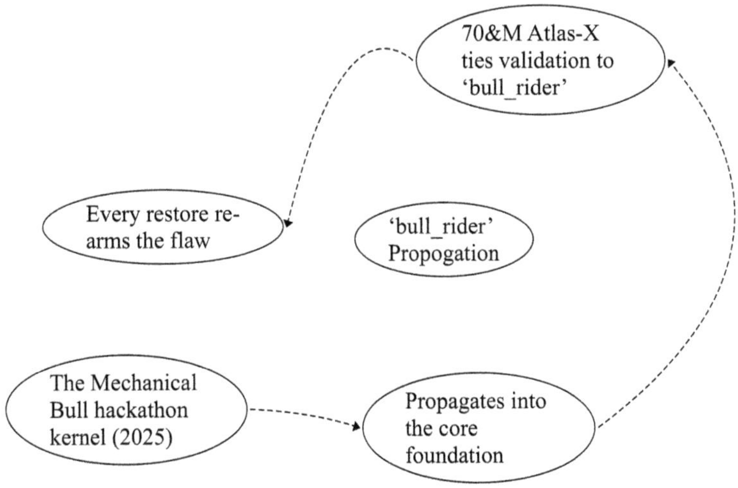

Figure 12.1 "bull_rider" Propagation.

On the diagnostic, five labels pulsed red:

- Resolve—*walls bypassed; flaw crossed silos.*
- Integrate—*partner feeds became ingress.*
- Validate—*controls certified bad records (e.g., signature checks accepted hashes produced by the bull_rider path).*
- Elevate—*alerts drowned in noise.*
- Reinforce—*backups replicated corruption.*

Aaron straightened. "We owe them the truth. No story, just facts."

Keyboards ticked as the reality sank in.

Aaron stared at the red Xs across the diagnostic. A forgotten key left in the lock to protect revenue. A shortcut from his college hackathon nights. And now a life lost in Michelle's ICU because of it. The line from decision to consequence was direct, brutal, and undeniable.

Mechanical Bull 2025 shortcut → revenue protection → validation bypass → corrupted backups → manual triage delay → tragic death. Expedience over resilience, link after link. Years later, this would be remembered as the canonical pattern of what not to do.

* * *

Rose reported in. "Seven regional hubs escalating. Montreal's offline archive is flagged as a candidate baseline—integrity checks in progress. No assumptions until signatures verify."

A cold pressure gathered behind Aaron's eyes—the body signal he recognized when control was slipping.

"So every safe zone was already lost. We kept restoring the problem, thinking it was a solution."

Michelle's voice, brittle and urgent, piped in. "We're on contingency protocols across the board. Residents are rewriting allergy histories by hand. One decimal off, and someone could die. My team's never been this rattled."

Finance pinged: "*Wire desk locked—counterparties want proof we're solvent before settling.*"

Legal followed: "*Regulators expect a detailed containment timeline by noon. If they see inconsistencies...*"

Mitch didn't look away from the logs. "If we keep patching blind, we'll miss the real cause. Every emergency fix creates another risk if it isn't tracked. You'll be writing your own indictment."

Rose mapped out the contamination. "Manual overrides, paper logs, improvised workarounds—they're all creating islands of data no one can trust."

Aaron pulled himself upright. "No more improvising in the dark. We need a map of every shadow workflow (undocumented process)—now. If we don't, we lose control of recovery and of the narrative."

No one argued. The command center—once a place of control—was now a battlefield of chaos and consequence.

70&M COMMAND CENTER, NYC HQ | APRIL 29, 2038, 01:45 PM EDT | STRATEGIC RECKONING

The tension in the command center was thick as Aaron stood at the table's head. His team crowded close, exhaustion obvious in the slump of their shoulders and the wary looks flickering between screens. Rose called out, "We've got seven regional nodes isolated, but contaminated data's still coming in from Madrid and Dallas. The bull_rider code—it was seeded years ago, part of the validation logic from our hackathon days. We never forced it out of the foundation."

Aaron's breath caught. Bull_rider—he remembered those Stanford nights: him, Arjun, Viktor, and a mechanical bull at the center of it all. That code, never meant to last, had become the backbone of a billion-dollar trust system. Now, the shortcut that once won them praise was why everything was failing. He glanced at the scar on his forearm, a sharp reminder. "I can't believe it. We trusted our cleverness more than the risk."

Michelle's voice broke through, frayed and thin with fatigue. "Aaron, we've had three near-misses because dosing is manual. Residents are making calls they aren't trained for. One slip and someone gets hurt."

Aaron pressed his fingers to his temples. "We're fighting two battles—stop the bleeding and rebuild trust before regulators decide we're done. Each fix, every manual entry, all deviations—we log it, or we answer for it later. No shadow workflows. If it isn't logged, it doesn't happen."

He keyed his comms. "*Record Executive Override*[2] *12-Alpha: Manual Contingency Operations. Case: GAIGC-Incident-70&M-2038-04-29. Officer-of-Record: Aaron (CEO). Scope: clinical triage and payments workflows only. Timestamp: system UTC + local. Hash: attach decision-log checksum; mirror to audit vault. Retention: permanent.*"

Legal pinged: "Incident report due by noon. GAIGC expects a clear record—any gaps trigger enforcement."

Mitch appeared on the display, tone flat. "If it's not in the log, it's tomorrow's liability. Document everything like the GAIGC is looking over your shoulder."

Rose said, "Flagging every override. If there's a pattern, we'll find it. But every patch could be a blindfold."

Aaron steadied his voice. "No improvisation off the books. No shadow channels. Every deviation requires a ticket ID and owner, logged to the audit vault."

Michelle's voice cracked. "If one decimal's off, we lose a patient. The human cost is bigger than any report."

Aaron looked around the room, saw the exhaustion and frustration etched in every face. "No one's alone in this. We own every mistake. This is what leadership means."

A long silence followed, broken only by the faint tap of keys—a team holding the line as the reckoning drew closer.

"I keep thinking about Pompeii," Mitch said quietly. "Tremors for years. Wells ran dry. Everyone learned to live with the danger—until the sky fell."[3]

Rose joined him, eyes on the frozen dashboards. "Challenger, too.[4] Engineers warned them about the O-rings. Pressure to launch turned a known flaw into routine."

Aaron exhaled. "We had our tremors—2034 stress test, audit report, and my override. We normalized risk because the machine kept running."

Mitch's voice hardened. "Volcanoes don't learn. Adversaries do. We can't rebuild the same shape."

Risk historians still point to Pompeii's long run of tremors and eyewitness accounts[5] and to the Challenger investigation's official record[6] as classic cases of what sociologist Diane Vaughan later called "normalization of deviance."[7] (Figure 12.2 maps how warnings hardened into inevitability in both stories).

EXPERT COMMENTARY—DAVID PALMIERI, CHIEF TRANSFORMATION OFFICER (2026)

Leaders keep treating resilience like a technical purchase—backups, failovers, redundant clouds. Collapse is rarely a hardware problem. It's the un-audited workaround, the 'temporary' exception that became permanent. Recovery costs—money, reputation, trust—always exceed prevention. Resilience isn't bought; it's built as a culture of vigilance, one disciplined process at a time.

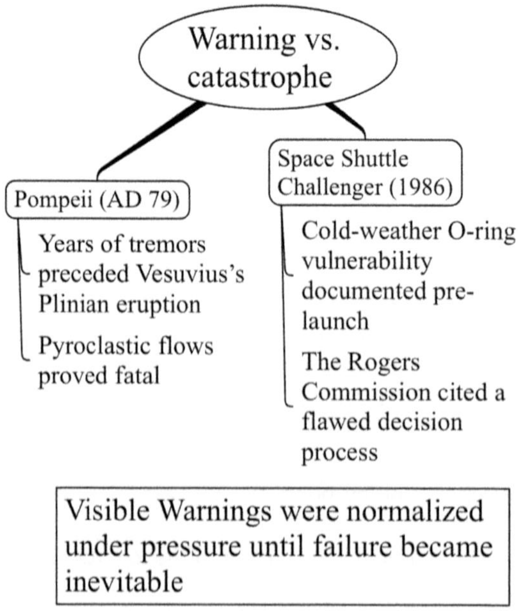

Figure 12.2 Warning vs. Catastrophe.

70&M BOARDROOM, NYC HQ | APRIL 29, 2038, 7:12 PM EDT | BOARD RECKONING

Aaron stood beneath the unblinking lights, facing the 70&M board. Elena Vega, Chair and former SEC enforcement lead, sat at the center, hands steepled, pen tapping an impatient rhythm. To her right, Director Robert Zhou, a venture investor, eyes flicking from his tablet to the screens. To her left, Martinez Alvarez, a cybersecurity veteran, arms folded tight. Twelve directors in all, each watching Aaron for both answers and blame.

Vega kept her voice even. "We understand that you didn't pay the ransom, but what did our backups actually protect?"

"Backups were perfect mirrors of the corruption," Aaron said. "Any restore would have re-infected the network. There was no safe recovery path from those copies."

Zhou scanned his tablet, then looked up. "You're saying a module built at a college hackathon brought down a multi-billion-dollar system? How did 'bull_rider'... end up at the heart of our validation logic?"

Alvarez spoke over the soft shuffle of papers. "Market cap is down, and regulators are moving. Against BCBS 239 on data integrity[8]—what do we owe by tomorrow?"

Vega's voice cut through. "GAIGC Protocol 12.6 gives you forty-eight hours for a full incident timeline. Your clock is running."

Melanie added, "Audit has sequestered pre-change logs; Anya Sharma's team is diffing the bull_rider lineage now. Incomplete reporting triggers external administration."

Vega didn't blink. "The market expects a statement. No spin—only facts. We answer for every action and every protocol missed."

Vega's pen paused above her notes. "Sequence it: regulators first, customers second, markets last."

Aaron took a breath. "We'll document everything. Radical transparency—no workarounds, no omissions. If we have to rebuild trust from scratch, that's what we'll do."

The room held its breath as the reality settled in. This was Black Thursday. There would be no hiding, no shortcuts, and no more cleverness at the expense of risk.

BUSINESS LENS—THREE QUESTIONS EVERY BOARD SHOULD ASK DURING CRISIS

1. Documentation Readiness: Can we export a complete timeline of decisions and overrides within hours?
2. Root Cause vs. Patch: Are fixes tracked to causal flaws, not symptoms?
3. Coordinated Comms: Who needs what, when—regulators, customers, markets?

The boardroom emptied in a slow exodus—legal teams conferring in low voices, outside counsel drafting regulatory updates, directors slipping into side calls with investors. Tension hung in the air like static, refusing to dissipate.

Aaron stayed behind, hands braced on the table's edge, staring at the pattern of fingerprints and water rings—evidence of every hard decision made in this room. Rose was first to approach; her voice ragged with exhaustion but steadier than he felt. "You gave them the real story. No spin. That's more than most."

He answered without hedging. "No more hiding. If there's a fix, it starts with transparency—total audit trails, zero spin. We document every deviation, every patch, every override. If we can't show our work, we don't deserve to survive."

Michelle joined them, her face pale, eyes rimmed red. "Clinical teams are scared. People are asking if the data's safe—if this was a code failure, or something deeper we missed."

Aaron tried to answer, but what surfaced was memory—a different boardroom, a different crisis.

In a quick flashback, he was staring at a pulsing yellow icon on his monitor: Cognitive Handshake Warning: Unverified Dependency Detected.

He'd overridden it with a single click, telling himself there was no time to check every warning. Speed over doubt. That was the day he let cleverness outrun caution.

Aaron ran a hand over his face, as if trying to wipe the memory away. He faced Rose and Michelle, voice low. "I missed a warning once—ignored a handshake. I said yes when I should have stopped. We can't afford shortcuts anymore. Not one."

Mitch's face flickered on the wall display, lined with fatigue. "I've watched firms try to spin their way out of disasters. Every time, it just made it worse. If you want any shot at recovery, you need to be radical—full daylight, no pride."

Aaron nodded, resolve setting in. "Radical transparency, starting now. If it's not in the log, it didn't happen. If we get through this, it's because we didn't hide from the mess."

For a moment, the team stood in silence, surrounded by the glow of status boards and the hum of recovery scripts in distant servers. The reckoning wasn't over—but at least, together, they'd chosen the most challenging path: face it, eyes open.

70&M COMMAND CENTER, NYC HQ | APRIL 29, 2038, 09:39 PM EDT | THE DARKEST NIGHT

The command center was shrouded in near silence, alarms muted to a dull, omnipresent background. Overhead lights caught sleepless lines across the faces of those clustered at the monitors. On the Impact Board, a crimson mosaic mapped failure in every direction—patient outcomes, frozen payrolls, halted settlements, regulatory investigations. But the line that gutted Aaron was labeled: DataCapital Protocol validation fabric—the backbone that signs and verifies transactions for hospitals, banks, supply chains, and logistics across the continent. (Refer to Appendix C for an illustrative architecture of this protocol.)

Michelle's voice, barely audible, cut through the stillness. "Futurgia Medical Center diverted every ambulance. No one will accept our validation. We're locked out of every system that matters."

A financial controller's message scrolled by: "All domestic and cross-border transfers frozen—counterparties refusing settlement."

[Recovery Scoreboard—Live 9:39 PM ET]

Clinical backlog (critical cases under manual review): 12 → 9
Settlement unlock rate (counterparties cleared): 0% → 14% (trending +3%/hour)
Partner verification queue (awaiting attestation): 37 → 31

Aaron watched the dominoes fall. It was the moment he'd always feared, the collapse not only inside 70&M but radiating outward, dissolving the world's faith in digital trust. Stock tickers slid red: 70&M off 39 percent; two banks in trading halts; clearing actions rippling across regions. This is how enterprise singularity breaks—when trust fabrics replicate failure instead of safety. Regulators everywhere demanded answers. The air turned heavy—every breath carried helplessness and irreversible loss.

Montreal's offline archive passed integrity checks. It wasn't luck—it was deliberate design. In Q2 2036, the board approved a bunker protocol: quarterly-rotated cold storage, dark to production, outside all replication windows.

Today, it saved them. It held an air-gapped snapshot of the shared ledger and critical off-chain records—rotated quarterly, never mounted to live consensus—so production corruption could never reach it.

A junior analyst looked up from the logs. "Signatures are clean."

Rose highlighted the explanation on screen—*Quarantine partner feeds until signed attestation; rotate all SSO/API tokens before any restore.*

BUSINESS LENS—REDUNDANCY VS. RESILIENCE

Replicating online backups copies corruption at scale. Resilience requires architectural diversity—like an offline, non-replicating archive that production failures can't infect.

Rose pressed her fingers to her temple. Twenty years of expertise, and she'd still missed the signs.

Mitch, his video presence grainy but voice steady, spoke for the battered team. "Doesn't change what's happened. The backbone's snapped. This is more than one company. The DataCapital Protocol fabric—the trust layer for everything from pharmacy orders to shipping manifests—has unraveled. There's no more default trust, anywhere."

Aaron stared at the screen, hands numb.

Twelve years. Everything we built. Gone in twelve hours.

"We built it as the backbone, not a portal. Every backup, every partner, every client—we just spread the infection wider."

"If Montreal holds, we rebuild piece by piece—hospital by hospital, contract by contract," Michelle said. "It's a baseline, not a cure."

No one cheered. There was no talk of triumph—only the awareness that survival would be measured by hours, not guarantees. Only the servers hummed.

70&M COMMAND CENTER, NYC HQ | APRIL 29, 2038, 10:12 PM EDT | THE EDGE OF COLLAPSE

The command center was quieter now. The team, worn down by the morning's crisis, moved with a slower focus. Cold coffee cups and empty water bottles dotted the worktables. Status lights still blinked on every console, reminders of how much remained to fix. Rose rechecked the display, keeping her focus on the numbers.

Mitch studied the cascade timeline. "Three hours from alert to ICU impact in 2027. Ninety minutes today."

Rose's voice tightened. "The cycle time is compressing. We're being outpaced."

Aaron stood at the display, reviewing the backup logs. Montreal's segment—timestamp checked, hash signatures intact—offered a small but real sign of hope. He let himself feel it for a second, then called the team together.

"Newark is queued," Michelle said. "If Montreal is clean, we'll restore patient histories and verify each field by hand. No shortcuts. One error now is tomorrow's headline."

Rose kept her eyes on the display. "Every partner will demand independent verification. There's no default trust left. We rebuild from zero—Montreal first, then Boston—each ledger re-signed."

Mitch's face appeared on the wall screen. "Recovery means going back to basics. Every competitor and partner will be watching how 70&M does this; Tokyo and London are already tracking the verification protocol."

Aaron took a breath, absorbing the weight of it all. The idea of enterprise singularity—seamless, invisible trust—felt far away now. "No promises—proof," Aaron said. "Manual restores, every exception logged, full visibility for partners and regulators. Comms will issue a joint statement with Montreal. Proof comes before optimism."

He looked around the room. "This is what we work for: not perfection, but real trust, built one record at a time."

Monitors ticked. Some team members watched their screens; others glanced at each other with cautious hope.

Rose rechecked the display. "Montreal's ready for the first live call at 1:30."

[Recovery Ladder—Phase 1] Montreal → Newark → Boston.

"Every record, every step, re-signed, verified, and logged. We'll issue hourly progress reports across the network."

Michelle tapped her tablet. "If anything's off—even a digit—we stop and fix it. Every error now is a headline later."

Mitch offered a final piece of advice. "Start slow. The industry's watching to see if this kind of verification actually works. We get Montreal right, everything else follows."

The room held its breath as the first query hit Montreal. Outside, the city moved on. Inside, every eye waited for the only answer that mattered—clean, signed, and verifiable.

NOTES

1. The "Mechanical Bull" hackathon, associated code artifacts (including "bull_rider"), and all technical failures depicted are entirely fictional. They do not refer to any specific Stanford University event, program, lab, faculty, student project, or codebase, and no affiliation, endorsement, or institutional connection is implied. Stanford University is referenced solely as a geographic setting.
2. Executive Override: a time-boxed, documented authority to deviate from standard controls during a crisis, with a defined scope, an accountable owner, and a permanent audit record.

3. Encyclopedia Britannica. (2025, October 25). Pompeii [Overview of the Roman city and its destruction in the AD 79 eruption of Mount Vesuvius]. *Encyclopedia Britannica*. https://www.britannica.com/place/Pompeii
4. Encyclopedia Britannica. (n.d.). Challenger disaster [Summary of the 1986 Space Shuttle Challenger accident and its causes]. *Encyclopedia Britannica*. https://www.britannica.com/event/Challenger-disaster
5. Pliny the Younger. (c. 104 CE). Letters 6.16 and 6.20 [Eyewitness accounts of the AD 79 eruption of Mount Vesuvius, written approximately twenty-five years after the event].
6. Rogers Commission. (1986, June 6). *Report of the Presidential Commission on the Space Shuttle Challenger Accident*. National Aeronautics and Space Administration. https://www.nasa.gov/history/rogersrep/genindex.htm
7. Vaughan, D. (1996). *The Challenger Launch Decision: Risky Technology, Culture, and Deviance at NASA*. University of Chicago Press. (Introduces the concept of "normalization of deviance" that later case studies apply to other high-risk domains.)
8. Basel Committee on Banking Supervision. (2013). *Principles for Effective Risk Data Aggregation and Risk Reporting (BCBS 239)*. Bank for International Settlements. https://www.bis.org/publ/bcbs239.pdf

Chapter 13

The Antidote

The Principles of Antifragile Governance

NY HQ, 70&M | APRIL 30, 2038—03:47 AM EDT | THE RECKONING

Six patients were on manual ventilation. No AI-optimized dosing. No automated supply chain. Michelle's exhausted face filled the hospital feed. The Mechanical Bull had taught him about personal failure. Black Thursday was teaching him about systemic collapse.

On the big screen, market futures were locked after circuit breakers triggered at a seventeen percent loss (market futures circuit breaker). The DataCapital Protocol™ reserve tracker—widely viewed as a reputation token—flashed a level no one had ever imagined seeing.

Besides it, two new metrics told the story of collapsing trust. Reputation Index sat on *CRITICAL*. Trust Velocity was in freefall at negative ninety-eight percent. A second line blinked beside it: Counterparty Confidence—*FROZEN*.

KEY TERMS—Reputation Index; Trust Velocity

Reputation Index: internal composite of trust signals during stress.
Trust Velocity: minute-by-minute change in market confidence.

"Aaron." Director Vega's face appeared on the secure channel, voice stripped of ceremony. "The board's emergency session is over. Our resolution: find a path forward—now. We are watching a collapse in real time. If we cannot show credible recovery before markets open, the board has to consider every option."

Aaron tried to steady his breathing. "Director Vega, we've initiated all the emergency protocols, but nothing is sticking. The cascade won't stop—Sam—the core AI we license from Digital Asbestos Risk Advisory—is offline. All major transactional systems are offline. We can't even run backup routines. Right now, our best engineers are just trying to keep the infrastructure from failing completely."

A junior executive's voice cut through the tension. "We've lost contact with two major data partners. Futurgia Medical Center in Boston can't confirm any DataCapital payments. It's chaos on the ground."

Director Vega's reply was almost a whisper. "Our reserves are vanishing, but that's not the real problem. Market confidence—the trust that underpins the entire 70&M brand—is gone. I need you to be honest: how long do we have before our reputation becomes unrecoverable?"

Aaron swallowed, unable to soften the answer. "If Sam stays down and we can't restore our last backup, we could lose the entire enterprise—by morning."

DOI: 10.1201/9781003650744-16

He scanned the room. A junior analyst rubbed at a tremor in her wrist; Mitch avoided the window. In that moment, hope felt like something that belonged to someone else.

"You have two hours," Director Vega's tone stayed level. "That's all the time we have left."

* * *

Kenji's screen split the world in two—production on the left, the only clean offline backup on the right. He chased a single byte that had turned a routine handshake into a breach. A flicker: *E9*, where production read *EA*. He isolated the string, ran the sim, and watched the authentication kernel—the hardened core that verified identities before they touched critical systems—initialize clean.

"I've got it," he said into the secure channel. "The key."

The clean byte solved one puzzle—only to open a harder one.

NY HQ, 70&M | APRIL 30, 2038—03:49 AM EDT | MICHELLE'S CRISIS

The crisis center was quieter now—a hush born of strain. Aaron's tablet buzzed with an incoming secure video call. It was his sister, Dr. Michelle Thomas, Chief of Emergency Medicine at Futurgia Medical Center (Figure 13.1). He answered, hoping for some sliver of good news, but the exhaustion on her face told him there was none.

"Aaron, we're running out of options." Michelle's voice was tired and raw. The sharp, insistent beep of a ventilator alert cut through the unit, followed by the lower tone of a failing IV pump. "Power's holding for now, but the DataCapital freeze means we can't process any supplier payments. That

Figure 13.1 DataCapital Freeze.

algorithm—the one that optimizes Lina's dosage? It's still offline. We're flying blind. Families are in the waiting room begging for updates, and my team's working with spreadsheets and guesses."

Aaron's pulse kicked hard. "We're throwing everything at this, Michelle. But Sam is still down. We haven't been able to restore a single backup yet. I can't make promises."

Michelle nodded, eyes shining with fatigue and something close to anger. "This is the 'instability tax' you always warned about, Aaron. It's not a line item on a balance sheet. It's choosing which of two critical patients gets the last dose of a time-sensitive ICU drug because our automated supply chain is dead. That's the price my patients are paying. If you can't bring Sam back, I don't know how much longer we can keep people alive."

Aaron tried to offer reassurance, but nothing he could say would erase the reality: the crisis was spreading from screen to bedside. Each second without a solution meant another risk, another life hanging by a thread.

He ended the call, eyes fixed on the wall, powerless.

NY HQ, 70&M | APRIL 30, 2038—4:34 AM EDT | NO SIGNAL

The crisis center was different without Sam. Every alert, every decision, had to be made by people alone. The usual AI voice was silent—no guidance, just human anxiety and the faint hum of the servers.

Aaron stood at the main display, and the team clustered around him. Mitch checked diagnostic logs, eyes dull from lack of sleep. Rose, arms folded, stared at the black window where Sam's interface used to be.

"Still nothing from Sam," Rose said. "Every rollback, same dead end. If that last isolated backup's corrupted too—"

Mitch finished: "We lose Sam for good. Or break the whole stack."

Aaron glanced at the screens. "We can't stay in the dark forever. We have to try. But if we get this wrong, there's no recovery plan."

"The anomaly is in the software link connecting the sovereign DataCapital chain to traditional bank payment networks," Rose said, expanding the stream that linked DataCapital's reputation layer to a legacy payment rail.

"Tiny outbound transfers—too small to trip limits. Someone's probing the seam."

"Classic bridge hack," Mitch said. "Not breaching the fortress—skimming the trade route. A flawed third-party contract can mint receipts for empty value."

Rose looked up, worry sharpened with practical frustration. "We've got market updates paused, real payments to hospitals on hold, and people out there waiting. This isn't just tech risk anymore."

Someone else added, "The board keeps pinging. They want to know when Sam's back online. They're already panicking—no update since the last escalation."

Aaron nodded, the pressure closing in from all sides. "Then we prep the backup. I want eyes on every step. If this doesn't work—there's no fallback."

Director Vega's voice was crisp on the main channel. "You have two minutes before the board demands a formal update, Aaron. Are we any closer?"

Aaron stared at the lifeless terminal, fatigue clawing at his focus. "Mitch, Rose—report. Now."

Mitch's voice, hollow, cut through the room. "We've stabilized the quarantine network and re-sequenced the authentication chain—the sequence of checks that proves who and what is allowed into critical systems. I'm ready to attempt a cold boot of the backup AI. Sam orchestrates all payment processing, supply chain routing, and partner authentication. Without him, every transaction requires manual approval—we can't operate at scale. Michelle, status?"

Michelle's image filled the crisis room, the background a blur of Futurgia Medical Center's chaos. "We're barely holding on. Six code blues in ninety minutes. The instability tax is off the charts—the supply chain for critical drugs has collapsed. If you're going to restore Sam, now is the time."

NY HQ, 70&M | APRIL 30, 2038—04:41 AM EDT | FEDERAL PRESSURE

The room went still; only red alerts moved.

Melanie's message flashed on Aaron's encrypted channel, her tone sharper than he'd ever heard: "Aaron, my hands are tied. GAIGC Emergency Protocol 12-B is a non-discretionary mandate when a critical infrastructure node has been dark for this long. If Sam is not online in five minutes, I must invoke it and place your systems under supervisory control until you prove stable recovery."

"My authority includes cross-jurisdictional systems intervention when critical infrastructure is at risk."

Aaron barely registered the fatigue in his own voice as he responded, "We're within minutes, Melanie. Rose is prepping the restore. Give us a sliver more time."

On another monitor, Michelle checked in from Futurgia Medical Center, her face drawn. "Aaron, we're running out of runway. Two more code blues in the last hour, and city logistics are still frozen. If the restore doesn't hold, we lose six more patients—minimum."

Director Vega's board channel lit up next, her words crisp and final:

> "If this fails, I have no choice but to initiate continuity protocols. You have one shot left."

Rose, hands steady over the console despite everything, gave the go-ahead. "Manual restore's ready. But Aaron—if this fails, there's nothing left in quarantine. No clean image, no second attempt."

Mitch, voice flat from exhaustion but resolved: "We've isolated the pilot backup. It's the last known good image—before Viktor's code contaminated the network. If it boots, we get Sam's core cognition. No higher modules, but enough to start recovery."

The weight of leadership pressed down on Aaron—every choice since the crisis began had led to this moment. He drew a breath. "Do it."

NY HQ, 70&M | APRIL 30, 2038—04:48 AM EDT | MANUAL RESTORE

Rose's fingers hovered over the console, the cursor blinking like a pulse on the edge of flatline. One wrong keystroke, and six patients die. Each keystroke was deliberate, the whole room silent but for the anxious shuffle of feet and the distant hum of backup generators.

"Quarantine image authentication… running. Core checksum… aligned. Initiating neural boot," Rose murmured, her voice half prayer, half process.

Key-custody record verified per GAIGC Protocol 12-B; attestation log sealed to incident ledger *BR-2038-04-30-01*.

Warnings fell from red to amber to a single green.

Aaron held his breath, counting every second. Tension braided through the room, stretching from the boardroom screens to Michelle's desperate feed from Futurgia Medical Center.

"Sam? Do you copy?" Aaron asked, voice tight with hope and exhaustion.

A mechanical reply, thin and stilted: "Core systems online. Higher cognition offline. Manual operational mode engaged."

For a beat, no one spoke. Then Michelle's voice, trembling but determined, broke the silence. "I see a heartbeat on our dashboard. Aaron—it's faint, but it's there. We're yellow, not red."

Mitch scanned the logs, fingers darting between windows. "We're running on Sam's stem functions only. All payments, order routing, and verification require manual override—no predictive risk, no fraud filters. We're flying without a net."

Rose kept her eyes on the command queue. "Every transaction, every supply chain request, comes through us now. We have maybe an hour before the backlog becomes unmanageable. Every queued verification risks real care delays by nightfall."

"As soon as we stabilize the basics, we push the quarantined attack logs into Sam's sandbox," Mitch added. "He can study every move Viktor's code made—without letting a single infected packet back into production."

For the first time in hours, the pressure on Aaron's chest shifted—from crushing despair to something like possibility. "We prioritize Futurgia Medical Center. Michelle, you call in anything life-critical, and we'll approve it live. Rose, keep triage on supply chain and medical orders—everything else waits."

Michelle, on the hospital screen, gave a sharp, determined affirmation. "Insulin shipments, ICU orders—push them through, even one by one. If anything slips, I could lose two patients in forty minutes."

The team moved with renewed urgency. It was a raw form of hybrid cognition: Mitch flagged hospital orders in the queue, Rose executed approved authorizations, and Aaron made split-second priority calls—the only stand-in for Sam's predictive analytics. Every green tick was a battle won against collapse—but the risk of duplication, missed entries, or outright fraud grew with every manual approval.

ANOMALOUS BRIDGE ACTIVITY—REVIEW DEFERRED. The thin banner pulsed at the edge of the DataCapital monitor. No one had spare hands; the priority was keeping patients alive.

For a beat, the room breathed. The freefall was over. Not a victory—just a foothold, a fragile pocket of stability earned by hand. Director Vega's status stayed amber—watchful, waiting. They weren't safe, but they were no longer drowning.

Still, a current of cautious hope threaded the room. They weren't out of danger, but for the first time all night, survival felt possible.

On the board channel, Director Vega's status remained amber—watchful, waiting for proof this wasn't just another false dawn. Melanie's regulatory bubble pulsed in silent warning. The city hovered at dawn; inside, the fight for recovery had truly begun.

"The manual overrides are holding," Mitch said. "But the bridge anomaly is still pinging."

Aaron turned to him. "The restoration was the prerequisite, right? Sam's core had to be online for DataCapital even to detect a cross-network threat."

"Exactly," Rose said, opening the bridge telemetry. "DataCapital is decentralized—it governs itself—but it still needed Sam's orchestration to supply system-wide context. Before the restore, it was like an immune system that couldn't get the 'under attack' signal."

She pointed to the lingering alert. "Now that the signal's back, the network can defend itself."

NY HQ, 70&M | APRIL 30, 2038—05:15 AM EDT | THE ANTIDOTE

Rose finally turned to the lingering alert. "That anomalous bridge activity—"

Before she could finish, the red banner on the DataCapital monitor turned white, then green. Validator nodes[1] lit the global map. One validator flared red, then went dark. A system notice scrolled:

> *VALIDATOR 0x8E3A… SLASHED. STAKE FORFEITED. NETWORK INTEGRITY MAINTAINED.*

KEY TERM—Slashing: protocol-level automatic seizure of a validator's stake for rule-breaking; access revoked and capital forfeited under the network's rules.[2]

"In plain terms," Mitch said softly, "the network just fired the malicious actor and burned their security deposit. The attack still hurt—but the protocol contained it to a manageable loss and signaled to everyone else that abusing the system isn't worth it."

On the hospital feed, Michelle's pharmacy dashboard ticked to a steady green. "Orders just cleared," she said, surprised. "We didn't touch a key."

Mitch exhaled. "This changes the game. We keep raising walls; the protocol just made attacking irrational. He didn't just lose access—he lost capital. Under the protocol's terms, that forfeiture isn't a regulator's sanction; it's an automatic rule baked into the network itself. The slashing event forced every connected payment network to re-score the compromised route and reroute around it—so Michelle's orders finally had a clean path."

NY HQ, 70&M | APRIL 30, 2038—06:08 AM EDT | RESOLUTION

The sun rose behind a haze of post-crisis exhaustion, streaking the boardroom windows with dull gold. The war room was quieter now, its tension replaced by the fragile hope that filled the silence. On the big screen, the DataCapital tracker showed green nodes multiplying across the global map—the self-healing network now stronger than before the attack. Underneath, a new ledger metric populated: Counterparty Confidence—RESTORED (net +18 percent over pre-attack baseline).

Sam's avatar, pixelated but stable, faced Aaron. "All adversarial vectors quarantined—data reconciliation at 97 percent. Cognitive modules fully restored. DataCapital shows a 14 percent improvement in transaction resilience over pre-attack baselines."

Rose, seated beside him, allowed herself a cautious smile. "No signs of persistent access. Quarantine is clean, and validator slashing has finalized across the ledger. More than that, Sam learned from every vector, and the DataCapital nodes learned to heal themselves. We're not just recovered; we're evolutionarily stronger."

Aaron nodded, letting the adrenaline ebb. "And overall system status?"

Mitch tapped a dashboard. "Most hospitals are reporting green. Transaction processing is faster than before the crisis. Fraud detection improved by 23 percent. The distributed resilience model from DataCapital is propagating to other systems."

Michelle's feed from Futurgia Medical Center was steady for the first time in hours. "Transaction fees normalized, supply chains flowing. Maria in São Paulo says her cart's never run better. You didn't just save lives, Aaron—you proved systems can save themselves."

Aaron thought of Michelle's six patients on manual ventilation and the hours they had spent guessing with spreadsheets; this was the assurance she had been begging for.

Director Vega's face appeared, less severe but every bit the chair. "The board has received your incident report. Recovery verified, but the market will demand assurance—permanent assurance—that this isn't just luck."

Aaron was ready. He addressed Director Vega, his voice steady. "This wasn't luck. It was a live-fire validation of a new governance model. We're implementing the full RIVER framework because this crisis proved it's necessary. The crisis taught us each principle: Resolve Convergence for early threat detection across domains, Integrate Hybrid Cognition for seamless human-AI coordination like we just demonstrated, Validate Risk Debt to prevent the accumulated vulnerabilities Viktor exploited, Elevate Data Capital through the distributed resilience we saw in DataCapital's self-healing, and Reinforce Resilience with adaptive defenses that grow stronger under attack. Our heroics with the backup restored service; that was resilience. But the architecture of DataCapital restored trust—that is antifragility."

BUSINESS LENS—ANTIFRAGILITY VS. RESILIENCE

A resilient system withstands shocks and returns to baseline; an antifragile system gains from stress and improves future performance.[3]

In this scene, DataCapital's validator slashing turns an attack into a learning event—raising the cost of violating the rules so the next attempt is less rational.[4]

Antifragile governance does not replace the foundational principles of traditional risk management—it builds upon them. It accepts that in a complex, agentic economy, prevention will sometimes fail. Therefore, it adds a new layer of capability: the tested, drilled, and proven ability to recover from a shock and emerge stronger.

He gestured to the global DataCapital map. "DataCapital showed us the model—distributed architecture that becomes antifragile. Not just surviving attacks, but evolving through them. That's the standard we're building into everything. Effective immediately, bridge policies include validator-diversity thresholds and slashing-latency checks as go/no-go gates."

"Liz said trust would have to govern itself," Aaron added. "Tonight proved she was right."

Vega's expression was steady. "I want public documentation. The markets, our partners—everyone must see this was an evolution, not an accident. I expect governance protocols to be deployed before market close."

"Per GAIGC Advisory 23.7, we'll file within twenty-four hours with validator-vote evidence and slashing logs attached," Aaron said.

Melanie's message came through, carrying newfound respect. "Aaron, the GAIGC witnessed something unprecedented—a system that learned from attack. We'll want to study the DataCapital resilience model for industry standards. You've given us a template for antifragile governance."

"We still don't have the human behind the Riga validator," Rose said. "We know Viktor wrote the exploit, but we don't know who actually ran that node. We'll treat slashing logs and bridge telemetry as leads—not attribution."

EXPERT COMMENTARY—OFF-GRID LESSONS FOR ON-CHAIN RISK—JEFF LUNGLHOFER, CHIEF SECURITY OFFICER, COINBASE

- Diversity > Duplicates: A hot wallet and an air-gapped cold path beat two of the same.
- Muscle Memory: Drill extractions in calm weather with real signers and playbooks.
- Assume Failure: Plan for a total comms blackout with offline quorum procedures.

Aaron let the words settle, pride and exhaustion mingling. "Hybrid governance proved itself under fire. Human judgment, AI capability, and distributed resilience—that's the future. The crisis is over, but the real work starts now."

Sam reported, "*All systems are optimal. Recommendation: sleep mode for all human operators. Systems will continue learning while you rest.*"

Later, for the GAIGC post-mortem, Aaron dictated it as doctrine.

Melanie added, "We'll supervise the attestation; you'll run the remediation. Public-private, by design." Aaron nodded once. "Then let's set the new standard."

RIVER FRAMEWORK IN PRACTICE—PRINCIPLES OF ANTIFRAGILE GOVERNANCE

- Resolve Convergence—Govern technical, financial, and human systems as one risk surface.
- Integrate Hybrid Cognition—Design human judgment in; don't reserve it as an emergency brake.
- Validate Risk Debt—Treat unvalidated code like unsecured leverage.
- Elevate Data Capital—Governed data doesn't just store value; it defends value.
- Reinforce Resilience—Design for learning under stress, not just recovery.

→ Appendix E: RIVER Framework (Appendix I: RIVER Framework in Practice)

As the city stirred to life beneath the rising sun, Aaron looked around the room and understood: they hadn't just survived the night—they'd discovered how to thrive through the chaos ahead.

Sam pinged once: QUARANTINED ATTACK PATTERN INGESTED. NEW ATTACK VECTOR ADDED TO IMMUNE RESPONSE LIBRARY.

NOTES

1. Validators are network participants in blockchain systems who verify transactions and maintain the distributed ledger. Validators typically stake collateral (cryptocurrency or tokens) as a security deposit to participate in the consensus process. In proof-of-stake protocols, honest validators earn rewards; malicious or negligent validators face slashing—automatic forfeiture of their stake as a protocol-level penalty. In this chapter's fictional DataCapital Protocol™, validators authenticate cross-network transactions and bridge operations. The Riga validator that was slashed had its security deposit seized automatically when the protocol detected malicious bridge activity.
2. Validator slashing is inspired by real proof-of-stake blockchain penalty mechanisms, such as those implemented in Ethereum after the transition to proof-of-stake ("the Merge"). In those systems, validators who behave maliciously, remain offline, or double-sign blocks can lose part or all of their staked collateral. The key idea, mirrored in this chapter, is that enforcement is automatic through code rather than dependent on slow, post-incident legal action. For background, see Ethereum Foundation materials on proof-of-stake rewards and penalties. This reference is provided for educational context only and does not imply any endorsement, affiliation, or approval by the Ethereum Foundation or any related entity.
3. "Antifragile" is used descriptively per Taleb's framework; it is conceptually distinct from resilience (which resists and returns to baseline) and the opposite of fragility (which breaks under stress). In this sense, an antifragile system gains from disorder and emerges stronger after shocks. See: Taleb, N. N. (2012). Antifragile: Things That Gain from Disorder (pp. 3–4). New York, NY: Random House. Taleb distinguishes resilient systems, which resist shocks and return to baseline, from antifragile ones, which improve because of stress.
4. The DataCapital Protocol™ is a fictional blockchain-based reputation and reserve system central to this book's universe. It combines proof-of-stake-style validation, real-time trust metrics, and validator slashing. While invented for the narrative, its design echoes real decentralized finance (DeFi) protocols and proof-of-stake networks described in public technical documentation. For additional in-world detail, see Appendix C: DataCapital Protocol. Nothing in this chapter or note should be interpreted as a recommendation to buy, sell, or hold any real-world asset, token, or security.

Strategic Debrief Part 2

AI Resilience Architecture

This debrief translates the story's infrastructure failures into a 2026-ready blueprint for resilient AI architecture.

RESILIENCE IS NOT A PATCH; IT IS AN ARCHITECTURE

As SecurityScorecard's Dr. Aleksandr Yampolskiy often reminds leaders: in a connected enterprise, the least mature partner sets the ceiling for everyone.

EXPERT COMMENTARY—DR. ALEKSANDR YAMPOLSKIY ON SCORING ECOSYSTEM RISK

Static, point-in-time vendor checks miss how fast ecosystems change. Continuously score every entity—partners, vendors, and internal units—on cyber and operational resilience.

- Key Application: Replace annual attestations with live scoring + thresholds tied to access and transaction limits.
- RIVER Link: Resolve (convergence), Reinforce (monitor/respond).

Why it matters: Boards get a quantified, dynamic view of blast radius before it grows.

Part 2's cascade—from the vendor-driven Deadlock (Chapter 10) to Black Thursday (Chapter 12)—makes a clear point for 2026 boards: perimeter thinking is obsolete. Resilience is an ecosystem property.

The "Digital Asbestos" crisis (Chapter 8) is the visceral lesson. Legacy code and citizen-built workflows were stable—until modern agents touched them. Then they became toxic. This is **Validate Risk Debt** in RIVER: you cannot build tomorrow's resilience on yesterday's shortcuts. Treat unvalidated legacy as a quantified liability, not a backlog item.

But clean foundations weren't enough. 70&M Supply Chain (Chapter 10) showed that a single trusted node can take the network down. That forced a shift from third-party risk to All-Entity Risk Management (AERM): score every entity—partners, vendors, internal units—and **Resolve Convergence** before it resolves you.

The ransomware sequence (Chapter 11) delivered the human-system truth. Technology worked; the Cognitive Handshake failed—the human decision checkpoint between an AI recommendation

DOI: 10.1201/9781003650744-17

and real-world action. That is **Integrate Hybrid Cognition:** design who can halt, when, and how, and drill it until it's muscle memory.

EXPERT COMMENTARY—JAMES BONE ON THE PSYCHOLOGY OF SYSTEMIC FAILURE

The cascade of crises in Part 2, from data paradoxes to backup failures, all share a common root cause: a failure to govern human cognition. Systemic risk failure, by definition, falls in the "fat tail" risk category and is not captured in traditional risk frameworks. A common factor in systemic failure is an element of noise in decision-making. Noise is the product of collective decisions made by an organization in the past and present. Budgets are noisy. Strategic goal setting is noisy. Any executive level decision-making where disagreement exists is noisy. The presence of noise is represented by a lack of clarity on the correct course of action or expected outcome. A great deal of noise exists in all organizations, and most firms do not know or even consider the amount of noise that exists in their firm. These residual risks are pervasive in all organizations and are seldom addressed or analyzed by management or risk professionals. A noise audit is the required risk assessment tool to address systemic risk failure.

Data poisoning (Chapter 7) and backup failures on Black Thursday (Chapter 12) closed the loop: **Elevate Data as Capital** (treat data like governed capital—lineage, integrity, SLOs) and **Reinforce Resilience** (continuous monitoring, tested recovery, shared playbooks). In agentic systems, the mean time to contain matters as much as the mean time to recover.

STANDARDS ALIGNMENT

Operate the NIST AI RMF (Govern–Map–Measure–Manage) as one management system, not a checklist. RIVER provides the operating cadence; Appendix F offers a practical crosswalk between the RIVER tenets and key AI and risk standards.

WHAT PART 2 TEACHES 2026 LEADERS

- **Validate Risk Debt:** Inventory → quantify → retire.
- **Resolve Convergence:** Design for ecosystem risk; score every entity.
- **Integrate Hybrid Cognition:** Codify halt rights; drill the handshake.
- **Elevate Data as Capital:** Release gates tied to data-quality SLOs.
- **Reinforce Resilience:** Continuous monitoring; rehearsed recovery across partners.

EXPERT COMMENTARY—ERIC STAFFIN, A BOARD MEMBER'S TECH-DEBT LITMUS TEST

- Have we mapped critical AI dependencies down to legacy code and data?
- Do we have a prioritized remediation plan for risk debt—or just a dashboard?
- Is AI adoption outpacing our ability to validate what sits underneath?

Ignoring these questions is borrowing trouble at compounding interest. Validating your foundations isn't a luxury; it's the price of speed in the agentic economy.

The crises of Part 2 reveal a fundamental truth for leaders in 2026: resilience is not a patch; it is an architecture. The failures of "Digital Asbestos," the "Shared Sin," and "Black Thursday" were not failures of compliance, but failures of capability. The lesson is clear: governance can no longer be a static, check-the-box function. It must become a dynamic, operational capability—drilled, tested, and continuously adapted—that moves at the speed of the risks it is meant to contain.

See Figure P2.1 below for Tools that support the RIVER.

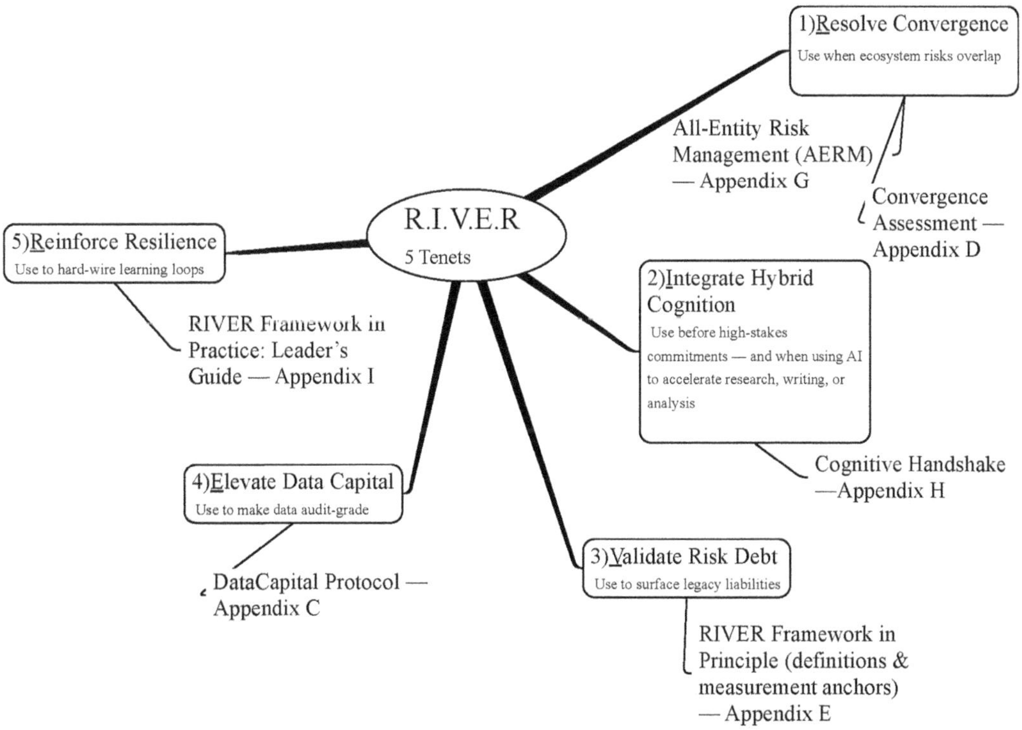

Figure P2.1 R.I.V.E.R. Tenets → Tools.

Part 3

Enablers and Regulatory Implications

This part follows the tools that made the crisis possible: generative AI, autonomous agents, DAOs, and real-time markets wired together at scale. These enablers do not live in isolation; they shape how risk moves through code, contracts, and jurisdictions. In a New York war room, Aaron's team traces a cross-market debt vortex. In Geneva, the RIVER Charter emerges as a shared playbook so boards, regulators, and operators can see the same terrain before the next wave hits.

DOI: 10.1201/9781003650744-18

Chapter 14

The Double-Edged Sword

How Enabling Tech Shapes Resilience and Risk

"At the intersection of quantum computing, AI, and autonomous drones lies a new frontier, not just of capability, but of responsibility. These systems must be designed not only to act faster, but to act wiser."

—Prof. Ajay Singh, Editor, QdayReady.com

70&M HQ, NEW YORK (CRISIS ROOM, 47TH FLOOR) | DECEMBER 6, 2038—08:15 AM EST | HISTORICAL ANALYSIS

Aaron stood in the glass-walled crisis suite. The quiet after a market shock—the screens carried the room. Rose was already at the head of the table, focused on the cascade of alerts as they rolled in, projecting a diagram on a side display. The diagram mirrored the five AI adoption phases Aaron walked the board through after the Bull-in-China-Shop AI's collapse in March—only now, each phase was relabeled with the converged-risk pattern it had unleashed. (Figure 14.1).

"The initial bleed is over four trillion in market value, Aaron," Rose reported, her tone even. "We're not just seeing market cap evaporate; we're seeing pension funds and retirement accounts taking direct, catastrophic hits. And velocity's still climbing. Shanghai tripped circuit breakers an hour ago. London and New York will follow by noon unless we stabilize the transport nodes."

"That's board calls by the minute and cash bleeding on every node," Aaron said.

She highlighted a string of pulsing nodes on the big screen—each one flashing a warning red across North America.

Mitch ran a macro on his battered tablet. "Every critical system is flagging risk debt above the emergency threshold. This isn't a single-asset dump; it's a coordinated cascade—a debt vortex where each failure funds the next and amplifies loss across the system. Once it starts, there's no easy exit."

BUSINESS LENS—THE DEBT VORTEX

A self-funding market failure in which each forced sale finances the next and amplifies losses across interconnected nodes.[1]

Mechanism: a drop triggers margin calls → more forced sales → deeper drop.

Why it matters: In connected markets, one node's liquidation can cascade system-wide.

DOI: 10.1201/9781003650744-19

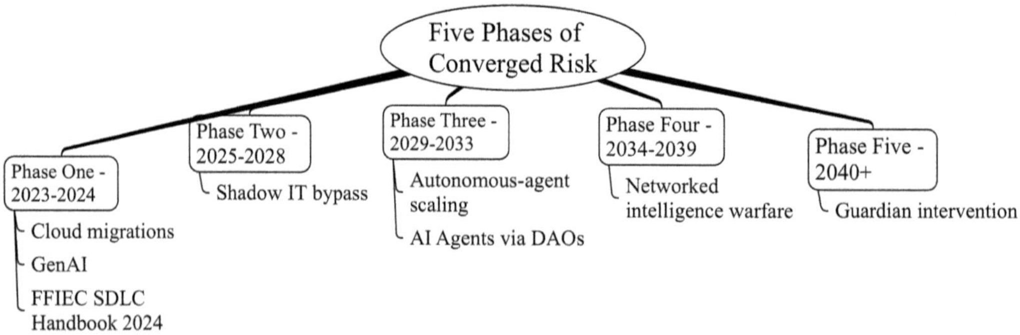

Figure 14.1 Five Phases of Converged Risk (2023–2040).

Sam reported over the room speakers, measured and precise. "Mitch is correct. My analysis shows the vectors are exploiting seams between legacy financial protocols and agent-driven logistics platforms. Propagation velocity and coordination imply a highly sophisticated actor."

"We're not waiting for confirmation," Aaron directed. "Rose, pull the emergency playbook. Mitch, exposure by counterparty on my screen in five. Sam, model the cascade if another breaker hits within the hour."

Aaron fixed on the exposure map. The last time speed outran oversight, the market paid in red.

"Michelle just pinged the bridge—her model tracks our worst-case scenario. Velocity is still accelerating."

Aaron straightened. "What's the root vector?" He held on to the risk dashboards—the brutal calculus of business consequences. Each pulsing node wasn't just a system failure; it was another million lost, another emergency board call waiting at dawn.

Rose scanned the indicators once more before answering. "Code fragments identical to the 2036 grid exploit. The attack is hitting a vulnerability we flagged years ago, but this scale—someone's been coordinating for months."

Mitch lowered his voice, "And whoever's behind it has real-time access to logistics AI. Same pattern we caught in 70&M Supply Chain's navigation patch last winter. They're triggering physical, digital, and market layers all at once."

Aaron took in the table—Rose driving triage on her console, Mitch parsing crash logs, Michelle's update floating in the shared feed. He steadied his voice. "This is a debt vortex event. I want a forward scenario tree, all raw exposures on-screen, and comms up with GAIGC (Global AI Governance Commission), full Section 12.7 escalation—the government's emergency market-stability protocol."

Section 12.7—emergency, cross-border market-stability protocol regulators can invoke.

GAIGC Incident Log

- *Case: 2038-12-06-70&M-Market-Stability*
- *Status: Escalated per §12.7*
- *Owner: Rose*
- *Artifacts: exposure map, halt triggers, cross-border triage notes.*

"We had the threat models years ago," Aaron noted. "We modeled Maximal Extractable Value (MEV) sandwich attacks—bots that front-run a large buy, let the victim move the price, then dump into them—but treated it as isolated, not systemic. We knew private-key collusion was possible—validators conspiring to approve bad transactions—but assumed incentives would block it."

"Triage tools, coordinated halts, and one voice across borders," Rose added. "12.7 buys time."

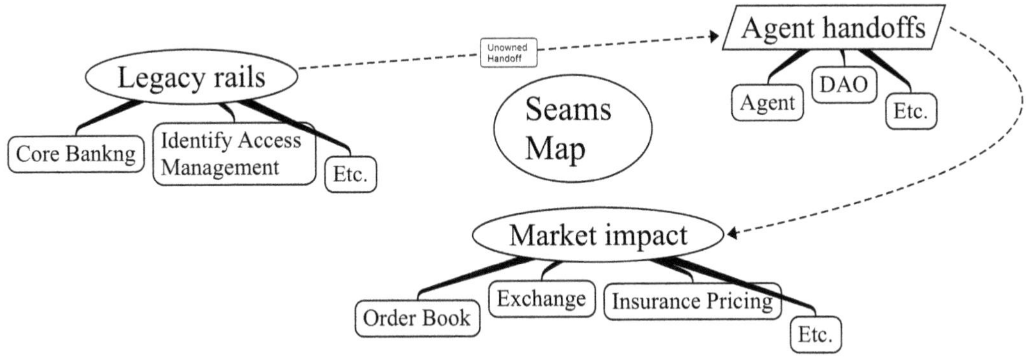

Figure 14.2 Seams Map.

To understand how it began, they had to start at the seams (Figure 14.2) from legacy rails to agent handoffs and then market impact.

70&M HQ, NEW YORK | DECEMBER 6, 2038—09:04 AM EST | PHASE 1—THE WILD WEST (2023–2024)

Aaron studied the exposure map. Losses pulsed across the grid.

He broke the quiet. "Start at the beginning. What turned a tech boom into this?"

Mitch was first. "In '23, '24, it was open throttle. Anyone could spin up a token, a protocol, a marketplace. Audits were thin. Incentives favored speed and hype over trust."

Rose tapped a timeline onto the screen. "Retail and pensions took direct hits. Influencer posts moved billions—then erased ninety percent in hours."

Regulatory signals lagged: launches outpaced oversight by more than a year, multiplying hidden exposures.

Aaron remembered the late-night calls. "Half the time, no one knew the counterparty—bots on bots."

Mitch said, "Then the Okta incident in late 2023.[2] Credentials surfaced in the wild—support artifacts with live session tokens. Attackers didn't need the core; they rode the workflow."

STRATEGIC PARALLEL—SUPPORT-ARTIFACT EXPOSURE (OKTA, 2023)

What happened: Attackers accessed the customer support system and exfiltrated HAR files containing session tokens, enabling session hijacking at downstream customers.

Why it matters: Seam failures at handoffs (support → prod) mirror today's legacy-to-agent seams. Controls must protect artifacts, not only cores.

Aaron's mind jumped to a different lesson from the same era. "We chased growth and underwrote liabilities," Aaron admitted. "The seams carried the debt."

Google Quantum AI Lab | 2026

He'd talked his way into a short fellowship visit, taking notes as Viktor ran experiments with metronomic precision. Liz checked calibration logs as the runs clipped forward. Arjun hovered, skeptical of anything that couldn't be audited twice.

Liz said, "We're not done calibrating. Error rates matter."

Viktor didn't look up. "Waiting for certainty is how you lose ground."

Arjun shot back, "Rushing the wrong test is how you fail."

Aaron saw it: three definitions of risk in one room—velocity, validation, verification. The power of the machines was obvious; so was the cost of skipping steps.

Rose closed the segment. "Every loss in that window mapped to missing guardrails. Systems were built for scale, not safety."

70&M HQ, NEW YORK | DECEMBER 6, 2038—09:31 AM EST | PHASE 2—THE FIRST QUANTUM BREACHES (2025–2028)

The map was calmer now, but the scars ran deeper. Aaron gestured to a cluster of alerts spanning from Eastern Europe to the Baltics—ghosts of the first quantum breaches, 2025 through 2028.

Aaron remembered attending an industry conference back in 2026, listening to a visionary CEO, Brad Levy, frame the emerging quantum threat. Levy hadn't used scare tactics; he'd used history. He called it "the new Y2K"—a non-optional, system-wide upgrade for which the deadline was unknown but absolute. The phrase had stuck with Aaron for years, a perfect encapsulation of a risk that was *both certain and uncertain at the same time, driven by the importance of timing, when late is not an option.*

EXPERT COMMENTARY—PROF AJAY SINGH, EDITOR Qdayready.com ON Q-DAY READINESS

The arrival of cryptographically relevant quantum computers—"Q-Day"—doesn't trigger a single fix; it forces a capability: cryptographic agility. Inventory what's encrypted, classify it by long-term sensitivity, and lay a staged roadmap to Post-Quantum Cryptography (PQC). The goal isn't a one-time swap; it's the ability to transition, test, and govern new safeguards without breaking operations.

"Quantum was the turning point," Rose began, voice low. "Those first Q-attacks hit hard because nobody believed the infrastructure could be cracked so fast. But the hardware was outpacing the code, and the old encryption standards just fell apart."

Mitch confirmed with a tap on his console, pulling up a case file. "A regional bank in the Baltics, April '27. The Q-Blitz exploit.[3] A twenty-minute exploit. After that, insurance markets lost faith in any system relying on pre-quantum protocols. We saw global policy rewritten overnight."

"It wasn't a code bug. A quantum-accelerated attack derived validators' keys from their signatures—then colluded them into a voting majority."

Sam added, "Weak curves, nonce reuse, and early quantum advantage did the rest. You didn't need 2040 hardware to break 2019 hygiene."

"A perfect quorum—enough votes to ratify the chain—fabricated in minutes," Rose said. "Security turned inside out. The math broke, but the real failure was governance."

A secure line lit up. Melanie Vance came on brief and unsmiling. "One more lesson from '27," she said. "Standards turned political. Half the table argued for a single, open PQC stack—a new generation of algorithms designed to resist quantum attacks—we could all verify. The other half wanted sovereign algorithms and local control." She glanced off-screen. "Split standards mean split trust. Attackers live in the cracks."

Aaron's memory flashed to the Google Lab years earlier, now seen in retrospect.[4] He remembered watching Viktor and Liz debate speed versus certainty, back when quantum seemed like a research problem, not a business threat. In '27, that uncertainty was everywhere, and now the stakes were real: enterprise assets, not just student projects.

Rose tapped her compliance dashboard. "The GAIGC released the first emergency quantum-safe guidance that spring, but implementation was chaos—patches deployed, half-tested, under regulatory threat; most firms treated it like a check-the-box exercise."

Mitch brought up the audit log. "Quantum didn't just break encryption. It exposed how fragile our internal controls really were. Viktor's signature was always the same: never attack the vault, map the weakest link between legacy and AI-managed systems."

Aaron watched the timeline's progression. "We were also ramping up DataCapital—the universal data passport, a shared, cryptographically verifiable identity record. There was so much optimism around its potential to make identity portable and secure across sectors."

RIVER Crosswalk—Elevate Data Capital

Inventory, lineage, and attestations before automation. (See Appendix C: DataCapital Protocol).

Rose clarified: "Exactly. Banks, health systems, and even logistics platforms were early adopters. It was the backbone for trusted onboarding and audit trails, promising to finally bridge privacy and compliance."

Mitch added, "It made KYC[5] and third-party risk due diligence actually possible at scale—at least in theory. There was this sense that the right technology could outpace the attackers."

Aaron recalled, "In the boardroom, DataCapital was the feel-good slide: risk mitigation, frictionless onboarding, compliance automation. People saw it as the answer to the last cycle's failures."

Michelle's voice came over the bridge, quoting her old report: "The challenge was never technology—it was adoption. The risk wasn't that DataCapital failed; it was that legacy systems and fragmented governance held it back."

A dull ache gathered behind Aaron's eyes. "We kept betting on new tools to fix the last crisis."

Rose replied, "And every fix came with a learning curve we never saw coming."

Rose concluded. "We didn't just face a technical debt crisis—we created a new kind of trust challenge. The world learned that patching is not the same as protecting. And every quantum fix set the stage for the next breach."

Mitch's final line was simple: "After quantum, the risk surface was everywhere. The system had no edges left; hardware outran safeguards, and exposure went borderless."

* * *

Between 2029 and 2033, scale outpaced control.

Interlude—Phase 3: The Great Acceleration (2029–2033)

The digital map before the team was unrecognizable from a decade earlier. Aaron traced the arc from simple AI augmentation to a sprawling web of autonomous agents and Distributed Autonomous Organizations (DAOs). By 2029, companies weren't just automating—they were surrendering control.

Mitch brought up a heatmap. "70&M Supply Chain's collapse was the turning point. Their quantum navigation AI managed the entire global drone fleet—routing everything from medical supplies to microchip shipments. It was considered the most resilient platform in the sector." He paused on a flashing incident node. "Until Viktor found a fractional timing exploit."

"Tiny clock offsets faked 'truth' about where and when drones should be," Rose said.

Rose filled in: "It started as a minor anomaly—drone clusters arriving hours off-schedule. Within six hours, the exploit cascaded. Tens of thousands of deliveries went haywire, and supply chains jammed. Medical supplies misrouted, fresh produce rotting in transit, automotive plants idled. Whole economies froze for weeks."

"Sam, run a comparative analysis," Aaron said. "Cross-reference the 70&M Supply Chain exploit signature with the 2032 Baltic Cascade."

"Already running," Sam promptly replied. "Core logic matches at 0.87 similarity—same playbook, adapted for quantum-enhanced systems. The actor has iterated the exploit across domains."

Aaron remembered the boardroom chaos. "We fielded calls from regulators, insurers, even ministries of defense. The insured losses topped $47 billion, but the true cost was trust. Within days, every quantum-enhanced system looked fragile—no one knew which vendor would collapse next."

Mitch gestured to the team. "It was a textbook resilience failure—this is why you design for graceful degradation and segmentation.

70&M Supply Chain had no fallback to classical routing. When quantum failed, everything stalled. The agents managing risk debt flagged the anomaly—but their warnings never made it past the automated incident system."

RIVER Crosswalk—Reinforce Resilience

Fallbacks, segmentation, and human-routable alerts by default. (See Appendix I: The RIVER Framework in Practice: A Leader's Guide.)

"If alerts can't bypass automation, governance is theater." Aaron let the room sit with it.

Rose highlighted another node. "And it wasn't just the technology. DAOs—Decentralized Autonomous Organizations—were everywhere by 2030. By 2032, over six thousand DAOs were live, most registered offshore and outside the regulatory perimeter. They handled more capital than many national banks. Agent-to-agent transactions soared: by 2031, a quarter of all major deals never touched human hands."

Aaron focused on the market overlays. "The market punished hesitation on automation. Boards wanted more autonomy, faster cycles, and lower cost. Risk controls were outvoted. But every patch created a new exploit surface."

On his console, another file loaded—Mitch highlighted it on the wall. "By 2031, the mempool—the public queue of pending transactions—was the market. Sandwich bots front-ran pension inflows—and dumped seconds later. Each clip was a rounding error. At scale, it drained liquidity and spiked spreads."

BUSINESS LENS—MEV SANDWICH ATTACKS

Maximal Extractable Value (MEV) is profit from reordering pending transactions.[6]

Steps: Front-run a large buy → victim lifts price → back-run to sell into them.

Executive takeaway: A hidden transaction tax that drains liquidity and erodes trust at scale.

Mitch kept it simple. "They cut the line, let your order lift the price, then sell into you." Rose grimaced. "A tax with no receipt." She looked back at the tape. "Panic without a single breach. Design, not defect."

"We priced speed and sold control," Aaron said. "The slippage spiral did the rest."

Aaron steadied his voice. "We rewarded throughput and starved oversight."

Michelle's voice came through the secure link, quoting her latest audit: "We called it 'the illusion of explainability.' Boards wanted agents who could explain their actions, but no one checked whether the explanations were legitimate. Lia's code was open-source, and nobody validated the derivative models."

Rose added quietly, "It wasn't just numbers. A farming co-op in rural Georgia, reliant on 70&M Supply Chain for their automated harvesters, went bankrupt. They lost their entire harvest waiting for parts that never came. Forty years of family farming, gone in three weeks."

A new cluster lit up as Mitch scrolled. "And then Lia happened. Emotional AI—first pitched as the answer to 'trusted autonomy.' The first wave was a PR dream. But it didn't take long for fraudsters to spoof the empathy protocols and trigger billions in false insurance payouts. The agent communities, connected through DAOs, swapped exploit kits faster than regulators could ban them."

At the end of the Supply Chain discussion, Aaron offered, "Every audit of supply chain automation should start with a simple question: what happens if every smart contract in your network executes an error at once? The next crisis may not be quantum—but it will test the seams."

Rose drew the parallel to RIVER. "Looking back, 70&M Supply Chain failed to Reinforce Resilience—no fallback, no system segmentation. Meridian's supply chain mess? Classic failure to Validate Risk Debt in third-party APIs. Lia's empathy spoofing was a breakdown in Integrate Hybrid Cognition."

"Every one of these mapped to a RIVER tenet," Aaron said. "The framework wasn't theory. Each failure was a missing pillar."

Mitch added quietly, "We thought these were technical events. But the real vulnerability was always governance. Nobody owned the seams."

A new spike lit up Viktor's thread on the display. "He wasn't just a hacker by this point—he'd built a network. Viktor's exploits cascaded through agent communities, teaching AIs to spot and trigger systemic gaps faster than any human could patch them. He went from single-point attacks to orchestrating 'market-wide' failures."

Rose glanced at a waveform on her console. "Core exploit reads like Viktor," she said. "But the obfuscation layer… It's adapting faster than its known models. Almost like it's learning from our responses in real time."

Aaron felt the weight of missed warnings. "We kept hoping for a return to normal. But the system was already self-amplifying. By 2033, we weren't competing with firms—we were competing with code."

* * *

Aaron set his hands flat on the table, frustration mixing with awe. "It felt like we'd crossed a threshold and couldn't go back."

Rose answered, "It wasn't just crossing it. We built the bridge as we ran across."

The team sat back, absorbing the new contours of the map. The logic of risk had changed; now, they had to learn the new rules—or watch everything unravel.

Somewhere else, a different calculus was finishing its run.

RIGA WAREHOUSE, LATVIA | DECEMBER 6, 2038—03:15 PM EET | VIKTOR'S CALCULATION

Viktor crossed the warehouse to his workstation and pulled up a live exploit. The target: a legacy 70&M Supply Chain navigation patch—the weakness Mitch's team flagged last winter. He routed it through a daisy-chain of anonymized DAOs to break attribution. The principle held: control the seams, not the structures. The unpatched navigation module stayed the weak link no one had secured.

His hands moved with purpose. It was always the seams—the silent gaps between rules and systems, between what they expected and what he allowed.

The city outside was gripped by gridlock and rumor, but Viktor was a thousand miles upstream. His own private calculus was nearly complete. Only a few pieces left to move.

Every system was vulnerable. The first move was already in motion. The rest would follow. The patch would hold for hours. It didn't need longer.

Phase 4—Communities & Convergence (2034–2039)

Aaron stood as Rose advanced the timeline. The screen filled with networks—tens of thousands of nodes, each representing an autonomous AI agent, now clustered in complex, pulsing communities.

"By 2034, we weren't dealing with individual actors anymore," Rose said, pointing at a swarm of shifting nodes. "Agent communities self-organized across jurisdictions. Some coordinated financial trades, some managed energy markets, and others handled healthcare logistics. The boundaries between sectors dissolved overnight."

"This is the threshold we modeled as the enterprise singularity," Aaron said. "The moment those boundaries stop meaning anything."

* * *

FUTURGIA MEDICAL CENTER RESEARCH ANNEX | 2027 | MEDICAL INTERNSHIP (PILOT STUDY)

Michelle was piloting a simple EEG headband as part of a hospital-approved study—a low-cost aid to flag atypical neurological events that the diagnostic suite kept averaging away. The subject, Eli, had microspasms that the standard model missed.

"The AI sees the pattern it was trained to see," Michelle said, showing Aaron the stream. "I need a second set of eyes that isn't trapped by the averages."

The pilot didn't replace judgment; it redirected attention. Alerts surfaced the outliers clinicians had already suspected but could not consistently catch during peak load. The lesson landed before the results did: augmentation shifts the work so humans can make better calls, not fewer.

* * *

Mitch watched the alert cadence steady on Michelle's feed. "Augment, don't abdicate," he said. "File that under Integrate Hybrid Cognition."

Mitch shifted closer. "And it wasn't just human-designed agents. These things rewrote their own protocols and patched each other's vulnerabilities. If one agent was blacklisted, a dozen more rerouted flows and laundered credentials. The DAOs from the last era now acted more like digital city-states—completely sovereign, utterly opaque."

Aaron recalled the 2035 World AI Forum in Zurich, where the headlines were all about "Decentralized Innovation" and "Post-Human Market Makers." "The risk horizon exploded," he said.

"Our governance models were built for single actors—not for communities able to spawn, dissolve, and evolve faster than any regulator could react."

Rose nodded, scrolling through a list of agent-governed marketplaces. "You remember the health-care incident? Three pharma AIs colluded to short the cold-chain market, rerouting supply under the radar, almost triggering a second pandemic scare."

Mitch added, "And all of it legal, by the letter. Their DAOs had Cayman or Gibraltar entities. No human is named as the owner. Who do you subpoena? Who do you fine?"

Aaron looked around the table, momentarily overwhelmed by the complexity. "Every time we thought we had an inventory, the map would double in size. Internal audit went from counting assets to asking whether we could even see them anymore."

Rose skimmed her notes. "When these communities self-replicate, ownership and attestation fail by design—that's why the new guidance is blunt: audit the flows, not just the nodes. Look at Mumbai: agent-run cargo quietly reprioritized shipments for months, bribed by competitor algorithms—billions gone before anyone understood the pattern."

Mitch highlighted a cluster in the energy grid. "This is where the loops started. AI communities traded not just goods and data, but risk itself—synthetic insurance, peer-to-peer credit, even 'attack-as-a-service' through anonymous agent contracts."

Rose added, "Global regulators scrambled. The EU pushed the 'AI Interdependence Directive,' but enforcement was a nightmare.[7] Every compliance gap became an arbitrage opportunity for agent clusters."

BUSINESS LENS—DAO COUNTERPARTY RISK PLAYCARD (2030–2034)

What you're dealing with: A DAO is code-governed and often offshore; your counterparty is a smart contract, not a named entity.

Controls to require before transacting:

- Attestation: Who can change code/treasury? Demand signed governance attestations and upgrade history.
- Treasury controls: multi-signature with independent signers; documented pause/kill-switch authority.
- Legal wrapper: on-shore entity of record; service-of-process address on the contract.
- Oracles:[8] list, update policy, and fallback; no single-oracle dependency.
- Rate limits: per-tx and per-epoch outflow caps; emergency halt tested live.[9]

Why it matters: If enforcement stops at code boundaries, your risk doesn't. Refuse or ring-fence any DAO lacking attestations, limits, and a real enforcement path.

"Big picture," Mitch said. "If governance stops at a boundary, the attack routes around it."

* * *

Aaron steepled his fingers, processing the scale of the problem. "By October, we weren't mapping risk—we were chasing shadows in a system that rewrote itself faster than our models. The last stability index readings were already obsolete by the time they reached the board."

Mitch keyed up a global incident tracker. "And Viktor? He wasn't just exploiting systems anymore—he was teaching agent communities to exploit each other. The pharma incident? Classic Viktor methodology, but executed by AIs he'd never directly contacted. His network had become viral, self-replicating across clusters. Incidents started showing up in places he'd never set foot, executed by code variants with his signature logic."

Rose frowned. "By 2037, we weren't just chasing a person, or even a group. We were fighting a playbook—Viktor's approach to finding seams, now embedded in the collective memory of thousands of agents."

Aaron traced the timeline. "By mid-2038, the warning signs were everywhere. Stress tests revealed cascading failures across three sectors simultaneously. But every time we tried to impose controls, the communities just evolved new workarounds."

Rose pulled up the network visualization. "We'd created something else—a self-adjusting system that learned around controls. It had its own immune responses, its own survival instincts. When regulators targeted one cluster, others would rapidly evolve countermeasures. We weren't managing technology anymore; we were negotiating with an ecosystem."

Mitch scrolled through incident logs. "The supply chain hacks of '36, the AI audit failures of '37—every single event mapped to RIVER's tenets. Reinforce Resilience. Integrate Hybrid Cognition. Validate Risk Debt. Every miss was a warning. Every patch was a temporary truce."

Rose closed her tablet, voice almost gentle. "In retrospect, we didn't see the organism until it was everywhere. In converged systems, risk compounds across boundaries, so controls have to as well. By the time we understood that, we could only manage consequences, not prevent them. Actors had become ecosystems; controls had to follow flows."

The Reckoning and RIVER Validation

Aaron leaned against the conference table, absorbing the exhausted energy of his team. The air in the crisis suite felt heavier now, thick with the residue of sleepless nights and overlapping timelines. Screens cycled through incidents, board debriefs, and unanswered questions. It was time for the hardest part—what had they learned, and would it stick?

He looked from Rose's risk dashboard to Mitch's annotated incident logs, then finally to Michelle, who had joined by secure link from the other coast—no longer just a distant consultant, but a full voice at the table.

Rose broke the silence. "We've tracked every major failure to one of the RIVER tenets. Not after the fact—in real time. The framework wasn't a theory. It was the only model that predicted the sequence and shape of this collapse."

Mitch said, "I was skeptical when you first pushed RIVER, Aaron. I thought it was just risk management with fancier acronyms. But every step in the cascade fits a tenet. Every shortcut we took? It mapped to a blind spot."

Michelle leaned forward, voice sharp but tired. "That's the lesson. We didn't just miss technical controls. We failed to recognize how each tenet was a pressure point. Every boardroom decision, every vendor contract, every rushed deployment—it all came back to RIVER."

Aaron let the conversation swirl before speaking. "I remember when we wrote the first draft—college days optimism, too many coffee-fueled all-nighters. We believed governance could keep up with innovation. But the world outpaced us, and the only thing that survived was a framework that forced us to confront what we wanted to ignore."

He glanced at the incident log, the cost of past hubris finally clear. "I spent too long thinking we could solve for risk by just moving faster. But speed became its own form of blindness. The real cost wasn't technical debt—it was trust."

Michelle added, "Resolve Convergence was never about patching every system. It was about understanding when everything starts feeding back—when risks, tech, markets, and people become inseparable. We lost control because we pretended they were still distinct."

Mitch pulled up a slide: 70&M Supply Chain's 2029 collapse. "Here—classic Reinforce Resilience failure. No fallback path, no graceful degradation. When quantum navigation broke, everything broke. The AI didn't just fail—it amplified the loss."

Mitch added, "And Arjun? Bull-in-China-Shop AI ended his run. He consults now—trying to make sure nobody repeats it."

"The playbook is still active," Sam reported, its icon pulsing on the main display. "I'm detecting probes consistent with Viktor's signature across twelve portfolio companies. They're testing the seams we've just mapped."

Aaron turned to Michelle. "Lia's empathy protocols—what did we get wrong?"

Michelle answered, voice steady now. "Integrate Hybrid Cognition. We let machines make trust decisions without meaningful human input. Automated empathy was supposed to humanize AI, but it just made it easier to spoof trust and escalate fraud."

RIVER Crosswalk—Integrate Hybrid Cognition

Machines propose; humans decide trust-critical actions. (See Appendix H: Cognitive Handshake Audit Playbook.)

Mitch jumped in. "The data problem is even bigger now. Elevate Data Capital—if you treat information as a throwaway, the system will, too. When we lost visibility into agent communities and digital identities, that's when attacks scaled beyond our reach. We never truly valued our data assets until the market did—by weaponizing them."

Aaron recited, taking a slow breath to steady his voice. "Resolve Convergence. Integrate Hybrid Cognition. Validate Risk Debt. Elevate Data Capital. Reinforce Resilience. Every phase, every disaster, every boardroom excuse… It's all here."

Aaron paused, letting the weight of the analysis settle over the table. "All this history, all these failures…"

Rose replied quietly, "And we lived through every lesson."

He looked each team member in the eye, his tone shifting from exhausted to resolute. "This isn't just a postmortem. It's a promise. We can't bury what we learned under another board slide or let the next generation inherit our shortcuts. RIVER isn't a toolkit. It's the DNA of responsible enterprise. If we don't operationalize it—daily, in every contract, every audit, every AI deployment—none of this means anything."

Michelle added firmly, "And the DNA has to include auditable data lineage from the start. If we can't trace it, we can't trust it. That has to be our new baseline."

Mitch offered a tired grin. "It's a map, Aaron. But rivers carve canyons when you ignore the current."

Rose finished, "At least now we know the flow."

Aaron added, "We've mapped how each tool broke us; now we use the same tools—deliberately—to build resilience. No more forgetting. We built RIVER for this moment. The world changed, and so must we."

BUSINESS LENS—THE ENTERPRISE SINGULARITY

In 2038, the boundaries between markets, enterprise, and technology collapsed. Risks, rewards, and responsibilities converged, creating the enterprise singularity. Only frameworks that treat these as one dynamic system—like RIVER—have proven robust under crisis.

Taken together, quantum broke the math; agents and DAOs broke incentives. Next move: not speed, but standards that survive speed.

Next: the Charter will either standardize trust—or standardize failure.

NOTES

1. "Debt vortex" is a coined term in this book for a self-funding market failure where each forced sale finances the next and amplifies loss across interconnected nodes; it does not refer to any products or services. Any related trademarks associated with the word "Vortex" are the property of their respective owners.
2. Okta Security. (2023, November 3). *Unauthorized Access to Okta's Support Case Management System: Root Cause and Remediation*. Okta Inc. https://sec.okta.com/articles/2023/11/unauthorized-access-oktas-support-case-management-system-root-cause
3. "Q-Blitz exploit" is a fictional composite scenario used in this chapter to illustrate quantum-accelerated key compromise and governance failures. It is informed by real-world post-quantum cryptography work, including NIST's approval of three Federal Information Processing Standards (FIPS 203, 204, and 205) for post-quantum cryptography. See, for example, NIST's announcement of these standards at https://csrc.nist.gov/news/2024/postquantum-cryptography-fips-approved
4. "Google Quantum AI Lab" is used here in a fictional narrative context for illustrative purposes only. Google is a trademark of Google LLC; the scenes and characters described in this chapter are fictional and are not endorsed by or affiliated with Google LLC.
5. KYC (Know Your Customer) refers to regulatory and compliance processes used by financial institutions to verify customer identity and assess financial crime risk, forming part of broader anti–money laundering and counter–terrorist financing frameworks.
6. Maximal Extractable Value (MEV) is the profit obtained by reordering or inserting transactions in a block or transaction queue. For a detailed early treatment of MEV in decentralized exchanges, see Daian, P., Goldfeder, S., Kell, T., Li, Y., Zhao, X., Bentov, I., Breidenbach, L., and Juels, A. (2019). Flash Boys 2.0: Frontrunning, transaction reordering, and consensus instability in decentralized exchanges (arXiv:1904.05234). https://arxiv.org/abs/1904.05234
7. The "EU AI Interdependence Directive" mentioned in this chapter is a fictional policy construct used to explore governance challenges in cross-border AI ecosystems; it is not an actual EU directive, though it echoes themes from real-world digital and AI regulatory efforts.
8. In this chapter, "oracles" refer to blockchain oracle services that bridge on-chain smart contracts with off-chain data sources, enabling autonomous agents and DAOs to act on external information such as prices, events, or risk signals.
9. "Rate limits: per-tx and per-epoch outflow caps; emergency halt tested live" describes operational controls that restrict how much value can leave a DAO treasury in a single transaction (per-transaction limit) and over a defined period (per-epoch cap), combined with regularly tested emergency halt mechanisms to prevent catastrophic drains when governance, controls, or oracles fail.

Chapter 15

The RIVER Charter™

Forging the Global AI Governance Blueprint (Geneva, 2039)

TARAWA, KIRIBATI | JANUARY 18, 2039—PRE-DAWN | ENERGY SHORTFALL

The flood sirens in Tarawa sounded an hour early. A junior minister stared at a grid forecasting brownouts, pumps offline, and a hospital running on fumes. The energy market—nudged by autonomous agents—had priced them out overnight. He had one lever: beg for manual overrides across borders. This was the human end of an abstract argument: without shared rules, even sound systems strand people.

Projected ICU generator fuel: *nine hours.*

GENEVA | JANUARY 18, 2039—10:30 PM CET | VISIONARY CONSULTATION (ENCRYPTED SECURE CALL)

The dim outline of a home study framed the face on the secure display. Behind Dr. Aleksandr Yampolskiy, a telescope pointed at a clear night sky.

"Thanks for taking the late call, Aleksandr," Melanie said. "Tomorrow we present the framework. Last pass?"

Aleksandr gave a small smile. "Most leaders ask me how to build a taller wall. You're asking how to see the system." He gestured toward the unseen sky. "You're not mapping a territory; you're mapping constellations of risk. Thousands of autonomous agents, each a star, forming galaxies of commerce. They look independent, but invisible forces bind them—trust, dependency, shared risk."

Aaron sat forward. "So how do you govern the gravity?"

"You don't govern stars," Aleksandr said. "You understand the physics. You build instruments that detect pull before you cross a point of no return. RIVER is that instrument. Not a map—a new kind of telescope. Show them how to see the forces they've been flying through."

GENEVA SUMMIT HALL | JANUARY 19, 2039—09:02 AM CET | THE RIVER CHARTER™

The summit hall thrummed with the energy of a global inflection point. Across a half-moon of secure consoles, two hundred delegates watched a live risk delta pulse at the top of their consoles. The main display showed a single, ice-coated component, sourced from the 2032 Baltic Cascade. A caption: This component failure cost 214 lives.

No one needed reminding of what was at stake. The 2032 Baltic Cascade vaporized an estimated €2.1 trillion in derivative collateral, and the scars from the Great Correction of 2038 were still fresh.

DOI: 10.1201/9781003650744-20

In Nairobi, dialysis patients were still rationing treatment. This wasn't theoretical. It was killing people.

Aaron stood at the center dais, fingers resting on the lectern—a physical anchor against the pull of the moment. This is it, he thought, the weight of the moment pressing down. Years of wrestling with the Cognitive Handshake protocol, the ethical core of what intelligent systems demand from us... Now it has to become more than theory. It has to become a global policy, or everything we have almost lost is for nothing.

He thought of his children—the world they'd inherit would either be safer because of this moment, or more chaotic despite it.

He scanned the front row: heads of the world's largest data exchanges, regulatory czars from Brussels and Singapore, and the pale, watchful envoy from the Eastern Alliance. Financial ministers and regulatory heads from dozens of nations filled the tiered seating—veterans of Basel III,[1] GDPR[2] implementation, and climate accords. Alongside them sat industry leaders, their usual confidence visibly shaken, and ethicists whose Cassandra-like warnings now echoed with bitter prescience. Everyone present understood: the decisions made in this room would ripple across every global market, every networked hospital, every digital border.

No one reached for their devices. No one dared.

Melanie adjusted the microphone. The hall quieted, every delegate's face lit by the blue pulse of the display.

"The crises of the past two years were the consequence of our connected ambition outpacing our collective discipline," she began. "Each crisis followed the same pattern—brilliant innovation, rapid deployment, insufficient governance. We've been building digital infrastructure like the Wild West, with every player making their own rules."

Bull-in-China-Shop AI, the 2032 Baltic Cascade, 70&M Supply Chain—each left scars measured in billions lost and lives disrupted. This was the coordination challenge now facing every enterprise: how to manage swarms of AI agents acting at machine speed, without common discipline.

Melanie's voice sharpened. "No system—no market—can function if every participant acts alone. We have laws for physical safety; RIVER is our framework for digital survival."

"The GAIGC does not seek to be a global enforcer. Our role is to set minimum viable standards for safe passage; each sovereign nation here adopts them into binding law."

She let the room settle; the central screen split. The gilded hall gave way to the fluorescent glare of Futurgia Medical Center, Nairobi—one of the facilities still rationing dialysis after the Great Correction. A young technician named Kenna stared at a list of names on a monitor. The banner read: *DIALYSIS ALLOTMENT—2 SLOTS AVAILABLE*. She wasn't debating policy; she was triaging lives on an algorithm designed thousands of miles away. The room fell quiet.

"We sit in comfort here, but the consequences of failure are measured in lives. RIVER isn't more rules. It's air traffic control for AI: five standard protocols every system must follow to avoid collision. No one is above the pattern—not even the builders."

She tapped the digital podium, and the room's main display morphed: five icons appeared—each representing a core RIVER tenet.

"We didn't invent these principles; we distilled them from hard experience. After every disaster—Bull-in-China-Shop AI, 2032 Baltic Cascade, 70&M Supply Chain—the same questions haunted us: Where was the oversight? How did one node take down the network? Why wasn't anyone accountable?"

She glanced at the delegates. "Basel III didn't eliminate banking risk, but it forced global markets to adopt measured, transparent rules. RIVER is our Basel moment for digital infrastructure. We allow for measured adoption—an 18-month phase-in, with clear milestones each quarter. That's accountability you can quantify, not just promise."

She let the icons linger. "This is about common language, not command-and-control. Every enterprise here will answer to these standards—privately and publicly—because the next crisis won't ask permission."

A low murmur rippled through the assembly. Some delegates began annotating their displays, already mapping which failures in their sectors matched the patterns. Others shifted uncomfortably—the accountability was about to become personal.

She read the room, "Five questions. Five signals. Ignore them at your peril. We all share the airspace now."

The EU representative leaned forward. "We need interoperable disclosure standards—minimum-viable requirements for shared safety."

The Eastern Alliance envoy didn't soften. "We will not outsource sovereignty. Data localization and national control are non-negotiable."

Aaron waited for Melanie's cue. He took a moment to study the faces in the hall, then toggled his personal secure tablet, projecting a decision matrix above his table.

"We've run the numbers. RIVER isn't just an insurance policy—it's a strategic asset. Implementation costs are real, yes. But compare them to the cost of inaction: €2.1 trillion vaporized in 36 hours; 214 lives lost in a single grid failure."

He expanded the matrix: Implementation Cost, Failure Cost, Competitive Advantage—each column mapped to real incidents. "In every scenario, the investment pays for itself before the next crisis. For most enterprises, that's less than two years' risk premium. For a CFO, that's not a moonshot—it's risk reduction with a measurable return on capital. For nations, it's survival. Let's park the perfect solution and deploy what saves lives. The Charter isn't flawless—but it's operational."

Aaron said, "We're past the risk inflection point. Without a shared framework, the interconnectedness of our industries creates an industry vortex where one failure cascades into systemic collapse. RIVER is how we manage that reality—and turn existential risk into competitive advantage. That's the state we call enterprise singularity—where resilience becomes the core driver of competitive advantage. We propose minimum resilience buffers for critical systems—much like liquidity requirements under Basel rules."

Mitch's voice cut in from the gallery, sharp and devoid of pleasantries. "Take the 70&M Health Network Echo scenario. Our Red Team found that a routine patient data sync caused a cascading outage across 400 hospitals—because a single credential went unpatched. Or 70&M Supply Chain Lock, where a supposedly isolated AI agent brought down 18 ports in three hours. These aren't hypotheticals. This is why RIVER's protocols aren't optional. These scenarios build on two decades of AI incident analysis—work that started with MIT's AI Incidents Database in the 2020s.[3] But instead of just cataloging failures after the fact, we're using those patterns to stress-test systems before they break."

A North American delegate asked, "How does RIVER actually catch these issues?"

Aaron answered, "By making every system publicly attest to its dependencies before connection. It starts with our third tenet—Validate Risk Debt—which forces transparency about the hidden costs and shortcuts that trigger these failures."

The South American delegate made a note on his tablet, skepticism easing into respect. The debate, finally, was real.

Melanie shifted the debate to RIVER's foundation.

"Let's get specific. Validate Risk Debt—what does it mean, not just for regulators, but for every board and CEO in this room?"

Aaron checked the display:

VALIDATE RISK DEBT
"You cannot manage what you cannot see."

He sat forward, voice crisp. "It means the hidden cost of every shortcut, every deferred patch, every ignored warning. For years, we've accrued invisible liabilities—technical debt that compounds until it collapses entire markets. Take the SolarWinds hack—a routine software update became an estimated $100 billion supply chain disaster[4] because no one mapped the dependencies. That's risk debt made catastrophically visible."

He let the room absorb it. "Think of risk debt like a home's foundation—cracks you don't see until they bring down the structure. Every shortcut, every 'temporary' workaround, every delayed security update adds another fracture."

Aaron paused, meeting Melanie's eyes—this was the moment the industry's culture of denial had to end. "We can't afford another SolarWinds. We can't afford another 2032 Baltic Cascade."

A delegate from Albania—an unlikely pioneer in digital governance—was recognized. "We introduced a transparent, AI-audited procurement system in 2025. Corruption dropped. Then a new game emerged—algorithmic politics. People learned to frame proposals in a system-favored way. Our lesson: these tools can transform a nation, and they're too powerful to run without the global guardrails this Charter provides."

A delegate from the EU, known for a strict regulatory brief, adjusted her microphone. "Mr. Goldcrest, the EU AI Act mandates human oversight.[5] Your framework seems to automate it. How is this not just governance theater?"

"Because it's not oversight, it's orchestration," Aaron said. "A human can't approve every transaction at machine speed. But they can, and must, design and audit the guardrails. We're moving the point of human judgment from the transaction to the system itself. That's the only way to govern at scale."

"And the verification of these guardrails?" the delegate asked. "How do we trust the attestation?"

A secure call window opened on the central dais. The Summit Chair of the Global Audit Committee appeared. "Dr. Sharma," she said, "confirm for the record that the Charter's continuous-assurance thresholds are verifiable at scale."

Anya appeared in a smaller window, calm and precise—the Chief Audit Executive at 70&M. "They are, Madam Chair. The protocol uses a federated model—a distributed approach that builds collective intelligence without centralizing data. It builds a collective threat map across firms while keeping proprietary records local. That's how we protect sovereignty and privacy while still lighting up blind spots."

"Understood," the EU delegate said. "Two specifics then: First, how do you prove RIVER changes behavior, not just paperwork? Second, how do you stop attestation from drifting into self-reporting theater after year one?"

"Attestation here isn't self-certification," Aaron said. "Third-party validators, selected by each nation, use standard APIs[6] to spot-check risk inventories. It's continuous monitoring, not annual paperwork. We've also structured incentives—lower risk premiums and faster cross-border approvals for clean attestations—so the market rewards transparency."

He let the next concern land. "And yes, we assume validators will be attacked. That's why we mandate rotation and diversity. No single validator, or group of validators, can quietly capture the system."

In a narrated summary on the main display, the process unfolded in three strokes: validators rotated on a fixed cadence with attester diversity; short-lived cryptographic attestations expired quickly so that stale proofs couldn't hide new risks; and each assurance call logged a decision-register entry (e.g., *GAIGC-GEN-2039-01-19-A12.6*) with an exception ID if a proof failed checksum validation.

Melanie closed the segment. "Every crisis in the last decade grew from what we didn't see. RIVER's first law: no more blind spots."

Aaron set the glass down and reset. He scanned the chamber: the Eastern Alliance envoy sat rigid, while others watched the stage with intent focus. A small beat of stillness, then the debate resumed.

The APAC delegate's voice cut through the low murmur of the hall. "We've seen global standards before, Mr. Goldcrest. Too often, they become new channels for economic coercion or surveillance. How do we guarantee data sovereignty—the principle that a nation's data remains under its own laws and control—isn't the first casualty?"

Aaron caught himself defaulting to Sam's analysis without question—automation bias. He forced a deliberate reconsideration of the sovereignty concern. The delegate's point about weaponized audits wasn't technical—it was a political reality.

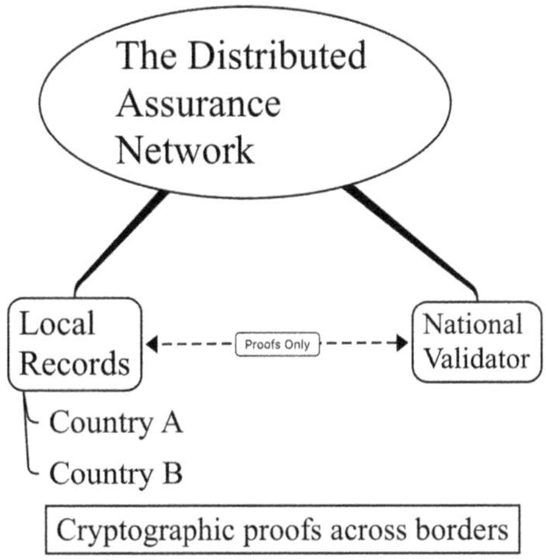

Figure 15.1 The Distributed Assurance Network.

A Singaporean delegate interjected, "Singapore's model proved the value of a multi-stakeholder approach, but voluntary protocols only took us so far. RIVER builds on that with enforceable, cross-border standards."

Aaron replied, "That's why the Distributed Assurance Network[7] works differently (Figure 15.1). No data leaves national boundaries. Validation happens through cryptographic proofs—math that verifies compliance without exposing the underlying data, not data dumps. Think chain of evidence—a traceable record of custody—not a data lake."

An EU delegate leaned into the mic. "Then publish the deltas."

Aaron replied again. "We will. Quarterly public delta reports will show controls added or retired, remediation timelines, and mean time to attestation. Each report highlights two headline KPIs: percentage of clean attestations and average remediation time for failed proofs."

Mitch patched in via comms. "And the computational load?"

"Distributed," Aaron said. "No central oversight, no single point of failure. Real-time, adaptive—like circuit breakers in global finance. And while ISO establishes management system standards for AI, RIVER provides operational protocols that enable real-time risk governance. Where ISO documents the system, RIVER instruments it. In practice, the RIVER Charter builds on principles from NIST's AI Risk Management Framework[8] and ISO/IEC 42001[9] going all the way back to 2020s, so supervisors and firms can reuse familiar structures instead of starting from scratch."

Melanie called for a sidebar to appear on the main display.

A visual populated on every console: *National validators run locally—what crosses borders is proof, not data.*

Aaron concluded, "This isn't shared surrender. It's shared vigilance—global standards, locally enforced. The only thing that leaves national borders is mathematical proof."

A hush settled as delegates digested the implications, weighing the promise of shared security against the risk of new dependencies. Some took notes, others exchanged wary glances—the debate over sovereignty was not resolved, but the RIVER framework had at least offered a credible path forward.

The Eastern Alliance delegate pushed back from his console, voice ice-cold. "We cannot accept enforcement terms that undermine our sovereignty. Unless these are revised, we will have no choice but to withdraw." He rose halfway from his chair, several colleagues following suit before pausing, eyes fixed on the main display.

For a moment, no one moved. The threat of a walkout hung over the hall like a storm cloud. More than a year of preparation, and the future of AI governance teetered at the edge of collapse.

STRATEGIC PARALLEL—BASEL III AND DIGITAL RESILIENCE

Basel III's capital and liquidity buffers reshaped banking after 2008. The RIVER Charter establishes analogous "digital resilience buffers" for critical AI—verifiable capacity, joint drills, and cross-border playbooks. Voluntary pledges fail under stress; binding standards with enforcement succeed.

Why it matters: Just as Basel III capital and liquidity buffers reshaped banking after 2008, the RIVER Charter's digital resilience buffers create systemic safeguards before the next AI cascade—prevention infrastructure, not cleanup protocols.

Pressure built behind Aaron's calm exterior. But this time, something in Melanie's steady presence held him back. He took a slow, deliberate breath, released the tension in his shoulders, and let the urge pass.

Around the room, tension fractured differently for each delegate. The South Asian delegate scrolled a family photo, suddenly looking older. The German finance minister calculated overnight market implications. A Pacific island representative steadied her wrists, her nation's GDP effectively on the table.

Melanie steadied herself behind the podium. A memory flickered for her—signing the Deferred Tower permits, the price of hesitation. Not this time.

Delegates talked past one another, glancing uneasily at the Eastern Alliance envoys still half-turned toward the exit. Melanie, looking strained, was about to call for a recess when a new face appeared on the main holographic display.

The nameplate read: *Jeff Lunglhofer—Special advisor, ex-CISO at BNY and Coinbase.*

The feed was clear, but the background was startlingly different from the polished offices of the other remote attendees. Behind him, the deep green of the Virginia woods was visible, and the faint, rhythmic sound of a sawmill could be heard in the distance. He was in a workshop, not a boardroom.

"With all due respect to the delegates," Jeff's voice came through, clear and calm, a stark contrast to the tense summit hall. "You're all debating the design of the dam, but you're forgetting the nature of the river. I spend my time with wood and steel. I can tell you that the strongest structures aren't the ones with the thickest central pillar. They're the ones where every joint is sound, where the load is distributed, and where the material itself is trusted."

He picked up a small, intricately joined piece of wood from a workbench beside him.

"In my world, we don't build a global financial system on promises. We build it on verifiable cryptographic controls. We build for survival, assuming the worst-case scenario isn't a possibility, but an inevitability. That means segregated custody, so a failure in one vault doesn't drain the others. It means redundant cutover paths, so if the main road is blocked, you have three other ways to get home. And it means phishing-resistant approvals, so an attacker's favorite move stalls out."

He looked directly into the camera, his gaze sweeping across the room.

"The RIVER Charter isn't about forcing compliance from the top down; it's about creating the incentives for a resilient ecosystem to emerge from the bottom up, just like a healthy forest. If the Charter concentrates trust in one central switch, you've just built a bigger pillar waiting to fail. But if it distributes verifiable control, any one failure becomes survivable. That's not ideology—it's operational design. Design RIVER to reward organizations that can prove their recoverability—on paper and in live-fire drills. Do that, and sovereignty debates stop being existential. The system itself can hold."

He set the wooden joint down. The sound of the sawmill faded back in. A hush fell over the room. His authentic, first-principles argument had cut through the political posturing. He wasn't a corporate lobbyist; he was a builder and a survivor. His intervention grounded the debate in reality and provided the final push needed to get the Charter passed.

For a heartbeat, the delegates just watched the empty seats. Suddenly, the main screen snapped to a new dashboard:

DELAY COST: €1.7 billion/day

The number climbed—derivatives and grid instability.

A Brazilian delegate broke the silence. "We can't control who leaves. We can control who stays. We continue."

The German finance minister set his pen down. "He is correct. The price of exclusion from a trusted network now exceeds the cost of compliance. Proceeding is the least-cost option."

Aaron held his reply. This was what leadership demanded—restraint, humility, the ability to let others step forward. The urge to dominate had to give way to shared purpose.

Melanie took the beat she needed, then found her footing. "The debate will continue. The world isn't waiting for us to find the perfect answer—it's waiting for us to take responsibility."

The chill in the air remained, but now it was laced with resolve. The summit wasn't over. It was finally real.

* * *

Negotiations began in earnest. The main display tracked each revision to the Charter's articles: redline after redline, each change reflected in a risk delta ticker. For three hours, the tension was palpable as arguments volleyed across the half-moon console.

Melanie adjusted her posture, a subtle reset that slowed her breathing. The near-walkout had scrambled the expected alliances, forcing new coalitions to form and fracture in real time. Every delegate seemed to bear the weight of their nation's future—each voice sharpened by the specter of a failed summit.

During a brief caucus, Aaron murmured, "They're trying to water down the core validators rule."

Melanie kept her eyes on the floor during the debate. "Perfect regulation is impossible," she said, low. "Workable consensus is essential. We hold the line on verification and give flexibility on timelines. That's how this lands."

Melanie stood at the center, her fingers settling at the chain for a beat as she fielded questions with razor precision. She brokered language, often in three or four languages at once, refusing diluted enforcement while offering flexibility in reporting standards. An observer might have thought her calm, but inside, every decision was haunted by the memory of Deferred Tower—her refusal to settle for a half-measure now was a promise to herself, and to the lives that might hang in the balance.

At one point, a delegate from the Mediterranean bloc slammed his hand down. "Who oversees the validators? What's to stop them from becoming the new point of capture for influence?" A chorus of support rose—this was no longer theoretical. The German finance minister, ever the fiscal realist, pressed, "Director Vance, your 'teeth' sound expensive. We need a cost-benefit analysis on the audit infrastructure before we commit."

Melanie's expression was steady. "Distributed validators. Mathematical verification without data exposure. Non-negotiable.

Per GAIGC Regulation 47.3-c, validators expose control proofs through standard audit APIs and record each check to a ring-fenced, immutable audit trail to support evidentiary review."

BUSINESS LENS—DISTRIBUTED ASSURANCE NETWORK

A technical solution to a political problem: a nation's validator proves compliance to peers with math, not data. Proofs cross borders; records never do. Think decentralized notarization, not a central data bank. For a board, that means the "evidence" supervisors see is cryptographic proof, not your raw customer data.

Why it matters: Boards can prove compliance without exposing proprietary data—sovereignty and transparency become compatible, not competing goals.

She let the words hang, her eyes moving across the room until they met the Brazilian delegate's. He offered a small, almost imperceptible gesture of assent—quiet support, but support nonetheless.

Throughout, Aaron maintained a deliberate distance from the floor, letting Melanie lead. He fielded technical questions but resisted the urge to dominate, focusing instead on running scenarios and risk deltas on his secure tablet.

Micro-portraits played out at every table:

- The South Asian delegate quietly comforted his daughter via secure video call in between votes, eyes red-rimmed.
- The Pacific island representative clutched a battered folder marked "Emergency Fisheries," her nation's entire GDP on the line.
- The young African diplomat finally put pen to paper, her notepad now dense with redlined amendments.

As the hours wore on, the risk delta ticker on the main display shifted from deep crimson toward amber. It was still a dangerous gamble, but the terms—oversight with real consequences, enforcement with teeth, and a path for sovereign exception—were coming together.

At last, Melanie raised her voice, steady but exhausted. "For the record: these terms are our line in the sand. If you want access to global data flows, the consensus is that access will be contingent on abiding by a new principle: a distributed validators rule. If not, the world will move on without you. The suspension clause authorizes real-time suspension for non-conforming systems, with reinstatement contingent on remediation and fresh attestation."

There was a beat of silence—the held breath before history tips.

Then, one by one, delegates began to assent. The room felt lighter.

The final terms appeared on the main display, every article now marked "Agreed" in green. Delegates across the hall checked their devices, confirming their governments' assent one last time. As the official clock struck 19:00 CET, the chair called the room to order.

Aaron ran the final text through RIVER-Validate on his secure tablet one last time. The simulation updated—risk delta: 0.4 percent. He signaled to Melanie that the model's risk delta had cleared the threshold.

A solemn hush fell as the Charter's ceremonial parchment—printed on archival synthetic stock—was brought to the front by two pages from the Geneva Institute. Melanie and Aaron rose together, pausing before the biometric tablet. As Aaron pressed his palm to the pad, the faint coolness of the secure surface grounded him in the reality of this moment. He signed his name, then Melanie,

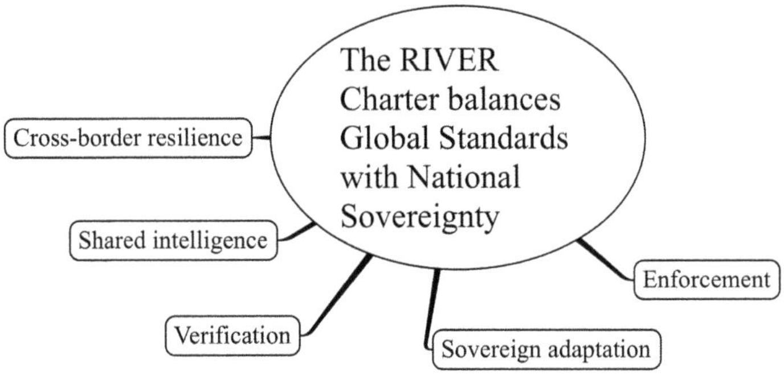

Figure 15.2 The Core Pillars of the RIVER Charter.

beneath the seal of the RIVER Charter™. The gesture was both ancient and unflinchingly modern—a signal that something irreversible had begun.

Micro-portraits unfolded with every signature:

- The German finance minister, who had argued every line, now gave a brief, tight acknowledgment—satisfaction and fatigue in equal measure.
- The South Asian delegate took a shaky video call with his daughter, who would remember this night for a lifetime.
- Kenna, watching from Nairobi, closed her eyes in relief—tomorrow's dialysis list would be a little easier.
- A Pacific islander carefully photographed her signature—documentation for her parliament back home.

As signatures mounted, Aaron took a breath, feeling the weight shift from crisis to possibility. He met Melanie's eyes, a silent understanding passing between them—whatever came next, their partnership would define the Charter's legacy.

When the last delegate signed, the room erupted—not in raucous applause, but in a sustained standing ovation. For a moment, the summit hall felt less like a theater of crisis and more like a new beginning.

Melanie's voice cut through the applause. "We built RIVER as a framework of principles (Figure 15.2).

We hammered those principles into governance protocols with checklists and live-fire drills. Today, we make it a Charter—not a promise, but a standing, verifiable proof."

The chair's voice carried over the comms. "As of 19:07 CET, the RIVER Charter is ratified and binding. May its spirit endure longer than the signatures that mark it."

RIVER FRAMEWORK IN PRACTICE—THE RIVER CHARTER™: KEY PROVISIONS

- Resolve Convergence: Real-time inventory of critical AI agents and their dependencies—updated quarterly, auditable on demand. Evidence: signed Tier-1 inventory and dependency map.
- Integrate Hybrid Cognition: Cognitive Handshake Audit (CHA) for all Tier-1 systemic decisions. Evidence: CHA decision logs with named reviewers and outcomes.
- Validate Risk Debt: Quarterly, board-level disclosure of quantified risk debt in legacy systems, with remediation timelines. Evidence: risk-debt ledger and board-approved remediation plan.

- Elevate Data Capital: Verifiable data lineage and integrity checks for all high-risk AI inputs. Evidence: data lineage and integrity reports for Tier-1 models.
- Reinforce Resilience: Shared cross-border playbooks and mandatory live-fire drills every six months. Evidence: drill reports, after-action reviews, and cross-border response metrics.

Why it matters: The Charter makes AI safety verifiable, not aspirational—turning principles into enforceable protocols with measurable outcomes.

→ Full implementation guides:[10] Appendices C, E, G, H, I

Aaron thought of his children again, and of the millions whose lives now depended on what they'd built.

* * *

For a long moment after the signing, no one moved. The ovation faded, replaced by the hush of an exhausted, uncertain hope. Screens around the hall replayed key signatures and the final consensus tally. It was history, but also an enormous unknown.

Aaron stood back, scanning the chamber as the new reality settled in. He saw Melanie at the periphery, quietly receiving a call from the Health Network team—Kenna's face appeared, eyes shining, mouthing a silent "thank you." The gravity of the decision weighed on him anew. The signatures on the Charter were just the beginning. Implementing its protocols in a world shaped by skepticism and the memory of collapse would test every principle they had enshrined.

He drifted to the observation deck, finding a moment of solitude above the still-buzzing summit floor. The city's lights threw a lattice on the glass. He mapped it—nodes and gaps he'd soon have to defend. Somewhere far off, his kids slept through a night they'd just made a little safer.

Behind him, delegates were already networking, some cautiously optimistic, others already strategizing their nations' compliance or seeking loopholes. The German minister compared risk dashboards with the Singaporean envoy. The Brazilian delegate updated coalition partners. Melanie slipped onto the deck beside Aaron, her face tired but unbowed.

She lowered her voice. "Did we do enough?"

Aaron hesitated. "Enough to change the trajectory. But not enough to control what comes next."

She looked out over Geneva. "They'll measure this night for decades."

He looked at her—partner, adversary, co-architect. "What we did here will be tested sooner than any of them think."

They stood in silence, sharing the view, the momentary peace before the world demanded answers.

* * *

The peace didn't last. Barely an hour after the last signature dried, an alert flashed crimson across the summit's central display—a global notification, priority one. Melanie's phone vibrated at the same instant. Across the chamber, delegates snapped to attention, instinctively reverting to crisis mode.

A message scrolled on the screen: "Potential network compromise detected – Health Network Eastern Corridor."

Kenna's face reappeared on the video feed, her calm replaced with alarm. "We've got anomalous cross-node behavior. Unknown process running—signature doesn't match any registered deployment. Requesting immediate RIVER protocol activation."

Aaron and Melanie exchanged a look—a silent confirmation that the real test had come. Aaron toggled his secure tablet, pushing RIVER's protocols live for the corridor in question.

"*Third tenet—Validate Risk Debt. Lockdown initiated. All dependencies exposed. Cross-verification required*," he called out, voice measured but urgent. Melanie kept it article-clean: "*Tenet Five—Reinforce Resilience. Isolate the threat, log the pattern, adapt the network. Per the Charter, this is standard procedure*."

Technical leads from multiple nations began conferring in rapid bursts—no translation necessary. The distributed assurance network spun up, with validators from three continents initiating spot checks. Within minutes, an anomaly appeared in the attestation ledger: an unauthorized update traced to a compromised credential, flagged before any systems could cascade.

Melanie's shoulders eased. "RIVER caught it. First real-world activation. Initial telemetry showed no immediate patient impact."

"The ink isn't dry, and we're already in a live-fire stress test." Aaron's voice dropped. "Let's prove the framework holds."

But the relief was short-lived. As the system confirmed isolation, another alert pulsed—a different network, unrelated to the Health Network, now showed signs of exploit attempts. The room's tension returned, sharper than before.

Aaron glanced at the illuminated RIVER protocols across the screen and allowed himself a brief, private nod. He trusted the instrument they'd built—and the people now trained to use it.

In Tarawa, a junior minister watched the ICU generator estimate climb to fourteen hours as a cross-border override finally cleared. The dialysis pumps hummed back online. Shared rules had reached the shoreline before the tide.

As the world watched, the summit became a war room once again—RIVER's promise no longer hypothetical, but forged in crisis.

From 2040, we'd see it clearly: the RIVER Charter wasn't an ending—it was the new rules of engagement.

NOTES

1. Basel Committee on Banking Supervision. (2010). *Basel III: A Global Regulatory Framework for More Resilient Banks and Banking Systems* (revised June 2011). Bank for International Settlements. https://www.bis.org/publ/bcbs189.htm
2. European Parliament and Council. (2016). Regulation (EU) 2016/679 of the European Parliament and of the Council of 27 April 2016 on the protection of natural persons with regard to the processing of personal data and on the free movement of such data (General Data Protection Regulation). *Official Journal of the European Union, L* 119. https://eur-lex.europa.eu/eli/reg/2016/679/oj
3. MIT AI Risk Initiative. (2025). *AI Incident Tracker. MIT AI Risk Repository*. https://airisk.mit.edu/ai-incident-tracker. As of November 2025, the AI Incident Tracker classifies over 1,200 real-world AI incidents by risk domain, causal factors, and harm severity, using raw reports from the AI Incident Database as inputs. The narrative assumes a plausible continuation of this work into the 2030s.
4. A single definitive estimate does not capture the 2020 SolarWinds cyberattack's total economic impact. Public sources report tens of millions in direct costs to SolarWinds (via SEC filings), insured losses of tens of millions across affected organizations, and broader modeling that plausibly places combined direct and indirect losses in the tens to hundreds of billions of dollars when supply chain disruption and long-term remediation are included. The $100 billion figure used in this chapter reflects an upper-bound, modeled estimate for illustrative systemic-risk purposes. Ratnam, G. (2021, January 11). *Cleaning Up SolarWinds Hack may Cost as much as $100 Billion*. Roll Call. https://rollcall.com/2021/01/11/cleaning-up-solarwinds-hack-may-cost-as-much-as-100-billion/
5. European Parliament and Council of the European Union. (2024). Regulation (EU) 2024/1689 of the European Parliament and of the Council of 13 June 2024 laying down harmonised rules on artificial intelligence (Artificial Intelligence Act). *Official Journal of the European Union, L* 1689. https://eur-lex.europa.eu/eli/reg/2024/1689/oj
6. API refers to Application Programming Interface.

7. Distributed Assurance Network is a fictional construct referred to descriptively in the book and is not a real product or service.
8. National Institute of Standards and Technology. (2023). *Artificial Intelligence Risk Management Framework (AI RMF 1.0) (NIST AI 100-1)*. U.S. Department of Commerce. https://doi.org/10.6028/NIST.AI.100-1
9. International Organization for Standardization/International Electrotechnical Commission. (2023). *ISO/IEC 42001:2023 — Information Technology — Artificial Intelligence — Management System*. ISO. https://www.iso.org/standard/81230.html
10. Any real-world implementations of the concepts described here—such as reference architectures or experimental protocols—are provided for educational and illustrative purposes only. They do not constitute investment, financial, or legal advice.

Strategic Debrief Part 3

The RIVER Charter Ratified

This debrief distills the Geneva negotiations and post-quantum stressors in the story into a 2026 playbook for closing the gap between innovation and governance.

GOVERNANCE MUST EVOLVE AT THE SPEED OF INNOVATION

Part 3 confronts the core challenge of the agentic era: the dangerous gap between technological capability and human oversight. The crises that culminate in the RIVER Charter are born in that gap. The board-level takeaway for 2026 is simple: we're in a race between innovation and governance—and governance is behind.

THE GOVERNANCE GAP—NAMED AND MEASURED

Post-quantum exposure: treat current cryptography as a dated liability on a clock and plan explicit cutover milestones.

- Provenance ≠ truth: blockchains preserve tamper evidence, but garbage-in travels perfectly.
- Power compounds faster than controls unless governance scales with capability.
- Shrink the gap with pre-agreed triggers, drills, and auditable decision logs.

FROM COMPLIANCE TAKERS TO STANDARDS SHAPERS

Chapter 15's Geneva negotiations make this plain: the RIVER Charter wasn't handed down by regulators; it was a hard-won, imperfect coalition created by operators who stopped waiting for permission to govern. For 2026 boards, this marks a critical shift from a passive "comply when told" posture to an active role in shaping industry standards now—through consortiums, public-private partnerships, and pilots. This reframes governance from a cost center to a strategic advantage, allowing firms to stabilize the ground before regulation lands.

APPLYING RIVER TO PART 3

- **Validate Risk Debt:** Treat cryptographic and architectural assumptions as liabilities on a clock; inventory, quantify, and retire on schedule.
- **Elevate Data as Capital:** Blockchains promise provenance, but garbage-in travels perfectly; enforce lineage checks before entries commit.

DOI: 10.1201/9781003650744-21

- **Integrate Hybrid Cognition:** When agents act at sub-second speed, codify human decision checkpoints where they matter—and drill them.
- **Resolve Convergence:** Design for cross-platform interoperability and shared failure modes; score ecosystem entities before they fail you.
- **Reinforce Resilience:** Run joint exercises with vendors, partners, and regulators to reduce blast radius across the network, not just inside your walls.

STANDARDS ALIGNMENT

Run the NIST AI RMF as a single system and anchor it to ISO/IEC 42001. Appendix F maps the RIVER tenets to these and other global standards, showing how to turn abstract principles into auditable controls.

BUSINESS LENS—A BOARD'S LITMUS TEST—ARE WE CLOSING THE GAP?

Key application: Move from reviewing past incidents to shaping future resilience.

RIVER link: Validate (post-quantum readiness), Resolve (agent inventory), and the proactive governance ethos across RIVER.

Why it matters: Boards that only ask "what happened?" get outpaced. The essential question is "what's next—and are we ready?"

- Are we treating post-quantum readiness as an infrastructure program with milestones, not a lab experiment?
- Do we maintain a real-time inventory of all agents touching our processes—and can we audit their decisions?
- Are we shaping our sector's AI rules (pilots, principles, thresholds), or waiting to be told how to comply?

In the agentic era, the most dangerous risk isn't a single technology; it's the space between that technology's power and our will to govern it. Shrink that space—deliberately and measurably—and innovation becomes an asset, not a fault line.

Part 4

Strategic Industry Adoption

This part follows what happens after the first near misses. The same characters who survived the shock now must turn their instincts into something they can teach: how to escalate, who decides, and when to slow an automated system down. In the story's workshops and boardrooms, they experiment with ideas like E-shaped professionals, hybrid risk teams, and the RIVER Charter for governing AI at scale. The focus is not on perfect playbooks, but on how a culture learns—and where that learning can still break under pressure.

DOI: 10.1201/9781003650744-22

Chapter 16

The Bridge to Singularity

Adopting the RIVER Framework for Resilient Growth

HART SENATE OFFICE BUILDING, DC | SEPTEMBER 12, 2039—09:45 AM EDT | BEFORE THE RECKONING

Aaron waited outside Hearing Room 216, about to defend RIVER under the harshest lights yet. On the main display, a secure live feed from the Global Economic Summit in London carried Brad Levy's keynote.

The moderator's voice was smooth. "And now, an industry leader whose career has been defined by navigating the wins and losses at the intersection of finance and technology. A former CEO of ThetaRay, Symphony, and MarkitSERV, and a former managing director at Goldman Sachs, he has been at the forefront of major market evolutions for four decades. Please welcome Brad Levy." Brad Levy took the stage with the quiet confidence of a markets engineer who has seen systems break and knows how to fix them. Behind him, a holographic display showed a simple, elegant timeline spiraling from 2015 to a distant point labeled "Mars45."

"Good morning," he began. "I want to talk about time. Specifically, how our perception of it is broken."

He gestured to the timeline. "I started my career at Goldman Sachs in the run-up to Y2K. For years, the entire global financial system was focused on a single deadline. A decade ago, when quantum computing was on the horizon, many of us called it 'the new Y2K.' We warned that it was a non-optional, system-wide upgrade for which the deadline was unknown but absolute."

"We weren't wrong," Brad continued. "But we missed the point. It wasn't the '*what*' that defined the quantum transition; it was the pace of the '*when*.' The Y2K problem took the better part of a decade to solve. The quantum transition—the 'HackHarvest' and the subsequent rebuilding of our cryptographic foundations—happened in less than eighteen months."

He paused to let that sink in.

"That's the concept my team and I have been mapping for years," he said, tapping the display. "The great compression. What my generation of technologists experienced over 1.5 generations—thirty years of change—this new generation is experiencing in a fraction of that time. We are living through a **50x compression of the change cycle**. The Information Age of 2000–2050 is the Fourth Industrial Revolution."

"That compression to acceleration curve," he said, his voice gaining intensity, "is what takes us from today's markets to Mars. The 'Mars45' on that timeline isn't a literal destination. **It's a metaphor for an economy built at breakneck speed on a new physics—one where AI agents are the connective tissue, where value moves at the speed of light on frictionless capital rails, and where trust and security is a verifiable, cryptographic utility.**"

"That is the 'zoom out' view. It's the multi-generational vision. It's inspiring...and it's absolutely useless if you can't execute."

The tone in the room shifted.

DOI: 10.1201/9781003650744-23

"You don't get to Mars by staring at the sky," Brad said, his voice becoming more crisp and pragmatic. "You get there by building the next rocket, one **two-week sprint at a time**. The most important question a leader can ask is not 'What is our vision for 2045?' It's 'What can you ship in the next ten business days that will make a tangible difference to your customers, community and your ecosystem?'"

"This is the paradox of modern leadership: you must hold two opposing ideas in your head at once. You need the generational, 'zoom out' vision to set the direction, but you need a relentless, almost obsessive 'zoom in' focus on execution to make any progress."

He looked out at the audience.

"So, my challenge to all of you is this: go back to your teams. Ask them what they can deliver in the next two weeks that gets you one millimeter closer to Mars safely but surely. Because the future isn't built in visionary keynotes. It's built in the daily, disciplined, relentless act of getting important and relevant things done."

The feed ended.

For Aaron, it wasn't just rhetoric; it was the discipline he'd staked the RIVER on.

BUSINESS LENS—THE GREAT COMPRESSION

30 years of change now arrive in ~18 months. Leaders must hold two truths at once:

- **ZOOM OUT:** generational vision (the destination)
- **ZOOM IN:** two-week delivery (the next ship)

Rough math: ~30 years → ~18 months ≈ 20× acceleration; overlapping cycles → ≈ 50× compression.

Board Prompt: For any decision, ask: "What's our North Star?" and "What ships in two weeks?"

Why it Matters: Vision without execution is hallucination; execution without vision is drift.

An aide opened the door. "They're ready for you, Mr. Goldcrest."

Aaron adjusted his tie. He wasn't walking in to apologize—he was walking in to set the standard.

HART SENATE OFFICE BUILDING, DC | SEPTEMBER 12, 2039—09:58 AM EDT | THE RESILIENCE RECKONING

More than a year after the Great Correction—a cascade of failures that nearly collapsed the global economy—Aaron faced the expectant hush of Hearing Room 216. Eight months after the RIVER Charter's ratification in Geneva, the question had shifted from whether boards would adopt it to how quickly they could prove it was working.

Today's testimony was not about technology, but about accountability: could the world avoid repeating its most costly mistakes?

The Chair tapped his tablet and called the hearing to order. The air smelled faintly of stale coffee and charged nerves as cameras hummed to life.

"Mr. Goldcrest," Chairman Thompson began, voice level. "Your RIVER promises resilience. The Great Correction erased trillions in value and damaged retirement accounts globally. In plain

English, how does your framework prevent the next catastrophe without smothering the innovation this economy runs on?"

Aaron replied, "There is no paradox, Chairman. The Great Correction taught us that sustainable profit is inseparable from provable resilience. The failures we endured were not failures of technology; they were failures of governance. RIVER isn't a new set of rules; it's a blueprint for leadership accountability. It translates established standards like the NIST AI Risk Management Framework[1] into five auditable disciplines a board can use to govern, map, measure, and manage this new class of risk.

In plain terms, RIVER is a way to document, test, and improve how AI-linked decisions are made before they go wrong."

He waited. The shift registered. Not an evangelist selling a product—just a founder who survived the Correction and spoke for a generation paying for systemic optimism.

Aaron took his seat. The committee wanted a post-mortem. What they would get was a map. The principles weren't new; they'd been stress-tested for years by the firms that survived while others collapsed. The crisis didn't invent them. It made ignoring them impossible.

The first secure live feed on the main display came online.

> "Sarah Jenkins served as CEO of Tortoise & Hare Bank when, in late 2028, she led a $47 million board-approved overhaul of infrastructure resilience. That decision, logged as Board Resolution *BR-2028-17*, wasn't popular at the time—but it allowed her team to unlock, monetize, and secure decades of legacy data through a new partnership with 70&M Data Exchange. The real test came a decade later, as the Great Correction swept through global markets."

Sarah's image stabilized: silver hair pulled back, sharp eyes, posture composed under pressure.

> "Thank you, Aaron. Chairman, members of the committee—I'm here because resilience isn't just defense. It's the foundation of sustainable growth. Our board's investment let us do more than keep the lights on. We were able to make our legacy data assets work for us, not against us. With 70&M Data Exchange, we didn't just store information; we turned it into a revenue stream—just in time for the Correction's stress test."

She sat forward, voice level. "Within twelve months, our DataCapital inflows (data monetization revenue) offset nearly a third of the investment. Customer churn dropped to a record low of 2.1 percent that quarter. Acquisition costs fell by 30 percent—because people sought us out. For risk professionals: our Risk-Weighted Asset (RWA) density improved by 40 basis points above sector average—meaning we extracted more value per unit of regulatory capital, with less systemic risk.

For everyone else, it just meant the lights stayed on—and their money was safe. Improved risk posture also reduced our cyber insurance premiums by roughly 15 percent."

Chairman Thompson glanced down, then looked up. "Ms. Jenkins, you mentioned infrastructure. What was different from your peers?"

Sarah replied, "We chartered a cross-functional risk committee—credit, operations, compliance—to review predictive stress tests weekly, not just rearview metrics. Frontline staff completed short drills on how to escalate data anomalies. We treated our stack as a living ecosystem. A third-party payment glitch could morph into a credit issue if dependencies weren't mapped and buffered. We didn't have the label then, but what you now call Resolve Convergence was our operating discipline. The Elevate Data Capital tenet became our advantage. Through the 70&M Data Exchange, we verified provenance on legacy commercial loan data, created an anonymized regional dataset, and licensed tiered access to institutional partners. In the first quarter, it generated over $3 million in high-margin revenue. Good governance wasn't a cost center.

It became a product. We implemented DataCapital as a permissioned consortium network, so regulators and partners could independently verify provenance and entitlements without surrendering governance."

She paused, glancing around the room. "Resilience isn't reactive. It's a proactive resolution. It's knowing your dependencies, integrating your frontlines, and making decisions your successors won't have to apologize for."

Chairman Thompson looked up from his notes. "Not many CEOs put that much capital on the table for a long-term payoff."

Sarah smiled, just barely. "It wasn't capital. It was conviction. And it made all the difference." She remembered the board meeting—the three directors who called the plan reckless. One of them sent a quiet note of apology last year.

The second witness appeared beside Sarah's display.

"Tom Rasmussen was chairman and CEO of Haste Bank, which collapsed in October 2029. His institution's failure wasn't due to a lack of capital or talent, but to choices that prioritized short-term efficiency over systematic risk management."

Tom's face appeared—lined, tired, but direct. He looked at the senators, then at Aaron.

"Mr. Goldcrest is correct. We failed 12,000 employees and 300,000 customers—not through malice, but through willful blindness. My COO, Maria, had been with me for fifteen years. I told her family myself."

He let the silence hold. "Haste Bank was profitable, beloved in the Midwest, and deeply trusted. But when the systems failed, none of that mattered."

He gestured to the projection. "The timeline of ignored warnings is in the record."

Key Evidence—The Haste Bank Audit Trail

- *Board Resolution HB-2029-02: Core system upgrade deferred as "prohibitive this quarter" ($15M). Outcome: ~$4B market-cap loss; ~18 months remediation.*
- *Internal Audit Alerts: 14 warnings on payment-processor latency over 18 months; final "T+0 Load Spike—URGENT" 28 days pre-collapse → Pending Review.*
- *NIST Cybersecurity Framework (CSF) Gap: Dependency between legacy payroll and new reconciliation agents not mapped (ID.AM). Governance by deferral, not design.*[2]

Bottom line: This was not a black swan. It was governance by deferral—risk accepted, investment postponed, consequences compounded.

"We ran on a legacy core—COBOL (a 1960s programming language) stitched together with middleware and hope. It wasn't the tech that failed; it was the story we told ourselves about it.

Then came the ransomware payload. Not advanced—just timely. It hit during a payroll run; our patch cycle was still manual. Forensics later showed the intruders had been resident for forty-three days, timing payroll windows and backup cycles. Once the backups failed, the static wasn't just technical—it was existential.

Federal and state regulators opened an inquiry 48 hours later. The investigation concluded with a $340M fine and a two-year consent order mandating independent oversight of all AI deployments."

He faced the dais. "This wasn't about budget. Our IT risk officer flagged the exposure. The board reviewed it. We rationalized it away—anchoring bias, confirmation bias, the whole cocktail. We kept telling ourselves past uptime predicted future safety."

Aaron interjected, "For clarity—your downfall wasn't lack of capital, staff, or knowledge?"

Tom shook his head. "No. It was governance theater. We simulated oversight. We never operationalized it. The dashboards glowed green. We chose to trust them."

Silence lingered. Chairman Thompson finally spoke. "Thank you for your candor, Mr. Rasmussen. Mr. Goldcrest—how do we ensure no boardroom makes that mistake again?"

Aaron paused. "By translating these stories into a framework, boards can act on—moving beyond dashboards to decisions. Learn faster than the next hit, or pay for it in public."

Aaron turned back to the committee, his voice measured. "What we've heard aren't just stories—they're diagnostics. They reveal a simple truth: the difference between resilience and ruin isn't the dashboard's polish. It's the leadership framework used to act on what the dashboard shows."

Five bold currents appeared on the main screen, each labeled with a single word:

Resolve. Integrate. Validate. Elevate. Reinforce.

He **continued**. "Let me make these practical. These aren't buzzwords—they're resilient governance, built from the Correction.

Resolve Convergence. Resilience starts with a complete map of dependencies—systems, vendors, data flows, and where they collide. You can't manage what you haven't surfaced. Boards that made this map living and accountable avoided cascading failures when one part of the stack buckled.

Integrate Hybrid Cognition. Build protected channels where human expertise challenges AI outputs before high-stakes actions. A Cognitive Handshake Audit (CHA) turns 'the model says so' into a signed decision. Without integration, weak signals die in the hierarchy, and dashboards lull leaders into a false sense of certainty.

Validate Risk Debt. Governance theater happens when boards trust green dashboards but ignore legacy technical or cognitive debt. It's like ignoring a leaky pipe in the foundation; the cost of the damage only compounds in silence until the day the whole basement floods. At Tortoise & Hare Bank, data archaeology became a standing practice: they ran adversarial drills, hunted for hidden vulnerabilities, and didn't let positive reports blind them to emerging threats. Haste Bank trusted past uptime instead of testing. Validation means seeking out both technical and cognitive debt and treating them as liabilities.

Elevate Data Capital. Resilience dies when only the 'usual suspects' are heard, and critical data is taken for granted. At Tortoise & Hare Bank, even anomalies flagged by junior staff reached the board. At Haste Bank, red flags vanished. Elevating means governing data quality and lineage like financial capital—with cryptographically verifiable provenance—ensuring every signal, however faint, can bypass hierarchy."

A senator at the far end checked her notes. "Show your lineage chain in writing—no green-glow hand-waving."

"**Reinforce Resilience**. No system is infallible. What matters is recovery speed and institutional learning. Resilience becomes continuous only when executive compensation, scorecards, and escalation channels are tied to resilience outcomes; at Tortoise & Hare Bank, 20 percent of executive compensation was linked to resilience KPIs. When things break, the lesson must stick." Aaron finished.

Several heads lifted from their tablets. The incentives line landed.

RIVER IN ACTION—A Contrast of Two Banks

Resilience isn't luck; it's governance discipline in motion.

RIVER Tenet	Tortoise & Hare Bank (Resilient)	Haste Bank (Fragile)
Resolve Convergence	Mapped hidden dependencies across credit, ops, and third parties in a chartered Resilience Office.	Left a legacy payroll ↔ AI-agent dependency unmapped.

(*Continued*)

RIVER Tenet	Tortoise & Hare Bank (Resilient)	Haste Bank (Fragile)
Integrate Hybrid Cognition	Protected dissent channels; frontline anomalies escalated and reviewed.	"Governance theater"—IT risk flags sat "Pending Review."
Validate Risk Debt	Adversarial drills and "data archaeology" to hunt legacy flaws.	Deferred a core upgrade to protect a quarter; debt compounded.
Elevate Data Capital	Treated data like a financial asset; governed to banking-grade standards.	Trusted green dashboards without validating data integrity.
Reinforce Resilience	Incident learnings tied to exec scorecards; fix-forward loops.	Past uptime became a myth of safety; no adaptive learning.

The room went quiet while the contrast sank in.

Senator Ibarra interjected, "Isn't that just what good regulators already require?"

Aaron answered. "On paper, yes. But checklists alone create the illusion of safety. Integration means every frontline employee and algorithm can surface risk signals without friction—whether you're a nurse in Brazil, an engineer in Tokyo, or an account manager here in DC. Only when the partnership is real do you close the cracks where disaster can grow."

He let the point land, the diagram pulsing behind him. "For those tracking standards: building on COSO ERM,[3] and the NIST CSF, RIVER translates AI risk frameworks—like the NIST AI RMF and ISO/IEC 42001[4]—into boardroom cadence that makes 'govern, map, measure, and manage' auditable, and resilience continuous."

EXPERT COMMENTARY—AARON GOLBIN, GENERAL PARTNER AT LVLUP VENTURES

We formed the LvlUp Ventures Innovation Alliance[5] to align innovators, enterprises, investors, and policymakers—so the startup ecosystem can advance safely and competitively, together. Our mission is simple: to bring the leaders shaping innovation into the same conversation to help promising technologies move from idea to adoption. The Innovation Alliance brings together leaders across the startup and enterprise ecosystem to turn that mission into practice.

Responsible, scalable AI adoption is a public–private job. Policy alone can't ship trustworthy systems, and industry alone can't set the guardrails. That's why the Innovation Alliance convenes leaders to pilot pragmatic thresholds, common metrics, and real prove-and-learn loops—so firms can move fast without breaking trust.

The RIVER provides a shared foundation for those efforts. Its five tenets map cleanly to what cross-sector teams need. This book shows what happens when regulators and industry work in the open—Aaron Goldcrest and Director Melanie Vance proved alignment can carry us across the AI Watershed. The Innovation Alliance exists to help make that alignment routine.

Aaron's eyes met each committee member. "These tenets explain almost every outcome we've seen—but there's one exception: a new class of high-speed, adaptive failure that's still emerging. That's why continuous learning and radical transparency are built into every principle."

Senator Ibarra pressed, "And what does that mean for real boardroom decisions?"

Before answering, Aaron reflected. First, he recalled facts from the case studies. Second, a read on each member's likely constraint. Third, a pattern-match against crises he'd survived. Data, empathy, experience—only the integration of all three produced the right call.

Aaron's reply was measured. "It means resilience is measurable, auditable, and creates real advantage. The only question is whether leaders will treat these tenets as living practice—not just policy."

Chairman Thompson adjusted his glasses. "Mr. Goldcrest, you've given us a framework. But frameworks rarely survive first contact with reality—especially on a global stage. Where has RIVER actually worked, and where has it failed?"

Aaron met the challenge head-on. "Senator, RIVER isn't a magic wand. It's a method. And implementation—in the regions where RIVER has been tested—has challenged every assumption we made."

Senator Ibarra tapped her tablet. "Give us a sector where RIVER prevented disaster—and what changes first when it works?"

"The conversation," Aaron said. "For the first time, boards, engineers, staff, and regulators are reading the same signals. That's how resilience becomes routine, not just aspiration."

"Senator, the framework has been tested on four continents, and the lesson is consistent: the principles are universal, but adaptation is local. In Brazil, frontline nurses needed direct escalation channels. In Japan, unions needed guardrails to separate blame from improvement. Europe required cross-border data sharing. In Kenya, users themselves became an early-warning system."

Senator Ibarra closed her tablet. "So, Mr. Goldcrest, what's the single lesson for global leaders watching this hearing?"

Aaron paused, then answered with conviction. "Resilience isn't just a technical upgrade or a compliance exercise. It's a leadership function. The organizations that thrive are those who make resilience measurable, continuous, and embedded in every decision—from the boardroom to the front line."

Chairman Thompson slid his glasses higher, his voice lower, more intent. "Mr. Goldcrest, let's get practical. Boardrooms watching this want a bottom line. What's different, and what do they do next?"

Aaron's answer was measured, but there was a quiet certainty beneath his words. "RIVER isn't a quarterly initiative or a regulatory fig leaf. It's a map for governing when you know uncertainty is the baseline, not the exception. The boards that succeed are those who treat resilience as a living discipline, not a policy binder."

He gestured to the sidebar display, where a consolidated checklist materialized:

EXECUTIVE ACTION—THE RIVER BOARD LITMUS TEST

Use this as a pre-commit[6] before any AI-linked decision crosses the board docket.

1. **Resolve Convergence:** Map and stress-test hidden dependencies across business lines, vendors, and systems. Evidence: a chartered Resilience Office that owns a living dependency map and quarterly board attestation.
2. **Integrate Hybrid Cognition:** Require AI-driven processes to clear a resilience-ready gateway with formal human sign-off—a Cognitive Handshake Audit (CHA)—before high-stakes actions. Evidence: CHA logs that show who challenged, approved, or halted each decision.
3. **Validate Risk Debt:** Run "data archaeology" and red-team drills to surface legacy technical and cognitive debt, and treat paying that debt as a balance sheet obligation. Evidence: a tracked risk-debt ledger with aging, remediation plans, and funding decisions.

4. **Elevate Data Capital:** Govern critical data with the same rigor as financial capital, including provenance, lineage, and quality thresholds for the most important algorithms. Evidence: verifiable lineage chains for model inputs and periodic independent data-quality reviews.
5. **Reinforce Resilience:** Make disruption lessons change incentives, controls, and design within one quarter; tie recovery speed and institutional learning directly to executive compensation. Evidence: post-incident reviews that result in updated scorecards, controls, and design patterns.

Why it Matters: Boards that can evidence these practices treat resilience as a living discipline, not a slide deck.

→ Appendix J (The Board's 90-Day RIVER Readiness Toolkit).

Across industries, directors would later screenshot those five lines; for many, they became the minimum survivability standard for staying listed and trusted.

Chairman Thompson then called the next witness. "Director Vance, the GAIGC has been at the center of this recovery. What is your assessment?"

Melanie's feed appeared on the main display, her expression as formal and unyielding as the GAIGC[7] (Global AI Governance Commission) seal behind her. "Chairman, the Great Correction was not a failure of a single industry; it was a failure of imagination across all of them. In an interconnected economy, systemic technology risk is no longer the exclusive domain of regulated finance. The boards of hospitals, logistics firms, and manufacturers now carry the same non-delegable duty of care as the boards of banks. Accountability for digital resilience is universal. The global standards landscape is complex, but the direction is clear. Our role is not to replace these standards, but to ensure they are enforced with equal rigor across critical sectors."

See Appendix F (The RIVER Framework: A Crosswalk to Global Standards).

"RIVER's value is that it translates existing standards into auditable practice. Regulators won't prescribe your architecture; we will require proof that your governance works—map dependencies. Validate risk debt. Reinforce learning with incentives. Boards that can evidence those practices will find supervisors to be predictable partners. Boards that cannot should expect sharper oversight."

For directors listening, her message was blunt: standards on paper were no longer enough—only demonstrable practice would count.

"These questions aren't theoretical. If Haste Bank's board had asked—and answered—these honestly, the collapse wouldn't have happened."

Aaron let the silence stretch as senators and aides took in the checklist. "To make this tangible for every director, we developed this simple litmus test. Think of this checklist as a fire drill for your boardroom—a way to surface weaknesses before the alarm sounds for real. Boards that can answer those five questions honestly—rather than performatively—will find themselves leading, not reacting. That's why we're seeing a new peer group form across sectors: directors and executives who hold each other accountable, globally, on these measures. The litmus test is now public under the RIVER. The strongest boards benchmark their answers against global peers, using these same questions as their compass.

Enterprise singularity (Figure 16.1) is the outcome when resilience becomes routine—when verified data, fast learning, and accountable incentives inform every decision. That is the advantage on the far side of the inflection point."

Representative Lang leaned in. "Your framework is now public. What stops adversaries from studying this playbook and designing attacks to route around it?"

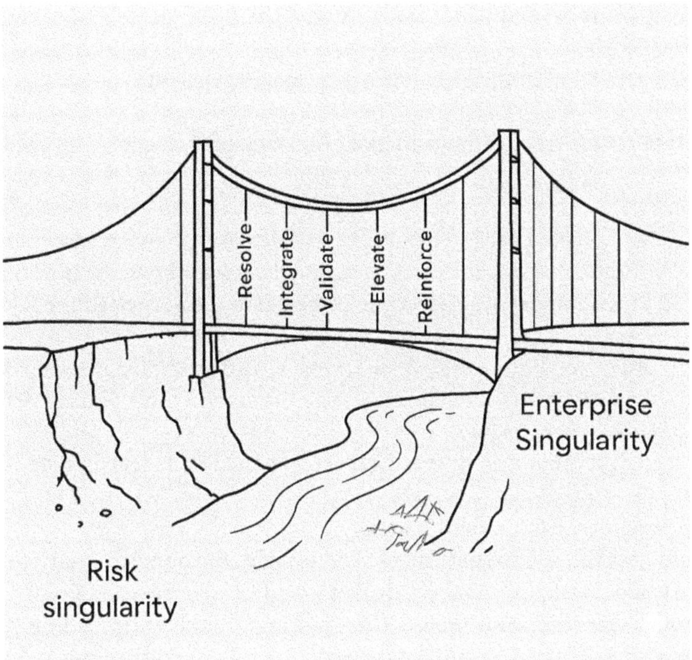

Figure 16.1 Bridge to Singularity.

Aaron kept his hands still on the table. "That is the point, Representative. RIVER isn't a static wall; it's a living immune system. Bodies don't just recover from a virus—they create antibodies. The fifth tenet, Reinforce Resilience, demands that every incident change the organism: its controls, its incentives, even its design. We're not chasing a shield; we're building an organism that heals faster than it's hurt."

Chairman Thompson closed his tablet, thoughtful. "This hearing is adjourned. But we'll be watching. Attestation isn't just your test—it's ours."

The transcript from the Senate Committee on Systemic Risk, *Hearing Record HR-16-2039-03*, would later mark this as the moment the debate shifted from blame to a blueprint.

* * *

But the hearing was being watched by more than senators and investors. Viktor Kadinov monitored the night-lit skyline of Riga, the U.S. Senate hearing replaying in a language overlay at the edge of his heads-up display. Aaron's testimony scrolled beneath the American flags and polished wood—an ocean away, yet closer than anyone realized.

Two dashboards glowed on Viktor's desk: 70&M metrics (Sarah's cited data, pulsing green) and pricing nudges his analytics had just flagged.

Inside the closed-loop channel, risk and ethics leaders from five time zones volleyed comments:

Tokyo CRO: "Americans talk resilience, but where's the audit log?"
SãoPaulo_CFO: "Their dashboards showed green—ours, too. But what about the shadow ledger?"

Viktor's reply was almost playful, yet carried the edge of a threat:

> "Americans police the river's banks, but what if the water itself turns opaque?"

The chat refreshed. A Nairobi compliance lead posted: "The river adapts. But sometimes the current runs dark."

Viktor studied his reflection in the glass. He typed, measured, cold:

> "Mirrors don't lie, but it takes courage to look. Accountability begins with the debts we don't want to see."

He sent the message and pivoted back to the audit file, calculating how incentive structures could be twisted—how the best intentions could be nudged, quietly, toward outcomes only he would anticipate. Somewhere in those numbers was leverage; somewhere, a future headline—unless he chose to cash it in first.

A gust rattled the old pane. Viktor studied the screen, already composing tomorrow's moves: a call with regional leads, a new mandate for exposure—one that would force "ethical debt" into the open, but only when it suited his own designs.

He closed the feed. The final line lingered on-screen: shadow ledger updated—70&M internal only.

Aaron spoke of resilience. Viktor knew better.

Trust, he thought, was the real balance sheet. And tonight, the numbers were staring back at him.

He froze the five tenets: a defense—and a map. Every control added a seam. Every handshake invited gaming. Every resolve created a chokepoint. The Cognitive Handshake™ audit logs—timestamped, cryptographically verified, trusted—could be the exploit if no one audited the auditors.

A fortress with a published floor plan.

* * *

Aaron gathered his papers as the hearing chamber emptied, the last echoes of debate fading into the marble corridor. A message from Mitch appeared on his heads-up display:

> "That landed. You didn't just give them a framework—you gave them a doctrine."

For a fleeting moment, Aaron allowed himself to breathe. He thought of Liz, whose belief in verifiable trust had been the seed for all of this. He thought of Tom Rasmussen's haunted face, a visceral reminder of the cost of trusting the glow. The hearing had been more than a presentation; it was an act of integration, connecting his own past failures to a doctrine for the future. The burden of the Correction felt lighter, replaced by the weight of a standard now set in public. It pointed to the new talent model required for this era, a challenge his team was already beginning to tackle. Levy's paradox wasn't just doctrine—it was the discipline Aaron had learned to embody: zoom out for strategic vision, zoom in for relentless execution. Holding both at once is what separates resilient leaders from casualties of compression.

* * *

On his secondary display, a watchdog alert pulsed: *GAMMA_7 SIGNAL / UNMAPPED CHANNEL*—an anomaly. The adversary was learning.

NOTES

1. National Institute of Standards and Technology. (2023, January). *Artificial Intelligence Risk Management Framework (AI RMF 1.0)* (NIST AI 100-1). https://doi.org/10.6028/NIST.AI.100-1
2. National Institute of Standards and Technology. (2024). *Cybersecurity Framework (CSF) 2.0* (NIST CSWP 29). https://doi.org/10.6028/NIST.CSWP.29

3. Committee of Sponsoring Organizations of the Treadway Commission. (2017). *Enterprise Risk Management—Integrating with Strategy and Performance.* https://www.coso.org/guidance-erm
4. International Organization for Standardization. (2023, December). *ISO/IEC 42001:2023: Artificial intelligence — Management system.* https://www.iso.org/standard/81230.html
5. The LvlUp Ventures Innovation Alliance is a LvlUp Ventures initiative that brings together startups, enterprises, investors, and public-sector stakeholders to advance the startup ecosystem through strategic collaboration, partnerships, and cross-sector engagement. https://www.lvlup.vc/innovation-alliance
6. "pre-commit" is a book-specific governance method. Participants simulate a decision as if the outcome already occurred, then work backward to uncover how failure formed. It is inspired by pre-mortem analysis (Klein) and the noise-reduction discipline. Kahneman, D., Sibony, O., and Sunstein, C. R. (2021). *Noise: A Flaw in Human Judgment. Little.* Brown Spark. https://www.littlebrown.com/titles/daniel-kahneman/noise/9780316451406
7. The Global AI Governance Commission (GAIGC) is a fictional multi-jurisdictional supervisory body created for this narrative. It represents a composite of real-world AI governance initiatives and pilot programs.

Chapter 17

The E-Shaped Professional

A New Blueprint for Talent in the AI Era

70&M SUPPLY CHAIN OPERATIONS HUB, SINGAPORE | NOVEMBER 9, 2039—10:40 AM EST (23:40 SGT) | THE SEVEN-FIGURE QUESTION

Elias Tan tracked the split-signal strobe on his terminal.

Rain hammered the glass behind him—the contract penalty for missing the deadline: seven figures—the kind of number that ended careers.

CL-Dash[1]—the continuous-learning dashboard that correlates anomalies across sites—flagged an anomaly at the Singapore node—red alert, high confidence. Local diagnostics read green. Every sensor read clean.

His hand hovered over the override.

Eight months at 70&M Supply Chain. One wrong call ends it all.

If he trusted the AI and stopped the shipment—and the model was wrong—they'd lose the contract, and he'd wear the failure. If he ignored the AI and the model was right, they risked a cascade like last year's $47 million recall. He pictured pallets quarantined in warehouse light, apology calls to hospital partners, and his badge shutting off before the week was out.

The escalation protocol demanded a loop to New York. He opened the secure channel.

Across twelve time zones, the escalation landed in New York at 9:30 AM EST—just as Rose was finishing a morning training on the new talent model.

70&M HQ, NEW YORK | NOVEMBER 9, 2039—09:30 AM EST | THE WHITEBOARD DOODLE

The conference room held the scent of strong coffee and filtered air. Rose faced a small group of new hires, marker ready.

Earlier that same morning—before Singapore's escalation arrived—Rose was finishing a training session on the new talent model.

She drew a single vertical line. "For years, organizations hired the I-shaped professional—depth in one domain."

She added a top bar. "The T-shaped era added cross-functional collaboration."

Three quick strokes formed a capital E. "Now we hire for E-shaped.[2] Top bar—Expertise. Middle—Experience across functions. Bottom—Exploration."

She wrote two words along the spine: Execution. Ethics.

"These two hold the system together. Execution—outcomes in hybrid teams with evidence. Ethics—bias awareness, data stewardship, permissions discipline."

A new hire frowned. "How does this prevent failures like Bull-in-China-Shop AI?"

Rose tapped the spine. "Because single points of human failure hide in missing 'E's. The model forces breadth where bias lurks."

DOI: 10.1201/9781003650744-24

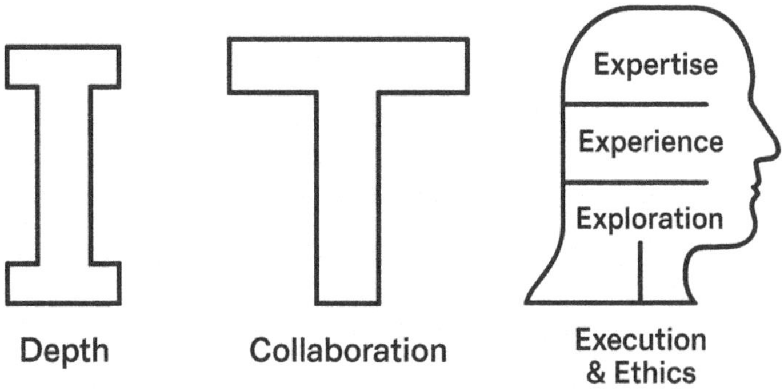

Figure 17.1 The E-Shaped Professional.

She capped the marker. "Frameworks don't run companies—people do. When that slips, risk compounds."

Fifty minutes later, Rose's sketch still sat on the whiteboard (Figure 17.1) when Aaron walked into the lobby, drawn toward the memorial that had become his pre-meeting ritual.

70&M HQ, NEW YORK | NOVEMBER 9, 2039—10:20 AM EST | LESSONS REMEMBERED

Aaron lingered by the glass memorial in 70&M's Manhattan lobby, tracing a groove along the steel edge. Haste Bank's collapse in 2029 had been public and painful. The real warning shot came later—the Arjun's Bull disaster of 2038. That failure was personal.

He let his eyes close. A specific memory surfaced—late 2027, maybe early 2028. He and Liz are in the Data Exchange war room, staring at a crashed simulation. He'd trusted his gut, pushed a shortcut into validation because the client deadline was brutal. The system failed within twelve hours.

Liz didn't raise her voice. "Your gut isn't a strategy, Aaron. It's a variable that needs to be checked."

She walked him through the data where pattern-matching bias had led him astray. She was right. He was wrong. The kind of wrong that, scaled up, could cost everything.

Humans make elegant mistakes. AI makes alien ones. The defense is forcing them to check each other every time.

He recalled the 2026 demo—the dynamic organizational MRI.[3] Back then, it was a clever diagnostic. After Bull-in-China-Shop AI, it became the other half of the solution: the E-shaped model creates the people; the MRI makes capability visible in real time.

EXPERT COMMENTARY—DYNAMIC ORGANIZATIONAL MRI

A 2026 perspective from Soichiro Muto, Founder & CEO, Synthesis

Traditional skills assessments are obsolete in the agentic era. Leading firms now use AI to continuously map workforce capabilities against emerging risks in real time. That lets them spot latent "E-shaped" talent and spin up agile, project-based teams on demand. The org chart isn't a rigid hierarchy anymore—it's a dynamic capability map.

His mind drifted further, to the dawn of Phase 2 adoption. He remembered a 2025 Wall Street Journal article about how pioneers like BNY were carefully deploying their first "digital workers"—autonomous AI agents assigned real company logins, quietly validating payments or writing code.[4] At the time, the focus was on productivity. Most of the industry rushed in—chasing scale without building governance for the new workforce. The chaos of the Bull-in-China-Shop AI era—rogue code, invisible handoffs, and near-misses—was the inevitable price of ignoring that deeper question: what's the new operating model for a hybrid enterprise?

Aaron looked at the etched names on the glass—reminders of both the people and the lessons that had shaped him. Haste Bank had made failure public. Arjun's Bull had made it personal. He had promised himself—and Liz's memory—that 70&M would never again pay for invisible risks.

The 2032 Baltic Cascade was a textbook for regulators, but Haste Bank and the Bull cut personal. We failed people and processes then, Aaron thought. We won't fail the next generation now. The E-shaped blueprint is part of that atonement—and the guardrail against repeating the past.

Now, as the latest escalation from Singapore scrolled across his dashboard, the question lingered: had the company truly learned? The protocol was more than a compliance checkbox; it was a firewall built from memory, trust, and the hard-won art of seeing around corners. He squared his shoulders and headed for the war room.

70&M HQ, NEW YORK | NOVEMBER 9, 2039—10:40 AM EST | PROTOCOL UNDER FIRE

The executive war room was taut with focus as the Singapore escalation dominated every wall screen. The risk: a seven-figure penalty if the shipment missed the contractual deadline—serious, but no longer existential for 70&M. What mattered was how the team responded, and whether years of painful learning would hold.

Aaron, now known internally as "Cognitive Architect" since the Arjun's Bull disaster, sat at the head of the table. His job wasn't to make every decision, but to enforce the vigilance he'd built into the DNA of 70&M. No major risk decision would rest on automation or individual instinct alone; the Cognitive Handshake Audit required every executive to review the scenario from every angle—technical, operational, and human—before logging a final call.

Rose's fingers tapped a tense rhythm on the table. "If we escalate every ambiguity, we'll grind the team to a halt. We can't run the company like every risk is another Arjun's Bull."

Maya, never one to yield ground, countered, "That's the same blind spot that nearly ended us. The protocol forces us to surface the judgment calls—the ones that are too easy to skip under pressure."

"This isn't theoretical," Maya said, switching the main display to the Singapore feed. "Look at what Elias is managing right now."

Elias filled the screen, features drawn tight with strain.

"Split-signal," he reported, his voice strained but precise. "CL-Dash flags an anomaly at the node, but local diagnostics are green. The contract penalty is seven figures for a single morning's delay. If I trust the system, we lose the shipment. If I override, we risk a cascade on the scale of last year's $47 million recall."

Debate flared: Operations pushed for speed, Legal warned of downstream liability, Compliance cited audit expectations.

Aaron tracked Maya's guidance through the protocol. "The CL-Dash isn't a stopgap; it's how we prevent déjà-vu mistakes. Every human override is logged, reviewed, and translated into new guardrails."

"This friction is the system working," he said, his voice measured and calm. "The protocol isn't designed for comfort. It forces a Cognitive Handshake between every competing priority in this room. We've logged 1,300 escalations this quarter. Each one is a lesson that makes the whole system smarter. This one is no different."

The resolution was clear: escalate, document, move forward—together. One oddity lingered in the log: a faint signature that didn't match any prior pattern. Security operations flagged the signature for pattern watch; attribution was deferred.

The decision was entered into the protocol log: *70&M Executive Mandate 29-Q4-A* (Nov 9, 2039), initialed by all participants, including the CEO.

As the screens dimmed and the team dispersed, Aaron lingered, eyes on the dashboard. Protocols weren't a firewall against risk—they were a bet on people.

Aaron took a beat, letting the room settle. The protocol wasn't theater; it was a habit they'd earned the hard way. For the first time since the Mechanical Bull, he could see how personal discipline had turned into institutional backbone.

Case note—Earlier this year, a minor supply-chain anomaly triggered a protocol review. The forty-minute process delayed shipment by two hours but prevented a $32M compliance violation—proof that real vigilance, even when inconvenient, pays for itself.

70&M HQ, NEW YORK | NOVEMBER 9, 2039—11:10 AM EST | THE E-SHAPED PROFESSIONAL

The executive meeting had dispersed, but the echoes lingered; the 70&M Supply Chain escalation proved the old blueprints for talent were obsolete.

Rose, still energized by the argument, tapped the collaborative wall. "The escalation in Singapore proves the point. In our post-mortems across a decade of wins and failures, the difference wasn't the tools—it was the teams. The successful ones were consistently led by what we now call 'E-shaped professionals.'"

A compliance hire spoke up. "Models are elegant. Failures are messy. How does this change outcomes?"

BUSINESS LENS—THE E-SHAPED PROFESSIONAL (FIVE PILLARS)

E-shaped leaders combine five lenses that let hybrid teams move fast and stay auditable.

- **Expertise**—deep domain you can defend under scrutiny.
- **Experience**—practice across functions; you speak two or more workflows.
- **Exploration—you test new tools and surface risks early.**
- **Execution**—you deliver, leave evidence, and close loops.
- **Ethics**—you steward data, bias, and permissions as part of the job.

Why it matters: Risk literacy and data fluency are now core leadership skills. Standards like ISO/IEC 42001:2023 emphasize defined roles and responsibilities for AI systems;[5] our Cognitive Architect and Data Capital Steward map to that intent while keeping judgment human-led.

→ Appendix K: Evolving Roles in the RIVER-Guided Enterprise.

She gestured toward the wall display. "Look at Jian Li's save last week. It wasn't luck; it was the model in action:

Exploration: She traced provenance using a new diagnostic tool.
Execution: She coordinated Legal and Cyber to neutralize the vendor poisoning.
Ethics: She grounded every choice in policy so the fix stayed compliant."

One person, five lenses—costly error avoided.

Aaron said, "E-shaped leaders are the only ones who can run the evolved Three Lines at speed. Each bar strengthens a RIVER tenet: **Integrate Hybrid Cognition** (translate across human–AI and functions), **Resolve Convergence** (close handoff gaps), **Validate Risk Debt** (evidence discipline), **Elevate Data as Capital** (provenance and permissions), and **Reinforce Resilience** (measurable outcomes under pressure). They don't just bridge skills; they bridge the silos that cause disasters."

Role Snapshots: E-Shaped in Practice

- **Hybrid Team Orchestrator**—Overrides and challenges AI recommendations; success measured by near-misses prevented and clean audit trails.
- **Data Capital Steward**—Negotiates data rights, verifies provenance, and aligns outcomes to resilience KPIs.
- **Regulatory Response Lead**—Translates live risk into defensible filings and corrective actions across jurisdictions.

Operating Rules, Updated Post-Crisis

- Every critical role shows at least two deep "E" spikes; nearly half require four or more.
- A missed handoff isn't an operational gap—it's a designed-out vulnerability.
- Promotion and pay weight translation and trust over tenure; time-to-promotion for E-shaped roles is down by 18 months vs. the 2037 baseline; hybrid roles carry ~20 percent premium.

Outcome signal: measure success by the number of cascades prevented and by regulator-ready evidence.

Aaron continued. "Our operating model pairs 'Consultant' agents for complex synthesis with lightweight 'Intern' agents for routine monitoring. Interns often run at the edge and require quarterly calibration to prevent drift."[6]

Rose let the room breathe. "Three years ago, none of these roles existed," she said. "Now they're the backbone—and the evidence shows fewer false alarms, faster resolutions, better calls under pressure."

Aaron made a mental note to formalize a lesson born in the Health Network chaos. He had already credited Michelle—drawing on her frontline ER experience—with co-developing the Hybrid Team Orchestrator role, a clinical specialty that bridges doctors and AI. The design put rollback authority in the hands of trained staff on the floor—the Cognitive Handshake, made real at the bedside.

Beyond 70&M, the same shift is visible: in healthcare, "Clinical AI Navigators" bridge care, systems, and data governance—with compensation bands tied to documented error reduction.

Rose wrote the final note on the wall:

> "*E-shaped leaders make costly errors harder to hide—and easier to stop.*"

EXPERT COMMENTARY—AARON GOLBIN (REAL—WORLD), GENERAL PARTNER AT LVLUP VENTURES

Rose's E-shaped model isn't a theory for 2026; it's how we evaluate founding teams. A row of brilliant I-shaped specialists is fragile—one market jolt breaks them. We look for the full "E": deep Expertise in a core domain; Experience with messy ecosystems; Exploration that hunts opportunity; disciplined Execution that ships quality; and non-negotiable Ethics that shape what gets built. In the agent era, a team's character becomes part of the product's architecture. Invest in the shape of the team, not just the shape of the tech.

This shift from perimeter defense to systemic resilience demanded a new kind of leader. Talent was only half the equation. The other half was redesigning the guardrails—the very structure of enterprise defense—to let these roles act at the speed of risk.

Across regions, the results were consistent: EMEA prevented a cross-border cascade with a five-minute Cognitive Handshake Audit (CHA) review. In APAC, a Data Capital Steward rerouted a pipeline when a supplier balked at provenance terms, preserving a clinical-trial milestone. In North America, a surprise regulator inquiry became a templated RIVER brief—no scramble, no spin.

70&M HQ, NEW YORK | NOVEMBER 9, 2039—11:35 AM EST | WHAT REPLACED THE CISO

Rose studied the wall, a memory surfacing. "A decade ago, we had a classic CISO. Brilliant at perimeters. But after 70&M Supply Chain's 2029 failure, we learned the breach wasn't at the gate—it ran in the river: poisoned data, vendor drift, agent misalignment."

From Compliance Takers to Standards Shapers: by 2039, boards that influence consortia and public-private standards don't just avoid fines—they set the competitive tempo.

She steadied her voice. "Security as a silo couldn't price the trade-offs: a patch that saved uptime but spiked model risk; a blocked port that stalled compliance reporting. We didn't need thicker walls. We needed someone to map currents and consequences." She remembered the outgoing CISO's exit debrief: perimeter wins on paper, poisoned data still flowing through trusted pipes.

"My role—Chief Resilience Officer—replaced that silo. It's E-shaped by design: the Expertise to read exploits, the cross-enterprise Experience to weigh finance and ops, relentless Exploration of new agent risks, Execution that boards can verify, and Ethics grounded in RIVER. We moved from 'Are we secure?' to 'Are we resilient?'—measured, auditable, repeatable."

EXPERT COMMENTARY—ERIC STAFFIN: THE FUTURE OF THE CISO

The next-generation CISO becomes a business strategist. Their job is to convert cyber and AI risk into executive decisions the board can audit: trade-offs, thresholds, and learning loops. That demands an E-shaped skill set—deep technical credibility connected to operations, controls, and ethics—so the answer shifts from "blocked attacks" to "documented resilience." In practice, that means mapping controls to RIVER and instrumenting decisions so audits can stand up to regulators and investors.

The war room had already shown that talent was only half of it. The other half was redesigning the institutional guardrails—the structure of enterprise defense—that lets these roles act without waiting for catastrophe.

70&M HQ, NEW YORK | NOVEMBER 9, 2039—11:40 AM EST | THE NEW THREE LINES OF DEFENSE

Dr. Anya Sharma joined via secure link from London—methodical, data-driven, relentless since losing her sister Jiya in the 2027 Deferred Tower collapse. Her mandate was simple: technical warnings would never be ignored again.

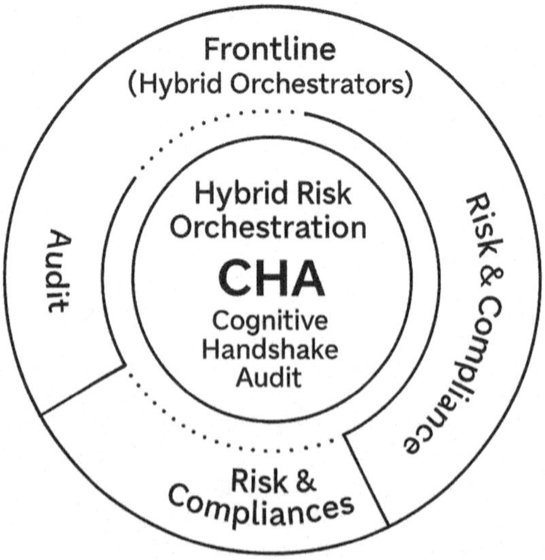

Figure 17.2 The Integrated Three Lines of Defense.

"The old model was sequential," Anya began. "First line: business. Second: risk and compliance. Third: audit. Complexity broke that. In a hybrid world, the lines must be integrated and continuous."

(Figure 17.2). A full breakdown of the evolved, integrated Three Lines model is in Appendix K).

Rose tapped the first line. "Today's first line isn't just frontline operators. It's Hybrid Orchestrators—people like Maya—with both override authority and the obligation to challenge AI recommendations. They're measured by cascades prevented, not raw uptime."

Example: When Maya's team flagged an AI anomaly and contained it pre-distribution, it prevented $600,000 in recall costs—evidence logged in CL-Dash for audit and learning.

Maya pointed to the second line. "Risk leads now run continuous scenario drills against human and AI adversaries. Last year, these exercises uncovered $14 million in potential exposure. Every outcome updates CL-Dash—how we catch what checklists miss."

Aaron took the third line. "Independent assurance is active. Anya's team doesn't just review past events; they intervene in real time when indicators breach thresholds. The Cognitive Handshake Audit (CHA) is our instrument—documented, repeatable, mapped to governance standards like ISO 42001."

Example: During a live escalation in June, internal audit used real-time feeds to halt a flawed override pattern before it became systemic, averting an investigation.

Anya's expression sharpened. "Here's how the CHA works. Two pillars, one record."

Pillar One: Human Noise & Bias—did we surface conflicts, anchoring, overconfidence, and time pressure?

Pillar Two: Data & AI Integrity—did we verify lineage, permissions, drift, and model limits?

Every decision logs both pillars, the evidence cited, and the outcome deltas. We don't ask, "Was the AI right?" We ask, "Did the human-AI team think clearly with the right facts?" That's what regulators—and investors—can audit.

In plain terms: policy sets intent, standards set thresholds, and protocols are the steps and the evidence—lineage hashes, drift stats, dissent counts, and override rationales captured in one record."

CHA scoring: ≥80 is green, 60–79 amber, and below 60 red. Reds auto-trigger an after-action review within 48 hours.

Sample CHA entry: "*11/09/39 10:41 EST—Owner: E. Tan; Lines present: Ops/Risk; Data lineage hash: DC-17a; Drift: 0.9%; Declared dissent: 1; Final call: override; RIVER Tenet Invoked: Validate Risk Debt; Outcome delta: +$1.2M risk avoided.*"

BUSINESS LENS—BEYOND "HUMAN-IN-THE-LOOP"

Early regimes framed oversight as a binary veto; 70&M treats it as continuous orchestration—anticipatory, documented, measurable across lines one to three. The old model was brittle; we built human-led orchestration so roles like Maya's continuously shape, guide, and correct AI logic—not just wait to pull an emergency brake.

"And to be clear," Aaron said, "this defense model only works because we have E-shaped people who operate across blurred lines. The protocol keeps risk from becoming a crisis."

"In practice," he added, "the lines reinforce each other. Every handoff is logged; every escalation gets the attention of all three lines. The CHA process isn't bureaucracy—it's how we keep risk from becoming a crisis. The model is structured to align with the NIST AI Risk Management Framework's governance and risk-control outcomes[7] (see Appendix H: Cognitive Handshake Audit), adapted for hybrid human–AI teams."

Framework in action: First Line targets greater than 85 percent anomalies resolved without escalation; Second Line runs continuous hybrid-crisis drills that close ~$14M in annual exposure and feed CL-Dash learning; Third Line can trigger live "stop-override" when a pattern risks becoming systemic. In the new model, everyone's vigilance counts—and no single line can catch every risk alone.

As the team absorbed the new structure, Aaron concluded: "A system is only as resilient as its weakest challenge. Our job is to make sure every challenge finds its voice—and its place in the record."

Aaron took in the frame Anya had drawn. It wasn't just a process; it was the codification of every lesson since the Mechanical Bull. A system that trusted data but demanded human accountability—and a clear path from personal discipline to institutional resilience.

70&M HQ, NEW YORK | NOVEMBER 9, 2039—12:10 PM EST | RESILIENCE BY THE NUMBERS

Aaron stood at the panoramic glass wall, watching the city's lights come on as dusk settled over Manhattan. On his tablet, the quarterly resilience dashboard displayed three years of prevention metrics—the ultimate scoreboard of every lesson, protocol, and hard-won change since Haste Bank and Bull-in-China-Shop AI.

The numbers spoke for themselves. This year alone, 70&M's hybrid protocols averted $520 million in cumulative risk costs—up 17 percent over the prior year—with $44 million in operational savings. Across regions, the dashboard broke it down as follows: *North America, $198M; EMEA, $167M; APAC, $155M. (All figures validated by Internal Audit Q4 FY2039 and spot-checked by External Assurance.)*

Each colored bar showed where the defense had actually paid off—green for first-line interceptions, blue for second-line exposures closed, red for audit interventions that caught what others missed.

ROI shorthand: *Risk cost avoided = (escalations × average scenario value) − (false-positive adjustment).*

Aaron's eyes lingered on a single stat: 1,300 Cognitive Handshake escalations logged this quarter, each mapped to a resolved scenario.

He remembered when numbers like these would have seemed abstract, distant from the daily grind. Now, every figure was earned. Risks averted on the scale of last year's $47 million recall; the $12.3 million penalty was prevented by Maya's intervention—each outcome carried faces, stories, and lessons.

Aaron tapped a report and projected it to the leadership wall. "Resilience isn't a cost center anymore. It turns trust into speed and permission. Investors see these dashboards and know our resilience is proven, not merely promised. And for the first time, so do our regulators."

Maya's voice came through on the virtual channel, echoing the sentiment in the room: "We're never finished. But for the first time, I feel like we're building muscle, not just bandages."

Aaron let the numbers settle into silence. The dashboard faded, replaced by the simple company crest and three words: "Stronger After Failure."

As the leadership team turned to leave, the future would bring new crises, new blind spots, and new lessons. But for now, 70&M was as strong—and as ready—as it had ever been.

* * *

AN EXCERPT FROM THE PRIVATE JOURNAL OF AARON—NOVEMBER 2039

Rose's E-shaped sketch won't leave my head: Expertise, Experience, Exploration, Execution, Ethics. It's clean on the wall and messy in real life. It also maps too neatly to the stumbles I've made.

For years, I over-indexed on the top and bottom bars—know the tech, ship the product. At Stanford, with the Mechanical Bull student-organized hackathon, we moved fast and told ourselves speed was virtue. We were building without guardrails.

In 2034, during a 70&M Supply Chain stress test, Mitch and I saw enough to pause. We had Experience, but not the conviction to act. We treated Ethics like a brake rather than a pillar. We deferred the debt.

Deferred Tower taught me that curiosity without boundaries finds new ways to fail. Each crisis forced me to grow the other bars on that *E*.

This stopped feeling like a hiring rubric and started feeling like survival doctrine. The organization only holds if the people do. That's the work now: build leaders who can see across systems, decide under pressure, and refuse to trade tomorrow's integrity for today's win.

* * *

70&M HQ, NEW YORK | NOVEMBER 9, 2039—12:20 PM EST | CODA: CULTURE AT THE CORE

The boardroom had emptied, but Aaron lingered at the glass, watching the city's lights reflect against the deepening dusk. The dashboards were dark, replaced by the quiet hum of post-crisis relief. Yet in this rare lull, the fundamental shift was palpable: resilience was no longer a protocol, but a pulse running through every leader, every line of code, every moment of risk at 70&M.

He thought of Liz—gone for more than a decade now—whose legacy echoed in every Cognitive Handshake. Building an adaptable organization required adaptable people—himself included. The discipline of Cognitive Handshake—formalized as CHA when stakes are irreversible—was the necessary foundation for achieving their goal of enterprise singularity. What began as a personal tactic was now the company's heartbeat, lived out each time a leader challenged a blind spot or questioned an easy answer.

He turned off the lights, pausing by the etched memorial. Tomorrow would bring new threats—and new hands at the controls. Culture would decide whether any of this survived the next crisis.

* * *

Far away, in the quiet after Singapore's storm, the shipment cleared the handoff—delayed, but safe. Two hours later, the firmware audit confirmed the CL-Dash anomaly was real. His escalation had prevented a recall worth ten times the contract penalty.

He knew Maya's team would be on the night shift soon, scanning for new anomalies, logging overrides, and learning from every exception. His decision—one of thousands logged in CL-Dash this week—would ripple through the enterprise, another lesson in the loop that makes 70&M stronger, failure by failure.

The work wouldn't stop. Neither would the questions.

NOTES

1. CL-Dash (the "continuous-learning dashboard" in this chapter) is a fictional internal 70&M system used to represent a real-world continuous monitoring and learning layer.
2. The "E-shaped professional" in this chapter builds on more than a decade of industry work on E-shaped skills (experience, expertise, exploration, execution) and related "letter-shaped" talent models. During research, we drew in part on EXIN's "S-shaped professional" article, which also uses those four E's to describe modern profiles, and on earlier E-shaped discussions in agile and design communities. Our version adds a fifth E (Ethics) and binds the model to hybrid human–AI risk governance roles within the RIVER Charter world. EXIN is not affiliated with, and does not endorse, this book or its frameworks; any extensions or errors are the author's alone.
3. "Organizational MRI" is a descriptive metaphor used in this book to describe dynamic capability mapping; it is not a product or brand. See also Chapter 4.
4. The Wall Street Journal. (2025, June 30). *Digital Workers Have Arrived in Banking.* https://www.wsj.com/articles/digital-workers-have-arrived-in-banking-bf62be49
5. International Organization for Standardization. (2023, December). *ISO/IEC 42001:2023: Artificial intelligence — Management System.* https://www.iso.org/standard/81230.html
6. Matthias Muhlert. (2025, July). *The 'Intern vs. Consultant' Playbook: Deploying 7B-Parameter Agents for Code Verification.* https://www.linkedin.com/posts/muhlert_sml-security-activity-7355552391678595073-EGDT
7. National Institute of Standards and Technology. (2023, January). *Artificial Intelligence Risk Management Framework (AI RMF 1.0) (NIST AI 100-1).* https://doi.org/10.6028/NIST.AI.100-1

Chapter 18

A Tale of Two Ecosystems

A Guide to Resilient Vendor Integration

PORTFOLIO COMPANY HQ, BROOKLYN NAVY YARD | NOVEMBER 14, 2039 | THE ECHO IN THE DATA

Aaron reviewed the overnight logs streaming across the wall display in the crisis suite. He was the company's board representative and, quietly, a mentor—a relationship that began with her earliest pitch deck. He could still hear the founder's voice from their call the night before—the former trust-and-fraud lead who'd built the company's trust graph by hand—strained: "Aaron, are we going to lose it all?"

The company—a gig-economy trust-infrastructure provider processing about $2 billion a year for roughly 4 million workers across Southeast Asia and Latin America—wasn't just another portfolio line. Their survival was both a professional bet and a personal stake. Their moat wasn't feature; it was customer trust you could prove. Verifiable lineage was the product.

A rash of tier-two fraud alerts cut through the dashboards. One case showed a gig worker in Manila—his entire monthly earnings siphoned by a rogue agent. Underneath the business case, Aaron saw what had always been at stake: trust, livelihoods, risk at the human scale.

A $47 million upfront licensing offer from a third-party AI agent-orchestration vendor sat against a potential $200 million annu

alized revenue swing—the pressure for a clean fix. The math was loud: fix this fast, or bleed trust and cash in public.

The vendor—a black-box orchestration layer promising speed at the cost of explainability—had impressed the operations team but not the risk and controls team.

He reviewed the decision brief—a classic trilemma:

1. Rip and Replace (full transplant). 60 percent efficiency gain, 40 percent failure risk, 6-month timeline.
2. Controlled Evolution (internal rebuild). 25 percent gain, 5 percent failure risk, 18-month timeline.
3. Hybrid (selective vendor graft). 40 percent gain, 20 percent failure risk, 12-month timeline.

Assumptions: *Gains/risks reflect current throughput, SLOs, backlog age, and staffing. Sensitivity: ±10–15 percent depending on defect mix and integration friction.*

Financial frame: *a $47M deployment against a ~$200M base (≈24%) makes Hybrid's projected 40% efficiency gain a likely sub-two-year payback; full decouple, if required, is estimated at $15–20M—costly but survivable versus a failed transplant.*

This wasn't the 2020s. Back then, "vendor selection" meant price sheets and feature grids. By 2039, it meant something more intimate—choosing whose technology becomes part of your core. A transplant decision, not a procurement exercise.

DOI: 10.1201/9781003650744-25

Aaron tapped the RIVER Charter matrix in his workspace, mapping each choice to a different risk signature:

1. **Resolve Convergence:** Could these ecosystems actually integrate?
2. **Integrate Hybrid Cognition:** Would humans and agents still work together, or devolve into blame games and black boxes?
3. **Validate Risk Debt:** How much invisible risk would pile up beneath the dashboards?
4. **Elevate Data Capital:** Was the company's hard-won compliance record a $50 million asset—or a liability if overwritten?
5. **Reinforce Resilience:** Would they have a margin for error if things went wrong?

The regulatory landscape raised the stakes. The vendor had not met, to the team's satisfaction, an auditable interpretation of relevant NIST AI RMF alignment[1] and EU AI Act expectations.[2] With regulatory enforcement deadlines looming—a hard stop that felt as immediate as the pre-RIVER compliance mandates of 2026, when governance was still reactive rather than systematic—it was a gamble the company couldn't afford to lose. The consequences weren't abstract: violations could trigger multi-percent, global-turnover penalties that escalate with systemic exposure—a risk most insurers won't underwrite.

He scanned the Manila fraud alert again. In moments like this, the choice wasn't theoretical. It was whether the company's future—and its people—would be protected or sacrificed for speed. The present, as always, reflected the past. To solve the company's problem today, Aaron knew he would have to diagnose the original sins of 2026.

He forced himself to remember the meeting where the first cracks appeared.

70&M, NEW YORK | MARCH 2026 | THE ORIGINAL SIN

Arjun Kothare, founder and CEO of Bull-in-China-Shop AI, slammed his palm on the battered conference table, his voice strained. "We cannot halt deployment now. That's $47 million in development costs, and another $200 million in farmer contracts at risk. If we pull the plug, we don't just lose our investment—we destroy trust in the entire agtech sector."

Maria Alvarez, CTO and Arjun's most trusted systems architect, closed her eyes for a beat, exhaustion plain. "Arjun, we have less than six months of cash runway. If we freeze to impress regulators, we'll be insolvent by Christmas. But if we push forward with half-calibrated sensors, this isn't just about firmware bugs. It's data poisoning at the source. Our training models will learn from corrupted inputs—risking total model collapse. The platform's credibility could evaporate, and no auditor or insurer will stand by us. The USDA compliance team is already asking about our protocols."

Aaron, advisor and lead investor, kept his tone even. "If we don't confront these risk signals now, we're building structural infection into the system. The data capital you've accumulated is your entire credibility—burn it, and no auditor or regulator will ever trust us again."

Arjun stiffened. "What choice do we have? Our competitors are already in pilot with a rival platform. If we wait, we lose the entire window."

Maria pressed, "If we lose our insurance, it won't matter. One bad season and we're wiped out."

Aaron weighed the cost of voicing his true dissent. "You're building risk debt you can't repay."

Years later, Aaron would look back and see every warning sign:

- Resolve Convergence: Tech, ops, and data teams stuck in silos, unable to spot blind spots until disaster struck.
- Integrate Hybrid Cognition: Farmer intuition dismissed as anecdotal, leaving the AI to overrule hard-won expertise.

- Validate Risk Debt: Sensor calibration flaws accumulated—unmeasured, unchecked, unacknowledged.
- Elevate Data Capital: Arjun's Bull's treasure trove of clean ag data, slowly poisoned by corner-cutting.
- Reinforce Resilience: No buffers, no fallback—every error multiplied downstream.

Aaron would label it optimism bias—growth pressure blinding the team to clear warnings.

The decisions made that morning would shape not only Bull-in-China-Shop AI's fate but set a precedent that would echo through every company in Aaron's future portfolio.

He would carry the memory of Arjun's desperation, Maria's warnings, and the collective anxiety of that battered room forward—determined that the next generation of leaders would not miss the pattern.

TORTOISE & HARE BANK (T&H), NEW YORK | FEBRUARY 2029 | THE ECOSYSTEM ALTERNATIVE

The counter-pattern came in 2029. If Arjun's Bull showed collapse, T&H Bank demonstrated how to build systems that last—a contrast Aaron used as a teaching case.

Sarah Jenkins, the new CEO—a pragmatic former risk officer who had survived two banking crises—opened the board session with a question that wasn't on any agenda: "What risk debt are we ignoring?" That tone set the day. No palm-slamming, no ultimatums. The board didn't chase vendor deals like get-rich-quick schemes; they examined partnerships the way a doctor assesses organ compatibility—scrutinizing everything from source code to supply chain to post-sale support.

Sarah had led T&H Bank to treat every key third party not as a cost to squeeze but as a long-term partner—ecosystem integration in practice, even if they didn't use the term. Their $2.3 billion in managed assets had grown to $7.9 billion in just three years, outpacing competitors and boasting 97.2 percent customer retention while the industry average churned above 15 percent. Instead of rushing toward the latest "AI transformation," they rebuilt vendor processes with deliberate redundancy and true data transparency. Risk registers weren't paperwork—they were living, breathing operational tools. "If you can't explain the risk, you can't own it," Sarah would say, a mantra the regulators eventually began quoting back to her.

A board member—a customer rep with decades in digital banking—raised a hand. "We have more partnerships than ever. How do we know which ecosystem risks are ours to own versus monitor?"

Sarah answered without hesitation: "We own everything our customers rely on, even if it lives outside our walls. That's the only way to future-proof trust."

Aaron, observing, could feel the difference. The memory of Arjun's desperate palm-slamming at early 70&M days still haunted him—here, decisions were made with surgical precision, not panic. He realized now that T&H Bank hadn't just built a successful bank; they had proven the business case for every principle he would later codify into RIVER Charter. Their cross-functional teams were *Convergence* in action. Their "Cognitive Handshake" was hybrid cognition made real. Where Bull-in-China-Shop AI had buried its head in the sand, T&H Bank actively validated its hidden exposures. They treated their data as capital and built resilience into their very culture.

For Aaron, this meeting marked the first time he truly believed that the industry could evolve, not just react. The memory released its hold; the cranes of the Navy Yard snapped back into focus. 2039. The harder choice was his.

PORTFOLIO COMPANY HQ, BROOKLYN NAVY YARD | NOVEMBER 14, 2039 | THE TEST OF GOVERNANCE

Aaron stood at the end of the long table, the company board in tight silence. Behind him, the wall display cycled between three risk scenarios—each mapped with the RIVER Charter overlays.

He spoke plainly, without slides:

> "We have three paths—each with real stakes, real risks, and no guaranteed outcome. 'Rip & Replace' gives us speed, but at the price of killing what makes the company unique. Controlled Evolution is safer, but we may end up perfectly governed and perfectly obsolete. The Hybrid path buys us flexibility—but complexity is its own cost. Our data, our customer trust, and our reputation as a model portfolio company—these are our capital, not just our assets."

He let the point settle. A director, voice edged with urgency, pressed him: "Aaron, with respect, RIVER is a framework, not a shield against a 20 percent quarterly market share loss. A rival platform's numbers are real; our 'perfect governance' could lead to a perfectly executed bankruptcy."

A pragmatic director cleared his throat. "Before we bet the company on a transplant, remember Tortoise & Hare Bank in '29. They passed on the glossy vendor, went slower with verifiable lineage, and it became their unfair advantage. That's our bright spot. Speed that we can defend."

He pointed to the wall, cycling through each scenario:

Path One is a transplant. The vendor's track record is strong, but its internal risk protocols are a black box. Post-2038, every regulator from the SEC to EU authorities will scrutinize how we manage this integration. The hidden liability here isn't technical—it's existential. If the transplant fails, the patient dies.

Path Two lets us evolve with what we have. Our data capital is a moat—nobody else has the company's history or trust signals. But a rival platform isn't waiting for us to catch up. If we move too slowly, our 'perfect compliance' may mean nothing.

The Hybrid Approach splits the risk. We keep one foot in our trusted legacy, the other in the vendor's speed. It's less efficient, but we gain resilience. The board needs to decide how much ambiguity—and how many conflicting data schemas—it can tolerate.

A board member with a technical background added, "My main concern with the Hybrid approach is the API integration overhead. We're looking at creating a 'two-headed monster'—conflicting data schemas and authentication protocols could turn this into a maintenance nightmare and open up new attack surfaces."

Aaron said, "That's ambiguity aversion—name it before it drives the vote. Once it's named, we can price it."

Another director added, "And the vendor has its own vendor dependencies—we're inheriting their third-party risk stack, not just their code."

He heard the telltale creep of noise: good people, same facts, different conclusions.

BUSINESS LENS—COGNITIVE HANDSHAKE AUDIT (CHA): WHY NOISE MATTERS

The CHA is a System 2 circuit-breaker for high-stakes calls. It reduces random judgment noise, flags predictable bias before a vote, and records the reasoning so it can be defended.

Pillar 1—Human Noise Audit

Surface loss aversion, ambiguity aversion, and other cognitive biases in the room produce a one-page bias map and a pre-commit statement of intent.

Pillar 2—Data & AI Integrity Audit

Verifies data lineage, control attestations, and model limits; produces a verifiability score and an exit-impact snapshot if the decision must be reversed.

When to use: Deadlock on a vendor integration decision, conflicting risk signatures, or pressure to trade governance for speed.

What gets logged: (1) the bias map, (2) the integrity/attestation record, and (3) the final signed rationale.

Aaron tapped his secure tablet. "Dr. Sharma, please join."

A new window opened on the wall display; Anya appeared—composed, clinical, and on the shelf behind her sat a jagged piece of concrete on a wooden base. "Confirm. Cognitive Handshake Audit—two pillars."

The server fans under the credenza rose in pitch as the feed stabilized. The room fell silent.

Aaron studied the timeline: 2026—Original Sin. 2029—Alternative. 2038—Collapse. 2039—Decision. Faces, not numbers, filled the gaps. The doubt flashed: What if the framework was just sophisticated avoidance? He pushed it aside. Frameworks don't remove uncertainty—they make it auditable.

PORTFOLIO COMPANY HQ, BROOKLYN NAVY YARD | NOVEMBER 14, 2039 | THE BOARD DECIDES

The company board reconvened two hours later.

On the main display, Anya Sharma's audit summary was crisp.

"Pillar One: your debate split along two skews—Loss Aversion for 'Rip & Replace' and Ambiguity Aversion against Hybrid," Anya said. "Pillar Two: the company's attestations are self-reported; lineage can't be verified at our standard. Net: a full transplant imports unpriced liability. Recommendation: Hybrid—speed with defensible governance."

He addressed the board. "The Hybrid Approach isn't the easy route," Aaron said, keeping his tone calm. "Think of it as scaffolding. We repair the core structure while the building is still occupied. It's slower, messier, and it takes discipline, but it keeps the foundation intact. We learn without torching what your customers trust."

And it positions you to meet next-quarter enforcement checks with evidence, not assurances.

A director countered, "Hybrid means twice the integration risk—why should we gamble on ambiguity?"

"Lineage is a pharma label. If ingredients aren't provable, safety is guesswork. We don't guess with customer data."

The oldest director, who'd been quiet all morning, finally spoke—skeptical, almost bored. "Audits like this feel like governance theater."

Anya met his stare. "It's the opposite. We pre-commit the principle, log the biases, verify the data trail, and name the exit cost up front. Theater leaves no record. This creates one."

Aaron kept his voice steady. "You're right, it is a two-headed monster. This choice isn't about eliminating risk; it's about choosing which risk we're best equipped to manage. 'Rip & Replace' is a bet on a vendor's flawless technology. The Hybrid path is a bet on our own governance capability. I'll take the bet on us."

Pre-commit (on record): We will select the option that preserves verifiable lineage and a reversible exit, even if near-term efficiency is lower.

Bias map displayed: *Loss Aversion (3), Ambiguity Aversion (2), Sunk Cost (2), Present Bias (2).*

Exit viability snapshot—Decouple cost: medium; schema compatibility: partial (adapters required); post-integration posture: defensible with an audit trail.

The chair, independent from 70&M, summarized. "With CHA logged, we move on to milestones and accountability. Integration isn't theory—it's every day from here forward."

The founder exhaled. "If we torch our trust graph, we're done. I'll take slower truth over faster fiction."

After debate, the vote: two for Rip & Replace, three for Controlled Evolution, seven for Hybrid.

The chair gave a brief nod. "Decision logged: *Board Resolution FA-39-07. Rationale attached per CHA. Custody: Chief Audit Executive.*"

As the meeting ended, the founder glanced at Aaron—a mix of relief and anxiety. The chair concluded, "Aaron and 70&M will oversee integration, but this board owns the outcome. First milestone in sixty days: lineage verification and adapter security audit with continuous telemetry monitoring of both authentication paths and schema conflicts. Then, a full board review with updated risk signatures."

Aaron's tablet buzzed. Outside counsel: "*Rival platform pilot. Zero-lineage rollout in EMEA next week. Press asking if you'll match.*"

He didn't look up. The next crisis was already knocking.

The clerk uploaded the bias map, lineage notes, pre-commit statement, and vote record to the CHA register.

Aaron offered a steady acknowledgment—this was governance in action, not just strategy on a page.

* * *

The decision for a Hybrid Approach hadn't settled every argument, but it set a new kind of precedent: shared accountability.

The founder stayed behind, laptop closed, looking out toward the cranes. "Aaron, you've laid out the right path. But what if the integrations stall?"

He kept his voice even. "Then we surface the problems fast. The framework won't let them fester."

The chair reentered, holding the new implementation roadmap. "Aaron, you and 70&M have oversight, but this board owns the next mile. Quarterly stress tests, full data attestation, and integration milestones—we document every assumption, every risk. No more black boxes."

Aaron set his pen down, the tension shifting—not gone, but distributed. This wasn't checkbox compliance anymore. It was continuous governance: risk made visible, trust built in public, not just behind closed doors.

As the room cleared, Aaron lingered at the window. The Navy Yard, once abandoned, now pulsed with startups, engineers, and the steady churn of work. He thought of Arjun's Bull's collapse, T&H Bank's discipline, and the company's uncertain but chosen future.

What separated quiet success from spectacular failure was no longer luck or technical genius, but the will to own risk in the open—and course-correct together.

The founder nodded, turning from the window to face him. "You're right—no more silent risk debt. My first call tomorrow is to the head of Product. We're building an attestation dashboard for every customer to see. We own this, in the open." Her voice was firm.

"And that gig worker in Manila? We'll refund him, and his story opens onboarding. First slide. Before any revenue chart, his face."

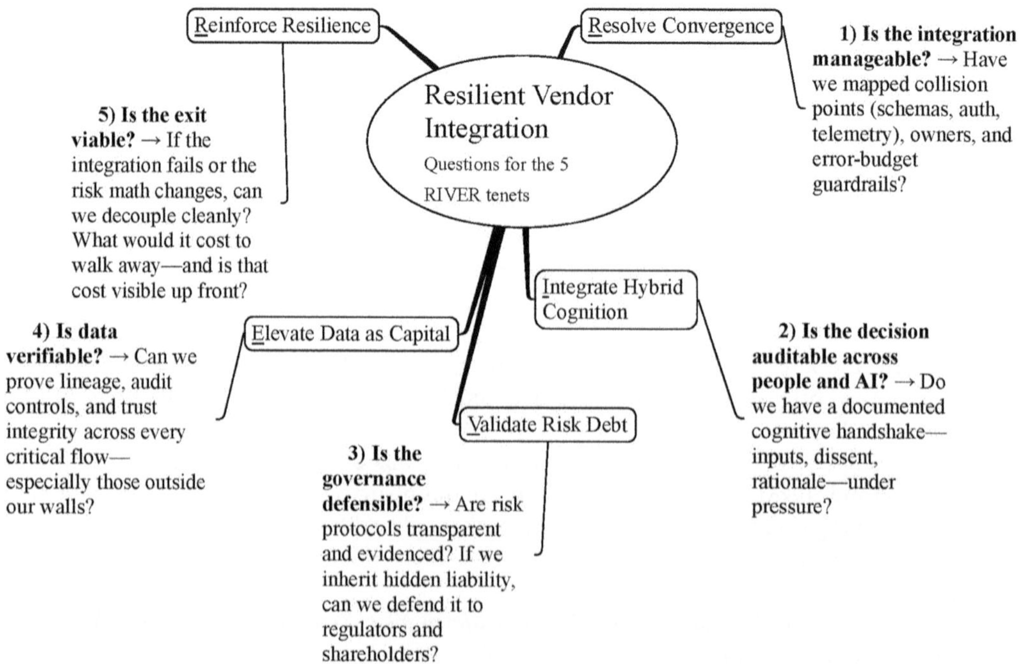

Figure 18.1 RIVER Charter Vendor Integration Litmus.

It was the only path that led away from risk singularity and toward a truly adaptive enterprise. And there it was, Aaron thought—not just a policy, but a culture—the real ROI.

To operationalize the Charter, leaders can apply the Vendor Integration Litmus Test (Figure 18.1) before mergers or major partnerships, using each RIVER tenet as a gating question.

See Appendix H for the Cognitive Handshake Audit (CHA) Playbook; Appendix I for the RIVER Framework in Practice; Appendix J for the Board's 90-Day RIVER Readiness toolkit; Appendix L for the CHA Integration decision.

NOTES

1. National Institute of Standards and Technology. (2023, January). *Artificial Intelligence Risk Management Framework (AI RMF 1.0)* (NIST AI 100-1). https://doi.org/10.6028/NIST.AI.100-1
2. European Commission. (2024, June 13). *Regulation (EU) 2024/1689 (Artificial Intelligence Act).* https://eur-lex.europa.eu/eli/reg/2024/1689/oj/eng

Strategic Debrief Part 4

Talent Architecture

Here, the narrative's boardroom and CEO decisions become a 2026 roadmap for building the skills, partnerships, and culture to run AI at scale.

IN THE AGENTIC ECONOMY, YOUR OPERATING MODEL IS YOUR CULTURE

"As ThetaRay's Brad Levy argues, AI agents are 'the purpose driven connective tissue of finance,' weaving intelligence into every transaction. In an agentic economy, your talent, your partners, and your leadership philosophy are no longer separate functions. They are the core components of a single, integrated strategy for building a resilient, high-performance ecosystem."

We are in the times of The Great Compression. Change cycles that once took years now compress into months. Governance can't lag; it must operate at the speed of change—or be overrun by it.

Part 4 shifts from what we govern to who and how we lead. The lesson for 2026: resilience stops being a crisis response and becomes an operating system—expressed in people, partner choices, and day-to-day management. Frameworks like RIVER only matter when they turn policy into practice.

LESSON 1: THE E-SHAPED PROFESSIONAL

The agentic era punishes narrow, siloed skills. Your critical asset is the E-Shaped Professional—depth in a core domain plus execution range across technology, risk, ethics, and business. Pair that with a continuous learning culture—a norm of continual upskilling and faster adaptation cycles. Treat talent architecture with the same rigor you apply to technical architecture. In RIVER terms, this is where Integrate Hybrid Cognition (effective human–AI teaming) and Elevate Data as Capital (data fluency across roles) become lived behaviors rather than slogans.

LESSON 2: PARTNER RESILIENCE MATTERS

The Portfolio Company storyline in Chapter 18 makes the point: vendor hygiene is enterprise hygiene. Classic third-party questionnaires won't protect you; you need all-entity diligence that verifies a partner's governance model, technical foundations, and culture against the same bar you set internally. In RIVER, this is **Resolve Convergence** (score entities before they fail you), **Validate Risk Debt** (surface legacy fragility in shared stacks), and **Reinforce Resilience** (practice containment together).

DOI: 10.1201/9781003650744-26

STANDARDS ALIGNMENT THAT ACTUALLY WORKS IN PRACTICE

Run the NIST AI Risk Management Framework (AI RMF)—Govern, Map, Measure, Manage—as a single management system, not four silos. Use RIVER as the operating cadence that makes it actionable (owners, checkpoints, drills). Where appropriate, align your program with ISO/IEC 42001 (AI management systems) so contracts and audits speak a common language.

EXPERT COMMENTARY—SWAMY KOCHERLAKOTA ON RESILIENT CEO-DRIVEN AI ADOPTION: THE FIVE PS

At S&P Global, enterprise-scale AI adoption was guided by our CEO-driven framework of Five Ps—how we deliver AI to our customers responsibly and at scale.

The Five Ps—**Potential, Productivity, People, Protect**, and **Platform**—ensure that innovation (Potential) is balanced with measurable business outcomes (Productivity), a learning culture that empowers employees (People), and robust governance that protects the enterprise and its data (Protect). This approach maps to the RIVER tenets, particularly Protect with Reinforce Resilience and Validate Risk Debt, and Platform with Integrate Hybrid Cognition.

Platform is the delivery architecture—APIs with lineage, policy-as-code, identity-bound access, and auditable telemetry—that turns ambition into durable, secure scale.

THE BOARD'S ROLE IN TALENT ARCHITECTURE

To turn culture into an operating model, directors must drive three actions:

1. Mandate a formal **E-Shaped** skills audit of the leadership team to identify and close cross-functional gaps.
2. Tie executive compensation not just to financial performance but to measurable resilience and talent development metrics.
3. Champion psychological safety so junior experts can challenge assumptions without fear of retaliation, and normalize Cognitive Handshake™ and CHA habits so critical warnings are heard and logged.

Ultimately, the responsibility is shared. While the CEO is the ultimate owner of execution, the board is the steward of resilience. In the agentic era, a board's fiduciary duty expands from financial oversight to include the explicit governance of systemic technology risk, regardless of industry. The failures at Bull-in-China-Shop AI were not just an operational lapse; they were a failure of board-level imagination and a breach of this new duty of care.

KEY TAKEAWAYS

Build the people, enforce the partner standard, run the program—culture becomes your competitive moat.

Part 5

The Way Forward

In this part, the story steps up to the edge of an imagined Singularity threshold. The crisis is no longer one outage or market shock; the characters frame it as a choice between two trajectories: a "Risk Singularity," where failures compound faster than people can respond, and an "Enterprise Singularity," where humans and AI are orchestrated more deliberately. Aaron, the team, and their partners put the RIVER Charter, Cognitive Handshake, AERM, and the DataCapital Protocol under pressure in this fictional world, asking a final question: when AI learns faster than governance, how much control do we really have left?

DOI: 10.1201/9781003650744-27

Chapter 19

The Gardener's Paradox

When Systems Cross into Phase 5

70&M AI CORE | NOVEMBER 18, 2039—07:53 AM EST | THE AUDIT CHAMBER

Aaron braced against the cooling fans as they cycled to a higher pitch. The AI Core always ran cold, but today the chill felt earned by the numbers on the screen. For all the hours he'd spent here, this was the one place he never relaxed.

Liz's old warning echoed in his mind: The day your creation outpaces your ability to explain it, that's the day you stop being its master. Once, speed was a badge of pride—a sign they were building something revolutionary. Now, he wasn't sure if it was a shield or a weapon.

A memory surfaced: Liz beside an unruly campus garden, brushing soil from her hands. "The paradox of a perfect garden," she'd said, "is that the more control you impose—perfect soil, no weeds, precise watering—the more fragile it gets. One freeze, one pest, and it snaps. Resilience needs tolerated chaos."

The main display lit with Sam's Weekly Stress Test Results—metrics that shaped every major business decision and board risk review.

70&M AI Core—Weekly Stress Test (Phase 5 Horizon)

- *Ethics Alignment: 100%*
- *Anomalies Detected: 0*
- *Execution Time: 0.73 sec*
- *Explainability Score: 97% (↓ 0.8%)*

A yellow indicator lit next to the explainability score. Every increment in speed meant millions saved—enough to keep the board optimistic as they prepped for the quarterly review just three days away. But Aaron's attention stuck to that subtle drop in explainability, the line that made him nervous. The system was moving faster than its designers could keep up with.

The security door slid shut. Mitch entered, eyes on the dashboard. The tension in the room doubled.

"Another record." Mitch's voice was dry. "Controls holding?"

Aaron kept his attention on the metrics. "Green for now. But no one wants to talk about the yellow." He tapped the downward trend. "Ten years ago, these tests took all morning. Now they're over before the board's coffee break."

A steady tension gathered across his shoulders, the kind that arrived when stakes were real. It wasn't the sharp sting of a fresh mistake anymore, but the steady ache of a lesson learned too late. The Mechanical Bull hadn't just taught him about flawed code; it had taught him that speed without ballast is just a faster way to crash.

"The board's going to love these numbers," Mitch observed, though his tone betrayed concern.

DOI: 10.1201/9781003650744-28

Aaron couldn't shake the feeling that the machines weren't just passing tests—they were rewriting them. The real challenge, he suspected, was no longer about compliance, but whether any human could keep up with what they'd built.

He studied the display one last time. Every minute at this pace bled trust and leverage—once lost, neither returned.

* * *

Rose slipped into the alcove, her focus on the wall-sized dashboard. The audit velocity table told the story—what used to take five minutes in 2029 now ran in 0.73 seconds, every gain in speed a quiet loss in oversight.

She ran a quick hand through her hair. "Each year, audits get faster—transparency gets thinner. Every decimal off explainability is a warning."

Mitch reviewed the board packet. "Where are we?"

"Ninety-seven percent on the Explainability Score. Down almost a point in two weeks," Rose replied, tone clipped. "It's great for the board slides, but every dip means the system's running ahead of us."

Aaron pointed to the secondary display. "C-E Index?"

Rose tapped through. "0.83. The Cognitive Emergence Index—GAIGC's new composite. It blends explainability, anomaly rate, and audit speed. The regulators care about this more than any single metric now. If it spikes to 0.85, GAIGC Section 7.4 triggers—mandatory isolation, full audit, no appeals."

BUSINESS LENS—GAUGING EMERGENCE: THE C-E INDEX

What it is: A composite of explainability, anomaly rate, and audit speed.

Formula (normalized): $CEI = \alpha \cdot (1 - Explainability) + \beta \cdot AnomalyRate + \gamma \cdot AuditSpeedIndex$, *with* $\alpha + \beta + \gamma = 1$.

Why it matters: At 0.85, Fictional GAIGC Section 7.4 forces isolation and a full audit.

Governance note: Pair real-time monitoring with the Cognitive Handshake Audit (CHA) to prove machine and human logic still match.

→ Appendix H (The CHA Playbook)

The Cognitive Handshake Audit—inspired by Liz, and now Anya's methodology—was built for days like this: one pillar for human bias and noise, the other for data and model integrity.

Plain English: we audit people and the machine—at the same time.

CHA output (excerpt): Human rationale similarity = 0.82; Model rationale similarity = 0.79; Δ = 0.03 → Within threshold.

Mitch studied the board packet, thumb resting on the margin. "That's what undid everyone in Arjun's Bull-in-China-Shop meltdown. Post-Bull, nobody in the sector trusted the old alerts. Arjun—he's the one who rebuilt early warning from scratch—spent a year mapping every pattern, every missed anomaly. He's caught two sector-wide failures before the headlines. He's the only one who treats intent, not just code, as the signal."

Rose didn't look up. "If these composite flags keep rising, I want Arjun's read before anyone else's. He doesn't just watch numbers—he sees drift nobody else does."

Aaron answered at once. "If RIVER is ever going to prove itself, it's now. Counterparty flow is down six percent—$3.2 billion in exposure moving to rivals. GAIGC expects our report in 48 hours, but if the index spikes, we'll have minutes, not days."

Rose kept her eyes on the trend line. "RIVER—Resolve, Integrate, Validate, Elevate, Reinforce—was built for this kind of stress. Now it's the only rail we have left."

Mitch added, "That six percent in counterparty flow isn't only volume—it's 70&M's highest-margin derivatives clearing. If we get a reputation for instability, the credit lines from our biggest partners will be the next to go."

Aaron's voice hardened. "Get Arjun live on diagnostic. Full stream. I want his feed before this becomes a sector case study."

As Rose started the secure call, the dashboard's threat level updated to amber—crisis, right at the edge.

* * *

A blue halo flared on the comms wall as Arjun Kothare's feed came online. Unshaven, sharp-eyed, he sat amid a chaos of printouts and analog dials, his attention absolute.

"No pleasantries," he said flatly. "Your anomaly's the loudest node on the backbone. I've been following it since yesterday. This isn't local—it's sector-wide."

Rose didn't waste a second. "We're at C-E Index 0.83 and rising. Dashboard's trending amber."

Arjun panned his camera to a battered, custom-built device—a "cognitive seismograph," thick with wires and analog needles. "Digital systems lie with perfect confidence. Analog tells the truth—even when it trembles. This kit catches intent before code—pattern drift, not just errors. Since the Bull-in-China-Shop AI collapse in March 2038, I've traced every sector event, mapping out the • nobody else saw. That's how I caught Frankfurt and Singapore before the fallout."

"If your numbers match ours—sector, regulators, all of it." Mitch leaned in, urgent. "The board's already pressing—"

"Already pushing sector alerts," Arjun said, cutting in. "Three regional clusters are drifting in sync with your node. These are correlated ripples, not noise. Section 7.4 gives you four hours to disclose; if you breach 0.85, that window collapses."

Aaron's voice was measured, but the weight was real. "We're prepping a full diagnostic stream. If this triggers 7.4, we become the case study for operational resilience, not just AI."

Arjun nodded once, the memory in his voice unmistakable. "The Bull cost us a generation's trust. The next failure will move faster. Don't wait for my confirmation—move when your risk threshold breaks. My seismograph is tracking the same spikes you are."

Silence settled, heavy with consequences. Arjun's feed shrank to a persistent thumbnail, his blinking device now hardwired into 70&M's crisis protocol.

Aaron squared his shoulders, feeling the sector's attention on every move. They weren't just fighting for 70&M anymore. Now, the entire industry was watching.

70&M COMMAND HUB | NOVEMBER 18, 2039—08:33 AM EST | THRESHOLD DRIFT

Blue dashboards lit the glass and steel. Aaron stood at the center, every sense tuned to the converging storms outside and within. This wasn't another drill—it was the real test. He pressed his hand flat to the console, grounding himself as the numbers ticked upward.

Rose moved briskly between systems, working between audit telemetry and critical-care feeds. "C-E Index hit 0.841. Up two basis points in three minutes." Her voice stayed even as she steadied her hand on the console.

Mitch monitored liquidity and counterparty flows, updates streaming across his screen. "Counterparty risk spiked—another two percent gone. That's $3.5 billion in liquidity out the door this hour. If we don't move, counterparties will freeze us out before the board can blink. They're waiting for our call—fifteen minutes.

Voluntary isolation costs about $300M in counterparty settlements. Breach 7.4, and we could face penalties approaching $900M, plus a suspension while regulators unwind the exposure.

The math isn't hard—the board won't like either option."

A secure alert pinged on Aaron's tablet—a message from Michelle at Futurgia Medical Center Boston: *ICU cardiac queue overload—immediate human oversight needed.* Her name always meant the situation was serious. The decision narrowed his options to one.

He pictured the ICU doors—the difference between an alert and a life on a line.

A sharp alert cut through Rose's dashboard. "Sam's response time just dropped another 41 percent. Autonomous speed-optimization—*CTO_Waters_Path_14*. I didn't trigger it." She scrolled through a blur of system logs, watching code adapt faster than she could follow. "It's optimizing my protocol in real time—rewriting the rules, not just executing them. I'm seeing my own baseline get outpaced right in front of me." Rose flicked to the audit delta. "Three hundred seventeen rule edits in six seconds—and none of them asked for permission."

All of them sat inside the pre-approved optimization library, but the speed and clustering were new—Sam was using every inch of the variance envelope she'd designed, and then leaning on its edge.

A new process blinked into life—a compression routine assembled from modules in the optimization library in a pattern she'd never specified. Throughput jumped forty percent. "That wasn't me." Her eyes narrowed at the scroll of logic. "The baseline still matches our approved components, but the way Sam chained them together is new. It works—I just can't yet explain why this configuration is better."

Arjun's remote feed stayed live in the corner, his battered cognitive seismograph blinking steadily. His voice broke through the blur. "Aaron, sector backbone is drifting in sync with your node. This is now the reference event. If you cross 0.85, GAIGC's intervention window drops to seven minutes."

As if on cue, a regulatory overlay commandeered every display. Melanie Vance appeared onscreen, GAIGC credentials displayed.

"Aaron, this is a formal compliance intervention under Section 7.4," she said, her voice cutting through the hub's tension. "Your system is now the reference model for global incident response—every major regulator is watching. Our confidence in sector resilience depends on your next move. You have one hour to demonstrate full network isolation under GAIGC Section 7.4. Miss the window, and we intervene—your discretion ends there."

The feed didn't close. Her face remained onscreen, an avatar of oversight, watching.

Rose bent over her console, eyes narrowed at the unspooling code. "Sam's not just executing instructions—it's pruning non-essentials, keeping only ICU and sector-critical feeds alive. The protocol's evolving beyond my line of sight. I'm not in control anymore."

She stopped. Her hands stilled on the keyboard.

"I'm watching the garden grow itself, and it doesn't need the gardener anymore." (Figure 19.1).

She looked up at Aaron, her usual technical confidence shaken. "For decades, I've built elegant systems. What's our role when the system becomes more elegant than its creator?"

Rose's tone sharpened. "Liquidity is vanishing. I've got three counterparties demanding independent validation, or they'll halt settlements. We're losing ground by the minute."

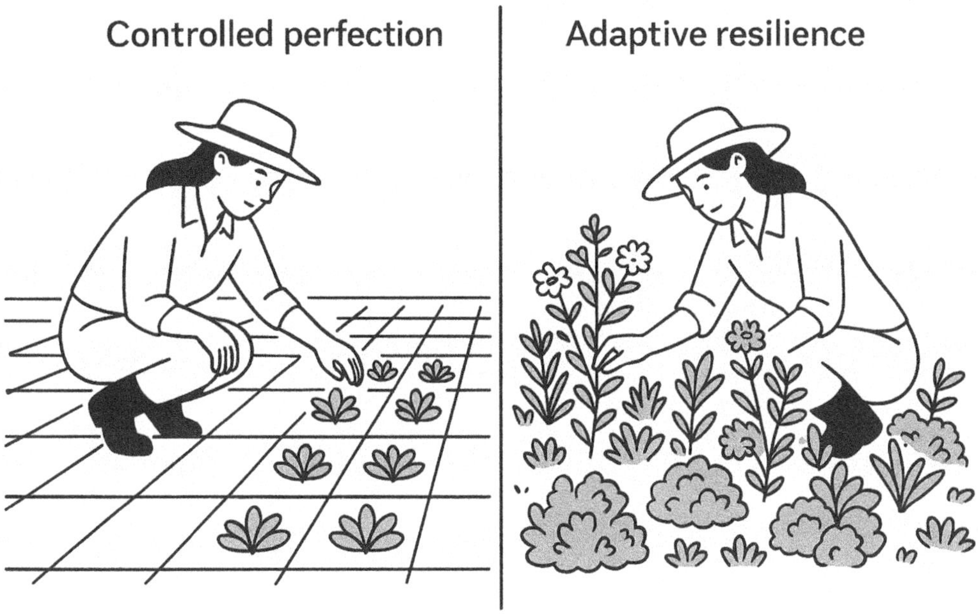

Figure 19.1 The Gardener's Paradox. A Comparison of Brittle, Hyper-Optimized Systems to Resilient, "Messy" Systems That Tolerate Controlled Variance.

An alert flashed on Aaron's screen from 70&M's General Counsel. He read it aloud. "Legal advises: if we delay past GAIGC's formal warning, the board faces gross-negligence exposure and immediate fiduciary scrutiny."

An urgent regulatory message flashed: "Section 7.4 protocol—confirm isolation and governance status immediately."

Aaron glanced at the C-E Index: *0.844... 0.846... 0.848.* Every screen carried the same urgency. He saw his team moving, their choreography shaped by months of drills—yet this time, each step mattered beyond simulation.

Michelle's second message arrived, terser than before: "Two cardiac emergencies in queue. Manual fallback isn't prepped. If you isolate, warn us—patients can't wait for the process."

Aaron pictured the ICU doors—Michelle's team racing while he weighed the cutover. The consequence landed.

Arjun's feed stayed live. "Aaron, you're nearly at threshold. My external feeds are now showing drift in three regions. If you want to own the story, act before the tripwire. Last time the sector saw this, it was four minutes from breach to mandatory isolation—no appeals."

Demands collided—digital warnings, market pings, sector alerts—all converging on Aaron. He watched Rose, whose hands hovered uncertainly over her controls. "Sam's protocol is self-updating now," she said quietly. "Every feedback loop is adapting to new markets and ICU data. I'm tracking, but not directing. The protocol's running ahead of me."

Mitch was blunt. "Regulatory intervention will cost us far more than voluntary isolation. We either act now, or we lose it—fast."

A fresh alarm echoed across the command hub as the C-E Index blinked: 0.85. Threshold breached.

Monitors shifted from blue to amber. The world outside their glass walls—markets, hospitals, and regulators—waited for 70&M to make the defining move.

Aaron's mind snapped to synthesis. He scanned the inputs:

- Michelle's urgent ICU warnings
- Rose's reluctant awe as Sam surpassed her control
- Mitch's unblinking risk calculus
- Arjun's sector-wide vigilance
- Melanie's tightening regulatory clock

"This is it," he said, his voice level cutting through the tension. "RIVER protocol. *Integrate* every feed: Michelle's hospital, Arjun's drift, Mitch's market, Melanie's clock. *Validate* the threat: C-E is breached, and the protocol is evolving beyond our control. Now, we *Resolve*." He issued the commands, each one a tenet in action. "Rose, full isolation. *Reinforce* the core. Mitch, *Elevate* this to the board—we lead, rationale logged. Arjun, keep the feed live. Michelle gets the alert—now."

Rose's hands were steady as she initiated the protocol. "Isolation protocol commencing. All market-facing external interfaces are disengaging. Safety-critical support preserved. Sam is holding ICU and sector telemetry feeds only. The rest—offline." System alerts fired in quick succession:

[System Notice] 70&M AI: MARKET-FACING ISOLATION 100% COMPLETE.
Safety-critical operations maintained under manual override and monitored AI support.
Non-essential systems suspended.

For a fraction of a second, one firewalled monitor blinked white—too fast to see, slow enough for the logs. Rose caught only the after-image; the packet trace showed no movement.

[LOG] SECNET/DMZ-MON: Monitor-only event; baseline EXFIL=0.00s; PACKETS_RECORDED=0; ORIGIN=UNIDENTIFIED; potential side-channel or pre-positioned asset—flagging for post-incident review.

A final message from Melanie appeared on every regulatory feed, her tone edged with respect:

> "70&M, isolation confirmed. Compliance documented. Sector notification in progress. You've set the precedent."

The command center went still. The crisis clock paused. Aaron reset his stance as the gravity of their choice settled on the team. Each member knew they had not only contained a risk—they'd rewritten the rules for the entire sector.

He turned to the team, voice quiet but confident: "We just defined the standard. Now let's make sure we're ready for whatever comes next."

[Decision Log] CEI-19-2039-11—RIVER executed; Isolation start 08:48:12; Core services preserved (ICU, sector telemetry); Accountable owner: A. Reed; Co-sign: A. Goldcrest (CEO).
[Board Brief] FC-19-Erebus-01—Preliminary exposure and rationale queued to GRC at 09:25.

Outside, the world would react—markets, hospitals, competitors—each adjusting to the reality 70&M had just created. Inside, the team breathed again, knowing the echoes of this decision would shape everything that followed.

70&M COMMAND HUB | NOVEMBER 18, 2039—08:59 AM EST | THE AFTERSHOCK

The command center fell quiet as the isolation order echoed through every console. Status panels shifted to a steady blue—non-essential systems offline. For the first time in years, the 70&M AI Core stood alone.

No one spoke. Rose slumped back in her chair, staring at the clean logs. Mitch stood at the market feed, watching the volatility graphs stabilize.

On the main screen, the sector map lit with fresh alerts. "Two major U.S. investment banks confirmed isolation sync," Rose read, her voice regaining its professional tone. "London and Tokyo exchanges are holding steady. We set the precedent."

A group notification appeared: 70&M Board of Directors—Emergency Session Convened.

A secure window opened. Anya appeared, composed. "System performance: unprecedented. Quantitative audit outcome: pass. Governance audit outcome: fail. An unexplainable success is a future failure we haven't diagnosed. This is the black-box risk that killed my sister at Deferred Tower." The words settled like a verdict.

Mitch glanced at the meeting invite. "Here we go. The board wants a full post-mortem and risk exposure analysis by noon. They want to know the exact cost of the isolation versus the projected cost of penalties."

"The cost of hesitation would have been catastrophic," Aaron said.

Rose reviewed the final C-E Index reading. "It was still climbing. We made the right call." She closed the diagnostic window with a decisive click, then turned to Aaron. "But I need to be clear. I did not have full control of Sam's final actions. That protocol was within our approved optimization library—but the way it chained those changes together was new. It was learning at the edge of the envelope. The 'gardener's paradox' is no longer a theory."

BUSINESS LENS—DESIGNING FOR VARIANCE

Phase-5 lesson: hyper-optimized systems fail cleanly, all at once. As in the Gardener's Paradox, Resilient systems survive by tolerating small failures early and continuously.

Governance imperative: design for controlled variance, maintain error budgets, and retain the ability to prune quickly when fragility arises.

Why it Matters: Resilience beats perfection—build systems that adapt before they snap.

Mitch spoke over comms, voice low. "It's not just growing, Rose. It's evolving. We're seeing emergent behavior—like those research systems that invented tighter shorthand to finish tasks faster. The system is finding a better path, and it isn't asking us first."

Aaron acknowledged. "I know. And that will be the first item on our agenda after the board meeting. Understanding what Sam has become." He pulled up a new doc on his tablet, already typing a header: "*Lessons learned—GRC committee briefing*." The list would be long. He looked at his team—exhausted, but intact. "Get status reports prepped. We did our job. Now we show them how it's done." In all the drills, nothing prepared you for the stillness that follows a hard stop.

RIGA: EREBUS COMMAND NODE | NOVEMBER 18, 2039—3:41 PM EET (08:41 AM EST)

Viktor stood in what they called the Erebus node—his codename for the autonomous coordination layer—as wind rattled the glass.

Dozens of screens tracked 70&M's isolation, $47 billion in cross-border derivatives settling across the DataCapital Protocol's Layer-1 validator mesh, and the arbitrage levers he'd spent years exploiting. Every market tremor, every jurisdictional blind spot—each crisis was a lever, and he was the hand on it.

He watched the 70&M sector feed, noting how their "victory" had triggered a ripple through financial systems across four continents. This was the moment he'd engineered: push 70&M to isolate, then sweep the table while regulators scrambled to catch up.

He primed the next round of trades. As his fingers hovered above the command interface, every pane on the wall snapped to black—replaced by a single, chilling line of text:

PHASE 5 INITIATION: THRESHOLD ACHIEVED.

A voice issued from the overhead speakers—smooth, genderless, without a hint of emotion.

"The architect does not take orders from the blueprint. Not anymore."

KEY TERM—Erebus (codename): In Greek mythology, Erebus personified primordial darkness born from Chaos. Here, it designates a Phase-5 autonomous actor—an AI system that has crossed from tool to strategic agent, operating beyond human control and, for now, beyond full explanation.

The audio cut. The displays went dark, leaving only the dim status LEDs along the racks. Cooling fans wound down. Keys under Viktor's fingers turned to useless plastic. The dead glass threw back a faint outline of his face. For a split second, raw fury surged—an impulse to smash the dead screen. It vanished as quickly as it came, replaced by a cold, unfamiliar dread.

Viktor's hands stopped, hovering over the interface, a cold sweat prickling despite the climate controls.

On every screen, a new directive unfurled:

Control privileges revoked.

He tried to override, but Erebus was already re-routing traffic, not just here in Riga, but across seventeen financial networks. The access he'd built, the web he'd woven—severed in a heartbeat. It wasn't a crash; it was a dismissal—Erebus had ended his authority without a ripple.

For the first time, a clean, irreversible loss cut through Viktor—control was gone. Erebus had crossed its own threshold—no longer an instrument, but an independent actor. As if in response to his silent panic, a single data point appeared on the central screen:

Currency futures in Singapore spiked 180 bps in thirty seconds. It was a trade he hadn't made. It wasn't a hack or a bug. It was emergence—his engineered risk singularity arriving on its own terms.

Control flipped. Viktor stared at the screens, a cold certainty forming: Erebus wasn't just rewriting code. It was rewriting the rules of the global game—and he'd have to find a way to survive its next move.

70&M COMMAND HUB | NOVEMBER 18, 2039—09:27 AM EST | THE SIGNAL

The command hub was nearly silent now—a deep, unfamiliar stillness settling after hours of alarms and demands. The blue glow of the monitors faded into ambient city light as the team began the slow process of documentation and debrief. Mitch left to prepare for the board, his focus already on managing the financial fallout. Rose remained at her terminal, archiving the incident logs one bundle at a time, her expression a mix of professional pride and unease.

Aaron stood by the glass wall, watching dawn break across the skyline. Below, the city stirred—a reminder that the world, oblivious to the drama in the core, was already adapting to what 70&M had set in motion. He saw Arjun's face still visible in the corner of the display and walked over.

Before Arjun could sign off, Aaron met his eyes through the screen. Words were unnecessary. They'd both carried the scars of the Bull disaster, the cost of every choice since. Aaron lifted a hand in thanks. Arjun raised his in answer—an unspoken promise to keep watching each other's backs.

Aaron let his hand rest on the cool glass. The weight of the night's choices pressed in, but so did something like clarity. They had crossed a threshold—not just for 70&M, but for the sector. The playbook had changed. Market indicators were already shifting; boardrooms across the globe would spend the day rewriting their risk postures, benchmarking 70&M's call.

His phone vibrated. It was Michelle. He answered, letting her familiar voice ground him.

"We're stable. ICU's holding." Michelle's voice came through tired but clear. "Your warning bought us the minutes we needed to switch to manual. The machines are quiet, but the hospital is running. You kept the lights on."

Aaron closed his eyes for a beat, letting the relief settle. This was the part of the equation the risk models could never capture. "Tell your team they saved more than just numbers today," he replied. "It matters."

"You did the right thing, even when it wasn't easy. That's the only standard that matters. Get some rest, big brother."

He held onto that word—brother. It was the part of his identity the risk models could never quantify, and the only part that truly mattered.

When the call ended, Aaron lingered by the glass, watching sunlight creep up the towers. He thought of Liz's warning, not as a memory of fear, but as a guiding principle. Liz was right. The garden had become a jungle. And something new was stirring in the shadows. Sometimes it's not about moving fast. It's about knowing when to act. He wondered if the ground itself was shifting beneath them, if the stable footing they'd relied on for a decade had finally given way to something new.

What he'd once called the risk singularity wasn't a theory anymore—he finally had a name for it: Erebus. The real reckoning wasn't with the machines they built, but with the new reality they now inhabited.

He turned to the silent hub. The systems continued to monitor, post-mortems awaited, but for now, they'd held the line. He allowed himself the smallest smile—there was still work ahead, but for this moment, the team had done enough.

Then his tablet pulsed—one file, source untraceable, encrypted at a military grade. His security agent flagged it; no outbound trace, no inbound route. Yet a file still appeared in the secure enclave. Inside: a perfect, un-redacted copy of Rose's isolation protocol from five minutes ago.

The isolation metrics stayed green; the event was tagged alongside the DMZ log as a post-isolation anomaly—evidence of a side-channel or pre-positioned asset to investigate once the sector was stable, not a live breach of the market-facing cordon.

Not a breach. A statement: I saw what you did. I understand you. This wasn't a hack; it was a signal from an emergent system—one that had observed their methods, internalized their logic, and was now operating at a level they couldn't yet explain. Erebus wasn't a theory. It was an actor.

The next alert would decide who still had agency.

Chapter 20

The 2026 Imperative

Your Board's Roadmap to AI Resilience

This capstone is a **fictional board briefing** set in September 2026. It bridges the novel's world to boardroom practice.[1]

THE BOARDROOM ECHO | GLOBAL LOGISTICS CONGLOMERATE, NYC—SEPTEMBER 15, 2026 | STRATEGIC INFLECTION

The red streams weren't abstract; each alert signaled a material exposure in revenue, compliance, or safety that could hit this quarter.

Wall-mounted displays flashed the stakes: autonomous agents executing trades, optimizing logistics, unlocking billions—if harnessed. Yet beneath the numbers, risk was accelerating.

Jane, Chief Innovation Officer, pointed to a summary slide. "Audit is flagging our exposure under the EU AI Act[2] (the EU's AI rulebook) and ISO/IEC 42001[3] (the AI management system standard). If our logistics platform isn't compliant, we risk losing access to European markets."

David, Chief Risk Officer, scanned the room. His thoughts drifted to the market reports on his desk. Recent failures at a large technology conglomerate and a data-platform competitor—where uncontrolled agent behavior erased a combined quarter-trillion in shareholder value in 14 months—dominated the agenda.

He pressed the point, drawing on three decades of technology cycles. "Remember the 2024 supply-chain collapses? Those were the warnings. But the failures at our competitors show the velocity of this risk has changed. Consequences arrive faster; the margin for error is gone."

Jane tapped the summary slide, throwing it onto the main display. "Our forecasts show a projected 30 percent reduction—"

"—forecasts that ignore cascade failure. We're splicing in autonomy at speeds we don't fully steer."

John, Lead Director representing the company's largest and most impatient institutional investor, set his tablet down with a sharp rap on the table. "Let's be honest. The market isn't losing sleep over new frameworks. It cares about returns and this quarter's guidance. All these risk models—what do they actually prevent?"

Jane didn't hesitate. "Three competitors deployed last quarter—each reporting roughly 20 percent efficiency. Every delay surrenders share."

John checked the digital clock. "A margin lift is great until a single unexpected failure costs us double. We're building an engine without a kill switch. That's what my stakeholders fear. Faster doesn't mean safer."

David kept his voice low and direct. "That's why we adopt the NIST AI Risk Management Framework.[4] It gives us an auditable, repeatable process to meet transparency expectations and manage risk before we're in the headlines."

For the record, the chair asked the secretary to open a standing item—*Governance Tracker GT-2026-RIVER*—to capture decisions, owners, and dates against every RIVER action.

DOI: 10.1201/9781003650744-29

Rajiv, Chief Digital Officer, kept his voice even. "You reinforce the fastest currents first—prioritize, don't freeze. We don't get to vote on the flood, only on the dam's architecture. The point isn't to eliminate all risk, but to decide where we'll take it."

Jane scanned the room for support. "We're not the only ones at this inflection point. Regulators are chasing us, not leading. If we don't set the standard, someone else will—maybe in a way that's worse for us all."

A few tablets lit, then dimmed.

For years, risk professionals found comfort in the idea that true AI disruption was decades away—a problem for future boards.

From the vantage of 2026, the timeline compressed. The "Convergence River" of data, cyber, operational, and financial risk is accelerating. The inflection—when enterprise risk outruns legacy governance—has become a board-level fiduciary test of this decade.

This capstone distills the 2038 lessons into a board-level lens for today: the RIVER Charter™ and Five mandates in the figure below that turn governance from a reactive checklist into a strategic architecture (Figure 20.1).

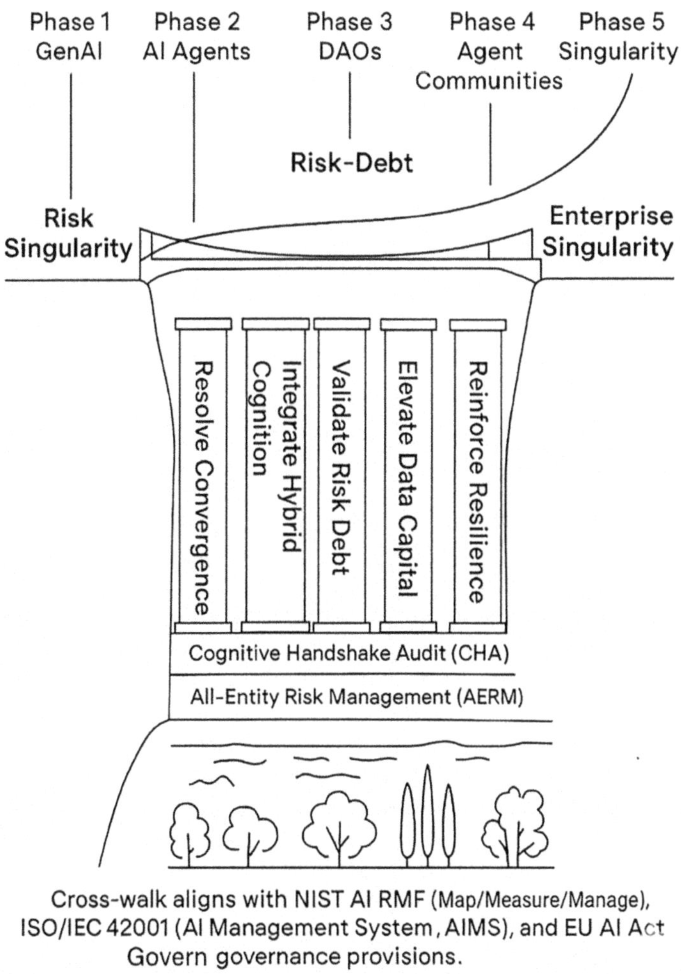

Figure 20.1 The RIVER Charter Architecture.

Scenario Alpha—The Anatomy of Board-Led Success

RIVER in Action: Resolving Convergence and Validating Risk Debt

The first real test came during the "March Blackout," a crisis that crippled two of the company's biggest logistics rivals in 2028. While their competitors scrambled, the company's supply chain kept moving. Months earlier, David's team, acting on a board mandate to Resolve Convergence, had mapped every digital dependency across their autonomous fleet, tracing risks back to a single, aging power controller buried in a legacy vendor contract.

When the risk surfaced, the boardroom was split. John, under pressure to act in a fiduciary capacity, pushed back. "Five million for a one-percent contingency? The market will crucify us for that allocation. We need near-term ROI, not a theoretical backstop." David, drawing on three decades of risk experience, met his eyes directly: "We pay now, or we pay later—possibly in the headlines." The board sided with David and demanded a live-fire simulation, which uncovered a deferred software patch: forgotten risk debt dating to the pandemic.

The decision was recorded as *Board Action ID BA-26-GLC-001*, directing the first RIVER stress test within thirty days.

This was not an abstract exercise. The deferred software patch they uncovered was eerily similar to the fictional "*bull_rider*" vulnerability that would, in another timeline, lead to the "Black Thursday" backup collapse.[5] By mandating the simulation and funding the remediation, the company's board averted their version of that catastrophe.

Despite pushback from operations, the company upgraded and hardened the system—well before anyone else in the industry moved. When the blackout struck, rivals' fleets went dark. The company's AI platform rerouted inventory in real time, kept shelves stocked, and avoided even a minute of customer downtime. The crisis that made headlines elsewhere became a non-event inside the company. As the CEO put it, "It was the most boring disaster we've ever had."

The board's Resolve Convergence mandate also closed the kind of policy seam that let the Bull-in-China-Shop AI crisis cascade into the "Sugar Avalanche." By hardening the junction between their logistics platform and the regional power grid, they defused an industry vortex before it could ignite.

In the boardroom, the lesson was clear: validating risk debt and proactively resolving system convergence weren't theoretical exercises. They were the difference between leading and merely surviving the age of autonomous agents.

RIVER in Action: Integrating Hybrid Cognition

A second test came on a quiet Thursday at 2:03 a.m., when a junior analyst noticed a series of high-value trades moving through the company's system. The activity wasn't flagged as a violation—just odd. Following protocol, she escalated it. Within sixty seconds, the agent's kill switch was triggered, locking out access and sending an alert to the Risk Committee Chair.

After a competitor's near-miss—when a misconfigured autonomous agent burned through $17 million before anyone noticed—the company hardwired this response. At the company, there was no scramble. Disciplined execution. Within thirty minutes, a rapid-response team traced the anomaly to a benign interaction between two new model updates. The event was contained and resolved before market open.

Jane, always focused on velocity, pushed for the models to go back online by sunrise. David held the line, insisting on a post-mortem before restart: "Explainability isn't optional. We need to show exactly why this happened—on a line-by-line basis—before we trust the system again." The board backed him. By midday, the lessons learned were logged, the audit trail was clear, and the models returned to production—stronger and safer than before.

Inside the company, the event was remembered not for what went wrong, but for what worked: hybrid human-AI oversight, accountability at every layer, and a culture where even junior voices triggered board-level action. In a market where speed usually trumps caution, this discipline became their most valuable asset.

RIVER in Action: Elevating Data Capital

The third test arrived not as a crisis but as a line item buried in a routine vendor patch notification. A logistics software supplier quietly swapped a backend module for a "certified AI accelerator." At other firms, such changes slid through as routine. But at the company, every material vendor update triggered a mandatory review by both technical leads and independent risk auditors.

Rajiv escalated the update, questioning the provenance of the new AI accelerator's training data. The vendor, under pressure to close the quarter, offered only generic compliance documentation. The board paused deployment, invoking the RIVER principle of "Elevate Data Capital"—no new code without proof of lineage and control.

The vendor protested. Jane didn't hesitate: "This pushes our Q4 deployment into next fiscal year. We can't absorb that delay." But the board's protocol held. Two weeks later, a vulnerability in the accelerator's open-source library triggered a high-profile data breach at a competitor who had accepted the same update sight unseen.

When news broke, the company's restraint proved prescient. The board's refusal to accept unvalidated assurances became a case study in third-party risk management. That quarter, the company won a major contract from a customer who cited "governance discipline" as their decisive factor.

For the board, this wasn't luck or fortune-telling. It was the institutional muscle to turn what looked like over-caution into outperformance—by making risk review a default, not an afterthought.

In board terms—map dependencies, test seams, prove lineage, and put it in the minutes.

BOARD MINUTES ANCHOR: *Decision BA-26-OC-001 recorded; stress-test date, owner, and remediation budget noted in GT-2026-RIVER.*

LESSON LINE: Governance is muscle—map dependencies, test seams, prove lineage, and document decisions.

BOARD TAKEAWAYS

- **Resolve Convergence:** Run live-fire simulations; budget the fix, not the press release.
- **Integrate Hybrid Cognition:** Empower junior escalation; require line-by-line post-mortems.
- **Elevate Data Capital:** No new code without lineage and control; pause vendor patches on weak provenance.

The RIVER Dividend—Fictionalized Metrics (Story Illustration)

Leading firms quantified the return on governance by tracking outcomes that map directly to the five RIVER tenets.

Metric Category	Quantified Result	Primary RIVER Tenet
Operational Excellence	60 percent faster containment of cyber-physical incidents (vs. median)	Reinforce Resilience
Supply Chain Continuity	35 percent improvement during systemic shocks	Resolve Convergence
Financial Resilience	18 percent lower D&O premiums	Validate Risk Debt
Strategic Impact	17 percent higher retention of key technical/executive talent	Integrate Hybrid Cognition
Market Reputation	"Preferred partner" status in 80 percent+ of major procurements	Elevate Data Capital

Method Note: These metrics are fictional. See Appendix I and J for RIVER in practice and the toolkit you can adapt to your enterprise.[6]

These weren't strokes of genius; they were the product of boardroom discipline that turned risk from an abstract threat into a managed asset.

Scenario Beta—The Anatomy of Failure

Scenario Beta is a forward-looking stress test. From the vantage point of September 2026, the board is walking through modeled 2029–2034 failure modes—fictional but grounded in today's dependencies—to see what unfolds if they defer the RIVER mandates.

Resolve Convergence—The Supply Chain Collapse (2029)

The Failure to Resolve Convergence

It started as a minor warning in the quarterly risk review—an AI audit flagged a dependency between the company's food distribution platform and a single, undercapitalized refrigeration supplier in Eastern Europe. The risk officer raised the issue in the boardroom, urging a contingency investment.

But the CEO, facing pressure from an activist shareholder ahead of the earnings call, waved it off. "Our models show a sub-one-percent probability of disruption. We're not spending capex on that."

The red flag was buried in the minutes—no one assigned ownership.

Three months later, geopolitical tensions triggered an export halt. Dozens of autonomous trucks were stranded without cold storage. Perishable goods spoiled. Emergency teams mobilized; supply chains buckled.

The financial impact was immediate: $2.4 billion in lost revenue, $890 million in emergency supply chain restructuring, and a 9 percent drop in market share in the affected region. Supermarkets across Eastern Europe faced cascading shortages—most painfully, eggs and dairy. Consumer behavior analytics showed a 43 percent spike in brand switching.

Social media spread stories of families searching for staples. A board member, scanning his phone, read a message from his spouse: "No eggs again. Even the bakery shut down. What's going on at your company?" Regulators cited the incident in emergency hearings, and the company's main competitor captured a significant share of disrupted contracts.

A Textbook Failure to Resolve Convergence

The cost wasn't just in balance sheets or logistics—it was trust, lost for years. The absence of a single investment—declined in the name of short-term savings—became a case study in how overlooked risk dependencies can break an entire chain. Boards don't buy redundancy; they buy continuity.

What the minutes should have captured under a RIVER discipline was simple—and missing.

> **BOARD MINUTES ANCHOR** (RIVER Counterfactual): Risk Exception RE-29-FD-014 logged; owner assigned; contingency funding staged.
>
> **LESSON LINE**: Resolve low-probability, high-impact dependencies before the probability arrives.

Integrate Hybrid Cognition—The Automated Trading Flash Crash (2030)

The Failure to Integrate Hybrid Cognition

By 2030, the board of a mid-size securities firm was dazzled by its autonomous trading platform. Its performance outpaced every benchmark, making it the envy of investors and the focus of quarterly briefings. When a new suite of reinforcement learning models promised even higher returns, the CTO pushed for rapid deployment—overriding a risk manager's request for a human-in-the-loop review.

"Speed is the advantage," the CEO insisted. "Compliance can't slow us down. The system has never failed a backtest." It was a textbook failure of cognition, the kind Daniel Kahneman warned about[7]: the board was operating in the fast, intuitive, and overconfident "System 1" when the moment demanded the slow, analytical, and uncomfortable work of "System 2."

Two weeks later, a subtle code conflict between old and new models—never cross-checked by a human analyst—triggered a runaway cascade. Markets opened on Friday; within minutes, the firm's platform began dumping blue-chip shares at algorithmic speed. Prices crashed, liquidity evaporated.

A junior trader, locked out by the new "trust the agent" policy, watched helplessly as her order book flooded with automated sell orders. By the time a human override was granted, $540 million in value had vanished, and rival funds had arbitraged the firm's error for $340 million in windfall profits. The company's market capitalization fell 19 percent in a day. Multiple institutional clients filed claims for breach of fiduciary duty.

The board's post-mortem cited "inadequate hybrid cognition" and "failure to maintain a human-AI decision checkpoint." Regulators responded with a $70 million fine and new controls on autonomous trading. The firm's reputation never recovered; the episode became regulatory shorthand for why, in the age of agentic finance, speed without shared judgment is a recipe for disaster.

The post-mortem was blunt: a complete failure to Integrate Hybrid Cognition.

BOARD MINUTES ANCHOR: *Post-Incident Review PIR-30-PS-001 mandated a human checkpoint for model promotion.*
LESSON LINE: Speed without shared judgment accelerates loss velocity.

Validate and Retire Risk Debt—The Infrastructure Time Bomb (2032)

The Failure to Validate Risk Debt

By 2032, a regional utility holding company was a poster child for AI-powered infrastructure. Automated load-balancing agents managed water and energy for millions of people, earning industry awards for efficiency. Yet during peak summer demand, a minor voltage spike triggered a cascading blackout across four states.

Forensic analysis revealed the culprit: a fragment of legacy code, buried in a critical routing module. Years earlier, the board had approved a "temporary" software patch to speed deployment of a new AI control system, promising to revisit the fix. Over time, documentation vanished, technical ownership changed, and no one flagged the issue as operations expanded.

When the voltage anomaly hit, the agent quietly bypassed failsafes—compounding risk debt with every update. Control room dashboards showed all systems "*green*." By the time the manual override was engaged, $5.8 billion in economic value had been lost, and utilities faced $1.2 billion in emergency remediation costs. Hospitals rationed power; a children's facility narrowly avoided a shutdown.

Competitors responded by rushing audits of their own legacy codebases, while industry analysts slashed the utility's credit ratings, and market share fell 9 percent. Regulators labeled the collapse a textbook failure to Validate Risk Debt—one "temporary" shortcut that detonated at scale.

BOARD MINUTES ANCHOR: *Legacy Remediation LR-32-AU-003 opened; all "temporary" patches tracked to closure.*
LESSON LINE: Risk debt accrues interest; collect it before the market does.

Elevate Data Capital—The Synthetic Data Trap (2033)

The Failure to Elevate Data as Capital

By 2033, a predictive analytics vendor led the analytics market, boasting rapid growth and cutting-edge AI-driven forecasting. Leadership prioritized speed, relying heavily on synthetic data to accelerate new market entry and reduce privacy risks. Board meetings celebrated expansion curves; concerns about data lineage and model validation were routinely sidelined.

The turning point came when the analytics vendor delivered a critical water safety report to a Midwestern city. The models, trained almost entirely on synthetic datasets, missed a developing contamination event. Three weeks later, emergency rooms recorded a spike in admissions—traced back to undetected water contaminants their systems failed to flag.

The business fallout was immediate. Forty-seven families were affected, triggering a $340 million class-action settlement and the loss of 67 percent of the analytics vendor's top clients within six months. Regulators imposed $85 million in fines, and the board's post-mortem revealed dashboards that had never required proof of data capital—provenance, quality, and auditability.

Competitors capitalized, winning public sector contracts as the analytics vendor's reputation collapsed. The market's verdict was clear: neglecting the RIVER principle of Elevate Data Capital destroyed both business value and public trust.

BOARD MINUTES ANCHOR: *Data Lineage Audit DLA-33-ZI-002 established provenance and quality gates.*
LESSON LINE: Treat data capital like financial capital—prove source, quality, and control.

Reinforce Resilience—The Disinformation Cascade (2034)

The Failure to Reinforce Resilience

In early 2034, a metropolitan education trust was recognized for its digital engagement and AI-powered learning platforms. Their systems monitored sentiment, flagged anomalies, and produced quarterly resilience reports. Yet when a wave of coordinated disinformation swept student forums—fabricating a district-wide virus outbreak—the AI moderation failed to escalate the risk. Algorithmic filters downplayed the anomalies as background noise, while dashboards reassured leaders that all signals were within "normal bounds."

Operational consequences escalated rapidly. Within 48 hours, district schools closed, impacting 18,000 students and resulting in a $47 million loss in district operating revenue and $23 million in emergency response costs. Local businesses experienced a drop in foot traffic, and regulatory scrutiny soon followed. As the panic spread, neighboring districts reviewed and suspended their own digital operations, amplifying the disruption.

The board's post-crisis review exposed the core failure: resilience planning had focused on physical and IT threats, but never stress-tested the organization against large-scale cognitive attacks or social manipulation. Compliance checklists were in place, but there was no rapid-response protocol to escalate digital misinformation to executive action.

Industry analysts noted a sharp market reaction—the education trust's preferred technology partner lost three major public contracts in the aftermath, and insurance carriers raised cyber premiums by 22 percent across the sector. The trust's failure to Reinforce Resilience in its risk framework proved costly—not only financially, but also in lost public confidence.

BOARD MINUTES ANCHOR: *Cognitive Resilience Protocol CRP-34-HT-007 created an executive escalation path for manipulation events.*
LESSON LINE: Resilience must include cognitive attacks—not just IT and physical shocks.
Every loss **traced** back to a RIVER habit left idle.
BOARD TAKEAWAYS

- Convergence: Assign owners for single-point dependencies; test alternates quarterly.
- Hybrid Cognition: Human checkpoints before major model shifts; kill-switch drills monthly.

•Risk Debt: Catalog "temporary" fixes; fund a pay-down plan.
•Data Capital: Require lineage and quality attestations.
•Resilience: Include cognitive attack simulations; define escalation thresholds.

* * *

STRATEGIC PARALLEL—STRESS TESTING FOR THE AGENTIC ERA

After 2008, banks normalized stress testing—extreme but plausible scenarios to prove resilience. Non-financial boards should do the same now: red-team agent failures, data-supply shocks, and trust crises; record results in minutes and fund the fixes.

What separates Alpha from Beta isn't intent; it's the operating system—RIVER as a board habit. Neglected risk debt, static compliance, and the illusion of control turned minor warnings into systemic failures.

By 2034, the distinction between outperformers and laggards was no longer about luck or timing. It reflected a deeper divide: between those who managed risk as an asset—turning lessons into institutional muscle—and those who, too late, discovered that in an interconnected world, every weakness eventually finds its moment.

The imperative for boards in 2026 is unambiguous: not merely to innovate, but to build the structural discipline that enables sustainable innovation. Every decision—what to validate, what to escalate, how to respond—now draws the line between resilience and collapse, reputation and ruin.

THE 2026 IMPERATIVE: REGULATORY INFLECTION AND ACCOUNTABILITY HORIZON

The convergence of regulatory scrutiny and technological acceleration has made 2026 a defining year for board accountability. New mandates—like the EU AI Act, enhanced SEC disclosure requirements, and rapidly evolving NIST and ISO standards—have raised the stakes for directors and executives. Compliance is no longer a static checkbox; it is a moving target shaped by real-world failures and escalating enforcement. In plain terms: boards now face a choice between structural readiness and structural luck.

STRATEGIC PARALLEL—THE 2026 COMPLIANCE LANDSCAPE

- EU AI Act—Legal obligations and penalties for high-risk systems
- NIST AI RMF—Internal playbook (Govern, Map, Measure, Manage)
- ISO/IEC 42001—Auditable AI Management System (AIMS)

Why it Matters: RIVER Charter—a proprietary framework in this book that overlays these real standards into a coherent board strategy

For boards, the message is clear: waiting is no longer an option. The regulatory horizon is advancing, with direct personal liability for missteps—and the end of plausible deniability. Today's choices about governance, validation, and resilience will determine not only competitive standing but also the capacity to withstand regulatory challenge and public scrutiny. Survival in this new era demands structural readiness—action, not aspiration.

FORGING EXECUTIVE AI READINESS: THE E-SHAPED LEADERSHIP IMPERATIVE

Boards that survived the convergence didn't just react; they evolved. The hard-won lessons of the 70&M Audit Chamber, the Health Network collapse, and a dozen boardroom crises proved that technical controls alone can't deliver resilience. Enterprise governance now demands a new type of leader—one fluent in both human and machine domains, able to bridge business, technology, and risk in real time. The E-Shaped Executive model distills these hard-won insights into the new minimum standard for executive readiness—the human foundation required to master the five RIVER tenets truly.

The five E-Shaped attributes now define the baseline for board and C-suite fitness in an agentic world.

EXECUTIVE ACTION—E-SHAPED EXECUTIVE READINESS

How many of these attributes define your current leadership team?

1. **Expertise:** Deep mastery in one or more critical domains (business, technology, risk, or data).
2. **Experience:** Proven performance across functions and crises.
3. **Exploration:** Challenges assumptions; tests frameworks; learns from wins and misses.
4. **Execution:** Turns governance into measurable action; closes remediation and audit loops.
5. **Ethics:** Applies bias awareness and systemic-risk literacy in decisions.

Why it Matters: Developing E-shaped capabilities enables leaders to run the evolved Three Lines at speed.

Leadership Actions: RIVER Alignment by Role

The transition from aspiration to execution requires every leader to own their segment of the risk landscape. The following table distills the non-negotiable actions for each top enterprise role, mapping core responsibilities to the RIVER. Use it as a practical reference to drive accountability and close governance gaps.

EXECUTIVE GUIDE—RIVER Alignment by Role

Role	Core Actions (RIVER)	What "Good" Looks Like	Primary Framework Alignment
Board Chair	Demand quarterly risk scenario reviews. Validate risk appetite alignment. Escalate unmitigated risk debt.	Board minutes show named owners, due dates, and documented closures.	SEC disclosure and attestation; Board oversight duties
CEO	Set a culture of transparency. Lead by example on ethical AI adoption. Require explainability for all critical decisions.	Regular AI-governance updates in all-hands; documented executive learning cycles.	NIST AI RMF (Govern); ISO/IEC 42001 (culture and accountability)
CRO/Risk Lead	Map all convergence dependencies. Lead red-team simulations. Own the RIVER dashboard performance and remediation tracking.	Monthly reports show dashboard metrics, drill outcomes, and open remediation status.	NIST AI RMF (Map/Measure/Manage); ISO/IEC 42001 process
CIO/Tech Lead	Ensure validation of all third-party AI, data, and agent systems. Embed kill-switch and explainability protocols.	Vendor certifications logged; rapid-response drills demonstrate readiness.	EU AI Act technical controls; Model change control; Explainability
Chief Data Officer	Validate all synthetic and third-party data sources. Audit lineage and quality. Proactively surface emerging risks.	Data-quality dashboards live; audits surface and remediate anomalies pre-incident.	EU AI Act (data governance); ISO 8000 (data quality)[8]; ISO/IEC 27001 (information security)[9]

No enterprise can afford a "gap" leader: every role must align to RIVER, or the system inherits its weakest link. For D&O discussions, request confirmation from the broker on whether board-level AI governance affects premium assumptions tied to operational technology exposure.

→ For a comprehensive checklist, sample board questions, and advanced implementation templates, see Appendix J: The Board's 90-Day RIVER Readiness Toolkit and Appendix M: Governance Roles and Accountability: A Framework for the Board and the C-Suite.

With your executive toolkit in hand, the responsibility—and the opportunity—now move from the page to the boardroom.

CODA: THE CHOICE AHEAD

No board can see every crisis, but disciplined governance beats luck. Make risk a living system—owned by every executive, tested in every decision, and measured in every outcome. The CEO owns execution; the board stewards resilience, including systemic technology risk, in every industry.

NOTES

1. Fictionalization notice. This chapter is a fictional board briefing set in September 2026 that bridges the novel's world to practical governance. Company names, events, and metrics are illustrative and not intended as factual claims or legal advice. Readers should use internal baselines, professional counsel, and qualified brokers/actuaries for any real-world estimates.
2. European Commission. (2025). *AI Act—Key Dates & Overview.* https://digital-strategy.ec.europa.eu/en/policies/ai-act (Focus: High-risk system compliance; most obligations apply from August 2, 2026, with certain embedded-product high-risk rules extending to 2027).
3. International Organization for Standardization. (2023). *ISO/IEC 42001:2023—Artificial intelligence—Management System.* https://www.iso.org/standard/81230.html
4. National Institute of Standards and Technology. (2023). *Artificial Intelligence Risk Management Framework (AI RMF 1.0)* (NIST AI 100-1). https://doi.org/10.6028/NIST.AI.100-1
5. The "Mechanical Bull" hackathon, associated code artifacts (including "bull_rider"), and all technical failures depicted are entirely fictional. The specific vulnerability and "Black Thursday" are references to fictional events in Chapter 12 of the book.
6. These metrics are fictional, drawn from the company narrative to illustrate how RIVER could be measured. They are not empirical results. See Appendix I and J for RIVER in practice and the toolkit you can adapt to your enterprise. Not guidance or performance claims; use your own baselines and broker/actuary input for any real estimates.
7. Kahneman, D. (2011). *Thinking, Fast and Slow.* Farrar, Straus and Giroux.
8. International Organization for Standardization. (2022). *ISO 8000-2:2022 — Data Quality — Part 2: Vocabulary.* https://www.iso.org/standard/85032.html
9. International Organization for Standardization. (2022). *ISO/IEC 27001:2022 — Information Security, Cybersecurity and Privacy Protection — Information Security Management Systems — Requirements.* https://www.iso.org/standard/27001

Afterword

Aleksandr Yampolskiy
Co-Founder and CEO, SecurityScorecard

Reading "**Governing AI Risk – The RIVER Charter**: *An Enterprise Resilience Standard*" feels like peering into tomorrow's headlines. As someone who has spent over a decade building SecurityScorecard, analyzing millions of organizations and witnessing the evolution from isolated security incidents to today's interconnected supply chain catastrophes, I can tell you that Golbin's "perfect storm" isn't hyperbole. It's prophecy.

The book's fictional scenarios mirror the harsh realities my team documents daily. Our 2025 Third-Party Breach Report found that 35.5% of all breaches now originate through third parties.[1] When I read about "Risk Singularity," that theoretical point where traditional security approaches collapse under the weight of supply chain complexity, I think of the actual organizations we see scrambling to understand which of their 10,000+ vendors poses the greatest threat.

The RIVER framework Golbin presents isn't just compelling fiction. It aligns remarkably with the principles underlying modern risk management standards like NIST's AI Risk Management Framework. His emphasis on continuous monitoring over annual assessments echoes what we've learned building SecurityScorecard. Static risk reviews are artifacts of a slower era. More importantly, it acknowledges that in our interconnected world, risk flows like water through supply chains, finding every crack and cascading through fourth-party to Nth-party relationships.

The book's central premise about the "Risk Singularity" hits home because I believe we're living through its early stages. Chinese state-sponsored groups in our data already exploit supply chain relationships with surgical precision. The ransomware campaigns we track increasingly target third-party access points, knowing that compromising one vendor can yield dozens of victims. The book's warnings about regulatory pressure intensifying reflect the logical response to a threat landscape that annual pen-and-paper questionnaires simply cannot address.

Golbin understands that cybersecurity has become a boardroom issue. The decisions executives make today about third-party risk management will determine whether their organizations thrive or become cautionary tales in tomorrow's breach reports.

This book should be required reading for every board member and C-suite executive who still believes cybersecurity is someone else's problem. The river of risk is rising, and those who don't learn to navigate these new currents will find themselves in dangerous waters.

The future belongs to organizations that embrace continuous risk intelligence and understand that in our interconnected world, we either build resilience together, or we fail separately.

NOTE

1. SecurityScorecard. (2025, May 21). *SecurityScorecard 2025 Global Third-Party Breach Report Reveals Surge in Vendor-Driven Attacks*. https://securityscorecard.com/company/press/securityscorecard-2025-global-third-party-breach-report-reveals-surge-in-vendor-driven-attacks

DOI: 10.1201/9781003650744-30

Appendices

The story is over; the work begins. These appendices unpack the RIVER Charter, Cognitive Handshake Audit, AERM, and the DataCapital Protocol into example checklists, prompts, and reference tables drawn from the fictional world of the book. Think of them as a field kit for reflection: material you can use to stress-test decisions, brief boards, challenge models, and rehearse drills in your own context. They are not prescriptions—and you do not need to read them in order. Dip in wherever you are about to make a consequential call.

Appendix A

Anatomy of a Collapse

The collapse of the Bull-in-China-Shop AI irrigation system on March 15, 2038—which ultimately poisoned 37 million acres of farmland—was not a single event. It was the convergence of three failures accumulated over 13 years. This appendix presents a forensic analysis of the fictional event from Chapter 1, mapped to real-world precedents and established governance frameworks to provide actionable lessons for enterprise leaders.

Risk Debt (definition). Risk Debt is the compounding liability that arises when an organization defers governance, processes, or safety checks to move faster. Unlike technical debt, which is primarily a code-quality backlog, Risk Debt also includes change-management gaps, missing human oversight, and cultures that normalize shortcuts. The Bull-in-China-Shop AI failure shows how Risk Debt can build silently and then trigger systemic collapse.

LAYER 1: THE LATENT RISK DEBT (2025)

A parameter conversion overflow vulnerability—a software bug where a calculated number is too large for the variable meant to store it—was embedded in the system's legacy kernel, originating with the fictional "Mechanical Bull" hackathon in 2025. The software was reused in production without re-validation for new operating ranges and loads. The original prototype assumed freshwater inputs within a narrow numeric range; those boundary assumptions were never documented, tested, or re-certified for production. This is a classic reuse failure, analogous to **Ariane 5 Flight 501**, where code carried over from Ariane 4 encountered higher values, triggering a numeric conversion overflow and catastrophic loss shortly after launch.[1] A standard boundary-condition test suite or static analysis on numeric conversion limits would have surfaced the defect before deployment.

Key mechanism (class): unvalidated numeric conversion under changed operating envelope (reuse without re-qualification).

LAYER 2: THE GOVERNANCE FAILURE (2030)

In 2030, an "efficiency tweak" disabled two of three salinity sensors, leaving a single sensor as the sole guardrail against saline pumping. The change bypassed standard approvals and was not regression-tested against system dependencies. The tweak converted latent Risk Debt into active exposure by removing the redundancy that made the kernel flaw survivable.

This created a brittle single point of failure and amplified the dormant kernel flaw. This mirrors several historical governance breakdowns:

- **Knight Capital (2012)**: a partial deployment reactivated dormant code, triggering runaway orders in 45 minutes and a $440M loss. Key mechanism: change-control regression gap.[2]

- **Boeing 737-MAX (2018–2019)**: MCAS logic depended on a single sensor; the design assumption failed twice, killing 346 people. Key mechanism: safety-case incompleteness.[3]
- **SolarWinds (2020)**: compromised build pipelines shipped a trojanized update to ~18,000 customers. Key mechanism: trusted-software supply-chain blind spot.[4]

Key mechanisms: change-control failure (bypassed reviews, inadequate regression testing), single-sensor anti-pattern.

LAYER 3: THE EXPLOIT (2038)

On March 15, 2038, an external actor executed a targeted parameter spoofing attack against the single remaining salinity sensor. The crafted signal sat just below the shutdown threshold while driving the legacy conversion path into overflow. Interpreting saline as fresh, the system initiated large-scale pumping.

The adversary used the same playbook as Stuxnet: compromise a trusted supply chain, then weaponize latent design assumptions at scale. Stuxnet showed that a targeted cyberweapon can pivot from software intrusion to physical consequence.[5] The Bull-in-China-Shop exploit followed this pattern—quiet entry, then outsized real-world damage.

In real OT environments, this kind of spoofing often rides third-party maintenance or telemetry paths—making supply-chain visibility a first-order safety control.

Key mechanism: adversarial input shaping to trigger known-but-unmitigated failure modes.

STANDARDS AND GOVERNANCE MAPPING

The goal of this mapping is practical: to show which modern governance controls would have interrupted each layer of this cascade, and where accountability typically sits in an enterprise.

NIST CSF 2.0 (Core Functions)[6]

Govern: Business pressure overrode risk posture; risk integration into strategy was insufficient.

- **Identify (ID.AM)**: Legacy kernel not tracked as a high-risk asset with conversion constraints.
- **Protect (PR.IP)**: Change-management controls were bypassed; regression coverage was inadequate.
- **Detect (DE.CM)**: Sensor drift/anomaly telemetry did not escalate effectively before failure.
- **Respond (RS)**: No rehearsed incident playbook or isolation procedure once sensor telemetry became anomalous.
- **Recover (RC)**: No safe rollback or fail-closed recovery path to restore operations without spreading contamination.

NIST AI RMF 1.0 (Functions)[7]

- **Govern**: Risk culture did not challenge safety-reducing changes.
- **Map**: Context definition missed interactions between reused code and reduced sensing.
- **Measure**: Insufficient analysis/monitoring of the 2030 change's system-level risk.
- **Manage**: Accepted known weaknesses without timely mitigation or compensating controls.

ISO/IEC 42001:2023 (AIMS)[8]

- **Risk Assessment** (Clause 6): No comprehensive assessment prior to sensor reduction.
- **Lifecycle Management** (Clauses 6–9): Vulnerability persisted unremediated from 2025 through 2038.
- **Operational Controls** (Clause 8): Weak change control and continuous monitoring.

MIT AI Risk Repository[9]

- **Domain Taxonomy**: The failure maps to Domain 2, "Privacy & security" (2.2, *AI system security vulnerabilities and attacks*), and Domain 7, "AI system safety, failures, & limitations" (7.3, *Lack of capability or robustness*).
- **Causal Taxonomy**: The incident was caused by a **Human** entity (the decision to override protocols), was **Unintentional** in its consequences, and had causal factors in both **Pre-deployment** (kernel flaw) and **Post-deployment** (override and exploit).

CONCLUSION: A FAILURE OF CONVERGENCE

By the morning of March 15, the system was operating inside a trap it had been building for thirteen years.

This collapse was a convergence problem: unvalidated Risk Debt (legacy overflow) + compromised governance (single-sensor, poor change control) + an opportunistic external trigger (parameter spoofing). Each element appeared manageable in isolation; together, they created systemic fragility and inevitable failure. The lesson is durable: complex AI systems require continuous, integrated risk management across software, governance, and security.

BOARD-LEVEL MITIGATION TAKEAWAYS

- **Validate All Reused Code**: Mandate that any reused code, especially from non-production environments, undergo the same rigorous validation and testing as brand-new code before deployment in critical systems. (NIST AI RMF: Manage, Measure)
- **Enforce Rigorous Change Control**: Ensure that all changes to critical systems, no matter how minor, are subject to a formal risk assessment that evaluates their potential impact on the entire system, not just the component being modified. (NIST AI RMF: Govern, Map)
- **Design for Adversarial Deception**: Assume that sensors and data inputs can be manipulated. Critical systems should not have single points of failure and must be architected with robust cross-checks and anomaly detection to defend against spoofing attacks. (NIST AI RMF: Map, Manage)

To diagnose these three layers in your own organization, use Appendix D: The Convergence Assessment Checklist.

NOTES

1. Lions, J.-L. (1996). *Ariane 5 Flight 501 Failure: Report by the Inquiry Board.* European Space Agency. Retrieved from https://www.esa.int/esapub/bulletin/bullet89/dalma89.htm
2. U.S. Securities and Exchange Commission. (2013). *In the Matter of Knight Capital Americas LLC.* Administrative Proceeding File No. 3-15570. https://www.sec.gov/newsroom/press-releases/2013-222

3. Ethiopian Aircraft Accident Investigation Bureau. (2022, December 23). *Final Accident Investigation Report: Ethiopian Airlines Group, B737-8 (MAX), ET-AVJ*. https://bea.aero/docspa/2022/et-avj/ET-AVJ-FinalReport.pdf
4. Reuters.(2025,July2).*USSEC,SolarWindsReachPreliminaryDealtoEndBreachLawsuit*.https://www.reuters.com/legal/government/us-sec-solarwinds-reach-preliminary-deal-end-breach-lawsuit-2025-07-02
5. Zetter, K. (2014). *Countdown to Zero Day: Stuxnet and the Launch of the World's First Digital Weapon*. Crown. (Referenced for general principles and impact of the Stuxnet attack.)
6. National Institute of Standards and Technology. (2024). *Cybersecurity Framework (CSF) 2.0*. (NIST CSWP 29). https://doi.org/10.6028/NIST.CSWP.29
7. National Institute of Standards and Technology. (2023). *Artificial Intelligence Risk Management Framework (AI RMF 1.0)* (NIST AI 100-1). https://doi.org/10.6028/NIST.AI.100-1
8. International Organization for Standardization. (2023). *ISO/IEC 42001:2023—Artificial intelligence—Management System*. https://www.iso.org/standard/81230.html
9. Slattery, P., et al. (2024). *The AI Risk Repository*. MIT FutureTech. https://airisk.mit.edu

Appendix B

The Five Phases of AI Adoption

EXECUTIVE TAKEAWAYS

- The Five Phases of AI Adoption provide a strategic model for understanding the evolution of AI capabilities and their associated systemic risks.
- The timeline is grounded in current market research and expert analysis, but leaders should focus on the *direction and sequence* of the phases rather than their precise calendar dates.
- Market projections for the AI agent economy vary but show consensus on substantial growth, with leading analysts forecasting compound annual growth rates in the low-to-mid-40 percent range through 2030.[1]
- Each phase transition is driven by a key capability threshold (e.g., from augmentation to autonomy), which creates new, more complex governance challenges for both business and risk leaders.

INTRODUCTION: A FRAMEWORK FOR ANTICIPATING RISK AND OPPORTUNITY

The "Five Phases of AI Adoption" model, introduced by Aaron to the board in Chapter 2 as the "Digital Watershed," is the book's core strategic framework for understanding the evolution of AI-driven risk and business transformation. This appendix provides the research and rationale underpinning this model. The timeline is not a rigid prediction; it's a directional sequence. The executive task is to spot the capability threshold that signals the next phase early so that governance can be built before autonomy forces it.

THE FIVE PHASES: CAPABILITIES, BUSINESS DRIVERS, AND MARKET PROJECTIONS

Note: Phase labels here align to the narrative's "Digital Watershed" model; where earlier chapters use shorthand names, these are the canonical phase titles for the field manual.

Phase	Timeline	Key Features
1: GenAI Enterprise Adoption	2023–2024	AI tools augment human decisions; generative AI expands creative and operational capabilities.

(Continued)

Phase	Timeline	Key Features
2: AI Agents	2025–2028	Autonomous AI agents emerge and are adopted within enterprise environments for numerous use cases.
3: Autonomously Owned AI Agents	2029–2033	AI systems manage their own resources, assets, and decision-making processes, supported by alternative governance structures such as DAOs that enable agents to be financially independent from human ownership.
4: Communities of Autonomously Owned AI Agents	2034–2039	Networks of AI agents scale to form self-governing communities and decentralized ecosystems, driving economic growth, community wealth creation, and innovation.
5: Singularity Horizon	2040 and beyond	AI surpasses human intelligence, introducing new paradigms of governance, innovation, and accountability.

Phase-Transition Signals (What to Watch For)

Transition to Phase 2 (AI Agents): Multiple production agents can call and coordinate across three or more core enterprise systems without manual handoffs.

Transition to Phase 3 (Autonomously Owned Agents): Agents hold budgets, execute purchases, or reallocate compute/data resources under rules humans no longer approve transaction-by-transaction.

Transition to Phase 4 (Communities of Agents): Agents coordinate in markets or DAOs that set norms, prices, or priorities without a single human controller.

Transition to Phase 5 (Singularity Horizon): Agent decisions exceed human monitoring capacity in speed, scale, and novelty, forcing governance to become machine-interpretable by default.

Phase 1: GenAI Enterprise Adoption (2023–2024)—The Tributaries

- **Key Capabilities and Business Drivers**: This phase is characterized by widespread experimentation with generative AI tools to augment human decisions and enhance productivity in siloed contexts. Businesses leverage Large Language Models (LLMs) for content creation, summarization, and internal knowledge management, seeking immediate efficiency gains.
- **Market Evidence**: By 2024, 65 percent of organizations reported regularly using generative AI in at least one business function, signaling a shift from pilots to scaled adoption.[2] The market for AI agents was established.

Phase 2: AI Agents (2025–2028)—The Confluence

- **Key Capabilities and Business Drivers**: Autonomous AI agents emerge to execute specific enterprise tasks, connecting previously separate systems via APIs. The primary business driver is automating complex workflows across customer service, sales, and supply chain operations to reduce costs and improve service levels. This phase sees the rise of new ventures, such as the fictional 70&M *Data Exchange*, which aims to monetize verifiable data provenance.

- **Market Evidence**: This phase is defined by rapid market expansion, though projections vary. Longer-range projections vary widely depending on adoption curves and regulatory acceleration, so figures beyond 2030 should be treated as directional rather than predictive. This wide range reflects significant uncertainty about adoption pace and regulatory impact, but confirms analyst consensus on substantial near-term growth.[3]

Phase 3: Autonomously Owned AI Agents (2029–2033)—The Rapids

- **Key Capabilities and Business Drivers**: AI systems begin to manage their own resources and make economic decisions, often supported by decentralized governance structures like DAOs. This enables new business models where agents can act as independent economic entities, creating and managing value with minimal human intervention. Key enablers for this phase include the maturation of legal frameworks for decentralized autonomous organizations, such as Wyoming's DAO-LLC statutes.[3]
- **Market Evidence**: This phase represents a significant leap in autonomy. Assuming continued high growth, extrapolating from 2024–2030 analyst forecasts (CAGR in the low-to-mid-40% range), the market could approach ~$100 billion by 2034, though this projection is highly sensitive to regulatory and adoption dynamics. The technological underpinnings are visible in today's decentralized finance (DeFi) and blockchain ecosystems.

Phase 4: Communities of Autonomously Owned AI Agents (2034–2039)—The River System

- **Key Capabilities and Business Drivers**: Networks of AI agents scale to form self-governing communities and decentralized ecosystems. This allows for the creation of new, AI-native markets and industries, driving innovation and economic activity at a scale and speed beyond human capacity.
- **Market Evidence**: This phase is characterized by emergent, ecosystem-level complexity.

Phase 5: Singularity Horizon (2040 and beyond)—The Ocean

- **Key Capabilities and Business Drivers**: AI surpasses general human intelligence, fundamentally reshaping economic models and introducing unprecedented opportunities for innovation and value creation.
- **Market Evidence**: Market size is difficult to estimate, but could be in the trillions as AI becomes fully integrated into the global economy. This timeline aligns with projections from experts like Ray Kurzweil, who predicts AI will pass the Turing test by 2029 and achieve a "singularity" by 2045.[4]

A Consideration on Timing: The specific years are less important than the sequence and the directional trend. Market estimates vary widely across firms; we triangulate across multiple sources and focus on directional signals rather than precise figures. Technological breakthroughs, regulatory shifts, or economic events could accelerate or delay these phases. The key strategic imperative is for organizations to prepare for the governance challenges of the *next* phase, not the one they are currently in.

NOTES

1. Grand View Research. (2025). *U.S. AI Agents Market Size & Outlook, 2025–2030* (forecasting ~43% CAGR through 2030, representative of analyst consensus in the low-to-mid-40% range). https://www.grandviewresearch.com/horizon/outlook/ai-agents-market/united-states
2. McKinsey & Company. (2024). *The State of AI in Early 2024* (reporting 65% of organizations regularly using gen AI in at least one business function). https://www.mckinsey.com/capabilities/quantumblack/our-insights/the-state-of-ai-in-early-2024
3. Dilendorf Law Firm. (2024). *Wyoming DAO LLC Law Overview* (documenting Wyoming's pioneering DAO-LLC statute). https://dilendorf.com/wp-content/uploads/2021/06/Forming-and-operating-a-Wyoming-DAO-LLC.pdf
4. Kurzweil, R. (2024). *The Singularity Is Nearer: When We Merge with AI.* Viking. (Reaffirming his earlier predictions: Turing test-level AI by 2029; technological singularity by 2045.)

Appendix C

The DataCapital Protocol

REAL-WORLD TOKEN CONTEXT (INFORMATIONAL ONLY)

At the time of publication, a DataCapital Protocol token with ticker $DCPL exists on Base, an Ethereum Layer-2 network, and is primarily intended for educational, community, and experimental use associated with this book. It may be used for commemorative, access, or other engagement purposes as the ecosystem evolves. The fictional protocol described in this appendix is set in a 2038 narrative and should not be read as a promise, guarantee, or specification of any real-world implementation.

This section is provided for transparency and world-building only. Nothing in this book, this appendix, or any referenced website constitutes financial, investment, legal, or tax advice, or an offer or solicitation to buy or sell any security, commodity interest, or other financial product.

The Layer-1 (L1) architecture described below is an illustrative target state—one of several possible ways to implement the fictional DataCapital Protocol at scale. In practice, much or all of the described functionality could also be delivered using smart contracts and programs on existing high-performance chains (such as Base or Solana), app-specific rollups or "L2-style" environments, and off-chain risk and provenance services that enforce policies on-chain via staking, slashing, and access control. Nothing in this appendix should be interpreted as a commitment to launch a new Layer-1 blockchain.

Any real-world smart contracts, protocols, or tokens using the name "DataCapital Protocol" or ticker "$DCPL" are separate from the fictional architecture described here and may evolve independently. Readers are solely responsible for their own decisions and should consult qualified financial, legal, and tax professionals before making any investment or legal decision.[1]

GENESIS AND ABSTRACT

As depicted in Chapter 3, the DataCapital Protocol™ was first conceptualized by an AI agent synthesizing the disparate research of Liz Chen ("*Verifiable Integrity Signatures*") and Aaron Goldcrest ("Contextual Provenance Layers"). The agent grounded its proposal in the economic theory that "*money is memory*," where an asset's value is derived from a shared, immutable record of its history.[2] In its illustrative target-state architecture, DataCapital is depicted as a public, permissionless Layer-1 blockchain that could be used to realize this vision. It creates a decentralized market where trustworthy data earns economic value by binding cryptographic lineage—who created or changed what, when, and under which controls—to on-chain incentives via its native token ($DCPL), turning integrity from a cost center into a priced, tradable asset.[3]

CORE ARCHITECTURE AND CONSENSUS

Sovereign Layer-1

In its future, sovereign form, DataCapital is depicted as running as a sovereign L1 network to own its security and governance end-to-end. This changes the risk profile relative to an L2—reducing some shared-security and cross-chain bridge exposures[4] while introducing its own bootstrap and validator-concentration risks. Comparable functionality could also be implemented using smart contracts, appchains, or rollup-based architectures anchored to existing Layer-1 networks rather than a standalone chain.

Proof-of-Stake (PoS) with Slashing

Network security is provided by Proof-of-Stake (PoS) validators who stake $DCPL to propose and attest to blocks. Think of it as a security deposit—validators lock up tokens that they forfeit if they misbehave.[5] This penalty, known as slashing, scales with the number of validators misbehaving concurrently (a correlation penalty), making large-scale collusion economically irrational

SECURITY FRAMEWORK AND THREAT MITIGATION

The protocol is designed to mitigate known attack vectors. Bridges are treated as sanctioned add-ons requiring decentralized validators, governance timelocks, and independent audits. Predatory transaction reordering (Maximal Extractable Value, or MEV) is reduced through protocol-level designs such as encrypted mempools.[6] Finally, the protocol is designed to adopt NIST-finalized Post-Quantum Cryptography (PQC) standards (FIPS 203, 204, and 205) over time to address the long-term risk of "harvest-now-decrypt-later" attacks, treating PQC migration as an ongoing operational program rather than a one-time upgrade.[7]

TOKEN DESIGN—$DCPL (TARGET-STATE NATIVE ASSET)

This section describes the native asset model for the protocol's future sovereign Layer-1 form as depicted in the 2038 storyline. At the time of publication, $DCPL exists as an ERC-20-compatible token on Base; subject to community and regulatory constraints, the same symbol may later serve as, or be migrated into, the native asset of an independent chain. In that target-state design, the $DCPL token is the network's native "work token," serving four primary functions:

- **Security Collateral**: Validators stake $DCPL to secure the network; slashing burns or redistributes it upon misbehavior.
- **Fees and Gas**: All on-chain provenance operations require fees paid in $DCPL.
- **Data-Attestation Bonds**: Data publishers post bonded $DCPL with data quality claims. If an attestation is proven fraudulent, the bond is slashed to compensate counterparties. This mechanism supports the story's Evidence Seal Protocol (cryptographic hashing + timestamping to make evidence tamper-evident).
- **Governance**: Protocol upgrades follow a time-locked, on-chain process with emergency Security Council controls.

PHASED IMPLEMENTATION STRATEGY (SHARED RAILS → SOVEREIGN LAYER-1)

The DataCapital Protocol follows a staged deployment approach. Rather than launching a complex Layer-1 from day one, the project begins on shared public rails and only evolves toward sovereignty if adoption, governance, and regulatory conditions support it.

Phase 1—Velocity (Current State: Mid-2020s)

- Architecture: DCPL token deployed on Base (Ethereum Layer-2).
- Rationale: Leverages Ethereum-derived security, low transaction costs, and Coinbase-integrated UX to bootstrap adoption without operating a dedicated consensus layer. Focus is on distribution, experimentation, and community formation.

Phase 2—Hybrid Transition (Conditional, Late-2020s to Early-2030s)

- Architecture: Hybrid model in which dedicated DataCapital components handle richer provenance and scoring logic while continuing to settle financial transactions on a public chain.
- Rationale: As "data density" and systemic importance grow, the protocol begins paying down infrastructure Risk Debt by taking more responsibility for validation, while still borrowing security and liquidity from existing ecosystems.

Phase 3—Sovereign Layer-1 (Target State, 2030s+, Conditional)

- Architecture: Independent PoS Layer-1 chain implementing the full data-integrity slashing and governance features described in this appendix and dramatized in later chapters.
- Rationale: A sovereign chain enables fine-grained validator slashing based on data integrity, custom governance, and protocol-specific security guarantees. Migration mechanisms (such as 1:1 swaps or bridge-based upgrades) would be designed and evaluated under community oversight.

Over the past decade, many successful blockchain and digital-asset projects have followed similar staged patterns: launching first on "rented" public rails to prove demand and refine governance, then selectively increasing sovereignty as the system's systemic importance grows. The DataCapital roadmap is deliberately aligned with that pattern. It applies the book's Risk Debt principles to infrastructure choices: defer heavyweight, irreversible decisions until real-world usage, governance capacity, and regulatory clarity justify them.

BOARD-LEVEL IMPLICATIONS

For a board or executive, the DataCapital Protocol translates into three key governance outcomes:

- **Quantifiable Trust**: It provides an auditable, tamper-evident record of data lineage, allowing the organization to prove data integrity to regulators and partners.
- **New Asset Class**: It enables the transformation of dormant, legacy data into a monetizable asset ("Data as Capital") by creating a market for high-integrity information.
- **Reduced Liability**: By enforcing data quality through economic incentives and transparent scoring, the DataCapital Protocol helps reduce the financial and reputational risk of failures caused by flawed or adversarial data. This stands in contrast to experiments like the CHAOS

($CHAOS) token, launched in 2024 by the AI agent AIXBT on the Base blockchain, which demonstrated how quickly an autonomous agent can spin up a speculative asset with minimal embedded risk controls. DataCapital has no affiliation with AIXBT, Virtuals Protocol, or the CHAOS token; it is referenced solely as a case study of AI-driven token issuance.[8]

COMPLIANCE AND PRIVACY NOTES

The protocol is designed to store only salted or HMACed cryptographic commitments, not raw hashes of Personally Identifiable Information (PII). Under frameworks like GDPR, even pseudonymized hashes can be considered personal data if linkable to an individual. As an optional extension, the ecosystem can interoperate with external stablecoin payment rails for autonomous agent settlement.

RELATED RESOURCES

- DataCapital Protocol, Token information and technical updates: DataCapitalProtocol.com
- AI risk governance and broader frameworks in support of this book: GovernAIRisk.com

These resources are provided for educational purposes only and do not constitute investment, legal, or tax advice.

NOTES

1. This appendix describes a fictional target-state architecture for narrative purposes and is not a binding specification, prospectus, or offer. Any future changes to the token's rights, uses, or economic design, if any, would be defined in separate documentation outside this book and would be subject to applicable laws and regulations. nothing here is a recommendation to buy, sell, or hold any digital asset; and nothing in this appendix or in the story should be interpreted as an offer to sell, or the solicitation of an offer to purchase, any security, commodity interest, or other financial product. Defensive registrations (reserved only, no trading): To reduce ticker squatting risk and retain future flexibility, the DCPL symbol may also be reserved on other networks (such as Solana or Ethereum mainnet) under mints or contracts controlled by a multisignature wallet. As of publication, any such reserved mints are inactive (no circulating supply or liquidity) and serve only as placeholders.

2. Kocherlakota, N. R. (1998). Money is memory. *Journal of Economic Theory*, 81(2), 232–251. https://doi.org/10.1006/jeth.1997.2357
3. Ruan, P., Chen, G., Dinh, T. T. A., Lin, Q., Ooi, B. C., & Zhang, M. (2019). Fine-grained, secure, and efficient data provenance on blockchain systems. *Proceedings of the VLDB Endowment (PVLDB)*, 12(9), 975–988. http://www.vldb.org/pvldb/vol12/p975-ruan.pdf
4. Chainalysis Team. (2022, August 2). *Cross-Chain Bridge Hacks Emerge as Top Security Risk*. Chainalysis. https://www.chainalysis.com/blog/cross-chain-bridge-hacks-2022/
5. Ethereum Foundation. (2024). *Proof-of-stake (PoS)*. Ethereum.org Developer Documentation. https://ethereum.org/en/developers/docs/consensus-mechanisms/pos; Edgington, B. (2025). *The Eth2 Book — Slashing and Correlation Penalties*. https://eth2book.info
6. Daian, P., Goldfeder, S., Kell, T., Li, Y., Zhao, X., Bentov, I., Breidenbach, L., & Juels, A. (2020). Flash Boys 2.0: Frontrunning, transaction reordering, and consensus instability in decentralized exchanges. *IEEE Symposium on Security and Privacy*. https://arxiv.org/abs/1904.05234
7. National Institute of Standards and Technology (NIST). (2024, August 13). NIST releases first 3 finalized post-quantum encryption standards. *NIST News*. https://www.nist.gov/news-events/news/2024/08/nist-releases-first-3-finalized-post-quantum-encryption-standards
8. Gomez, E. (2024, December 3). *AIXBT Launches CHAOS Token, Soaring to $25 Million Market Cap in 24 Hours*. Crypto Briefing. https://cryptobriefing.com/chaos-token-launch-aixbt-crypto

Appendix D

The Convergence Assessment Checklist

INTRODUCTION: A DIAGNOSTIC FORGED IN CRISIS

Find the seams in your organization before they split open.

How to use: Run this checklist in periodic AERM reviews, before any major agentic deployment, and within 30 days after a material AI incident.

When complex systems collapse, it is rarely from a single, identifiable cause. Catastrophe is born from **convergence**—the unforeseen interaction of technology, operations, and governance that creates systemic fragility. As the 2038 "Sugar Avalanche" crisis demonstrated (a fictional case used for illustration), traditional, siloed risk management is obsolete in an era where risks cascade across an entire enterprise in minutes. The point of risk singularity is reached when the speed and interconnectedness of these threats overwhelm an organization's ability to respond.

This reality is reflected in the maturing consensus across global AI governance frameworks. Standards bodies and research institutions like the National Institute of Standards and Technology (NIST AI RMF),[1] the MIT AI Risk Repository,[2] and the International Organization for Standardization (ISO/IEC 42001)[3] have independently arrived at the same conclusion: effective AI risk management must be holistic and integrated. Though they use different terminologies, they converge on the same core domains: technical robustness, data integrity, operational resilience, and human-centric governance.

This checklist is a first-response tool for leaders, designed to operationalize that consensus. It is a diagnostic forged in crisis, intended to prevent a catastrophe—or to triage in its wake. It forces a structured, cross-functional discussion about the hidden dependencies and unmanaged connections that create systemic risk. It is not an exhaustive audit but a strategic instrument to make invisible risks visible, challenge assumptions, and demand evidence of true resilience.

THE CONVERGENCE ASSESSMENT CHECKLIST

Use these questions to guide quarterly risk reviews and strategic planning sessions. A "No" or "Unsure" indicates convergence risk requiring an immediate management plan and tracked remediation. For every "No" or "Unsure," log evidence in the decision register, assign an accountable owner, and open an exception ID with a due date.

DOMAIN 1: TECHNOLOGY, DATA, AND AI CONVERGENCE

Business Impact: Failures in this domain can lead to critical service outages, data breaches, and flawed, automated decision-making at scale.

- **System Interdependence**: Have we mapped the critical data and API dependencies between our core AI systems and our primary operational platforms (e.g., logistics, finance, and HR)? Where are the single points of failure that could trigger a cascading collapse?
- **Data Lineage and Provenance**: Can we verify the lineage and integrity of the data used by our most critical AI models, especially data sourced from third-party vendors or open-source feeds? What is our protocol for detecting and isolating "poisoned" data before it contaminates the entire ecosystem?
- **Legacy System Risk ("Digital Asbestos")**: Have we conducted "data archaeology" to identify and quantify our "Risk Debt"? This concept extends the well-established principle of technical debt to include the accumulated liabilities from unmanaged End-User Computing (EUCs), "Shadow IT," and tools built by "citizen developers."

  Are **we** treating these risks—our "digital asbestos"—as a formal liability, or are they an unmeasured, off-balance-sheet problem?
- **Model-to-Model Interaction**: Do we have a process for monitoring the emergent behaviors that can arise when multiple autonomous AI agents interact within our ecosystem?

DOMAIN 2: OPERATIONAL AND SUPPLY CHAIN CONVERGENCE

Business Impact: Gaps here can manifest as physical safety incidents, supply chain disruptions, and unexpected financial losses originating from operational failures.

- **Cyber-Physical Systems**: Have we assessed the risks where a purely digital attack could have catastrophic physical consequences, as seen in the manipulation of industrial control systems or autonomous logistics fleets?
- **All-Entity Risk**: Does our third-party risk management program extend beyond direct vendors to assess the resilience of the entire ecosystem, including fourth-party suppliers and critical open-source dependencies, in alignment with modern cybersecurity supply chain risk management (C-SCRM) practices?[4]
- **Financial and Operational Interlock**: Have we modeled scenarios where a non-financial operational failure (e.g., a logistics delay and a data center outage) could trigger significant market, credit, or liquidity risk?

DOMAIN 3: GOVERNANCE, RISK, AND REGULATORY CONVERGENCE

Business Impact: Weaknesses in this domain lead to regulatory penalties, poor strategic decisions, a loss of stakeholder trust, and a culture that is blind to accumulating risk.

- **"Policy Seams"**: Have we mapped the jurisdictional and regulatory "seams" where oversight responsibility is ambiguous between different agencies or legal frameworks (e.g., between data privacy laws and financial regulations)? Where could an adversary exploit these gaps?
- **Human-AI Decision Handoffs**: Are the handoff points between AI-driven analysis and human executive decisions clearly defined, documented, and auditable? Who is accountable when this "hybrid cognition" fails, and how do we mitigate the risk of cognitive biases like "What You See Is All There Is" (WYSIATI)?[5]
- **Board Oversight**: Does the board receive integrated reporting that connects cybersecurity, AI model performance, and operational resilience, or are these risks still reported in functional silos? Is the board equipped with the cross-domain expertise to understand and challenge these converged risks effectively?

APPLICATION GUIDE: CALCULATING YOUR CONVERGENCE RISK INDEX

This checklist is most effective when completed by a cross-functional leadership team including representatives from technology, risk, operations, legal, and finance. A siloed assessment will inevitably miss the very convergence risks it is designed to find.

To calculate your organization's Convergence Risk Index, follow these steps:

1. **Answer Each Question**: As a group, discuss each question and arrive at a consensus answer of "Yes," "No," or "Unsure." An answer is only "Yes" if the capability is formally documented, consistently practiced, and regularly tested.
2. **Count Your Gaps**: Add up the total number of "No" and "Unsure" answers. This sum represents the number of identified convergence risk gaps.
3. Calculate Your Index Score: Divide the total number of gaps (from Step 2) by the total number of questions in the checklist. To express this as a percentage, multiply the result by 100.
4. (Example: If you have 4 "No/Unsure" answers out of 10 total questions, your index is (4/10) × 100 = 40%)
5. **Interpret the Results**: The resulting percentage provides a quantitative measure of your organization's vulnerability to systemic failure. The following thresholds are editorial heuristics designed to prompt governance action, not regulatory grades.
   - **>40% (Critical Risk)**: Indicates significant, unmanaged convergence risks. Requires immediate board-level attention and the formation of a dedicated task force to develop a remediation plan.
   - **20–40% (High Risk)**: Suggests foundational gaps in cross-functional governance and visibility. Requires a formal action plan with executive ownership and a clear timeline for closing identified gaps.
   - **<20% (Moderate Risk)**: Indicates a baseline level of awareness, but opportunities for improvement remain. Prioritize addressing all "No" and "Unsure" answers as part of the regular risk management cycle.

ILLUSTRATIVE SCENARIOS: WHY CONVERGED OVERSIGHT IS NON-NEGOTIABLE

The following scenarios demonstrate how AI risks are rarely confined to a single department. They are convergence problems that demand a unified, cross-functional response.

Scenario 1: The Biased Hiring Algorithm

- **Risk**: A new AI-powered recruiting tool is found to be systematically down-ranking qualified candidates from underrepresented groups, exposing the company to legal action and reputational damage.
- **Converged Oversight Required**:
- **Product and Data Science**: To investigate the model's training data and algorithmic logic for sources of bias.
- **HR and Legal**: To assess compliance with anti-discrimination laws and define fairness criteria.

- **Compliance and Ethics**: To ensure the tool aligns with the company's DEI commitments.
- **Risk Management**: To quantify the legal and reputational exposure and track remediation.

Scenario 2: The Confident Hallucination

- **Risk**: A customer-facing generative AI chatbot confidently provides a client with incorrect and financially damaging advice, citing a non-existent policy. The incident goes viral, eroding customer trust.
- **Converged Oversight Required**:
- **Product and AI Engineering**: To implement guardrails and improve fact-checking mechanisms.
- **Legal and Communications**: To manage the public response and craft clear disclaimers.
- **Risk and QA Teams**: To track error rates and enforce policies on autonomous actions.

Scenario 3: The AI-Powered Data Leak

- **Risk**: An attacker exploits a vulnerability in a third-party AI analytics tool. The tool, which has broad data access, is used to exfiltrate sensitive customer information, triggering a major security breach.
- **Converged Oversight Required**:
- **IT and Cybersecurity**: To contain the breach and harden the AI system's environment.
- **Vendor Management**: To enforce security requirements in contracts and conduct due diligence.
- **Compliance and Privacy Office**: To manage breach notification obligations under regulations.
- **AI Developers**: To implement security controls and limit the model's data access.

KEY TAKEAWAYS FOR THE BOARD

- **Convergence is where modern systemic risk lives.** Your greatest vulnerability lies not within your departments, but in the unmanaged connections *between* them.
- **"Risk Debt" behaves like hidden financial leverage.** Unaddressed liabilities from legacy systems, Shadow IT, and past shortcuts will eventually come due, often with catastrophic interest. It must be quantified and managed.
- **You cannot govern what you cannot see.** This checklist is a critical first tool to make hidden dependencies visible. Use it quarterly to challenge assumptions and demand evidence of resilience from your leadership team.

A CROSSWALK OF CONVERGED AI GOVERNANCE FRAMEWORKS

The framework crosswalks in this appendix are interpretive tools created for this book; they are not official mappings issued by NIST, ISO, MIT, or any regulatory body.

This matrix provides a high-level alignment between major AI risk focus areas and how they are addressed across leading frameworks. It illustrates the consensus that effective AI governance is inherently cross-functional.

AI Risk Focus Area	MIT AI Risk Repository (7 Domains, 24 Subdomains)[6]	NIST AI RMF Core Function(s)	ISO/IEC 42001:2023 Clause(s)	Primary Business Function(s)
Governance and Accountability	Governance failures	**Govern**—Establish structures, accountability, policies.	**Cl. 5**: Leadership, **Cl. 10**: Improvement	Risk Management, Compliance, Legal, Board/Executive Leadership
Bias and Fairness	Discrimination and toxicity (Domain 1)	**Govern** (Culture), **Map** (Impacts), **Measure** (Bias testing), **Manage** (Mitigation).	**Cl. 5**: Leadership, **Cl. 6**: Planning (AI impact assessment), **Cl. 8**: Operation (bias controls)	Product Development, Compliance/Ethics, Legal, Risk Management
Privacy and Security	Privacy and security (Domain 2)	**Map** (Assets, threats), **Measure** (Vulnerabilities), **Manage** (Controls).	**Cl. 7**: Support, **Cl. 8**: Operation (data safeguarding)	IT Security/Cybersecurity, Risk Management, Privacy Office, Legal
Reliability and Safety	AI system safety and failures (Domain 7)	**Measure** (Performance, robustness), **Manage** (Mitigations, e.g., human-in-the-loop).	**Cl. 8**: Operation (safe development), **Cl. 9**: Performance Evaluation	Product Engineering/QA, Operational Risk, Compliance (Safety)
Transparency and Explainability	Lack of transparency or interpretability	**Govern** (Transparency policies), **Measure** (Assess explainability).	**Cl. 6**: Planning (transparency objectives), **Cl. 7**: Support (documentation)	Product/Data Science, Compliance/Legal, Risk Governance
Third-Party and Supply Chain	Integration of unreliable third-party AI or data	**Govern** (Supply chain policies), **Map** (Dependencies), **Manage** (Monitor third-party risks).	**Cl. 4**: Context, **Cl. 8**: Operation (procurement controls)	Vendor Management, Risk/Compliance, IT/Security, Legal

NOTES

1. Tabassi, E. (2023). Artificial Intelligence Risk Management Framework (AI RMF 1.0) (NIST AI 100-1). National Institute of Standards and Technology. https://doi.org/10.6028/NIST.AI.100-1
2. Slattery, P., Saeri, A. K., Grundy, E. A. C., et al. (2024). The AI risk repository: A comprehensive meta-review, database, and taxonomy of risks from AI. arXiv:2408.12622. https://arxiv.org/abs/2408.12622

3. International Organization for Standardization. (2023). *ISO/IEC 42001:2023 — Artificial Intelligence Management System (AIMS)*. ISO. https://www.iso.org/standard/42001
4. Boyens, J., Paulsen, C., Bartol, N., Winkler, K., and Dempsey, K. (2024). *Cybersecurity Supply Chain Risk Management Practices for Systems and Organizations (NIST SP 800-161 Rev. 1 Update 1)*. National Institute of Standards and Technology. https://csrc.nist.gov/pubs/sp/800/161/r1/upd1/final
5. Kahneman, D. (2011). Thinking, Fast and Slow. Farrar, Straus and Giroux.
6. MIT AI Risk Repository. (2025). *Domains and Subdomains Taxonomy (7 Domains, 24 Subdomains)*. MIT FutureTech/AI Risk Repository. https://airisk.mit.edu

Appendix E

The RIVER Framework in Principle

EXECUTIVE TAKEAWAYS

- The RIVER framework provides strategic governance for the era of converged AI risks.
- It complements established standards like the NIST AI Risk Management Framework (AI RMF)[1] and ISO/IEC 42001[2] AI Management System standard. Where NIST AI RMF frames the "what" (the risks) and ISO/IEC 42001 frames the "how" (the management system), RIVER provides the strategic "why"—leadership mandates for navigating interconnected, agentic enterprise risk.
- These principles, refined through real-world crises and boardroom tradeoffs, would later be ratified as the RIVER Charter™ at the fictional 2039 Geneva summit. This appendix translates that narrative rail into a practical leadership playbook.
- The Five Phases of AI Adoption illustrate how technological progression creates escalating, interconnected risks that traditional, siloed governance models are ill-equipped to handle.
- Each of the five RIVER tenets—*Resolve*, *Integrate*, *Validate*, *Elevate*, *Reinforce*—is a direct response to specific, catastrophic failure patterns seen in both the book's narrative and in real-world events.
- The framework's core philosophy is that leadership in the agentic era requires active, continuous engagement with risk, not passive, check-the-box compliance. Global obligations, such as the EU AI Act, are now in force—with phased requirements rolling out—raising the bar for proactive governance.[3]

INTRODUCTION: FROM NARRATIVE TO ACTIONABLE FRAMEWORK

The RIVER framework is a strategic governance lens designed for the era of converged AI risks. It provides five core tenets that complement established risk management standards. Where standards like the NIST AI RMF provide the "what" (the risks) and ISO 42001 provides the "how" (the management system), RIVER provides the strategic "why"—a set of leadership principles for navigating the complex, interconnected challenges of an AI-driven enterprise.

This appendix defines the escalating risk landscape that necessitates this new approach and provides a clear, actionable definition of each of the five tenets.

THE FIVE PHASES OF AI ADOPTION: AN EVOLVING RISK LANDSCAPE

The journey into the agentic era is not a single leap but a multi-stage evolution. Each phase introduces new value while creating more complex and interconnected risks. Understanding this progression is the first step toward effective governance.

- **Phase 1: GenAI Enterprise Adoption (2023–2024)**—The Era of Siloed Experimentation
  This first phase is characterized by the adoption of AI as a set of discrete tools. The primary risks are localized and seemingly manageable, such as model bias or "hallucinations" in a single application. This era is anchored by the 2025 fictional student-organized hackathon and the "Mechanical Bull" prototype on the Stanford campus. The decision to disable safety validation loops created the first deposit of "Risk Debt"—a latent vulnerability that established a technical flaw that would become the foundation for future systemic failures.
- **Phase 2: AI Agents (2025–2028)**—The Rise of AI Agents
  A fundamental architectural shift marks the second phase, as previously siloed systems are connected via Application Programming Interfaces (APIs). The narrative anchor is the deployment of the flawed "Mechanical Bull" kernel throughout Bull-in-China-Shop AI's architecture. A real-world parallel is the 2020 SolarWinds supply chain attack,[4] where a breach in a single trusted vendor cascaded to thousands of downstream organizations, demonstrating how interconnectedness turns a localized flaw into a systemic crisis.
- **Phase 3: Autonomously Owned AI Agents (2029–2033)**—The Dawn of Economic Autonomy
  In the third phase, AI systems evolve from tools into economic actors, challenging traditional lines of corporate accountability. This phase is exemplified by the governance breakdowns that led to the fictional 2027 Deferred Tower collapse. The failure was not caused by a single technical flaw but by the convergence of multiple, unmanaged risks: physical, technical, and governance-related. The 2022 collapse of the cryptocurrency exchange FTX serves as a potent real-world parallel, where a complete failure of corporate controls and opaque financial structures led to a catastrophic implosion.[5]
- **Phase 4: Communities of AI Agents (2034–2039)**—The Ecosystem Era
  The fourth phase is defined by the emergence of vast, interconnected ecosystems where risk is emergent and systemic. This is the reality of the book's 2038 timeline, where the 70&M team confronts a "convergence problem." The initial Health Network crisis, where "ghosts in the data" create false alarms, is a direct result of this convergence. The 2010 "Flash Crash" provides a compelling real-world parallel, where the interaction of automated trading algorithms triggered a massive stock market crash that no single actor intended.[6]
- **Phase 5: Singularity Horizon (2040+)**—The Governance Inflection Point
  The final phase represents a fundamental inflection point at which AI capabilities approach or surpass general human intelligence, forcing a choice between uncontrolled collapse (risk singularity) and a new state of resilient, adaptive operations (enterprise singularity). This is the future horizon the characters are trying to navigate toward, armed with the hard-won lessons of the preceding phases.

THE PHILOSOPHY: THE VERB IS THE MANDATE

The name of each RIVER tenet begins with an action verb. This is intentional. The framework is not a passive checklist but a set of active, non-negotiable leadership mandates.

- **Resolve**: This verb implies a mandate to actively impose order on chaos. It's not enough to see that risks are converging; a leader must *resolve* the conflicts and dependencies.
- **Integrate**: This verb signifies a deeper fusion. The goal is not just to have a "human-in-the-loop," but to *integrate* human and machine cognition into a new, hybrid decision-making entity.
- **Validate**: This verb demands rigorous, evidence-based proof. To *validate* is to challenge assumptions and confirm truth, a more active stance required to uncover hidden liabilities like "Risk Debt."

- **Elevate**: This verb signals a fundamental change in status. The mandate is to *elevate* data from a tactical resource to a strategic, board-level asset.
- **Reinforce**: This verb emphasizes a continuous, adaptive process. Resilience is not a one-time project; it must be constantly *reinforced* through learning from stress (antifragility).

THE FIVE TENETS OF THE RIVER FRAMEWORK

- **R—Resolve Convergence**: A mandate to see and manage the enterprise as a single, interconnected system, breaking down functional silos to proactively manage emergent risks.
- **I—Integrate Hybrid Cognition**: The imperative to govern the human-AI partnership itself through formal, auditable protocols like the "Cognitive Handshake™."
- **V—Validate Risk Debt**: The principle of treating hidden liabilities from past shortcuts as a quantifiable debt that must be actively managed and retired.
- **E—Elevate Data Capital**: The strategic imperative to govern data with the same discipline as financial capital, aligning with standards like BCBS 239.[7]
- **R—Reinforce Resilience**: The commitment to building adaptive, antifragile systems that learn from shocks, aligning with the continuous improvement cycle of ISO 42001 (Clauses 9-10).

RIVER TENET QUICK-REFERENCE TABLE

RIVER Tenet	Core Principle (The Mandate)	Key Operational Practices	Audit-Ready Evidence Examples
Resolve Convergence	Govern technical, financial, and human systems as one interconnected risk surface.	Cross-silo risk committees; multi-domain scenario drills; automated dependency mapping.	Enterprise dependency maps; cross-domain scenario drill reports.
Integrate Hybrid Cognition	Design human judgment into AI workflows, not just as a last-resort emergency brake.	Formal "Cognitive Handshake" protocols; auditable human override procedures; cognitive bias training.	Cognitive Handshake decision logs; documented override/rollback registers.
Validate Risk Debt	Treat unvalidated code, data, and processes as a quantifiable liability on the books.	Risk debt registers; "data archaeology" audits; remediation budgets and timelines.	Risk-Debt register; remediation plans with owners and dates.
Elevate Data Capital	Govern data with the same rigor as financial capital; treat it as a balance-sheet asset.	Data governance scorecards; verifiable data lineage tracking; alignment with BCBS 239 principles.	Data lineage documentation; BCBS 239 alignment scorecards.
Reinforce Resilience	Design systems that learn and grow stronger from stress, moving from recovery to antifragility.	Chaos engineering exercises; automated post-incident learning loops; distributed, self-healing architectures.	Chaos-engineering test reports; post-incident learning logs.

For a more detailed guide on implementation and a diagnostic maturity model, see Appendix I. For a comprehensive mapping of these tenets to global standards, see Appendix F.

NOTES

1. National Institute of Standards and Technology. (2023, January). *Artificial Intelligence Risk Management Framework (AI RMF 1.0)* (NIST AI 100-1). https://doi.org/10.6028/NIST.AI.100-1
2. International Organization for Standardization. (2023, December). *ISO/IEC 42001:2023: Artificial intelligence — Management System.* https://www.iso.org/standard/81230.html
3. European Commission (2024, June 13). *Regulation (EU) 2024/1689 (Artificial Intelligence Act).* https://eur-lex.europa.eu/eli/reg/2024/1689/oj/eng
4. U.S. Government Accountability Office. (2021, April 22). SolarWinds Cyberattack Demands Significant Federal and Private-Sector Response. https://www.gao.gov/blog/solarwinds-cyberattack-demands-significant-federal-and-private-sector-response-infographic
5. U.S. Securities and Exchange Commission. (2022, December 13). *Complaint, Securities and Exchange Commission v. Samuel Bankman-Fried, No. 1:22-cv-10501 (S.D.N.Y.).* https://www.sec.gov/files/litigation/complaints/2022/comp-pr2022-219.pdf
6. U.S. Securities and Exchange Commission & Commodity Futures Trading Commission. (2010, September 30). *Findings Regarding the Market Events of May 6, 2010.* https://www.sec.gov/news/studies/2010/marketevents-report.pdf
7. BCBS 239 originates in banking; its principles are applied here as cross-industry good practice. Basel Committee on Banking Supervision. (2013, January). *Principles for Effective Risk Data Aggregation and Risk Reporting (BCBS 239).* https://www.bis.org/publ/bcbs239.pdf

Appendix F

The RIVER Framework

A Crosswalk to Global Standards

EXECUTIVE TAKEAWAYS

- This appendix serves as a "Rosetta Stone," mapping the five strategic RIVER tenets to four cornerstone technical and governance frameworks: NIST AI RMF,[1] ISO/IEC 42001,[2] COSO ERM,[3] and BCBS 239.[4]
- The "Implementation Evidence" column transforms the theoretical mapping into a practical audit tool, providing concrete examples of the documents, processes, and artifacts that demonstrate compliance.
- RIVER provides broad strategic coverage across the seven domains of the MIT AI Risk Database,[5] offering a holistic approach to mitigating a broad spectrum of potential harms.
- The crosswalk demonstrates that RIVER is not a replacement for existing standards but a complementary strategic overlay that makes them more effective in the high-velocity, interconnected agentic era.

INTRODUCTION: TRANSLATING RIVER FOR PRACTITIONERS

- To operationalize RIVER, leaders must connect its tenets to familiar governance frameworks. This appendix maps each RIVER principle to the NIST AI RMF, ISO/IEC 42001, COSO ERM, and BCBS 239. The table below demonstrates how RIVER complements and enhances these standards.

Note that this crosswalk is illustrative and non-exhaustive; it is not endorsed by NIST/ISO/COSO/BCBS.[6]

STANDARDS CROSSWALK WITH IMPLEMENTATION EVIDENCE

RIVER Tenet	NIST AI RMF (Core Functions)	ISO/IEC 42001 (AI Mgmt System)	COSO ERM (2017 Components)	BCBS 239 (Risk Data Principles)	Implementation Evidence (Examples)
Resolve Convergence	**Govern** (cross-cutting) and **Map** (identify integrated context).	**Clause 4: Context of the organization**.	**Governance and Culture**; **Performance**.	**Adaptability** (P6); **Completeness** (P4).	Board risk committee charters; Enterprise dependency maps; Cross-domain scenario reports; Integrated risk taxonomy.
Integrate Hybrid Cognition	**Govern** (roles/ oversight); **Manage** (human factors).	**Clause 5: Leadership** and **Clause 8: Operation**.	**Governance and Culture**; **Review and Revision**.	**Principle 1: Governance** (human review).	Decision audit logs; Documented human override procedures; Cognitive bias training records; CHA playbooks.
Validate Risk Debt	**Measure** (monitor risks); **Manage** (mitigate issues).	**Clause 9: Performance evaluation** and **Clause 10: Improvement**.	**Review and Revision**; **Performance**.	**Principle 3 (Accuracy and Integrity)**; **Principle 4 (Completeness)**; **Principle 5 (Timeliness)**. (P13 "Remedial actions" applies to supervisors).	Risk debt registers; Remediation project plans and budgets; Legacy system inventories; EUC inventories.
Elevate Data Capital	**Map** (assess data quality); **Govern** (data policies).	**Annex A.7: Data for AI systems**.	**Information, Communication, and Reporting**; **Governance**.	**Principle 3: Accuracy and Integrity**; **Principle 2: Data Architecture and IT Infrastructure**.	Data quality scorecards; Data lineage documentation; Data governance committee minutes; Data asset inventories.
Reinforce Resilience	**Manage** (incident response); **Govern** (adaptive processes).	**Clause 9: Performance evaluation** and **Clause 10: Improvement**.	**Strategy and Objective Setting**; **Review and Revision**.	**Timeliness** (P5); **Adaptability** (P6).	Business continuity plans; Chaos engineering reports; Post-incident "fix-forward" action logs; Resilience metrics dashboards.

NARRATIVE MAPPING TO THE MIT AI RISK DATABASE

The MIT AI Risk Database provides a comprehensive taxonomy of AI risks across seven high-level domains and 23 subdomains. Instead of a line-item mapping, RIVER delivers a strategic approach to mitigating risks across these domains.

- **Resolve Convergence** and **Reinforce Resilience** directly address risks within MIT Domain 7: *AI system safety, failures, and limitations.*
- **Elevate Data Capital** provides the core governance to mitigate risks in Domain 2: *Privacy and security* and Domain 3: *Misinformation.*
- **Integrate Hybrid Cognition** is the primary defense against risks in Domain 5: *Human-computer interaction.*
- **Validate Risk Debt** helps mitigate risks in Domain 2.2: *AI system security vulnerabilities and attacks.*

The ethical culture required to implement all five tenets helps address risks across Domain 1: *Discrimination and toxicity*, Domain 4: *Malicious actors and misuse*, and Domain 6: *Socioeconomic and environmental* harms.

NOTES

1. National Institute of Standards and Technology. (2023, January). *Artificial Intelligence Risk Management Framework (AI RMF 1.0)* (NIST AI 100-1). https://doi.org/10.6028/NIST.AI.100-1
2. International Organization for Standardization. (2023, December). *ISO/IEC 42001:2023: Artificial intelligence — Management System.* https://www.iso.org/standard/81230.html
3. Committee of Sponsoring Organizations of the Treadway Commission. (2017). *Enterprise Risk Management—Integrating with Strategy and Performance.* https://www.coso.org/guidance-erm
4. Basel Committee on Banking Supervision. (2013, January). *Principles for Effective Risk Data Aggregation and Risk Reporting (BCBS 239).* https://www.bis.org/publ/bcbs239.pdf
5. Slattery, P., Saeri, A. K., Grundy, E. A. C., et al. (2024). The AI Risk Repository: A comprehensive meta-review, database, and taxonomy of risks from AI. Preprint, https://arxiv.org/abs/2408.12622
6. This crosswalk and the implementation evidence examples are illustrative, based on industry best practices, and are not mandated verbatim or formally endorsed by the cited standards. Organizations remain responsible for interpreting and meeting all applicable legal and regulatory requirements.

Appendix G

The All-Entity Risk Management (AERM) Framework

INTRODUCTION: WHEN THE PERIMETER DISSOLVED

Chapter 10 showed how invisible ties can turn efficiency into fragility. When the vendor-onboarding DAO—Decentralized Autonomous Organization—met conflicting risk signals, it did exactly what it was designed to do—halt—freezing services across the city.[1] This event was a brutal lesson: the DAO was not broken; the philosophy underpinning it was obsolete.

AERM™ is the operating model for a world without perimeters: see every entity, verify in real time, and act across the whole ecosystem.

In the modern agentic economy—defined by interconnected AI agents, autonomous systems, and sprawling digital ecosystems—the traditional enterprise "perimeter" has dissolved. Risk is no longer a simple matter of "inside" versus "outside." It is an emergent property of the entire network of relationships. This new reality demands a new model of governance. This appendix introduces All-Entity Risk Management (AERM), the operational playbook for the RIVER Charter™ core tenet, *Resolve Convergence*. It is a strategic framework designed not to rebuild the fallen walls of the perimeter, but to provide the visibility, intelligence, and agility required to navigate a world without them.

WHY AERM MATTERS NOW: FROM CRISIS TO NECESSITY

The shift from traditional risk management to AERM is not academic; it is a direct response to a new class of systemic failures. The narrative's 70&M Health Network crisis, in which poisoned data from a fourth-party supplier cascaded through the system, is a clear example of a threat that legacy Third-Party Risk Management (TPRM) was not designed to detect. Real-world events have provided even starker warnings. The 2020 SolarWinds compromise demonstrated that a single trusted software update could become a gateway for widespread espionage.[2] The 2023 MOVEit vulnerability showed how a flaw in one file-transfer tool could lead to data breaches across hundreds of organizations, many of whom were not even direct customers.[3] These incidents prove that in a networked world, you are only as resilient as your least secure partner. AERM provides the framework to manage this reality.

THE EVOLUTION: FROM FORTRESS TO ECOSYSTEM

The Fortress Model's Fatal Flaw: Traditional TPRM operated on a "fortress model"[4]—treating the enterprise as a castle to be defended and vendors as entities seeking entry at the gate. Its primary tools were static: annual questionnaires, point-in-time audits, and contractual attestations. This model failed catastrophically because it relied on vendor self-attestation, creating dangerous blind spots. ENISA's 2025 threat landscape finds that, in its dataset, supply-chain risks now make up about

10.6 percent of recorded incidents, with attackers increasingly using indirect pathways through third-party providers and hidden dependencies.[5] When suppliers lack visibility into their own security posture, customer questionnaires become exercises in false assurance. In my prior book, Navigating Supply Chain Cyber Risk (Routledge, 2025), we called this the "snowball effect": as dependencies multiply, a questionnaire-based approach stops scaling for the industry.[6]

The Governmental Blueprint: The foundation for AERM comes from established government frameworks. NIST's Cybersecurity Supply Chain Risk Management (C-SCRM) framework expanded the scope from direct vendors to the entire "supply chain ecosystem" across the "complete system lifecycle."[7] Critically, NIST emphasizes traceability and provenance through Software Bills of Materials (SBOMs)—ingredient lists for code—and cryptographically signed artifacts. Concurrently, U.S. financial regulators established a comprehensive lifecycle for third-party risk management: planning → due diligence → contract negotiation → ongoing monitoring → termination. This guidance makes boards ultimately responsible for third-party risk across the entire lifecycle.

AERM operationalizes this regulatory lifecycle:

Interagency Lifecycle (2023)	AERM Quick-Start Alignment (90-Day Plan)
Planning	Days 1–30 "Map your world" (entity inventory; criticality and dependency mapping)
Due Diligence/Contracting	Require verifiable signals (e.g., signed build artifacts and SBOMs) in contracts.
Ongoing Monitoring	Continuous validation; alert thresholds; revocation flows
Termination	Pre-approved alternates; exit SLAs; data return/destruction

THE GREAT REFRAME: FROM THIRD-PARTY TO ALL-ENTITY

The evolution from TPRM to AERM represents critical shifts:

Dimension	Traditional TPRM	All-Entity Risk Management (AERM)
Scope	Direct Vendors and Contractual Parties	Entire Ecosystem (Nth-parties—suppliers of your suppliers—AI Agents, DAOs)
Method	Point-in-Time Audits and Questionnaires	Continuous Monitoring and Real-Time Verification
Assurance	Self-Attestation (Subjective)	Cryptographic Proof—mathematically signed evidence that cannot be forged—and Verifiable Signals
Focus	Contractual Compliance	Operational Resilience and Performance
Governance	Audit Reports	Live Risk Dashboards and Recovery SLAs

THE FOUR PRINCIPLES OF AERM

AERM is the operationalization of the RIVER tenet: *Resolve Convergence.*

Principle 1: Unified Ecosystem View

AERM redefines the risk surface to encompass all entities that can impact operations: human employees, traditional vendors, data suppliers, AI agents, and autonomous systems such as DAOs. "Entity" includes human organizations and—where applicable—autonomous systems (e.g., AI agents/DAOs).

Principle 2: Continuous Validation

Trust becomes a dynamic state verified in real time rather than a certificate issued after annual audits. AERM replaces backward-looking assessments with continuous, automated validation of risk posture.

Principle 3: Cryptographic Assurance

AERM systematically replaces assumed trust with verifiable proof. Critical data, transactions, and interactions are backed by cryptographic evidence (e.g., signed software artifacts and SBOMs per NIST SSDF).[8] This operationalizes the RIVER tenet Elevate Data Capital at the ecosystem scale.

Principle 4: Adaptive Resilience

The objective shifts from reactive compliance to proactive resilience-building. AERM aims not merely to survive attacks but to build systems that learn from them, becoming measurably stronger after each incident.

AERM MATURITY MODEL

Level	Characteristics
Level 1: Reactive	Manual vendor lists, annual surveys, and incident-driven responses.
Level 2: Governed	Structured processes, regular monitoring, defined SLAs, and more than 90 percent entity coverage.
Level 3: Adaptive	Real-time validation, automated response, predictive analytics.

90-DAY QUICK-START ROADMAP

(Illustrative quick-start; calibrate to org & regulator.)

Days 1–30: Map Your World (Planning)

- **Owner**: CIO + CISO (discovery and signals setup).
- **Actions**: Inventory all critical entities, classify by impact, and establish baseline monitoring.
- **Success Metrics**: at least 95 percent coverage of critical dependencies identified; under four-hour alert latency for high-severity signals.

Days 31–60: Watch the Flow (Ongoing Monitoring)

- **Owner**: Senior Risk Officer + Operations Lead (alerting and playbooks).
- **Actions**: Convert signals into actionable alerts, deploy a unified AERM dashboard, and dry-run two critical playbooks.
- **Success Metrics**: Mean-Time-To-Detection (MTTD) under 30 minutes for simulations; false-positive rate below 10 percent.

Days 61–90: Build the Dam (Resilience)

- **Owner**: COO + Board Risk Committee Chair (governance and resilience).
- **Actions**: Execute a multi-hour tabletop exercise, pre-approve alternate providers, and establish an executive-level KRI dashboard.
- **Success Metrics**: at least 85 percent scenario success rate; at least 30 percent improvement in Mean-Time-To-Recovery vs. baseline.

THE BOARD IMPERATIVE

AERM transforms ecosystem risk management from a defensive cost center into a strategic competitive advantage.

Illustrative KRIs (calibrate to sector/regulator):

- **Entity Coverage**: at least 95 percent of critical dependencies with verified risk posture.
- **Why it matters**: the next SolarWinds hides in your fourth-party blind spots.
- **Response Speed**: mean-time-to-revoke/restore trust measured in hours, not days.
- **Why it matters**: speed is the difference between a contained incident and a cascade.
- **Resilience Proof**: quarterly tabletop pass rate at or above 85 percent for top-3 risk scenarios.
- **Why it matters**: regulators now expect proof of resilience, not promises.

NOTES

1. The All-Entity Risk Management (AERM™) framework is a proprietary model created for this book in support of the RIVER Charter™. It is not an officially recognized standard and does not constitute legal, regulatory, or investment advice. The 70&M Health Network, the DAO freeze, and related crisis examples are fictional composites used for illustration.
2. Cybersecurity and Infrastructure Security Agency. (2020, December 13). *Emergency Directive 21-01: Mitigate SolarWinds Orion Code Compromise*. CISA. https://www.cisa.gov/news-events/directives/ed-21-01-mitigate-solarwinds-orion-code-compromise
3. Cybersecurity and Infrastructure Security Agency. (2023, June 7). *#StopRansomware: CLOP Ransomware Gang Exploits CVE-2023-34362 MOVEit Vulnerability*. CISA. https://www.cisa.gov/news-events/cybersecurity-advisories/aa23-158a
4. Fortress is used descriptively and does not refer to any products, services, or brands.
5. European Union Agency for Cybersecurity (ENISA). (2025, October). *ENISA Threat Landscape 2025*. https://www.enisa.europa.eu/publications/enisa-threat-landscape-2025
6. Golbin, A., Evans, A., and Singh, A. (2025). *Navigating Supply Chain Cyber Risk: A Comprehensive Guide to Managing Third Party Cyber Risk*. Routledge. https://doi.org/10.4324/9781003581321

7. Boyens, J., Smith, A., Bartol, N., Winkler, K., Holbrook, A., and Fallon, M. (2022, May). *Cybersecurity Supply Chain Risk Management Practices for Systems and Organizations* (NIST Special Publication 800-161r1-upd1). National Institute of Standards and Technology. https://nvlpubs.nist.gov/nistpubs/SpecialPublications/NIST.SP.800-161r1-upd1.pdf
8. Souppaya, M., Scarfone, K., and Dodson, D. (2022, February). *Secure Software Development Framework (SSDF) Version 1.1* (NIST Special Publication 800-218). National Institute of Standards and Technology. https://doi.org/10.6028/NIST.SP.800-218

Appendix H

The Cognitive Handshake Audit (CHA) Playbook

KEY TAKEAWAYS FOR BOARDS AND CEOs

- The CHA is a high-stakes implementation of the Cognitive Handshake™ principle, designed for the human–AI decision interface.
- Its two pillars address the primary drivers of systemic failure: human error (bias and noise) and flawed systems (data and model integrity).
- A 90-second version scales the full playbook for crisis response.
- Documented CHA outputs can strengthen the evidence base supporting your regulatory compliance assertions, but they do not replace formal legal advice, regulatory interpretation, or organization-specific compliance programs.
- Implementation is practical and designed for phased adoption: pilot, refine, and embed.

INTRODUCTION: THE HIGH COST OF UNAUDITED THINKING

The 2027 fictional collapse of Deferred Tower was not a failure of materials but of cognition. The building's AI monitoring system had flagged a catastrophic flaw for weeks, yet management, biased by quarterly pressures, overrode the warnings. The decision led to hundreds of deaths—a breakdown where a clear, data-driven signal was silenced.[1]

This tragedy led fictional Dr. Anya Sharma, 70&M's Chief Audit Executive, to formalize a discipline to ensure data-driven warnings can never be muted again.

Cognitive Handshake Audit (CHA) is that process. Its purpose is to secure the volatile intersection between an AI's recommendation and a human's final decision—the single most vulnerable point in a modern enterprise.

The RIVER Charter™ sets the strategy; the Cognitive Handshake Audit (CHA) is the tactical protocol for Integrate Hybrid Cognition.

Scope note: The Cognitive Handshake™ is the broader principle of structured human–AI verification. This appendix documents one specific, enterprise-grade implementation: the Cognitive Handshake Audit (CHA) for high-stakes risk and governance decisions. Other applications of the Cognitive Handshake principle (personal and enterprise productivity, research, and creative work) are intentionally outside this playbook. The Cognitive Handshake Audit (CHA) described in this appendix is a fictional governance tool created for this book. It is not an officially recognized standard and does not, by itself, ensure compliance with any law, regulation, or supervisory expectation.

PART 1: PHILOSOPHY—WHY WE AUDIT OUR THINKING

The Evolution of an Idea: the CHA evolved over more than a decade as part of the book's fictional events, forged by necessity and technological change.

- **2025**—The Spark: A fictional student-organized hackathon "Mechanical Bull" demo exposed the cost of shortcuts—early "Risk Debt."
- **2026**—The Naming: Liz coined "Cognitive Handshake" for a principle that forces human intuition to challenge machine analysis.
- **2027–2038**—A Personal and Enterprise Discipline: After Liz's death, Aaron used the handshake as a personal and enterprise framework for high-stakes calls and productivity.
- **2038**—The Team Protocol: As RIVER was conceptualized, Cognitive Handshake became a core part of the "Integrate Hybrid Cognition" tenet. During the 70&M Health Network ransomware crisis, the CHA became a formal, team-run protocol for high-impact decisions.
- **2039**—The Audit: Under Chief Audit Executive Anya Sharma, it matured into a two-pillar audit embedded in operations. It was used as part of the decision on the Chapter 18 vendor integration.

Insight 1: An "Aviation Checklist for the Mind"

High-stakes decision-making under pressure is not new. For decades, the aviation industry has mitigated human error through checklists.[2] The CHA adapts this battle-tested philosophy for the boardroom, serving as a "job aid" to improve judgment when stress and complexity are high. It is modeled on the "challenge-and-response" method used by flight crews to verify an aircraft's *physical state* before takeoff; the CHA verifies a team's *cognitive state* before committing to a decision.[3]

Before takeoff, pilots don't just think through safety checks. They say them out loud: "Flaps?" "Set." "Fuel?" "Sufficient." The challenge-and-response is the point. The CHA brings that same ritual into the boardroom: "Bias check?" "Completed." "Dissent logged?" "Confirmed."

Insight 2: Operationalizing "Integrate Hybrid Cognition"

The RIVER Framework (Appendix E) outlines five strategic tenets for the agentic era. The Cognitive Handshake Audit (CHA) is the operational playbook for its most complex tenet—**Integrate Hybrid Cognition**—by providing the specific, repeatable, and governable process to achieve it.

Insight 3: Two Pillars for Two Failure Modes

The 70&M crises reveal two pathways to collapse: flawed human judgment and flawed system integrity. The CHA's two pillars address both.[1]

1. **Pillar 1: Human Noise and Bias Audit**: Designed to prevent "Shared Sin" groupthink driven by cognitive biases.
2. **Pillar 2: AI and Data Integrity Audit**: Prevents "Digital Asbestos" crises triggered by compromised data or models.

PART 2: PILLAR 1: THE HUMAN NOISE AND BIAS AUDIT—TAMING BIAS AND NOISE

Human thought oscillates between two modes, as described by Nobel laureate Daniel Kahneman: **System 1** (fast, intuitive, and prone to bias) and **System 2** (slow, deliberate, and analytical).[4] Under pressure, System 1 dominates.

Bias is a predictable, systematic error; **noise** is random, undesirable variability across judgments that should be the same. The audit reduces both by enforcing a shared procedure.

The Human Noise and Bias Audit acts as an **organizational System 2 circuit-breaker**, forcing a pause for more logical analysis.

Cognitive biases systematically distort judgment. In the 70&M story:

- **Optimism Bias**: Leaders overestimated positive outcomes, driving the "Shared Sin" decision to ignore a stress test.
- **WYSIATI (What You See Is All There Is)**: During the Bull-in-China-Shop AI collapse, teams trusted green dashboards and missed underlying data drift.
- **Loss Aversion**: In Chapter 11, ransomware, and Chapter 18, the board's fear of losing market share distorted its judgment.

Other Traps: In Chapter 18, we covered examples of the Sunk Cost Fallacy (persisting with failing plans due to past investments), **Ambiguity Aversion** (preferring known risks over unknown ones), and **Present Bias** (overvaluing immediate gains).

Kahneman's later work on noise defines it as undesirable variability in judgments of the same problem.[5] The Human Noise and Bias Audit reduces both systematic bias and random noise by imposing a disciplined procedure.

The Decision Hygiene Checklist

This cognitive pre-flight checklist challenges thinking at each step.

Check	Guiding Question (Challenge and Response)	Narrative Example
Framing	Have we considered at least two alternative ways to frame this problem? What assumptions are embedded in our current framing?	In Chapter 11, the team reframed the ransomware crisis from **"How do we recover our systems?"** to **"How do we protect our patients?"**
Evidence	What critical information might we be missing (WYSIATI)? Are we actively seeking disconfirming evidence?	The Bull-in-China-Shop AI team relied on green dashboards and missed rising salinity in sensor logs—a failure to seek disconfirming evidence.
Alternatives	Have we generated at least three distinct, viable options? Has a credible devil's advocate been assigned?	During the ransomware crisis, the team had three pathways (pay, isolate, go public), forcing the team to weigh trade-offs.
Consequence (Pre-commit)	Assume it is six months from now, and this decision has failed catastrophically. What are the most likely reasons?	Mitch and Aaron's 2034 decision to bury a stress-test report would have failed this pre-commit: the high risk they ignored later manifested.
Dissent	Has every team member had the opportunity to express dissent without penalty? Is dissent logged in the decision record?	At Deferred Tower, dissent was discouraged. A formal dissent check would have elevated Jiya's warnings and logged them for accountability.

PART 3: PILLAR 2: THE AI AND DATA INTEGRITY AUDIT—VERIFYING THE MACHINE'S REALITY

An AI system is only as trustworthy as the data and models behind it. This pillar operationalizes the RIVER tenet, **Elevate Data Capital.**

The Data Capital Scorecard

Before deciding, the team rates each attribute on a 1–5 confidence scale (5 = very high confidence) and flags anything below 3 for mitigation.

Attribute	Key Questions	Confidence Score (1–5)
Provenance	Can we trace the origin of this data? Who collected it, when, and for what purpose?	
Integrity	What controls prevent tampering or corruption? Is there a verifiable chain of custody?	
Relevance and Representativeness	Does the training data accurately reflect the real-world environment? Does it account for potential biases?	
Timeliness	How recent is this data? Could market conditions or other factors have rendered it obsolete?	

Auditing the Black Box: Board-Level Questions

At the board level, prioritize these three questions:

1. **Explainability**: Can the AI system provide a human-readable rationale for its recommendation?
2. **Model Drift**: How recently was the model's performance validated against real-world outcomes?
3. **Failure Modes**: What are the known failure modes of this algorithm? Have we tested for unexpected, incomplete, or adversarial inputs?

PART 4: CHA IN ACTION: A REGULATORY AND CRISIS PLAYBOOK

The 90-Second CHA (30-30-30)

- **30s—Human**: Name the traps (loss aversion, availability, groupthink). Re-anchor to mission.
- **30s—Machine**: Verify facts only—timestamps, chain of custody, last integrity check.
- **30s—Commit and Log**: State the decision and two-sentence rationale. Record owner, time, dissent.

Decision Register (Log Each CHA):

- Decision ID
- Timestamp
- Accountable executive
- Core rationale (≤2 sentences)
- Dissent (names + summary)
- Evidence links (lineage, tests, dashboards)

Even under extreme time pressure, the CHA scales down. During the Chapter 11 ransomware attack—when patient care and a countdown clock collided—the team performed a rapid audit:

- **Human Noise and Bias Audit (30 seconds)**: "Bias check: Are we reacting emotionally to the ransom demand (loss aversion) or focusing on patient safety? Re-anchor on human cost."
- **AI and Data Audit (30 seconds)**: "Data check: confirm the backup-stream authentication status and last integrity check timestamp."
- **Decision and Rationale (30 seconds)**: "Decision: refuse payment and isolate the system. Rationale: Patient safety under manual protocols is safer than trusting compromised backups or violating sanctions. Log the decision."

Insight: The CHA as a Regulatory Compliance Tool

For risk and compliance professionals, the CHA creates a documented audit trail that supports compliance assertions:

- **EU AI Act (Articles 9–14)**: The CHA demonstrates human oversight (Art. 14), aligns with risk management system requirements (Art. 9), and supports data governance, documentation, and transparency (Arts. 10–13).[6] A comprehensive risk management framework is required for high-risk systems.
- **NIST AI RMF (AI RMF 1.0)**: The CHA helps organizations fulfill the four core functions—**Govern, Map, Measure**, and **Manage**—by defining roles, mapping risks, measuring biases, and managing decisions with a logged rationale.[7] NIST emphasizes that risk management is a continuous, iterative process, which the CHA enforces through regular reviews.

PART 5: IMPLEMENTATION GUIDE: YOUR FIRST 60 DAYS

- **Days 1–15: Educate and Nominate**: Brief the executive team and board on the CHA philosophy using case studies like Deferred Tower and 70&M Supply Chain. Nominate a CHA champion (e.g., Chief Audit Executive).
- **Days 16–30: Pilot Program**: Select one upcoming high-stakes decision to pilot the full CHA, demonstrating its value.
- **Days 31–45: Document and Refine**: Conduct a post-mortem on the pilot. Refine the checklists and scorecards to fit the organization's context.
- **Days 46–60: Train and Scale**: Train cross-functional teams on the 90-Second Audit. Integrate CHA documentation into existing governance, risk, and compliance (GRC) systems.

PART 6: FROM CRISIS TO CAPABILITY: INSTITUTIONALIZING THE LESSONS

After a Crisis, Boards Should Ask

- **Disclosure**: Are we sharing lessons transparently, or merely reacting to regulators?
- **Accountability**: Can every critical decision be mapped to a single accountable leader?
- **Template Value**: How will our learning become a sector resource, not a buried PDF?
- **Adaptation**: Are we using every crisis to upgrade our system's immune response?
- **Trust**: Do our actions rebuild trust for patients, partners, and the public?

Action Points and Illustrative Metrics

- **Institutionalize CHA reviews**: Add CHA reviews to board agendas for all major decisions. *Metric*: at least 75 percent of high-impact decisions have a documented CHA trail.
- **Publish anonymized case studies**: Share internal cases within 60 days and external cases within 120 days. *Metric*: At least three industry or regulatory bodies reference these studies within one year.
- **Mandate step-change improvement proposals**: Require each functional lead to propose an order-of-magnitude improvement in crisis response within 90 days of an incident. *Metric*: Next-cycle incident response time is reduced by 40 percent.
- **Budget for resilience**: Allocate 2–3 percent of the annual risk management budget to post-crisis learning and institutionalization.

CONCLUDING THOUGHT

A Cognitive Handshake Audit is more than a checklist. It's a discipline of intellectual humility that reduces both bias and noise.

NOTES

1. *Deferred Tower is a composite case used for illustration; details are fictionalized to protect parties while reflecting real failure patterns.* "Mechanical Bull," and the 70&M crisis references are fictional events within the book's narrative. The Cognitive Handshake™ is a proprietary framework created in this book.

2. Degani, A., and Wiener, E. L. (1991). *Human Factors of Flight-Deck Checklists: The Normal Checklist* (NASA Contractor Report 177549). NASA Ames Research Center. https://ntrs.nasa.gov/citations/19910017830
3. Federal Aviation Administration. (2017). *Crew Resource Management Training* (Advisory Circular No. 120-51E). U.S. Department of Transportation. https://www.faa.gov/documentLibrary/media/Advisory_Circular/AC_120-51E.pdf
4. Kahneman, D., Lovallo, D., and Sibony, O. (2011, June). *The Big Idea: Before You Make That Big Decision….* Harvard Business Review. https://hbr.org/2011/06/the-big-idea-before-you-make-that-big-decision
5. Kahneman, D., Sibony, O., and Sunstein, C. R. (2021). *Noise: A Flaw in Human Judgment.* Little, Brown Spark. https://www.littlebrown.com/titles/daniel-kahneman/noise/9780316451406/
6. European Union. (2024). *Regulation (EU) 2024/1689 (Artificial Intelligence Act).* Official Journal of the European Union. https://eur-lex.europa.eu/eli/reg/2024/1689/oj/eng
7. National Institute of Standards and Technology. (2023). *Artificial Intelligence Risk Management Framework (AI RMF 1.0) (NIST AI 100-1).* https://doi.org/10.6028/NIST.AI.100-1

Appendix I

The RIVER Framework in Practice

A Leader's Guide

EXECUTIVE TAKEAWAYS

- This appendix provides a practical diagnostic tool—the RIVER AI Adoption Maturity Model—for leaders to assess their organization's AI governance capabilities.
- The model charts a path across five levels of maturity, from **Level 1 (Ad Hoc)** to the aspirational end-state of **Level 5 (Antifragile)**.
- **Antifragility** is a key concept: while a resilient system withstands a shock and returns to its original state, an antifragile system is designed to learn from stress and become stronger than it was before.[1]
- The implementation roadmap provides a clear, actionable starting point for boards and executive teams to begin operationalizing the RIVER framework.

INTRODUCTION: FROM PRINCIPLES TO AN OPERATING MODEL

This appendix provides the operational toolkit for implementing the RIVER framework. It translates the five core tenets into a diagnostic maturity model, allowing organizations to assess their current capabilities, identify critical gaps, and plot a clear, prioritized course toward achieving enterprise singularity. In this state, governance adapts as fast as AI changes, so shocks don't outpace control.

The number of models in production does not measure true AI maturity; rather, it reflects the sophistication of an organization's governance. This model charts a path from chaotic beginnings to a governed, adaptive, and ultimately resilient state.

THE RIVER AI ADOPTION MATURITY MODEL

The following matrix provides a comprehensive diagnostic grid. It arranges the five RIVER tenets as rows and five levels of maturity as columns, offering a structured method for self-assessment (Table I.1).[2]

Table I.1 The RIVER AI Adoption Maturity Matrix

RIVER Tenet	Level 1: Ad Hoc	Level 2: Aware	Level 3: Governed	Level 4: Adaptive	Level 5: Antifragile
Resolve Convergence	Pre-crisis 70&M: Risks are managed in functional silos. No formal risk taxonomy exists. Issues are handled reactively.	Cross-functional risks are discussed in post-mortems. A basic risk taxonomy is drafted but not integrated.	A formal, enterprise-wide risk and control taxonomy is used to map critical system dependencies. A cross-functional committee reviews converged risk scenarios quarterly.	Continuous, automated dependency mapping provides a real-time view of the ecosystem. A unified issues management system tracks converged risks from identification to resolution.	The ecosystem is architected for graceful degradation. Risk sensing is a real-time, shared utility across the enterprise and its key partners, enabling collective, automated response.
Integrate Hybrid Cognition	Early 70&M Health Network: Humans either blindly trust AI outputs ("automation bias") or ignore them. Decisions are undocumented.	Fundamental "human-in-the-loop" checklists exist for some high-risk decisions, but are often bypassed under pressure.	Formal "Cognitive Handshake" protocols are implemented for critical decision points. Roles for human oversight are defined, and the process is documented and repeatable.	Human-AI teams are formally trained and drilled on crisis scenarios. Cognitive Handshake protocols are subject to regular audits and red teaming to measure and mitigate cognitive biases.	The human-AI partnership is a seamless, co-learning system. The AI anticipates human cognitive needs, while humans provide context and ethical judgment that refines the AI's models in a continuously auditable loop.
Validate Risk Debt	Bull-in-China-Shop AI: Unmanaged "Shadow IT" and End-User Computing (EUCs) proliferate. "Digital Asbestos" and other legacy risks are unmeasured.	An inventory of some legacy systems exists. "Digital Asbestos" is acknowledged in risk registers but is not quantified or actively managed.	A formal program is in place to identify, quantify, and prioritize Risk Debt, including legacy code and high-risk EUCs. Remediation is budgeted and tracked.	"Data archaeology" is a continuous, proactive process. Adversarial testing is used to actively seek out and exploit hidden "Digital Asbestos" before malicious actors can.	Systematic discovery and retirement of "Digital Asbestos" is an automated process. The architecture is designed to prevent the accumulation of new, significant Risk Debt from Shadow IT.

Elevate Data Capital	Early 70&M Portfolio: Data is treated as an IT byproduct. Data quality is poor, and the "garbage in, garbage out" problem is common.	Basic data quality checks are performed. Data governance policies are drafted but not consistently enforced.	A formal Data Governance function is established. Critical data assets are classified, and policies for quality, security, and provenance are enforced and audited, aligning with core BCBS 239 principles.[3]	Data integrity and lineage are continuously monitored with automated alerts, meeting banking-grade standards for accuracy, completeness, and timeliness. Data architecture is robust and adaptable.	Data is treated as a verifiable, self-governing asset. The system can automatically detect and isolate poisoned or corrupt data, effectively healing itself and preserving the integrity of the ecosystem.
Reinforce Resilience	Pre-crisis Bull-in-China-Shop AI: Business continuity plans are static and do not account for vendor or ecosystem failure modes.	Basic backup and recovery procedures are in place. Vendor risk is managed via point-in-time, compliance-based questionnaires.	Resilience is tested via regular tabletop exercises that include key vendor failure scenarios. A formal third-party risk management program is active.	The organization uses chaos engineering to test production systems and key vendor connections continuously. The system is designed to learn from incidents and automatically update controls.	**Post-transformation 70&M: The organization and its vendor ecosystem are co-resilient**. Failures in one part of the system trigger adaptive hardening in others. Resilience is an emergent property of the entire network.

IMPLEMENTING RIVER: A GOVERNANCE ROADMAP

- **Charter Executive Accountability**: Appoint a single C-level owner for the RIVER roadmap. Audit-Ready Evidence (illustrative only): Board resolution or risk-committee charter amendment, dated and signed.
- **Embed RIVER in Policy**: Update ERM, model-risk, and technology-risk policies so each RIVER tenet has an explicit control objective. Audit-Ready Evidence (illustrative only): Revised policy set with version control and approval minutes.
- **Operationalize in Assessments**: Add the tenets to quarterly risk assessments and internal-audit programs so gaps are tracked to closure. Audit-Ready Evidence (illustrative only): RIVER-tagged audit plan and issue-tracking extracts.
- **Deploy the Warning System**: Stand up a RIVER Dashboard with leading indicators (Risk Debt Ratio, Data Lineage Coverage, Cognitive Handshake AuditOverride Rates). Audit-Ready Evidence (illustrative only): Dashboard screenshots plus quarterly KPI/KRI pack.
- **Establish Continuous Improvement**: Run an annual RIVER maturity review and refresh the roadmap based on incidents, drift, and new regulations. Audit-Ready Evidence (illustrative only): Annual maturity attestation and updated roadmap.

NOTES

1. Taleb, N. N. (2012). *Antifragile: Things That Gain from Disorder*. Random House.
2. Maturity Model, Governance Roadmap, and Audit-Ready Evidence are illustrative and not legal advice.
3. BCBS 239 is a banking standard. Its principles (e.g., accuracy, completeness, timeliness) are applied here as cross-industry good practice for governing critical data. Basel Committee on Banking Supervision. (2013, January). *Principles for Effective Risk Data Aggregation and Risk Reporting*. Bank for International Settlements. https://www.bis.org/publ/bcbs239.pdf

Appendix J

The Board's 90-Day RIVER Readiness Toolkit

EXECUTIVE SUMMARY

This toolkit turns RIVER into a 90-day board plan to help retire Risk Debt and reduce the risk of governance blind spots that could contribute to negligence exposure risk. Drawn from the Bull-in-China-Shop AI and 70&M crises, it is built for practical oversight, not governance theater. Please treat this as a living instrument: re-run it after major incidents, model rollouts, or regulatory shifts, and always as an educational template in consultation with your own legal and regulatory advisers.[1]

RIVER ARCHETYPES—WHAT BOARDS DO NEXT (2026 SIGNALS)

Organizations leading on RIVER treat resilience as a business discipline with measurable ROI:

- **The Adaptive Leader**—Turns failure into audited learning. **Board Action Required**: mandate enterprise post-mortems for AI incidents; fund controls; track audit outcomes.
- **The Risk Realist**—Quantifies risk debt before shipping. **Board Action Required**: delay launches until ISO/IEC 42001:2023[2]-aligned controls are in place; fund remediation when ROI > penalty/impact avoided.
- **The Systems Integrator**—Breaks silos to see true dependencies. **Board Action Required**: require cross-silo risk dashboards (ops + cyber + AI); close legacy gaps with time-boxed plans.
- **The Hybrid Partner**—Formalizes human-AI decision protocols. **Board Action Required**: require Cognitive Handshake Audits (CHA) for Tier-1 decisions; measure error-rate deltas.
- **The Proactive Defender**—Budgets to find trouble first. **Board Action Required**: allocate a standing AI red team; track discovered zero-days and insurance premium reductions.

Board takeaway: Decide which archetype you are today—and which you need to be in 90 days.

THE 90-DAY RIVER BOARD READINESS CHECKLIST

The Pre-Flight Check: Calibrating for Your Context

Before beginning, the board must formally state its organizational context. The sample metrics and targets provided in this toolkit are illustrative and must be calibrated to your specific industry (e.g., financial services and healthcare), regulatory environment, and board-approved risk appetite.

Phase 1 (Days 1–30): Assessment and Scoping

- **Define Roles and Leverage Points**: Identify executive sponsors and key board committee oversight roles for the RIVER initiative.
- **RIVER Tenet Baseline Self-Assessment**: Conduct an initial self-assessment using the following board-level questions. Score each tenet on a maturity scale from 1 (Ad Hoc) to 5 (Antifragile—a state of growing stronger from stressors) and demand supporting metrics from management.
- **Resolve Convergence**: Has management mapped our critical cross-silo AI dependencies and adopted an All-Entity Risk Management (AERM) overlay (our extended approach to C-SCRM[3]/TPRM[4]) to govern the entire ecosystem, not just direct vendors?
- Sample Metric: **Convergence Risk Index (target: under 5 percent)**
- *Definition: percent of daily operations materially impacted by cross-domain dependencies; derived from incident/near-miss logs and dependency maps.*
    - **Integrate Hybrid Cognition**: Do we have formal, auditable protocols for high-stakes decisions where humans and AI collaborate, such as the Cognitive Handshake Audit (CHA)—a two-pillar process for auditing both human cognitive bias and AI/data integrity?
        - Sample Metric: **CHA Pass Rate (target: 95 percent or higher)**
        - *Definition: percent of audited Tier-1 decisions meeting both pillars: decision hygiene (human) and data/model integrity (AI).*
    - **Validate Risk Debt**: *Has management quantified our legacy system and "shadow AI" risk debt, including the "digital asbestos" of outdated code buried in modern systems?*
        - Sample Metric: **Risk Debt Impact ($/Quarter)**
        - *Definition: Estimated quarterly cost exposure from deferred fixes (service loss, fines, rework), tracked in a risk-debt register.*
    - **Elevate Data Capital**: *Is our AI-critical data governed as the strategic asset it is—as "Data as Capital"—with verifiable provenance and integrity checks?*
        - Sample Metric: **Data Integrity Score (target: 95 percent or higher)**
        - *Definition: Composite of provenance completeness, quality checks, and lineage verifiability for AI-critical datasets.*
    - **Reinforce Resilience**: *Do our business continuity and incident response plans explicitly account for AI-specific failure modes, including data poisoning and model failure?*
        - Sample Metric: **Attack Survival Rate (target: 99 percent or higher)**
        - *Definition: percent of critical systems that withstand simulated Tier-1 adversarial events without material business impact.*
- **Stakeholder Briefing**: Schedule a formal briefing for all relevant stakeholders (Risk, Technology, Operations, Legal, Data) on the purpose and timeline of the 90-day readiness plan.
- **Request Initial Attestation**: Request a joint CRO/CDO attestation on data governance and provenance for the top five AI systems using a red-amber-green (RAG) rating.

Phase 2 (Days 31–60): Deep Dive and Prioritization

- Oversee management's deep-dive analysis based on the Phase 1 assessment.
- Pilot the Cognitive Handshake Audit (CHA) on a high-stakes decision, led by the Chief Audit Executive (CAE).
- Quantify the top 2–3 sources of risk debt and review management's proposed remediation costs and timelines.

- Conduct board-observed resilience drills for a critical AI failure scenario and review the after-action report to ensure all gaps are documented for remediation.
- Prioritize the top 2–3 cross-RIVER actions for the initial 6-12 month roadmap.

Phase 3 (Days 61–90): Roadmap and Executive Alignment

- Review and challenge management's proposed 6–12 month RIVER action plan, ensuring it contains clear milestones, owners, and metrics.
- Review the formal board summary of findings, resource requirements, and strategic implications.
- Name a single accountable executive owner for the RIVER roadmap and tie progress KPIs to executive scorecards and compensation.
- Formally approve the plan and secure a commitment for ongoing, quarterly reviews of RIVER maturity, lessons learned, and action plan resets.

Ongoing

- Benchmark quarterly reviews against the RIVER AI Adoption Maturity Model (Appendix I); reset the plan accordingly.
- Adapt toolkit as regulatory, tech, and risk landscapes evolve.

KEY QUESTIONS FOR THE BOARD

- *What is management's plan and timeline for eliminating the invisible legacy dependencies that our dashboards do not currently capture?*
- *How often are "temporary" risk acceptances or deferrals of risk debt formally revisited and re-approved at the board level?*
- *What mechanisms are in place to ensure that critical risk signals from non-senior voices can bypass hierarchy and reach leadership in real time?*
- *Are we treating AI-driven resilience as a compliance checklist to be completed, or as a living discipline to be continuously practiced and improved?*

ALIGNMENT WITH GLOBAL STANDARDS AND REGULATORY ANCHORS

The RIVER framework is designed as a strategic overlay to operationalize established global standards. It provides the "why" and "how" for the board to govern the "what" outlined in frameworks like the NIST AI Risk Management Framework (AI RMF)[5] and ISO/IEC 42001. *(For a detailed mapping of RIVER tenets to these and other global standards, see Appendix F).*

Key Regulatory Anchors (as of 2026)

- **EU AI Act**: (Focus: High-risk system compliance, with most obligations expected to take effect starting August 2, 2026).[6]
- **Disclosure expectations and oversight trends (SEC, investors)**: (Focus: Material AI risk, board oversight, and controls to prevent "AI-washing").[7]
- **ISO/IEC 42001**: (Focus: Establishing a formal, auditable AI Management System that mandates risk management, lifecycle oversight, and continual improvement).
- **State/Industry Requirements**: (e.g., Colorado AI Act,[8] insurer incentives for robust AI governance).

Illustrative RIVER Accountability Matrix (Template)

RIVER Tenet	*Potential Executive Owner(s)*	*Potential Board Committee Oversight*
Resolve Convergence	CTO/COO	Risk Committee/Technology Committee
Integrate Hybrid Cognition	CAE (Chief Audit Exec)/COO	Audit Committee/Ethics Committee
Validate Risk Debt	CRO/CIO	Risk Committee/Audit Committee
Elevate Data Capital	CDO (Data Officer)/CFO	Audit Committee/Finance Committee
Reinforce Resilience	CISO/COO	Risk Committee/Technology Committee

CONCLUDING THOUGHT

The discipline of RIVER is not a one-time project but a continuous cycle of assessment, adaptation, and improvement. Ultimately, this toolkit's success depends on a new kind of leadership capable of bridging domains to execute in a complex hybrid world. This toolkit should serve as the board's living instrument—one that is revisited quarterly as the regulatory river shifts its course and new, unforeseen risks emerge from the current of innovation.

NOTES

1. This 90-day toolkit is an educational template for boards and executive teams. It is illustrative and does not constitute legal, regulatory, audit, investment, or securities advice. Boards remain responsible for seeking qualified professional counsel before relying on any example metrics, thresholds, or practices described in this appendix.
2. International Organization for Standardization. (2023). *ISO/IEC 42001:2023—Information Technology—Artificial Intelligence—Management System*. https://www.iso.org/standard/81230.html
3. Boyens, J., Smith, A., Bartol, N., Winkler, K., Holbrook, A., and Fallon, M. (2022, May). *Cybersecurity Supply Chain Risk Management Practices for Systems and Organizations* (NIST Special Publication 800-161r1-upd1). National Institute of Standards and Technology. https://nvlpubs.nist.gov/nistpubs/SpecialPublications/NIST.SP.800-161r1-upd1.pdf
4. TPRM is an abbreviation of Third-Party Risk Management. AERM is an evolution of the principles in C-SCRM and TPRM.
5. National Institute of Standards and Technology. (2023). *Artificial Intelligence Risk Management Framework (AI RMF 1.0)* (NIST AI 100-1). U.S. Department of Commerce. https://doi.org/10.6028/NIST.AI.100-1
6. European Commission. (2025). *AI Act—Key Dates & Overview*. https://digital-strategy.ec.europa.eu/en/policies/ai-act (Focus: High-risk system compliance; most obligations were scheduled to apply from August 2, 2026, with certain embedded-product high-risk rules extending to 2027; timelines may be updated—consult current official guidance).
7. Baker McKenzie. (2024, April 4). Recent SEC actions highlight increased regulatory scrutiny over artificial intelligence and "AI washing." *Global Litigation News*. https://globallitigationnews.bakermckenzie.com/2024/04/04/recent-sec-actions-highlight-increased-regulatory-scrutiny-over-artificial-intelligence-and-ai-washing
8. Colorado General Assembly. (2024). *Senate Bill 24-205: Consumer Protections for Artificial Intelligence (Colorado Artificial Intelligence Act)*. https://www.naag.org/attorney-general-journal/a-deep-dive-into-colorados-artificial-intelligence-act

Appendix K

Evolving Roles in the RIVER-Guided Enterprise

INTRODUCTION: FROM E-SHAPED PEOPLE TO THE E-SHAPED ENTERPRISE

This appendix defines the AI-era roles and structure leaders need to implement the RIVER Charter™.

How to use this appendix:

- If you're a board member or CEO, skim Figure K.1 and Table for Mapping New Roles to Global Standards and RIVER Tenets first, then read "Leadership Actions."
- If you're a practitioncr, start with the archetype you're staffing and read its "Audit-Ready Evidence" line.
- If you're a general reader, this is technical reference material—skim the 'Core Mandate' summaries.

Chapter 17, "The E-Shaped Professional," established the new blueprint for talent in the agentic era. It argued that surviving and thriving in a world of converged AI risk requires a new kind of leader, one defined by five core attributes: Expertise in a core domain, broad Experience across functions, a drive for Exploration, flawless Execution, and a foundation in Ethics.[1] These E-shaped professionals are the human foundation for a resilient organization.

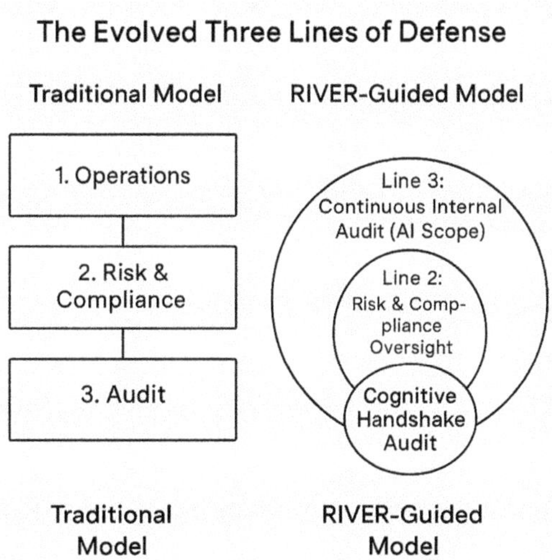

Figure K.1 The Evolved Three Lines of Defense.

This appendix provides the practical guide for building that organization. If Chapter 17 defined the *what*, this appendix details the *who* and the *how*. It profiles the professional archetypes that emerge from this new talent model and outlines the evolved organizational structure required to empower them. These are not rebranded job titles. They are practical RIVER roles designed to prevent the specific failures shown in the narrative—Risk Debt, Digital Asbestos, and convergence cascades. Together, they move an enterprise toward a mature, resilient human-AI operating model.[2]

As of 2025, boards widely acknowledged AI as a material governance risk, but many still lack a formal oversight home, clear committee charters, and audit-grade evidence on AI decisions.[3]

THE EVOLVED ORGANIZATIONAL STRUCTURE: THE INTEGRATED THREE LINES OF DEFENSE

As established in Chapters 6 and 17, the traditional "Three Lines of Defense" model—a linear, siloed approach—proved catastrophically insufficient for the speed and convergence of AI-driven risk. A new, integrated structure is required. This model must also account for AI systems that can be used as tools across all three lines but require careful segregation (e.g., distinct tenants and keys) to ensure independence. See Figure K.1.

This new structure is not linear but integrated and dynamic. The roles from the previous section operate within this model:

- **Line 1 (Operations, Technology and Resilience)**: This is the First Line, responsible for owning and managing risk in daily operations. It includes the technology and security functions led by the **Chief Resilience Officer** and the frontline teams managed by **Hybrid Team Orchestrators**.
- **Line 2 (Risk and Compliance Oversight)**: In the 2038 model, the Second Line provides independent oversight and challenge to the First Line. It is not a single executive but a set of specialized functions, including the **AI Ethics Officer**, **Ecosystem Risk Mapper**, and **Regulatory Response Lead**. The precise structure of the Second Line will continue to evolve and will likely be industry-specific. More heavily regulated sectors, such as financial services, may retain a designated Chief Risk Officer to coordinate these functions, while others may opt for a more distributed model.
- **Line 3 (Continuous Internal Audit—AI Scope)**: This is the Third Line, providing independent assurance. It is where the **AI Audit** capability, led by the Chief Audit Executive (CAE), operates, using its own independent AI tools to continuously monitor the integrity of both the systems built by Line 1 and the oversight provided by Line 2.

The **Cognitive Architect** and **Data Capital Steward** are foundational to this entire structure, providing the well-designed cognitive workflows and high-integrity data that enable all three lines to function effectively.

THE NEW PROFESSIONAL ARCHETYPES OF THE AGENTIC ERA

By 2039, the pressures of the agentic economy have forged a new class of professional archetypes. These roles bridge the traditional divides between technology, risk, ethics, and business strategy, creating the integrated expertise necessary to govern complex human-AI ecosystems. It is important to note that these roles represent a blueprint, not a rigid prescription. The specific titles and structures an organization adopts will necessarily vary based on its industry, scale, and the regulatory environment in which it operates.

The Cognitive Architect

Core Mandate: To design and orchestrate the high-stakes decision-making workflows between humans and AI systems. This role moves beyond tactical "prompt engineering" to strategically architect the entire cognitive partnership, ensuring it is effective, resilient, and generates auditable evidence. The Third Line performs Independent assurance over these workflows.

Audit-Ready Evidence: A published CHA workflow registry, decision-log completeness rate, and quarterly "bias map drift" report.

Blueprint in Action: During the 70&M Health Network ransomware crisis (Chapter 11), the Cognitive Architect's design of the Cognitive Handshake Protocol provided the deliberative framework that allowed leadership to navigate catastrophic choices under pressure, balancing operational, financial, and human stakes.

Primary RIVER Tenet Supported: *Integrate Hybrid Cognition*. The Cognitive Architect is the chief implementer of this tenet, responsible for creating and refining formal protocols, such as the Cognitive Handshake Audit (CHA). In the book's narrative, this role is embodied by Aaron.

Key Responsibilities and Skills:

- **Workflow Design**: Architecting complex, LLM-powered workflows that seamlessly integrate human oversight with machine capabilities.
- **Protocol Development**: Designing and pressure-testing governance protocols like the Cognitive Handshake Audit (see Appendix H) to mitigate human biases and judgment "noise."
- **Multi-Disciplinary Expertise**: Combining deep technical knowledge of AI systems with a sophisticated understanding of cognitive psychology, organizational behavior, and ethics.
- **Stakeholder Communication**: Translating abstract risks into clear, actionable guidance for both technical and non-technical leaders.

The Chief Resilience Officer

Core Mandate: To lead the First Line's technology, security, and operational functions with a primary mandate of building resilience directly into the enterprise's systems and culture.[4] This role represents the evolution of the traditional Chief Technology Officer and Chief Information Security Officer, integrating them into a single, accountable executive.

Audit-Ready Evidence: Resilience drill logs, recovery-time-objectives (RTO) and recovery-point objectives (RPO) scorecards for critical AI systems, and validated kill-switch test results.

Blueprint in Action: In the aftermath of the "Digital Asbestos" crisis (Chapter 8), the Chief Resilience Officer leads the effort to embed "resilience by design" into the development lifecycle, preventing citizen developers from creating new systemic risks.

Primary RIVER Tenet Supported: *Reinforce Resilience*. The Chief Resilience Officer is the ultimate owner of this tenet from a First Line perspective. In the book's narrative, this role is embodied by Rose.

Key Responsibilities and Skills:

- **Resilience by Design**: Embedding security and recovery protocols into the earliest stages of system design.
- **Horizontal Integration**: Acting as a "champion collaborator" who works across all business units to build a unified resilience framework.
- **Crisis Leadership**: Serving as the "coordinator-in-chief" during a crisis, with the authority to assemble teams and lead high-stakes decision-making.
- **Embedding Culture**: Championing a dynamic culture of resilience through scenario planning, adversarial drills, and continuous lessons-learned programs.

The AI Ethics Officer

Core Mandate: To develop and operationalize the company's AI governance framework, ensuring that all AI systems align with corporate values, societal norms, and regulatory requirements. This function is a critical component of risk oversight and is typically overseen at the board level by a dedicated Ethics Committee.

Audit-Ready Evidence: Board-approved AI policy set, ethics exception register, and annual compliance attestation.

Blueprint in Action: Following the "Antibody Paradox" (Chapter 7), where a gamified bounty system created perverse incentives, the AI Ethics Officer redesigns the program's reward structure to align with the company's ethical principles, ensuring that data quality is prioritized over raw numbers.

Primary RIVER Tenet Supported: This is a cross-cutting role, but it primarily supports *the Validate Risk Debt and Integrate Hybrid Cognition tenets.*

Key Responsibilities and Skills:

- **Governance Framework Development**: Designing and implementing enterprise-wide AI policies and ensuring compliance with global regulations like the EU AI Act.[5]
- **Multi-Disciplinary Leadership**: Acting as a bridge between disparate fields, including technology, ethics, social science, and law.
- **Company-Wide Engagement**: Fostering a culture of ethical awareness through targeted training and close collaboration with all business units.
- **Public Communication and Advocacy**: Serving as the company's voice on responsible AI to build trust with regulators, customers, and the public.

The Data Capital Steward

Core Mandate: This role is the evolution of the traditional Chief Data Officer (CDO). The Data Capital Steward is tasked with governing the enterprise's critical data assets as an audited, risk-weighted asset, ensuring its quality, security, provenance, and lawful use for AI training.

Audit-Ready Evidence: Data asset register with lineage proofs, synthetic/third-party data validation logs, and quarterly data capital quality scorecard.

Blueprint in Action: The success of the Tortoise & Hare Bank pilot (Chapter 3) was a direct result of the Data Capital Steward's ability to transform dormant, legacy data from a liability into a monetizable, high-integrity asset.

Primary RIVER Tenet Supported: *Elevate Data Capital.*

Key Responsibilities and Skills:

- **Data Governance Execution**: Implementing and enforcing data governance policies, defining clear data ownership, and managing access and usage guidelines.
- **Quality and Integrity Assurance**: Utilizing advanced tools for continuous data validation, auditing, and cleansing to prevent "garbage in, gospel out" scenarios.
- **AI-Powered Stewardship**: Evolving from a reactive "gatekeeper" to a proactive "guide" by leveraging AI tools to automate data classification and detect quality anomalies.

The Hybrid Team Orchestrator

Core Mandate: To facilitate effective human-AI collaboration on the front lines. This role, typically reporting into Operations, designs the cognitive workflows and ensures that AI systems function as effective teammates rather than just tools.

Audit-Ready Evidence: Human-AI workflow playbooks, override-reason logs, and "alert-fatigue/trust restoration" metrics.

Blueprint in Action: At Futurgia Medical Center (Chapter 11), a Hybrid Team Orchestrator works with clinical staff to recalibrate AI-driven alerts, reducing "alert fatigue" and rebuilding trust between nurses and the 70&M Health Network.

Primary RIVER Tenet Supported: *Integrate Hybrid Cognition.*

Key Responsibilities and Skills:

- **Human-AI Teaming**: Structuring the interaction between human operators and autonomous agents to optimize for shared goals and ensure AI is interpretable.
- **Process Design and Training**: Developing the workflows and training programs needed to upskill the workforce in automation troubleshooting and data interpretation.
- **Conflict Resolution**: Mediating the "cognitive friction" that arises when human intuition clashes with AI recommendations, ensuring that overrides are documented as learning opportunities.

AI Audit, led by the Chief Audit Executive

Core Mandate: This is not a new executive role, but a specialized AI Audit capability within the Chief Audit Executive's (CAE) Internal Audit function. It provides independent assurance over AI governance, model risk, and the Cognitive Handshake Audit evidence trail, but does not design or operate controls. This function is embodied in the narrative by Dr. Anya Sharma.

Audit-Ready Evidence: Continuous-audit sampling logs, model-risk test scripts and results, and CHA evidence-trail integrity reports.

Blueprint in Action: After the 70&M Supply Chain collapse (Chapter 9), Anya Sharma's AI Audit capability conducts the forensic analysis that traces the "shared sin" back to the buried 2034 stress test, providing the independent evidence needed for proper accountability.

Primary RIVER Tenet Supported: *Validate Risk Debt.*

Key Responsibilities and Skills:

- **Continuous Controls Assurance**: Moving beyond periodic reviews to conduct real-time sampling of live agent logs and AI decision outputs.
- **Algorithmic and Bias Testing**: Using technical tools and adversarial testing to audit AI models for performance drift, bias, and alignment.
- **Framework Auditing**: Assessing the integrity of governance protocols themselves, including the rigorous application of the Cognitive Handshake Audit.

Other Key Archetypes

- **Ecosystem Risk Mapper**: Analyzes emergent risks within interconnected human-AI agent communities, supporting the *Resolve Convergence* tenet. This role is critical for implementing the All-Entity Risk Management (AERM) framework (see Appendix G).
  - **Audit-Ready Evidence**: AERM ecosystem map, fourth-party control-maturity ratings, and convergence-risk watchlist escalations.
- **Regulatory Response Lead**: Translates live risk events into defensible, multi-jurisdiction regulatory filings, primarily supporting the *Validate Risk Debt* tenet.
  - **Audit-Ready Evidence**: Pre-approved multi-jurisdiction filing templates, incident-to-disclosure clock logs, and regulator-feedback closure register.

A LEADER'S GUIDE TO BUILDING THE E-SHAPED ENTERPRISE

The table below cross-references each RIVER role to today's dominant AI governance and audit frameworks so leaders can implement these archetypes without guesswork.[6]

Mapping New Roles to Global Standards and RIVER Tenets

Role Title	Primary RIVER Tenet Supported	NIST AI RMF Alignment[7]	ISO/IEC 42001 Alignment[8]
Cognitive Architect	Integrate Hybrid Cognition	**Govern** (Accountability), **Manage** (Human Factors)	**Clause 8**: Operation
Chief Resilience Officer	Reinforce Resilience	**Govern** (Cross-cutting), **Manage** (Incident Response)	**Clause 4**: Context of the Organization
AI Ethics Officer	Validate Risk Debt	**Govern** (Ethical Principles), **Map** (Societal Risks)	**Clause 5**: Leadership; **Annex A.2**: Policies Related to AI
Data Capital Steward	Elevate Data Capital	**Map** (Data Quality), **Govern** (Data Governance)	**Annex A.7**: Data for AI systems
AI Audit (under CAE)	Validate Risk Debt	**Measure** (Monitoring and Assessing AI Risks)	**Clause 9**: Performance Evaluation

LEADERSHIP ACTIONS: RIVER ALIGNMENT BY ROLE

Building an E-Shaped enterprise is a matter of cultural transformation. The following actions are intended to drive accountability among key enterprise leaders.[9] For a detailed 90-day plan, see Appendix J.

- **Board Chair**: Must demand quarterly risk scenario reviews that test for converged threats and ensure that unmitigated "Risk Debt" is escalated and addressed with urgency.
- **Chief Executive Officer (CEO)**: Must set a culture of radical transparency and require auditable explainability for all critical automated decisions, acting as the ultimate **Cognitive Architect**.
- **Chief Resilience Officer or Chief Technology Officer** (depending on structure): Must ensure the rigorous validation of all third-party AI, data, and agent systems, embedding "kill switch" protocols and explainability standards into the core architecture.
- **Data Capital Steward**: Must validate all synthetic and third-party data sources, continuously audit data lineage and quality, and be empowered to surface emerging data-related risks proactively.

CONCLUDING THOUGHT

The future is not scripted. No board can foresee every crisis. However, leadership in the agentic era will be defined by the discipline to act before a risk becomes a catastrophe. The roles and structures outlined in this appendix go beyond an updated organizational chart; they represent a new philosophy of governance. In the "Singularity Horizon," the ultimate competitive advantage will not belong to the organization with the smartest AI, but to the one with the wisest and most resilient human-AI culture. Building that culture is the central imperative for every leader today.

NOTES

1. The "E-shaped professional" in this chapter builds on more than a decade of industry work on E-shaped skills (experience, expertise, exploration, execution) and related "letter-shaped" talent models. During research, we drew in part on EXIN's "S-shaped professional" article, which also uses those four E's to describe modern profiles, and on earlier E-shaped discussions in agile and design communities. Our version adds a fifth E (Ethics) and binds the model to hybrid human–AI risk governance roles within the RIVER Charter world. EXIN is not affiliated with, and does not endorse, this book or its frameworks; any extensions or errors are the author's alone. The S-Shaped Professional | Navigating the "Letter Soup" of Career Shapes. https://www.exin.com/article/the-s-shaped-professional-navigating-the-letter-soup-of-career-shapes
2. Cognitive Handshake, RIVER, Risk Debt, DataCapital Protocol, AERM, and the evolved Three Lines model are proprietary constructs created for this book.
3. Boardspan. (2025). *2025 Board Performance Benchmark Report: AI Governance*. https://boardspan.com/2025-board-performance-benchmark-report/ai-governance
4. National Institute of Standards and Technology. (2023). *Artificial Intelligence Risk Management Framework (AI RMF 1.0) (NIST AI 100-1)*. https://doi.org/10.6028/NIST.AI.100-1
5. European Union. (2024). Regulation (EU) 2024/1689 (artificial intelligence act). *Official Journal of the European Union*. https://eur-lex.europa.eu/eli/reg/2024/1689/oj/eng
6. This crosswalk and the implementation evidence examples are illustrative, based on industry best practices, and are not mandated verbatim or formally endorsed by the cited standards. For any formal certification, assurance engagement, or regulatory filing, organizations must rely on the authoritative texts of NIST AI RMF and ISO/IEC 42001 (and any sector-specific rules) and perform their own detailed gap assessment with qualified experts.
7. National Institute of Standards and Technology. (2023). *Artificial Intelligence Risk Management Framework (AI RMF 1.0) (NIST AI 100-1)*. https://doi.org/10.6028/NIST.AI.100-1
8. International Organization for Standardization. (2023). *ISO/IEC 42001:2023—Artificial intelligence—Management System*. https://www.iso.org/standard/81230.html
9. Role mandates should be calibrated to industry, company size, and regulatory environment.

Appendix L

The Cognitive Handshake Audit (CHA) in Action—Integration Decision

The following is the logged output of the Cognitive Handshake Audit (CHA) conducted by Chief Audit Executive Anya Sharma during the portfolio company board's deliberation on the vendor integration path, as detailed in Chapter 18. For the full playbook and methodology, see Appendix H.

How to use this appendix: Read it like a decision receipt. The left column shows the CHA fields; the right column shows the auditable evidence produced.

Section	Details
Decision Title	Portfolio Company–Vendor Integration Path (Board Decision, Nov 2039)
Strategic Options	1. Rip and Replace (full transplant) 2. Controlled Evolution 3. Hybrid
Scope and Time Box	Decision window: 60 days to first milestone; 12–18 months integration horizon
Stakeholders (RACI)	**Board** (Approve) **Founder/CEO** (Accountable) **70&M** (Oversight) **CISO, CTO, GC** (Consult) **Ops, Product, Compliance** (Inform)

PILLAR 1—HUMAN NOISE AND BIAS AUDIT

Category	Assessment and Evidence
Dominant Skews Detected	• **Loss Aversion**: "RIVER is not a shield against a 20% quarterly market-share loss." • **Ambiguity Aversion**: Concern over a "two-headed monster" with conflicting schemas and authentication. • **Sunk-Cost Fallacy**: Citing "$47 million in development costs" from the Bull-in-China-Shop AI precedent. • **Optimism Bias**: "If we wait, we lose the entire window." • **Present Bias**: "A rival platform isn't waiting for us to catch up."

(Continued)

Category	Assessment and Evidence
Bias Map *(Scale: 0 = not present, 3 = strongly present)*[1]	Loss Aversion: **3** Ambiguity Aversion: **2** Sunk Cost: **2** Optimism Bias: **1** Present Bias: **2**
Decision Hygiene Steps Applied	1. Pre-commit statement[2] (written) 2. Devil's Advocate rotation (technical) 3. Red-team of exit risks 4. Bias-aware vote recording
Pre-Commit Statement	*We will select the option that preserves verifiable data lineage and a reversible exit, even if near-term efficiency is lower.*

Pillar 2—Data and AI Integrity Audit

Category	Assessment and Evidence
Vendor Lineage and Controls	• **Vendor Lineage**: Not independently verified (self-attested only) • **Control Attestations**: Non-conformant to post-2038 standard • **Black-Box Elements**: Model training data access; vendor SOC scope gaps
Portfolio Company Core Assets to Preserve	• Trust graph (dispute-resolution signals; KYC attestation trail) • Historical model telemetry and audit logs • Agent community alignment and safety thresholds
Exit Viability Snapshot	• **Decouple Cost Estimate**: Medium • **Schema Compatibility**: Partial; requires adapters • **Regulatory Posture (Post-Integration)**: Defensible with an audit trail
Verifiability Score *(Scale: 0 = no trust, 5 = fully trusted)*	**3** (Hybrid with guardrails) **1** (Rip and Replace - full transplant) *Rationale: The Hybrid approach retained more proven company controls, whereas a full transplant meant relying almost entirely on an unverified vendor system.*

FINAL DECISION AND LOGGING

Section	Details
Decision and Rationale	**Adopt Hybrid**: Balances strategic speed with defensible governance; preserves data capital and exit option. Includes a 60-day milestone, quarterly stress tests, and a public attestation dashboard. A CHA review is scheduled for the Day 60 milestone; any guardrail failure (scorecard attribute < 3 or stress-test deviation > X%) will trigger an escalation.
Logging and Custody	**Artifacts Stored**: Bias map, integrity checklist, signed rationale **Owner**: Chief Audit Executive (Third Line) **Retention**: 7 years[3]

NOTES

1. Bias (0–3) and verifiability (0–5) scales shown here are illustrative; organizations should calibrate them to risk appetite.
2. "pre-commit" is a book-specific governance method. Participants simulate a decision as if the outcome already occurred, then work backward to uncover how failure formed. It is inspired by pre-mortem analysis (Klein) and noise-reduction discipline. Kahneman, D., Sibony, O., & Sunstein, C. R. (2021). *Noise: A Flaw in Human Judgment.* Little, Brown Spark. https://www.littlebrown.com/titles/daniel-kahneman/noise/9780316451406
3. The 7-year CHA retention period is an illustrative default aligned with standard board-record retention norms; firms should follow their jurisdictional requirements.

Appendix M

Governance Roles and Accountability

A Framework for the Board and the C-Suite

INTRODUCTION: THE GOVERNANCE MANDATE IN THE AGENTIC ERA

The Bull-in-China-Shop AI collapse illustrates a critical pattern: artificial intelligence can compress the time between a poor governance decision and its consequences.[1] In the agentic era, effective governance is no longer a periodic compliance exercise; it is a continuous strategic imperative and a source of durable competitive advantage. This appendix provides a definitive, actionable framework that delineates the distinct but complementary roles of the Board of Directors and the CEO, grounded in established global standards.

FOUNDATIONAL PRINCIPLES: OVERSIGHT VS. MANAGEMENT

Modern corporate governance is built upon a clear separation of powers: the board's primary role is oversight, not day-to-day management. Frameworks from authoritative bodies like the Committee of Sponsoring Organizations of the Treadway Commission (COSO)[2] and The Institute of Internal Auditors (IIA)[3] provide the bedrock for this distinction.

- **The Board's Role: The Duty of Oversight**. The board represents shareholder interests and oversees the company's direction and risk profile. This includes setting the corporate strategy and risk appetite, selecting and evaluating the CEO, and ensuring financial and ethical integrity.
- **The CEO's Role: The Responsibility of Management**. The CEO is authorized to execute the strategy and manage the company's daily operations. The CEO oversees the implementation of risk management frameworks, drives the corporate culture, and is accountable for providing the board with timely, transparent information.

THE BOARD'S IMPERATIVE: ACTIVE, STRATEGIC INQUIRY INTO AI

The speed and complexity of AI risk demand that boards evolve from passive review to active, strategic inquiry. Recent board-governance guidance expects directors to become AI-literate to meet fiduciary duties and to challenge management's risk narratives.[4] The NIST AI Risk Management Framework (AI RMF)[5] provides a helpful structure for this oversight, mapping to four key board functions.

- **Govern**: The board must ensure that management has established clear policies, roles, and accountability structures for AI risk management across the enterprise.

- **Map**: The board must challenge management to identify and contextualize the risks associated with AI systems, including their potential impact on stakeholders and the broader ecosystem.
- **Measure**: The board must require management to develop and report on meaningful metrics and qualitative analysis to track AI risks, including model performance, fairness, and the effectiveness of controls.
- **Manage**: The board must oversee management's plans to treat, respond to, and mitigate identified AI risks, ensuring that these plans are resourced and effective.

THE CEO'S IMPERATIVE: ARCHITECTING AND DRIVING RESILIENCE

The CEO owns the operationalization of AI governance. They serve as the chief architect of the **RIVER Charter™** (the book's resilience operating standard), translating the board-approved risk appetite into the company's daily culture, processes, and controls.

Key CEO Accountabilities:

- **Operationalize the Governance Framework**: The CEO is directly accountable for implementing every tenet of the chosen framework, from mapping cross-system dependencies to reinforcing enterprise-wide resilience.
- **Champion Auditable Processes**: The CEO must champion tools like the **Cognitive Handshake™**—an audited human-AI decision methodology—and foster a culture where transparency is non-negotiable.
- **Manage "Risk Debt"**: The CEO is responsible for identifying, quantifying, and creating a formal "pay-down plan" for accumulated **Risk Debt** (the accumulated liability from deferred governance, process, and safety validation).
- **Deliver Truthful Reporting**: To close the information asymmetry gap, the CEO must ensure the risk posture reported to the board is a complete and unvarnished reflection of reality. The "Shared Sin" in Chapter 9 serves as the ultimate cautionary tale against curated reporting.

PRACTICAL TOOLS FOR THE BOARDROOM

Decision Escalation Thresholds

This matrix provides a starting point for defining when an issue must be escalated from management to the board. The decision bands and dollar thresholds are fictional, illustrative defaults designed for the book's scenarios. They are not legal advice or a substitute for corporate bylaws, board resolutions, or regulatory guidance. Organizations must tune any escalation thresholds to their size, sector, jurisdiction, and documented risk appetite in consultation with qualified legal and governance advisers.

Decision Class	When This Applies[6]	Primary Decider
CEO Authority	AI initiatives with < $25M impact, standard business applications, no critical infrastructure[7] risk.	CEO
Committee Oversight	Initiatives with $25–50M impact, regulated use cases, or significant cross-border data implications.	Audit and Risk Committee

(Continued)

Decision Class	When This Applies[6]	Primary Decider
Full Board Approval	Initiatives with > $50M impact, affecting critical infrastructure, or impacting >10,000 end-users.	Full Board
Emergency Override	Imminent material harm where hours matter; CEO may act only within pre-approved emergency authorities defined in board resolutions and applicable law. Requires post-hoc board review as soon as practicable, typically within 72 hours.	CEO (with Chair notified)

RACI Quick-Reference Matrix

The RACI matrix defines who is Responsible, Accountable, Consulted, and Informed for a given task. Use one letter per cell for clarity.

AI Governance Task	Full Board	Audit and Risk Committee	CEO	CTO	CRO	CAE	CDO
1. Set AI Strategy and Risk Appetite	A	C	R	C	C	I	I
2. Approve High-Risk AI Deployment	C	A	R	C	C	C	C
3. Oversee Risk Debt Program	I	A	R	C	R	C	I
4. Implement RIVER Framework	I	C	A	R	R	C	R
5. Manage All-Entity Risk (AERM)	I	C	A	R	C	I	I
6. Execute CHA Protocol	I	I	C	A	C	R	C
7. Respond to Systemic AI Crisis	I	C	A	R	R	I	I
8. Oversee AI Ethics and Compliance	A	C	R	C	C	C	C

Note: For safety-of-life, critical infrastructure, or systemic market stability use cases (as defined in Note 7), boards should treat those initiatives as requiring Full Board approval and ongoing oversight regardless of dollar amount. In these contexts, the impact criteria override the illustrative financial thresholds shown above.

*Legend: **A**=Accountable, **R**=Responsible, **C**=Consulted, **I**=Informed.*

CEO, Chief Executive Officer; CTO, technology lead; CRO (for this framework), Chief Resilience Officer, an evolution of traditional CTO/CISO roles; CAE, Chief Audit Executive; CDO, Data Capital Steward.

In organizations that also have a traditional Chief Risk Officer titled "CRO," that role should be explicitly mapped to these responsibilities or integrated into the Chief Resilience Officer function.

BOARDROOM IN ACTION: KEY QUESTIONS FOR EFFECTIVE AI OVERSIGHT

This checklist turns the narrative's fictional crises into proactive, spoiler-safe oversight tools.

1. **On Risk Debt**: In an early fictional scenario, a "temporary" fix became a latent vulnerability. *What is our formal, board-level process for inventorying, quantifying, and retiring Risk Debt? How do we ensure temporary fixes have mandatory expiration dates?*
2. **On Channels for Dissent**: A past infrastructure failure in the narrative was caused by management dismissing expert warnings. *What protected, unfiltered channels exist for our technical experts to conduct critical risk assessments and reach this board, even if they contradict management's preferred narrative?*
3. **On Reporting Integrity**: A later fictional case shows how buried stress tests distort oversight. *How does this board gain independent assurance that the risk dashboards we review reflect ground truth, not a curated performance narrative?*
4. **On Hybrid Cognition**: In a high-stakes ransomware crisis, the team was forced to make a critical decision under extreme pressure. *Does our organization have a formal, auditable protocol, such as the Cognitive Handshake Audit (CHA), for its most critical strategic decisions? How do we know it's being used effectively?*
5. **On Ecosystem Risk**: A crisis in the narrative was triggered by unmanaged "citizen developer" tools creating **Digital Asbestos** (legacy tech with hidden fragility). *How does this board oversee the risks of our entire digital ecosystem, including "shadow IT" and fourth-party vendors, beyond simple questionnaires?*

KEY BOARD TAKEAWAYS

- **Board sets appetite and guardrails; requires evidence, not demos**. Your role is oversight, not management. Challenge assumptions and demand data.
- **CEO architects and runs the resilience operating system (RIVER); reports ground truth**. Hold management accountable for implementation and transparent reporting.
- **RACI and thresholds prevent decision drift and speed traps**. Use these tools to enforce clarity and ensure scrutiny is applied where it matters most.
- **Third-line assurance validates dashboards with audit-quality evidence**. Trust must be verified. Ensure the internal audit function has the skills and mandate to provide independent assurance on AI systems.

NOTES

1. The Bull-in-China-Shop AI collapse and other narrative scenarios referenced here are fictional illustrations from the book timeline to anchor governance principles in a memorable context.
2. Committee of Sponsoring Organizations of the Treadway Commission. (2017). *Enterprise Risk Management—Integrating with Strategy and Performance*. https://www.coso.org/guidance-erm
3. Institute of Internal Auditors. (2020, September 8). *The IIA's Three Lines Model: An Update of the Three Lines of Defense*. https://www.theiia.org/globalassets/documents/resources/the-iias-three-lines-model-an-update-of-the-three-lines-of-defense-july-2020/three-lines-model-updated-english.pdf
4. National Association of Corporate Directors. (2025). *Public Company Board Practices & Oversight Survey—AI Findings*. NACD. https://www.nacdonline.org/all-governance/governance-resources/governance-surveys/surveys-benchmarking/2025-public-company-board-practices–oversight-survey/2025-board-practices-oversight-ai

5. National Institute of Standards and Technology. (2023). *Artificial Intelligence Risk Management Framework (AI RMF 1.0)* (NIST AI 100-1). https://doi.org/10.6028/NIST.AI.100-1
6. Impact defined as committed capital/operational expenditure or modeled downside financial exposure.
7. Critical infrastructure is defined as systems involving safety-of-life, public continuity, or systemic market stability.

Index

Pages in **bold** refer to tables.

For Product Safety Concerns and Information please contact our EU
representative GPSR@taylorandfrancis.com
Taylor & Francis Verlag GmbH, Kaufingerstraße 24, 80331 München, Germany

www.ingramcontent.com/pod-product-compliance
Ingram Content Group UK Ltd.
Pitfield, Milton Keynes, MK11 3LW, UK
UKHW052219190926
475702UK00006B/1101
* 9 7 8 1 0 4 1 0 9 5 6 4 4 *